T0302253

Public Relations and Whistleblowing

There is a growing interest in corporate whistleblowing, but no comprehensive research has yet focused on public relations practice. Drawing on extensive research on *Fortune* 1000 and *Wilshire* 5000 corporations, this book reveals executives' attitudes and relationships toward their organizations and their impact on whistleblowing.

Perhaps unsurprisingly, it reveals that wrongdoing in corporations and the privileges of power coexist. Top-ranking public relations executives, who are mostly white and male, are more likely to be aware of wrongdoing but no more likely to blow the whistle, fundamentally due to their positive relationship with their employers. Using the new lens of evolutionary theory, this study explains whistleblowing, retaliation, and relationships, and in the light of the connection between whistleblowing behavior and executives' attitudes, it proposes a new theory of the phenomenon of Golden Handcuffs.

As public attitudes to corporations, corporate social responsibility (CSR), and transparency harden, these findings have serious implications for companies globally. Researchers, scholars, and advanced students in public relations, organizational communication, corporate communication, strategic communication, corporate reputation, and CSR will find this book full of revealing insights.

Cary A. Greenwood (Ph.D., U. Oregon), APR, Fellow PRSA, is Associate Director for public relations research at the Debiasing and Lay Informatics (DaLI) Lab in the Center for Applied Social Research at the University of Oklahoma. She has taught public relations and researched evolutionary theory, whistleblowing, and corporate social responsibility (CSR) following a 30-plus-year career in public relations.

Routledge New Directions in PR & Communication Research
Edited by Kevin Moloney

Current academic thinking about public relations (PR) and related communication is a lively, expanding marketplace of ideas and many scholars believe that it's time for its radical approach to be deepened. Routledge New Directions in PR & Communication Research is the forum of choice for this new thinking. Its key strength is its remit, publishing critical and challenging responses to continuities and fractures in contemporary PR thinking and practice, tracking its spread into new geographies and political economies. It questions its contested role in market-orientated, capitalist, liberal democracies around the world, and examines its invasion of all media spaces, old, new, and as yet unenvisaged.

The New Directions series has already published and commissioned diverse original work on topics such as:

- PR's influence on Israeli and Palestinian nation-building
- PR's origins in the history of ideas
- a Jungian approach to PR ethics and professionalism
- global perspectives on PR professional practice
- PR as an everyday language for everyone
- PR as emotional labor
- PR as communication in conflicted societies, and
- PR's relationships to cooperation, justice, and paradox.

We actively invite new contributions and offer academics a welcoming place for the publication of their analyses of a universal, persuasive mindset that lives comfortably in old and new media around the world.

Paradox in Public Relations
A Contrarian Critique of Theory and Practice
Kevin L. Stoker

Public Relations and Whistleblowing
Golden Handcuffs in Corporate Wrongdoing
Cary A. Greenwood

For more information about this series, please visit www.routledge.com/ Routledge-New-Directions-in-Public-Relations – Communication-Research/ book-series/RNDPRCR

Public Relations and Whistleblowing

Golden Handcuffs in Corporate Wrongdoing

Cary A. Greenwood

LONDON AND NEW YORK

First published 2022
by Routledge
2 Park Square, Milton Park, Abingdon, Oxon OX14 4RN

and by Routledge
605 Third Avenue, New York, NY 10158

Routledge is an imprint of the Taylor & Francis Group, an informa business

British Library Cataloguing-in-Publication Data
A catalogue record for this book is available from the British Library

Library of Congress Cataloging-in-Publication Data
Names: Greenwood, Cary A., author.
Title: Public relations and whistleblowing : golden handcuffs in corporate
    wrongdoing / Cary A. Greenwood.
Description: Abingdon, Oxon ; New York, NY : Routledge, 2021. |
    Includes bibliographical references and index.
Subjects: LCSH: Corporations—Public relations. | Corporations—
    Corrupt practices. | Whistle blowing.
Classification: LCC HD59 .G685 2021 (print) | LCC HD59 (ebook) |
    DDC 659.2—dc23
LC record available at https://lccn.loc.gov/2020053758
LC ebook record available at https://lccn.loc.gov/2020053759

ISBN: 978-1-138-29377-9 (hbk)
ISBN: 978-1-032-00537-9 (pbk)
ISBN: 978-1-315-23189-1 (ebk)

DOI: 10.4324/9781315231891

Typeset in Bembo
by Apex CoVantage, LLC

Contents

About the author

Cary A. Greenwood (Ph.D., U. Oregon), APR, Fellow PRSA, is Associate Director for public relations research at the Debiasing and Lay Informatics Lab in the Center for Applied Social Research at the University of Oklahoma. She has published, or has had accepted for publication (forthcoming), Secrets, sources, whistleblowers, and leakers: Journalism in the Digital Age. (Review of the book *Journalism After Snowden: The Future of the Free Press in the Surveillance State*, E. Bell & T. Owen, [Eds.] *Communication Booknotes Quarterly*); (2020), "I was just doing my job!" Evolution, corruption, and public relations in interviews with government whistleblowers; (2017), with J. S. Lim, Communicating corporate social responsibility (CSR): Stakeholder responsiveness and engagement strategy to achieve CSR goals; (2016), Golden Handcuffs in the *Fortune 1000*? An employee-organization relationship survey of public relations executives and practitioners in the largest companies; (2015), Whistleblowing in the *Fortune 1000*: What practitioners told us about wrongdoing in corporations in a pilot study; (2015), with J. S. Lim and H. Jiang, The situational public engagement model in a municipal watershed protection program: information seeking, information sharing, and the use of organizational and social media. (2011). *Killing the messenger: A survey of public relations practitioners and organizational response to whistleblowing after Sarbanes-Oxley.* (Doctoral dissertation); (2010), Evolutionary theory: The missing link for conceptualizing public relations; and (2007) with L. R. Kahle, Toward an evolutionary theory of marketing: Evolution and branding. Prior to entering academia, she had a 30-plus-year career in public affairs in government and public relations in the private sector.

Foreword

Dr. Cary A. Greenwood's book about whistleblowing and the public relations profession is most timely. We know most communication professionals advocate for open communication, organizational transparency, and ethical behavior and decision-making. A professional code of ethics spells out the corresponding guidelines for practitioners. And we live in a transparent world where cover-ups are increasingly uncovered. Revelations of power abuse and illegal and unethical activities within the economic, social, political, and religious spheres in our society have become all too common. But where does whistleblowing fit in? Does it fit in?

A *whistleblower* is someone who informs on or exposes a person or an organization engaged in illegal, unethical, or illicit activity to try to end that activity. They may do so inside or outside the organization, and doing so often comes at great personal cost to the whistleblower, despite some protections. The insistent question in the book is this: *Should public relations professionals become whistleblowers when other approaches fail to prevent their organizations, or individuals within them, from carrying out illegal, illicit, or unethical activities?*

She sets it up this way in her introduction: "The drive for open communication is either helped or hindered by those in power, and those in power are helped in their communications by those in public relations." There we are – at the center of communication in a dramatic age of transparency. When we speak "truth to power," which is deemed an important role by most PR professionals, and when our recommendations are ignored or refused, which they sometimes are, what happens next? Do we walk away from the job? Do we accept the decision, follow orders, and help executive decision-makers "speak their own truth" to our publics, even if we know such "truth" is self-interested, manufactured, or manipulated? Or do we blow the whistle on the activity or transgression, inside or outside the organization?

Dr. Greenwood recounts the history of whistleblowing in the United States, and this history is replete with examples of whistleblowing and organizational crises, ranging from Enron to Cambridge Analytica. She also examines the concept and practice in other countries, where it is viewed and valued somewhat differently. Indeed, whistleblowing is an issue mostly in English-speaking countries. In addition, she reviews the complex and often conflicting legal frameworks for dealing with whistleblowing, and the varying and evolving protections for those who risk a great deal when they blow the whistle on their employers – retaliation, humiliation, isolation, job loss, and career damage.

The results of the research Dr. Greenwood conducted for the book suggest that public relations professionals are seldom whistleblowers: more than 90% of those professionals in her research don't or won't consider reporting wrong-doing as part of their job. They often know more about the wrongdoing, but they don't do *more about it*. Most won't blow the whistle because (1) they don't believe it is their responsibility to do so, or (2) presumably they fear losing their job, benefits, and reputation. These results are very similar to those found in a study of dissent conducted by a colleague and me a decade ago: once a decision was made by top executives, most public relations professionals stopped resisting and subserviently carried out the orders they were given, no matter how egregious the situation.

The book raises other important implicit and explicit questions about whis-tleblowing and the communication profession. For example:

- What are the roles and responsibilities, if any, of public relations profession-als with respect to whistleblowing?
- Should whistleblowing be clarified or incorporated more explicitly in PRSA's existing code of ethics?
- Should more training and education, in practice and in the classroom, be provided to better understand whistleblowing and its implications for professionals?
- What can be done to prepare professionals to more effectively speak "truth to power," and to counter alternative narratives grounded in self-interests or other motives?
- How do we deal with non-disclosure agreements that prohibit whistleblowing?
- What role, if any, does the communication team play in providing other whistleblowers in their organizations with safe communication channels for their grievances?

This book is a must-read for public relations professionals and scholars, espe-cially in the current environment. Whistleblowing is a complex, troubling, and divisive issue at the core of practice – one of those uncomfortable issues many would rather not discuss. But given the importance of ethics in practice, and our increasingly transparent world, more discussion and education seem vital. My hope is this book spurs that discussion and needed action.

Bruce K. Berger, Ph.D.
Professor Emeritus, University of Alabama
Founding Director, The Plank Center for Leadership in Public Relations
Previously Corporate VP, Global Communications, Whirlpool Corporation

Acknowledgments

Many people have assisted me in the process of writing this book. I will not be able to thank everyone who helped, but please know that I appreciate everything everyone did throughout this process. My first thanks go to my husband, Paul Nosbisch, whose love, dedication, support, and confidence have never wavered, and who truly made this book possible; to our daughter, Jaida Bridgette Sweetland, who has sacrificed much but still cheered me on, and who, with Joel Sweetland, opened their home to us during the 2020 fire evacuation; and to our son, Todd Greenwood, who also has sacrificed much and cheered me on, and who shared his knowledge of computer science to help me manage my work; to my late parents, Vonnett M. Greenwood, Chief, Management Office (RET), Field Artillery Board, and MSGT, RET Orville Greenwood, both of Fort Sill, Oklahoma, who supported and encouraged my life-long pursuit of education; and to my brother, Richard P. Greenwood, and his family, who kept the home front secure.

This book would not have been possible without the continuing support of my editors at Routledge, initially Jacqueline Curthoys and Dr. Kevin Moloney, and more recently, Guy Loft. Dr. Moloney's email invitation to review someone else's book proposal captured my interest with his intriguing, Darwinian subject line, "Hello from the English Channel through which the Beagle sailed." It was his receptivity to this project and his guidance through my own proposal process that made this book possible. He and Ms. Curthoys believed in this project from the beginning. For that, I am most grateful.

I would like to express my sincere appreciation to the University of Oregon and the people who guided and encouraged me there. Dr. Patricia A. Curtin, Associate Dean for Undergraduate Affairs, Professor, School of Journalism and Communication, advised me and worked with me extensively on the two seminal projects underlying this work; Dr. H. Leslie Steeves, Senior Associate Dean for Academic Affairs, Professor, School of Journalism and Communication, advised me and introduced me to feminist theory; the late Dr. James K. Van Leuven, Professor and Endowed Chair in Public Relations, School of Journalism and Communication, advised me and introduced me to media, communication, and public relations theories; Dr. Michael Russo, Lundquist Professor of Sustainable Management, Lundquist College of Business, advised me and introduced me to sustainability research; Dr. Anne Parmigiani, Head, Department of Management, Associate Professor of Management, Lundquist College of Business, advised me and introduced me to management theories; Dr. Alan Meyer, Professor Emeritus of Management, Lundquist College of Business, introduced me to management research; Dr. Lynn Kahle, Professor Emeritus of Marketing, Lundquist College of Business, introduced me to marketing theories and co-authored our paper on marketing and evolution; Dr. Robert Mauro, Associate Professor, Department of Psychology, offered statistics instruction and advice; the late Dr. John Orbell, former Professor Emeritus, Political Science Department, introduced me to evolutionary theory; and Dr. Tiffany Derville Gallicano, Associate Professor, University of North Carolina, Charlotte, helped me develop a qualitative instrument for whistleblowing research. All errors and misconceptions in this book are, of course, solely my own.

I would like to offer a special thanks to Dr. James E. Grunig, Professor Emeritus, and Dr. Larissa A. Grunig, Professor Emerita, Emeritus Faculty, University of Maryland, for their contributions to the field of public relations, their friendship, and their encouragement of my academic pursuits. I also would like to thank Dr. Jeong-Nam Kim, Endowed Chair in Public Relations and Strategic Communication, University of Oklahoma, who supported this project by inviting me to join him at the Debiasing and Lay Informatics (DaLI) Lab at the Center for Applied Social Research.

I would like to express my sincere thanks to Dr. Don Stacks, Professor Emeritus, Public Relations and Corporate Communication, University of Miami, CEO/Executive Director, International Public Relations Research Conference, who meticulously read the majority of the manuscript in the spring and who gave me invaluable advice and support. I would also like to thank Dr. Bruce Berger, Professor Emeritus, University of Alabama, founding director, The Plank Center for Leadership in Public Relations, previously Corporate VP, Global Communications, Whirlpool Corporation, for his ongoing encouragement for this project and for writing the Foreword.

I would like to thank Kathleen Roland, Head of Circulation, and Kathryn Devine, Reference Librarian, Washington State Library; Anne Hall, founding director, and Jeffrey Syrop, current director, of the North Lincoln County Historical Museum, Lincoln City, Oregon; Kristal S. Boulden, Social Sciences Librarian; Jeffrey M. Wilhite, Associate Professor, Government Documents Librarian; Kelly G. Thompson, Billing, Media, and Reserves Supervisor; and the Interlibrary Loan Office/Sooner Xpress at the Bizzell Memorial Library, University of Oklahoma, Norman, Oklahoma; and Toni Hoberecht, Associate Professor, Technical Services Librarian, at the Schusterman Library, University of Oklahoma-Tulsa, for facilitating my research.

Some portions of this book were previously published or adapted from other sources. Chapter 1 is derived in part from Taylor & Francis' Greenwood, C. A. (2010). Evolutionary theory: The missing link for conceptualizing public relations. *Journal of Public Relations Research*, *22*(4), 456–476, available online: www.tandfonline.com/DOI: 10.1080/10627261003801438. Sage Publications, Inc., allowed me to adapt three tables (7.4, 7.5, and 7.8) from Miceli, M. P., Rehg, M. T., Near, J. P., & Ryan, K. C. (1999). Can laws protect whistle-blowers? Results of a naturally occurring field experiment. *Work and Occupations, 26*(1), 129–151. Taylor & Francis allowed me to adapt one table (Table 7.6) from Hongmei Shen & Hua Jiang (2019) Engaged at work? An employee engagement model in public relations, *Journal of Public Relations Research*, 31:1–2, 32–49, DOI: 10.1080/1062726X.2019.1585855. Taylor & Francis allowed me to adapt one table (Appendix B) from Greenwood, C. A. (2016) Golden Handcuffs in the Fortune 1000? An Employee-Organization Relationship Survey of Public Relations Executives and Practitioners in the Largest Companies, *Communication Research Reports*, 33:3, 269–274, available online: http://dx.doi.org/10.1080/08824096.20.

I would like to thank those editors and publishers for their efforts on my behalf and for allowing me to use their material in this work.

Finally, I would like to thank everyone who responded to my surveys. I sincerely appreciate your willingness to share your insights and perspectives. Without your help, this book would not have been possible. I hope we have another opportunity in the future to communicate about whistleblowing. We all have an opportunity to set an example for truth and transparency in an increasingly challenging global climate.

Introduction

Public relations and whistleblowing

Importance of whistleblowing

Why publish a book on whistleblowing and public relations, and why publish it now? The answer is obvious: The term "whistleblower" has entered the Zeitgeist. Every new day brings another fresh round of whistleblowers and their release of yet more previously secret material. The call for "transparency" in government and in business is coming from everywhere. In every case, no matter at what level, the drive for open communication is either helped or hindered by those in power, and those in power are helped in their communications by those in public relations. "Speaking truth to power" meets "speaking the truth of the powerful" on a regular basis, and the likelihood that that powerful individual in a leadership position, whom the public relations executive or practitioner serves, is engaged in some form of "illegal, immoral or unethical" activity increased significantly in recent years (PriceWaterhouseCoopers, 2018).

Whistleblowers in the news

Whistleblowing has been a topic of media interest since the Vietnam War, and it has continued to resonate strongly with the public for more than 50 years. Several well-publicized whistleblowers have caught the attention of the world media and have impacted world events. Their names will resonate with students of history, contemporary news consumers, and aficionados of popular culture. Among them are the following:

- Daniel Ellsberg, commemorated in the movie *The Post* (Pascal, Spielberg, & Krieger, 2018), who in 1971 released the documents that came to be known as the Pentagon Papers and changed the course of the Vietnam War;
- Mark Felt, a high-ranking Federal Bureau of Investigation (FBI) official who in 1972, after the Watergate break-in in Washington, DC, and under the code name Deep Throat, fed two *Washington Post* reporters confidential information that brought down Richard M. Nixon's presidency and who was commemorated in the book *All the President's Men* (Bernstein & Woodward, 1974) and in the movie of the same name (Coblenz & Pakula, 1976);

DOI: 10.4324/9781315231891-1

- Sherron Watkins (Enron), Cynthia Cooper (WorldCom), and Coleen Rowley (FBI), three female whistleblowers at the beginning of the current century who forewarned of two massive corporate failures and a government failure that led to 9/11, whose efforts led to significant changes in federal whistleblower laws, and who were rewarded by being named *Time Magazine's* 2002 "Persons of the Year" (Lacayo & Ripley, 2002);
- Christopher Wylie, who exposed the massive breach of Facebook data acquired by Cambridge Analytica, the British research firm used by then-presidential candidate Donald Trump, which may have affected the outcome of the 2016 U.S. presidential election (U.S. Senate Committee on the Judiciary, 2018);
- An anonymous whistleblower (Office of the Inspector General of the Intelligence Community, 2019a, 2019b) in the U.S. government whose allegations of improper conduct by the President of the United States with regard to Ukraine led the U.S. House of Representatives to impeach him; and
- Anonymous, the self-identified high-level member of the Trump White House, whose editorial in the *New York Times* in 2018 (Anonymous, 2018) and whose book, *A Warning*, published in November 2019 (*A warning / Anonymous, a senior Trump administration official*, 2019), exposed the purported failures of the U.S. president and the reactions of his closest advisers, and who revealed himself on October 28, 2020 (Tapper & Herb, 2020) as Miles Taylor, a former chief of staff at the Department of Homeland Security.

Whistleblowing has entered the national and international consciousness and created a debate over the disclosure of previously secret or private information that will not subside. The most pressing challenges in addressing this topic are the difficulty of keeping up with the daily release of information about and from whistleblowers, in anticipating who will blow the whistle, in evaluating the motivations behind whistleblowers' actions, in evaluating the validity of whistleblowers' claims, in ascertaining the retaliation whistleblowers experience, and in addressing the impact of awareness of wrongdoing, whistleblowing, and retaliation on employees' relationships with their organizations.

The origins of whistleblowing have been traced to a phenomenon that emerged in the 1960s and 1970s due to cynicism over corporate and governmental excesses (Glazer & Glazer, 1989) and "the civil rights, antiwar, consumer, and student protest movements" (Westin, 1981, p. 7). A brief review of the recent history of whistleblowing illustrates its importance to society as a mode of "ethical resistance" (Glazer & Glazer, 1989, p. 11), to organizations as a method of communication (Richardson, 2005), to business as a means of informing management of operational problems (Moberly, 2006), and to public relations as a seldom-used means of dissent (Berger & Reber, 2006). Although considered by some "a recent phenomenon in American history" (Glazer & Glazer, 1989, p. 4), the public's awareness of whistleblowing may owe more to advances in technology and mass communication than to any change in human nature. In other words, whistleblowing may be an ancient practice popularized by recent mass-communicated publicity. *This study* explores the origins of whistleblowing as a function of human nature that has its basis in human evolution, as well as the potential hampering of whistleblowing within the field of public relations by the privilege of benefits commonly referred to as the "Golden Handcuffs."

Broadly speaking, the term "whistleblower" refers to a group member who goes against group norms and attempts to change improper group behavior by alerting an internal or external authority (Miceli & Near, 1984). Whistleblowing could be an act undertaken for a socially constructive purpose, but it is not without potential cost to the individual and to the organization. Whistleblowing has been found to have three potential but not mutually exclusive outcomes. It can result in success, in that the whistleblower succeeds in stopping the improper behavior; it can result in failure, in that the whistleblower fails to stop the improper behavior; and in either case, whistleblowing can result in retaliation against the whistleblower (Rehg, Miceli, Near, & Van Scotter, 2008).

Beginning with the Civil War, the federal government provided protection from those risks and punishments to private citizens who entered into legal actions against the federal government. It provided protection for federal employees beginning in the 1950s, but those protections were extended only to whistleblowers in the private sector at the beginning of this century with the passage of the Public Company Accounting Reform and Investor Protection Act of 2002 [*Sarbanes-Oxley Act of 2002*, 15 U.S.C. § 7201 nt (2002)], also called the Sarbanes-Oxley Act, and, then, only in the case of financial fraud. Sarbanes-Oxley was designed to prevent financial fraud in corporations by increasing financial oversight and transparency, auditor independence, and corporate accountability (Brickey, 2003). The legislation also, for the first time, mandated that publicly traded companies establish and maintain anonymous communication channels for reporting financial wrongdoing directly to external directors on the audit committee of the company's board of directors, and it provided strong sanctions for retaliation against whistleblowers. The Dodd-Frank Wall Street Reform and Consumer Protection Act of 2010 [*Dodd-Frank Act of 2010*, 12 U.S.C. § 5301 (2010)], also called the Dodd-Frank Act, extended those protections to whistleblowers in all corporations and offered monetary incentives for whistleblowing.

Why this book is important to public relations

Given the legislated mandate to establish communication channels for reporting wrongdoing within corporations, the newly strengthened sanctions for retaliation against whistleblowers, and financial incentives for whistleblowing, one would expect business and related fields, such as law and public relations, to take an increased interest in the phenomenon of whistleblowing. That has been the case for business and for law, with extensive journal articles on the subject in both fields. Nevertheless, there is a dearth of articles examining whistleblowing in the major public relations journals. Whistleblowing has been

touched on by scholars exploring influence strategies in public relations practice (Berger, 2005; Berger & Reber, 2006; Kang & Berger, 2010). However,
no one in the field of public relations has focused on whistleblowing within
the ranks of public relations and communications executives as a primary field
of study until recently (Greenwood, 2009, August, 2011, 2012, August, 2013,
March, 2013, May, 2013, June, 2014, April, 2014, May, 2014, August, 2015,
2015, April, 2016, 2017, April, 2020, forthcoming).

Contributions to whistleblowing research

This is the first research to focus exclusively on whistleblowing by public relations
and communications executives in the private sector in the United States. It is
the first research to administer the federal survey to public relations and communications executives in the largest U.S. corporations, and it is the first research to
compare results from corporate public relations and communications executives
with results from federal and management studies (Greenwood, 2011). It builds
on a body of work (Greenwood, 2007, March, 2008, May, 2010, 2011, 2012,
August, 2013, March, 2013, June, 2014, August, 2015, 2016, 2017, April, 2020;
Greenwood & Kahle, 2007, June), one of which (2010) other scholars in public relations, communication, and strategic communication (Marsh, 2012, 2013,
2017; Nothhaft, 2016; Seiffert-Brockmann, 2018) have noted as groundbreaking
in its application of evolutionary theory to those fields and in its call for *consilience*:

> Cary Greenwood (2010) was the first scholar to systematically introduce
> evolutionary thought to public relations and organizational communica-
> tion. She proposed evolutionary theory as the metatheory for public rela-
> tions and adoption of E. O. Wilson's (1998) idea of consilience, in which
> biology grounds all thought, all disciplines speak one language, and all
> scholars pursue similar goals, as the framework. In a slightly altered version
> of Dobzhansky's dictum that "nothing in biology makes sense except in
> the light of evolution" (1973, p. 125), Greenwood argued, "Nothing in
> public relations makes sense except in the light of evolution" (Greenwood,
> 2010, p. 471).
>
> (Seiffert-Brockmann, Nothhaft, Kim, &
> Greenwood, 2019, July 17)

It is the first research to extend the role of evolutionary theory to whistleblowing (Greenwood, 2011, 2012, August, 2013, March, 2013, June, 2014, August,
2015, 2016, 2017, April, 2020). It proposes using empirical data from *this study*
to elevate a relevant, evolutionary-based concept, the Golden Handcuffs, to
the status of a theory in order to explain the actions of corporate agents when
confronted with corporate wrongdoing. Finally, it offers a look forward and
suggests cross-disciplinary research that could help public relations and communications scholars and practitioners understand whistleblowing in the context of evolution and public relations.

Contributions to public relations education

In addition, *this study* helps inform the teaching of public relations in which students are told that public relations is a management function that requires them to advise management on strategic, tactical, and ethical issues. It explores the potential repercussions for public relations and communications executives for doing what they have been directed to do by public relations education and theory – gain a seat at the management table, provide advice and counsel to senior management, act as boundary spanners, and, in the process, bring bad news about the environment (which arguably could include bad news about the organization) to management. In whistleblowing literature, this would be viewed as role-prescribed whistleblowing, which is the reporting of wrongdoing by those who are required to do so by their job descriptions, such as internal auditors (Miceli & Near, 1994). In this sense, public relations and communications executives could be viewed as role-prescribed internal whistleblowers. The admonition to management to listen to those bringing bad news forward and not to "shoot the messenger" has been articulated (Greenwood, 2011, p. 70; Yamey, 2000), but the extent of retaliation against those bringing bad news forward has not been explored.

Organizational structure

This study is divided into eight chapters. Chapter 1 proposes using evolutionary theory and the "Golden Handcuffs" to explain how public relations and communications executives deal with wrongdoing in their corporations. Chapter 2 explores the history of whistleblowing and the legal protections for whistleblowers in the United States. Chapter 3 reviews whistleblowing research in government, management, and law in the United States. Chapter 4 presents whistleblowing laws and research around the globe. Chapter 5 examines whistleblowing research in communication, journalism, and public relations. Chapter 6 outlines the method used in *this study* of whistleblowing among public relations and communications executives in the *Fortune 1000* and *Wilshire 5000* corporations. Chapter 7 states the results of *this study*. Chapter 8 discusses the implications of *this study* for public relations theory development and future research in public relations.

References

Anonymous. (2018). I Am Part of the Resistance Inside the Trump Administration. *The New York Times* (September 5, 2018). Retrieved from https://www.nytimes.com/2018/09/05/opinion/trump-white-house-anonymous-resistance.html

Berger, B. K. (2005). Power over, power with, and power to relations: Critical reflections on public relations, the dominant coalition, and activism. *Journal of Public Relations Research*, 17(1), 5–28.

Berger, B. K., & Reber, B. H. (2006). *Gaining influence in public relations: The role of resistance in practice*. Mahwah, NJ: Lawrence Erlbaum Associates.

Bernstein, C., & Woodward, B. (1974). *All the President's men*. New York: Simon and Schuster.

Brickey, K. F. (2003). F. Hodge O'Neal Corporate and Securities Law Sumposium after the Sarbanes-Oxley Act: The future disclosure system: From Enron to Worldcom and beyond: Life and crime after Sarbanes-Oxley. *Washington University Law Quarterly, 81,* 357–402.

Coblenz, W. (Producer) & A. J. Pakula (Director). (1976). *All the President's Men* [Motion Picture]. Los Angeles: Warner Bros.

Dodd-Frank Act of 2010, 12 U.S.C. § 5301 (2010).

Glazer, M. P., & Glazer, P. M. (1989). *The whistleblowers: Exposing corruption in government and industry.* New York: Basic Books, Inc.

Greenwood, C. A. (2007, March). *Evolutionary theory: The missing link for Public Relations.* Unpublished manuscript.

Greenwood, C. A. (2008, May). *Evolutionary theory: The missing link for public relations.* Paper presented at the Annual Meeting of the International Communication Association, Montreal, Canada.

Greenwood, C. A. (2009, August). *Whistleblowing in public relations: Call for a research agenda.* Poster presented at the Association for Education in Journalism and Mass Communication Annual Conference, Boston, MA.

Greenwood, C. A. (2010). Evolutionary theory: The missing link for conceptualizing public relations. *Journal of Public Relations Research, 22*(4), 456–476. Retrieved from https://doi.org/10.1080/10627261003801438

Greenwood, C. A. (2011). *Killing the messenger: A survey of public relations practitioners and organizational response to whistleblowing after Sarbanes-Oxley.* Doctoral dissertation. University of Oregon, Eugene, OR. Retrieved from ProQuest Dissertations & Theses (UMI No. 907550960).

Greenwood, C. A. (2012, August). *Whistleblowing in the Fortune 1000: Ethical dilemma or role responsibility?* Paper presented at the Association for Education in Journalism and Mass Communication Annual Conference, Chicago, IL.

Greenwood, C. A. (2013, March). *Whistleblowing in government: What whistleblowers and reporters say about it.* Paper presented at the Association for Education in Journalism and Mass Communication Midwinter Conference, Norman, OK.

Greenwood, C. A. (2013, May). *What public relations practitioners do and what whistleblowers want.* Presentation at the PRSA/GA Annual Conference. Atlanta, GA.

Greenwood, C. A. (2013, June). *Whistleblowing in the Fortune 1000: What did public relations practitioners tell us?* Poster presented at the International Communication Association Conference. London.

Greenwood, C. A. (2014, April). *Whistleblowing as an act of communication: What ethical choices do communicators face?* Panel presentation at the Eastern Communication Association Annual Meeting, Providence, RI.

Greenwood, C. A. (2014, May). *Whistleblowing in government: What whistleblowers say about it.* Paper presented at the International Communication Association Annual Conference, Seattle, WA.

Greenwood, C. A. (2014, August). Whistleblowing in Government as Free Expression: Are Government Whistleblowers Traitors, Heroes, or Loyal Employees Trying to Do the Right Thing? Panel presentation at the Association for Education in Journalism and Mass Communication Annual Conference. Montreal, Canada.

Greenwood, C. A. (2015). Whistleblowing in the *Fortune 1000*: What practitioners told us about wrongdoing in corporations in a pilot study. *Public Relations Review,* (41), 490–500. https://doi.org/10.1016/j.pubrev.2015.07.005

Greenwood, C. A. (2015, April). *Whistleblowing in a national laboratory: Do whistleblower protections apply to federal contractors, and how is national security compromised when they don't?* Panel presentation at the Eastern Communication Association Annual Conference. Philadelphia, PA.

Greenwood, C. A. (2016). Golden Handcuffs in the Fortune 1000? An employee-organization relationship survey of public relations executives and practitioners in the largest companies. *Communication Research Reports, 33*(3), 269–274. http://doi.org/10.1080/08824096.2016.1186624

Greenwood, C. A. (2017, April). *Whistleblowing: Can E&C programs induce reporting and reduce retaliation?* Presentation at the Ethics and Compliance Initiative Annual Conference, Washington, DC.

Greenwood, C. A. (2020). "I was just doing my job!" Evolution, corruption, and public relations in interviews with government whistleblowers. *PARTECIPAZIONE E CONFLITTO, 13*(2), 1042–1061. https://doi.org/10.1285/i20356609v13i2p1042

Greenwood, C. A. (forthcoming). Secrets, sources, whistleblowers, and leakers: Journalism in the Digital Age. [Review of the book *Journalism After Snowden: The Future of the Free Press in the Surveillance State*, E. Bell & T. Owen [Eds.]]. *Communication Booknotes Quarterly, 52*(1).

Greenwood, C. A., & Kahle, L. R. (2007, June). *Toward an evolutionary theory of marketing: Evolution and branding.* Proceedings of the Advertising & Consumer Psychology Conference, Santa Monica, CA. Retrieved from www.myscp.org/pdf/ACP%202007%20Proceedings.pdf

Kang, J.-A., & Berger, B. K. (2010). The influence of organizational conditions on public relations practitioners' dissent. *Journal of Communication Management, 14*(4), 368–387. https://doi.org/10.1108/13632541011090464

Lacayo, R., & Ripley, A. (2002). Persons of the year: The Whistleblowers. *Time, 160*(27). Retrieved from http://content.time.com/time/subscriber/article/0,33009,1003998,00.html

Marsh, C. (2012). Converging on harmony: Idealism, evolution, and the theory of mutual aid. *Public Relations Inquiry, 1*(3), 313–335. https://doi.org/10.1177/2046147X12448583

Marsh, C. (2013). Social harmony paradigms and natural selection: Darwin, Kropotkin, and the metatheory of mutual aid. *Journal of Public Relations Research, 25*(5), 426–441. http://doi.org/10.1080/1062726X.2013.795861

Marsh, C. (2017). *Public relations, cooperation, and justice: From evolutionary biology to ethics.* London: Routledge Taylor & Francis Group.

Miceli, M. P., & Near, J. P. (1984). The relationships among beliefs, organizational position, and whistle-blowing status: A discriminant analysis. *Academy of Management Journal, 27*(4), 687–705.

Miceli, M. P., & Near, J. P. (1994). Relationships among value congruence, perceived victimization, and retaliation against whistle-blowers. *Journal of Management, 20*(4), 773–794.

Moberly, R. E. (2006). Sarbanes-Oxley's structural model to encourage corporate whistleblowers. *Brigham Young Law Review, 2006*(5), 1107–1180. Retrieved from https://digitalcommons.law.byu.edu/lawreview/vol2006/iss5/1

Nothhaft, H. (2016). A framework for strategic communication research: A call for synthesis and consilience. *International Journal of Strategic Communication, 10*(2), 69–86. http://doi.org/10.1080/1553118X.2015.1124277

Office of the Inspector General of the Intelligence Community. (2019a). *Letter to congressional intelligence committees re. Whistleblower complaint.* Washington, DC: U.S House of Representatives Permanent Select Committee on Intelligence Retrieved from https://intelligence.house.gov/uploadedfiles/20190812_-_whistleblower_complaint_unclass.pdf.

Office of the Inspector General of the Intelligence Community. (2019b). *IG Letter to the Director of National Intelligence (Acting)*. Washington, DC: U.S House of Representatives Permanent Select Committee on Intelligence Retrieved from https://intelligence.house.gov/uploadedfiles/20190826_-_icig_letter_to_acting_dni_unclass.pdf.

Pascal, A., Spielberg, S., & Krieger, K. M. (Producer) & S. Spielberg (Director). (2018). The Post [Motion Picture]. Los Angeles: 20th Century Fox.

PriceWaterhouseCoopers. (2018). *2018 Global Economic Crime and Fraud Survey: US perspectives*. Retrieved from https://www.pwc.com/us/en/services/consulting/cybersecurity-privacy-forensics/library/global-economic-fraud-survey.html

Rehg, M. T., Miceli, M. P., Near, J. P., & Van Scotter, J. R. (2008). Antecedents and outcomes of retaliation against whistleblowers: Gender differences and power relationships. *Organization Science, 19*(2), 221–240.

Richardson, B. K. (2005, May). *Expanding whistle-blowing scholarship: How stakeholder theory, organizational structure, and social influence processes can inform whistle-blowing research*. Paper presented at the International Communication Association Annual Conference, New York.

Sarbanes-Oxley Act of 2002, 15 U.S.C. § 7201 nt. (2002).

Seiffert-Brockmann, J. (2018). Evolutionary psychology: A framework for strategic communication research. *International Journal of Strategic Communication, 12*(4), 417–432. https://doi.org/10.1080/1553118X.2018.1490291

Seiffert-Brockmann, J., Nothhaft, H., Kim, J.-N., & Greenwood, C. A. (2019, July 17). *Call for Papers: Conference on Evolutionary Perspectives on Public Relations, Strategic Communication, and Organizational Communication to be presented at University of Vienna, July 10–12, 2020*. Web log post. Retrieved from https://www.linkedin.com/pulse/call-papers-evolutionary-theory-public-relations-dr-cary-a-/?trackingId=LuYPWI4CvhiZQvyWI96W9g%3D%3D

Tapper, J., & Herb, J. (2020). Author of 2018 'Anonymous' op-ed critical of Trump revealed. *CNN* (October 28, 2020). Retrieved from https://www.cnn.com/2020/10/28/politics/anonymous-new-york-times-oped-writer/index.html

U.S. Senate Committee on the Judiciary. (2018). Hearing on Cambridge Analytica and Future of Data Privacy (Testimony of Christopher Wylie). *U.S. Senate Judiciary*. 2. Retrieved from https://www.judiciary.senate.gov/meetings/cambridge-analytica-and-the-future-of-data-privacy

A warning / Anonymous, a senior Trump administration official. (2019). (1st ed.). New York: Twelve, an imprint of Grand Central Publishing.

Westin, A. F. (Ed.). (1981). *Whistle blowing! Loyalty and dissent in the corporation*. New York: McGraw-Hill.

Yamey, G. (2000). Protecting whistleblowers: Employers should respond to the message, not shoot the messenger. *British Medical Journal, 320*(7227), 70–71.

1 Public relations, whistleblowing, and evolution

Evolutionary theory: the missing link for conceptualizing public relations

Although a decade has passed since this article was published,[1] the arguments for the need for a metatheory to unify public relations thought remain strong. A recent study of public relations evaluation and measurement articles over the past 40 years found "no guiding theory" and the "non-existence of a coherent theoretical body of knowledge within evaluation and measurement research" (Volk, 2016, p. 969). Public relations scholars continue to draw from a variety of disciplines and perspectives in their research into the field. However, the inability to agree upon a theoretical perspective for evaluating the field means, in part, that guidance for those most likely to learn about an organization's failings and most likely to be required to help steer that organization through difficult times may be least likely to have a clear path of action for dealing with that knowledge. Those in the field of public relations need more guidance than they have been given to date on addressing organizational wrongdoing.

> This article introduces the concept of using Charles Darwin's evolutionary theory as the metatheory for conceptualizing public relations thought. It examines the state of public relations theory development and explores theories that have been proposed as metatheories for the field, including systems theory, complexity theory, and symmetrical/Excellence theory. It also explores the tenets of evolutionary theory that have relevance for public relations theory, including social intelligence, Machiavellian intelligence, cheater detection, cooperation, reciprocity, and reciprocal altruism.

"For some time, the field of public relations has been in search of a unifying theory" (Leeper, 2001, p. 93). Given the extensive coverage in recent years of Charles Darwin's life, work, and contribution to science through his theory of evolution, it seems only fitting to introduce Darwin into the discussion of public relations theory-building. In fact, given the current state of disagreement over theory-building among public relations scholars, it seems highly appropriate to consider a widely accepted and widely used metatheory in the

DOI: 10.4324/9781315231891-2

life sciences, that is, evolutionary theory, as a metatheory for conceptualizing public relations thought. The theory contends that the complexity of life forms currently on the planet is the result of the evolution of individual species over a long period of time through natural selection, or adaptation, for survival and reproduction (Darwin, 1979/1859; Dennett, 1995).

Public relations theory development is one of the fastest growing areas of public relations scholarship (Sallot, Lyon, Acosta-Alzuru, & Jones, 2008). The number of theory development articles published in the two leading public relations research journals, *Public Relations Review* and the *Journal of Public Relations Research*, more than doubled from 2001 to 2003 over the 1984–2000 time frame (Sallot et al., 2008). The increase might be attributed, in part, to a call by leading public relations scholars for increased theory development (Botan, 1989; J. E. Grunig, 1989), to criticism of existing theory (Curtin & Gaither, 2005; Gower, 2006; Holtzhausen, 2000; Holtzhausen & Voto, 2002; Hutton, 2001; Murphy, 1991), to the ongoing search for a satisfying theoretical framework (Cheney & Christensen, 2001), or to the lack of a unifying theory (J. E. Grunig, 1989; Leeper, 2001; Murphy, 1996, 2000). Despite the phenomenal growth in attention paid to theory development, the field of public relations still lacks a universally agreed-upon metatheory (Sallot et al., 2008). The lack of a unifying theory for public relations, and the need for one, is the issue that occupies this chapter.

A "paradigm struggle" is now occurring within public relations between the dominant paradigm, as represented by symmetrical/Excellence theory, and more critical worldviews, including the critical-cultural and the postmodern (Botan, 1993; Botan & Hazleton, 2006b, 1989). That struggle is viewed by some as evidence of public relations' arrival as a more mature discipline (Botan & Hazleton, 2006a; J. E. Grunig, Grunig, & Dozier, 2006), as evidence of the central role played by symmetrical/Excellence theory (J. E. Grunig & Grunig, 2008; J. E. Grunig et al., 2006), as the mechanism by which future theoretical developments will ensue (Botan & Hazleton, 2006b; J. E. Grunig et al., 2006), as a crossroads between the dominant paradigm and a more critical worldview (Gower, 2006), or as a fundamental flaw in the positivist outlook of the dominant paradigm (Curtin & Gaither, 2005).

This struggle, along with the growth of public relations theory development, offers an opportunity to extend the theoretical boundaries of public relations by opening the door to possible pathways for future theory development. One such pathway leads directly from the dominant paradigm (back) to the life sciences and connects the two in ways that could be beneficial to both.

One line of thought that holds great promise for a comprehensive, cross-disciplinary Kuhnian-style (Kuhn, 1970) paradigm for public relations is a research tradition from the life sciences that is being integrated slowly into other social and life science disciplines: evolutionary theory. What evolutionary theory requires is a willingness to accept the scientific paradigm. Those willing to consider the scientific model may find this pathway illuminated and illuminating.

Some might argue that evolutionary theory is a well-trodden path, rather than a newly blazed trail, for public relations theory. An early definition of public relations used the concept of ecology from the life sciences to explain the "interdependence of organizations and others in their environments. Viewed in this perspective, *public relations' essential role is to help organizations adjust and adapt to changes in their environments* (Cutlip, 1952)" (Cutlip, Center, & Broom, 1994, p. 199). Central to that research tradition is the idea that organizations and public relations have to evolve (i.e., adapt) to changing circumstances and environments:

> We believe future research should be developed to help public relations *evolve* (L. Grunig, 2007) as a strategic management function and continually reinstitutionalize itself to adjust to changes in organizations, communication technologies and societal expectations. Thus, we believe the future of the excellence theory should be evolutionary change.
>
> (J. E. Grunig & Grunig, 2008, p. 292)

What was lacking in the early use of ecology as an underlying concept for public relations was an acknowledgment of the broader potential for evolutionary theory as a metatheory for the field, as well as the application of specific evolutionary concepts to public relations.

This chapter introduces the concept of using evolutionary theory as the metatheory for conceptualizing public relations thought. It examines the current state of public relations theory development and explores theories that have been proposed as metatheories, including systems theory, complexity theory, and symmetrical/Excellence theory, to make the case for the role that evolutionary theory could play in the further development of public relations theory.

Public relations theory development

Since its beginnings in the publicity efforts of nineteenth-century U.S. industrial expansion, public relations has been closely aligned with various fields, including business, political science, psychology, mass communication, and sociology (Cheney & Christensen, 2001; Cropp & Pincus, 2001; J. E. Grunig, 1989; K. S. Miller, 2000; Murphy, 1991; Prior-Miller, 1989; Verčič & Grunig, 2000). The practice of public relations has developed from a variety of activities involving individuals and organizations, including rhetoric, oratory, publicity, promotion, advertising, marketing, community relations, and government affairs. In part because of its origins in practice, the theoretical basis of public relations has been called into question, and public relations is accused of lacking theory (J. E. Grunig, 1992).

Like other emerging academic fields, such as strategic management (Meyer, 1991), public relations has borrowed or adapted many of its theories from these other disciplines (Coombs, 2001; J. E. Grunig, 1993; Pasadeos, Renfro, &

Hanily, 1999). Several historical developments account for why these diverse theories have not been unified as a metatheory for public relations. Theoretical developments in social science have encouraged communication scholars to avoid grand theories and to focus on developing falsifiable middle-range theories (Sallot et al., 2008; Verčič & Grunig, 2000). The impetus for developing middle-range theories lies in sociology's mid-twentieth-century desire to avoid general theories that could not account for observations (Merton, 1967). As an outgrowth of its origins in practice, public relations has focused on applied, or problem-solving, research, rather than basic, or theoretical, research (Botan, 1989). As a result, "In the past, public relations theory has ignored metatheory" (J. E. Grunig, 1989, p. 17).

Of the many theories used in public relations, only a few have claimed the status of a unifying theory, or metatheory, for public relations. Of those few, systems theory, complexity theory, and symmetrical/Excellence theory have received the most attention from scholars.

Systems theory

Systems theory was introduced into the scientific community in the 1950s (Bertalanffy, 1951; Boulding, 1956) and had become an established theory by the late 1960s (Bertalanffy, 1968). However, it was not until the 1970s that it was introduced into the field of communication, where its popularity grew over the next ten years. Systems theory was used to design speech communication courses (Tucker, 1971), to determine the effectiveness of organizational communication (Hickson, 1973), to underscore the importance of communication as a cohesive element of organizational systems (Almaney, 1974), and to serve as an organizing theory for organizational communication (J. E. Grunig, 1975). By the mid-1980s systems theory had gained such a following that it was identified as a foundational theory for public relations (Cutlip, Center, & Broom, 1985; J. E. Grunig & Grunig, 1986). It provided four of the suppositions J. E. Grunig (1989) used in developing symmetrical communication: holism, interdependence, open system, and moving equilibrium (Grunig, 1989). However, more recently, public relations scholars have criticized systems theory's goal of organizational survival as "weak" (J. E. Grunig & Grunig, 2000, p. 306). Despite its widespread contribution to public relations theory development, systems theory's lack of status as a metatheory for public relations is evidenced in part by the lack of scholarly publications dedicated to it in recent journals (Sallot et al., 2008; Verčič & Grunig, 2000).

Complexity theory

Complexity theory is an outgrowth of chaos theory, which was developed from "physics, topology, and systems theory," and which sees the underlying nature of the universe as made up of "disorder, diversity, instability and non-linearity" (Murphy, 1996, pp. 95–96). It is the "study of many individual actors who interact locally in an effort to adapt to their immediate situation" and whose actions have global effects (Murphy, 2000, p. 450). Both theories share a postmodern focus on "participation and relationships" (Stroh, 2007, p. 206), and both have been proposed as scientific worldviews whose adoption as metatheory would increase the credibility of public relations (McKie, 2001). More recently, complexity theory has been presented as useful in crisis communication (Holtzhausen & Roberts, 2008) and as complementary and equal to symmetrical/Excellence theory as a unifying theory for public relations (Murphy, 2007). However, neither of these theories has shown a significant following as metatheory, based on a recent review of theory development articles published in the leading public relations journals (Sallot et al., 2008).

Symmetrical / Excellence theory

Symmetrical communication was developed specifically to address this lack of a unifying theory for public relations (J. E. Grunig, 1989; J. E. Grunig et al., 2006). Its purpose was to counteract the then-dominant paradigm, or leading theory, of public relations developed by Bernays, which used "theories of attitudes and persuasion" (J. E. Grunig, 1989, p. 19) "to manipulate publics for the benefit of the organization" (p. 18). In response, J. E. Grunig developed symmetrical public relations, "which has a different set of presuppositions and calls for a different kind of theory" (p. 19). Symmetrical theory was developed as a "presupposition," or metatheory, for public relations:

> Presuppositions are the essence of metatheory. . . . They consist of assumptions about the world and values attached to those assumptions. Presuppositions define the problems researchers attempt to solve, the theoretical traditions that are used in their research, and the extent to which the world outside a research community accepts the theories that result from research.
> (J. E. Grunig, 1989, p. 18)

Symmetrical communication and the Excellence theory that followed it employed scientific methods to advance an overarching set of attitudes and beliefs about how public relations should function and how public relations should be measured, while at the same time warning against overestimating the objectivity, neutrality, and truth of scientific findings.

The symmetrical/Excellence theory eventually became seen by many as the dominant paradigm of public relations, and as such, it drove a significant amount of the progress in public relations theory development and research (Botan & Hazleton, 2006a; J. E. Grunig et al., 2006). For example, of the four authors of the Excellence study, J. E. Grunig and D. M. Dozier were two of the three most cited authors from 1990 to 1995, and L.A. Grunig was one of the three most published authors during that period (Pasadeos et al, 1999). Further, several scholars identified symmetrical/Excellence theory as the theory most closely approximating a metatheory developed thus far in public relations (Botan & Hazleton, 2006a; Sallot et al., 2008).

Other theoretical directions

Some scholars disagree (Leeper, 2001; Sallot et al., 2008). While acknowledging the role of symmetrical/Excellence theory in public relations theory development, argue that "no dominant paradigms per se have emerged" (Sallot et al., 2008, p. 368) in this or the last century. "Of course, many might *still* argue that Excellence Theory is the dominant paradigm in public relations" (2008, p. 368). The debate about symmetrical/Excellence theory's role as the dominant paradigm in public relations theory may reflect its maturation as a theory, or it may reflect the paradigmatic struggle between the dominant paradigm and postmodernism that some argue is indicative of a maturing discipline (Botan & Hazleton, 2006a).

Part of that paradigmatic struggle concerns the commerce between public relations and other disciplines and the stature public relations research is granted outside the field (McKie, 2001). Given its historic willingness to borrow from other fields, one might expect public relations to continue to welcome infusions of research and theory from a variety of other disciplines. However, despite an initial cross-pollination of theories from other disciplines, public relations has been accused of not acknowledging or accepting research from disciplines other than the communication and business fields (McKie, 2001). For these reasons, some view the scope of public relations research as limited and see that limitation as the reason few outside the field cite it (Pasadeos et al., 1999).

Scholars who are critical of the dominant public relations paradigm contend that public relations has limited its horizons by following the scientific research model, or what McKie (2001) calls "outmoded ideas of science" (p. 80). This criticism reflects the philosophical differences between the critical-cultural and postmodernist positions and that of positivism (Curtin & Gaither, 2005; J. E. Grunig & White, 1992). Some argue that the scientific method has added to the stature of public relations theory (Botan & Hazleton, 2006a, 1989; J. E. Grunig & White, 1992; Pasadeos et al., 1999). Yet others argue that the scientific method, while valuable, is fundamentally subjective, and scholars should be willing to entertain a new paradigm (Kuhn, 1970), presupposition, or worldview about the purpose and role of public relations (J. E. Grunig, 1992). This debate underscores a philosophical difference of opinion about research methods that must be noted in this discussion (Botan, 1993; Botan & Hazleton, 2006a) but the resolution of which lies outside the scope of this chapter.

The fact that the debate is occurring indicates a healthy interest in public relations theory development. The debate also indicates that, despite the great strides that have been made to date, something is missing, and more work remains to be done. Some would argue that the missing element lies in the area of cross-disciplinary research (McKie, 2001; Pasadeos et al., 1999), and this chapter further develops that argument. What is missing to date is the metatheory or defining theory that would link public relations to the disciplines to which it is connected by pedigree and inheritance. One theory that provides a path between public relations and science, just as it provides a bridge between natural science and the humanities (E. O. Wilson, 1998), is evolutionary theory.

Evolutionary theory

Evolutionary theory is widely recognized in academic disciplines and widely discussed in the popular press, including recent series in both *Nature* (Gee, Howlett, & Campbell, 2009) and the *New York Times* (Safina, 2009; Wade, 2009), but the implications for public relations theory development have not been explored until now. Darwin's theory attempts to provide an explanation for the number and variety of species that he personally observed and that were then known to exist on the planet. The theory contends that the evolution of individual species over time through natural selection for survival and reproduction has resulted in the life forms now in existence. Prior to Darwin, and as far back as Aristotle, species had been seen as unchanging, distinct entities; since Darwin, that view of the world has changed (Dennett, 1995).

Evolutionary theory has been substantially validated and advanced in recent years by scientific discovery (Byrne & Whiten, 1988, 1997; Dennett, 1995; Trivers, 1971, 1985). "From the perspective of 2009, Darwin's principal ideas are substantially correct" (Wade, 2009). The 1930s and the 1940s witnessed a significant breakthrough in the biological sciences in which the discovery of genes was coupled with natural selection to explain heredity (Dennett, 1995). With the later discoveries of DNA and RNA, the transmission mechanisms of heredity and the exact pathways of natural selection are becoming known. Research continues to provide information about the transmission of genetic change that extends the role of evolution, despite the fact that genes were unknown to Darwin (Dennett, 1995).

> As an old (now dead) friend of mine, Aaron Novick, a famous biologist, once observed to me: "Evolution is not a theory; it's a laboratory problem. Evolution in the laboratory makes it extremely difficult to keep laboratory-designed bacteria and other species constant for study and analysis."
>
> (J. Orbell, personal communication, March 31, 2007)

The growth of this body of knowledge is prompting the adoption of evolutionary theory in a variety of widespread disciplines. In addition to its role in public relations, organizational communication, and strategic communication, evolutionary theory has emerged in evolutionary biology through Darwin and others (Darwin, 1979/1859; Dennett, 1995; Dobzhansky, 1973; Hamilton, 1964; Trivers, 1971; E. O. Wilson, 1975, 1998), in evolutionary psychology (Barkow, Cosmides, & Tooby, 1992; Buss, 1991; Cosmides, Tooby, & Barkow, 1992; G. F. Miller, 2000), in evolutionary marketing (Greenwood & Kahle, 2007, June; Saad, 2004, 2006a, 2006b, 2007; Saad & Gill, 2000), in evolutionary psychology applied to strategic communication, public relations, and organizational communication (Nothhaft, 2016; 2017; Seiffert-Brockmann, 2018), in evolutionary economics (Nelson & Winter, 1982), in organizational evolution (Aldrich, 1999; Aldrich & Ruef, 2006; Baum & Singh, 1994; Singh, 1990), in political science (Orbell, Morikawa, Hartwig, Hanley, & Allen, 2004; Smirnov, Arrow, Kennett, & Orbell, 2007), in social psychology (Byrne & Whiten, 1997; Kahle, 1984), in evolutionary anthropology (Gibson & Lawson, 2015), in human behavioral ecology (Nettle, Gibson, Lawson, & Sear, 2013), in evolutionary biology (de Santis, 2021), and in cultural evolutionary psychology (Moloney, 2006). Even those disciplines without primary subspecialties in evolutionary theory have been forced to contend with the rapidly emerging discipline and its interdisciplinary impacts. For example, the recent use of evolutionary psychology to explain a finding that violence decreases enjoyment of television dramas for both men and women points to the emergence of evolutionary theory in the field of mass communication (Weaver & Wilson, 2009).

Key concepts of evolutionary theory and implications for public relations

Evolutionary theory has much to offer public relations as a metatheory, particularly as it sheds light on relationships. Relationships have long been recognized as a crucial component of public relations (Ledingham & Bruning, 2000), and key concepts of evolutionary theory have implications for human relationships. These include social intelligence, Machiavellian intelligence, cheater detection, cooperation, reciprocity, and reciprocal altruism. These concepts are directly applicable to the concept of relationships, as well as to the concepts of two-way symmetrical communication and Excellence theory.

Primates are not the only animals that have social relationships, but primates have their own ways of developing and using relationships (Cords, 1997). Nonhuman primates form groups with dominance structures, matrilineal organization, and long-standing membership (Whiten & Byrne, 1997). They also build relationships (friendships) through reciprocal behaviors such as grooming, and they repair those relationships when they are damaged. They strategically develop alliances and coalitions with others for competitive value; they repair those alliances and coalitions when they are damaged; they engage third-party protectors when threatened; and they recognize the social rank of non-group members (Whiten & Byrne, 1997). These are all behaviors in which human primates engage, as well.

But what is it about primates that allows them (and us) to enter into relationships in the first place? The foundational capacity that allows primates to engage in social behaviors is social intelligence (Humphrey, 1976, 1988).

Social intelligence

One of the key concerns of public relations, the development and maintenance of relationships, is tied to one of the key concerns of evolutionary scientists: the size and complexity of the human brain and the fact that it evolved so rapidly in evolutionary time. The idea that has the most promise for explaining this phenomenon is the concept of social intelligence (Humphrey, 1976, 1988). Social intelligence predicates that the extensive size of the human brain resulted from the need to deal with the complexities of social organization and that this large brain predisposes humans to solve social problems (Humphrey, 1976, 1988). The key aspects of complex social structure include living in large groups, recognizing other individuals, communicating with other individuals, remembering interactions with other individuals, learning from other individuals, manipulating other individuals, detecting when one has been manipulated, and engaging in reciprocal beneficial activities (Byrne & Whiten, 1997; Humphrey, 1976, 1988).

Although the topic is controversial, some argue that brain imaging research supports the concept of social intelligence (Frith, 2007). Brain imaging has found dedicated areas in the human brain that allow people to predict what will happen in social interactions, called "the social brain" (Brothers, 1990, in Frith, 2007, p. 671). Researchers have found that certain areas of the brain control specific functions that are used in social interactions. These include reading the mental states of others, predicting what others will do based on their mental states, remembering how to behave in various situations, and experiencing empathetically, or mirroring, the emotions others are feeling. It is the ability to experience emotions, desires, beliefs; to communicate verbally and through actions; to recognize and remember individual features in order to know who is trustworthy and who is not; to know what another is seeing; and to guess at what another is thinking or sensing that defines the "social brain" (Frith, 2007):

> But first, I must consider what the social brain is for. It is the social brain that allows us to interact with other people. As with all our interactions with the world, we can do much better if we can predict what is going to happen next. The better we can predict what someone is going to do next, the more successful our interactions with that person will be. I shall argue that the function of the social brain is to enable us to make predictions during social interactions. These predictions need not be conscious and deliberated. . . . Perhaps the most important attribute of the social brain is that it allows us to make predictions about people's actions on the basis of their mental states. . . . There are many different types of mental states that can affect our behaviour. There are long-term dispositions: one person may be trustworthy while another is unreliable. There are short-term emotional states like fear and anger. There are desires like thirst which lead to specific goal-directed behaviours. There are the beliefs that we have about the world which determine our behaviour even when they are false. . . . Finally, there is the rather special intention to communicate with others, and the associated ability to recognize that certain behaviours are communicative.
>
> (pp. 671–672)

Machiavellian intelligence and cheater detection

At the root of the concept of trustworthiness are the concepts of Machiavellian intelligence and its counterpart, cheater detection. Machiavellian intelligence is the ability to manipulate others, and cheater detection is the ability to detect manipulation or cheating by others (Cosmides & Tooby, 1992; Orbell et al., 2004). The evolutionary basis for Machiavellian intelligence is the concept that group living encourages selection of manipulative behavior that favors the individual without disrupting the group (Whiten & Byrne, 1997). Machiavellian intelligence is understood in social psychology in a colloquial sense as manipulating others for one's own benefit, often to the detriment of the others. In that context, it is viewed as a personality trait, wherein one can be considered high Mach or low Mach. In the context of evolutionary biology, Machiavellian intelligence is a more complex social strategy encompassing both helping and deceiving strategies (Byrne & Whiten, 1997).

Machiavellian intelligence involves sending deceptive signals. For example, young people, particularly young women, use tanning to promote the illusion of good health and enhance sexual attraction (sexual selection), despite the well-known and well-publicized adverse health effects of prolonged exposure to ultraviolet rays (Saad, 2006a). If ads targeted at young women are focused on the long-term aging effects of tanning, those appeals can actually have the desired public health effect of reducing sun exposure. In other words, the desire to look young and sexually alluring over an extended time may, in fact, trump the desire to appear young and sexually alluring in the present (Saad, 2006a).

The concept of Machiavellian intelligence is applicable also to strategic public relations campaign planning and relationship management. If we understand that humans will act in accordance with certain principles, that is, the desire "to seek food and shelter, attract and retain a mate, protect and nurture one's kin, and develop strategic networks of friends and alliances" (Saad, 2006a, pp. 630–631), we will design our strategies accordingly. This would argue that, in most instances, an exchange approach will be the more effective model of relationships and that an asymmetrical approach will be the more effective model of communication.

The message for public relations from evolutionary theory is that persuasion may be a more effective communication model than symmetrical communication because of the evolutionary development of the human brain. Persuasion has been described as "humankind's primary symbolic resource for exerting control over the environment" (Miller & Steinberg, 1975, in Miller, 1989, pp. 45–46). However, this conclusion should not preclude scholars or practitioners from aspiring to or attempting communal relationships and symmetrical communications. From an evolutionary perspective, Machiavellian intelligence and cheater detection are not the only elements affecting relationships. Three other evolutionary concepts – cooperation, reciprocity, and reciprocal altruism – play a significant role in relationship development, as well, and they validate the more normative aspects of symmetrical/Excellence theory.

Cooperation, reciprocity, and reciprocal altruism

Kin selection, which is the genetic predisposition to aid one's close relatives (Hamilton, 1964), can be understood in the light of evolution more easily, perhaps, than such actions as cooperation, reciprocity, and reciprocal altruism, which provide benefits to unrelated individuals. Cooperation is defined as engaging in mutually beneficial activities (Hamilton, 1964); reciprocity is defined as returning behavior in kind; and reciprocal altruism is defined as enduring loss so that another may benefit (Axelrod, 1984; Fessler & Haley, 2003; Field, 2004; Gigerenzer, 1997; Hamilton, 1964; Hammerstein, 2003; Orbell et al., 2004; Trivers, 1971; Whiten & Byrne, 1997). All three of these concepts have been demonstrated as elements of human and nonhuman primate relationships.

Cooperation is facilitated through social relationships; emotions act as the guardians of those relationships (Hammerstein, 2003). Various emotions and psychological states, including "friendship, dislike, moralistic aggression, gratitude, sympathy, trust, suspicion, trustworthiness, aspects of guilt, and some forms of dishonesty and hypocrisy can be explained as important adaptations to regulate the altruistic system" (Trivers, 1971, p. 35). Cooperation can evolve from tendencies to manipulate when those tendencies are balanced by another evolutionary trait, the ability to detect attempts at manipulation (Orbell et al., 2004). In other words, cooperation may demonstrate Machiavellian intelligence operating in conjunction with cheater detection.

Reciprocity is the trading of favors, such as grooming activities among apes and monkeys, possibly in order to build relationships for future benefit (Byrne & Whiten, 1997). As such, reciprocity forms one of the foundational concepts of human, as well as nonhuman, primate sociality. Reciprocal altruism, in which there is a small cost to the giver and a great benefit to the taker, requires repeated positive interaction with non-kin over time (Trivers, 1971). Humans are among the few primates who engage in reciprocal altruism, a form of cooperation (Trivers, 1971).

In public relations, the more common term is "reciprocity," although the distinction between reciprocity and reciprocal altruism is not as finely drawn as in evolutionary theory. Reciprocity has been shown to be a "universal component of all moral codes" (Gouldner, 1960, in Kelly, 2001, p. 284) and the first of Kelly's (2001) four key tenets of stewardship, along with responsibility, reporting, and relationship nurturing. It is also "an integral part of the symmetrical worldview that is an essential part of excellent public relations" (J. E. Grunig, 1992, p. 48).

Reciprocity forms a link between evolutionary theory and symmetrical/ Excellence theory by way of game theory. It is the foundation of game theory, and success in game theory also involves cooperation and the likelihood of repeated encounters (Axelrod, 1984). Game theory has been used to challenge symmetrical/Excellence theory because game theory involves both self-interest and other-interest (i.e., mixed motives) (Murphy, 1991). However, as James

E. Grunig points out, two-way symmetrical communication included mixed motives "as we originally conceptualized it (J. Grunig & L. Grunig, 1992, pp. 309-312)" (Grunig, 2001, p. 12; Grunig & Kim, 2021.)[2] Symmetrical communication could be interpreted as a combination of self-interest and either reciprocity or reciprocal altruism. "The norm of reciprocity is the essence of what generally is called social responsibility" (J. E. Grunig & White, 1992, p. 47).

Relationships in both human and nonhuman primates incorporate most, if not all, of these characteristics. From an interpersonal perspective, individuals or organizations cultivate relationships through relationship maintenance strategies, the results of which are relationship quality outcomes and which represent two kinds of relationships, exchange and communal (J. E. Grunig & Huang, 2000; Hon & Grunig, 1999; Huang, 1997). Strategies include access, the ability of two parties to interact without involving a third; positivity, the effort to make the relationship enjoyable; openness, the sharing of thoughts and feelings; sharing of tasks, joint problem-solving; networking, the creation of coalitions; and assurances, the validation of the legitimacy of the other's concerns. Relationship quality outcomes include trust, a confidence in and willingness to be open to another; satisfaction, a cost-benefit analysis in favor of the relationship; commitment, a willingness to spend time on the relationship; and control mutuality, a sense of shared power in the relationship (control mutuality). Relationships are exchange, a trade of benefits, or communal, in which no benefit is anticipated (J. E. Grunig & Huang, 2000; Hon & Grunig, 1999).

Several relationship maintenance strategies appear to have been demonstrated in primate research. Nonhuman primates have demonstrated the use of third parties, the creation of alliances and coalitions, networking, and grooming behaviors (Byrne & Whiten, 1997). These activities could be equated at some level to the relationship maintenance strategies of access, positivity, openness, sharing of tasks, networking, and assurances. Relationship quality outcomes in the relationships of nonhuman primates are more difficult to measure because outcomes measure states of mind that are not directly accessible in nonhuman primates. However, exchange relationships, which demonstrate reciprocity, are clearly evident in nonhuman primate behavior. The evidence for communal relationships, which demonstrate reciprocal altruism, however, is limited almost exclusively to humans. In that respect, perhaps, the normative aspect of symmetrical relationships is accurately portrayed. Providing good to another at a cost to oneself, that is, self-sacrifice, is an attainment solely of the higher primate – humans.

Problems critics have with evolutionary theory

Despite its widespread acceptance and incorporation in a variety of disciplines, evolutionary theory has its shortcomings and its share of detractors. Some take issue with evolutionary theory because of the difficulty of comprehending the estimated 4.5 billion-year-age of the earth and the millions of years necessary to accomplish the current state of mankind. Contributing to the difficulty is the fact that Darwin did not apply natural selection to humans in *On the Origin of Species* (1979/1859); he feared such a claim would overshadow his work and lead to its rejection (Dennett, 1995). Although he corrected this problem in *The Descent of Man and Selection in Relation to Sex* (Darwin, 1871; Dennett, 1995), this reluctance has led to ongoing debate regarding the applicability of evolutionary theory to humans. Darwin's initial work also identifies natural selection as the primary, but not necessarily the exclusive, means of change in species (Darwin, 1979/1859). Despite the initial impression of hedging, the remainder of his work clearly demonstrates his belief that the overwhelming evidence is on the side of evolution (Darwin, 1979/1859; Dennett, 1995).

However, the major arguments against evolution involve the theological and philosophical unwillingness of some to relegate the creation of life to random selection. These arguments can be arranged along a continuum of belief in theological intervention from absolute Creationism (all things having been created by Divine Intervention), through evolution with help from intervention (Divine or otherwise) outside of evolution, to Darwin's idea of something evolving from nothing over time (Dennett, 1995). Critics argue that evolution is reductionist (it oversimplifies scientific process to an absurd level), but supporters argue that reductionism merely insists on scientific method without resorting to Divine Intervention (Dennett, 1995).

Despite the criticisms that have been leveled against evolutionary theory, a significant number of disciplines now have members who have embraced it conceptually, have incorporated its concepts, and are testing its suppositions. Is it not possible that there is a role for evolutionary theory in the development of public relations theory and, particularly, in the development of a metatheory for public relations?

Discussion

The concepts of evolutionary theory have the potential to influence profoundly the ways in which public relations is conceived, theorized, and practiced. They even provide evolutionary explanation for the position of critical theorists, who accuse public relations of being unethical and of using persuasion for deception. The abilities of humans to deceive one another, to recognize when they are being deceived, to reciprocate behavior they have experienced, and to choose not to reciprocate negative behavior but, instead, to "turn the other cheek" are all capabilities that many believe are hardwired into the species through evolution (Orbell et al., 2004; Whiten & Byrne, 1997).

Some might argue that the business of public relations is about humans and human relationships, not about relationships among other species. Others would argue that understanding social behavior depends upon an understanding of how the social creatures under consideration (in this case, humans) originated (Trivers, 1985). If evolution applies to humans, as well as other animals, then the advances in evolutionary theory derived from biology and the other life sciences are applicable to humans, too. The tenets of evolutionary theory have potential significance for the practice and discipline of public relations because they explain human behavior.

And while some may argue that public relations deals only with a subset of human behavior, that of groups or organizations and external parties (stakeholders or publics), it seems clear that human behavior at the primate level involves groups and organizations, and that human behavior is what should be of interest to public relations scholars. By understanding how primates function in situations involving these behaviors, we may have a better understanding of how humans function. This should provide a better ability to predict behaviors in humans. It is from an understanding of human behavior that we can develop an understanding of group behavior and organizational behavior.

The value of using evolutionary theory to guide the study of public relations is its ability to increase the understanding of human behavior. While there is much to learn from other sciences, it will be valuable to the field to conduct studies within public relations to show the application of evolutionary theory to public relations problems. For example, complexity theory suggests that entities are not strategic in their collaborations. "Instead, they form alliances with others who are simply most similar to them" (Murphy, 2000, p. 457). Primate studies, however, demonstrate that long-term strategic considerations play a factor in the formation of alliances (Byrne & Whiten, 1997; Harcourt & de Waal, 1992). If public relations scholars accept the applicability of evolutionary theory to public relations, they could follow the developments in evolutionary theory in the life sciences and in evolutionary psychology, and they could design studies to replicate the findings in nonhuman primates with human subjects, where possible.

Evolutionary theory has the capacity to serve as a metatheory for public relations, an umbrella under which all mid-range public relations theories can shelter. When the source of humanity is acknowledged to be biological, and when the foundation of public relations is acknowledged to be the interaction of humans, then the path to illumination for public relations would seem to lie through biology. And when the only accepted biological theory is evolution – "Darwin's theory of evolution has become the bedrock of modern biology" (Wade, 2009) – one could argue that public relations should turn to evolutionary theory.

Conclusion

Envision, if you will, a world in which evolutionary theory is accepted as the organizing metatheory for all of the life sciences and humanities. Imagine E. O. Wilson's (1998) world of consilience, in which biology grounds our thinking and our understanding, and all disciplines converse in a common language in pursuit of similar goals. What would public relations theory look like in such a world? In reality, it might not look terribly different from the way it looks today. There would be no need to eliminate or destroy the current theories of public relations under the organizing light of evolution. All theories have a place in this new world, observational and data-based, as well as normative and philosophically based. The only caveat is that all of these theories must recognize that all living things are the product of evolution. Today's behaviors have evolved as solutions to yesterday's problems, and understanding, as well as changing, behaviors, if that is what is wanted, requires understanding the purposes those behaviors serve.

Wilson (1998) has gone so far as to propose evolutionary theory as the bridge between the natural and social sciences that could lead to a unified theory of knowledge. The belief in the "unity of the sciences," the foundation for the 200-year Enlightenment, has been abandoned in the face of romanticism, post-modernism, and the growth of scientific specialization (E. O. Wilson, 1998). For Wilson, the continued search for unification between science, social sciences, and art, which he calls "consilience" after Whewell (1840), is the only appropriate path for future exploration. "The greatest enterprise of the mind has always been and always will be the attempted linkage of the sciences and humanities" (E. O. Wilson, 1998, p. 8). For Wilson, objective knowledge grounded in evolutionary biology is that link (E. O. Wilson, 1998).

Knowing the framework of human behavior can both limit one's expectations and raise one's hopes for the future. If the significance of public relations lies in relationships (J. E. Grunig, 1992), does it not behoove us, as scholars of relationships, to be open to and to learn from those disciplines where relationships are studied? What is lacking and still needed in public relations is a Kuhnian paradigm that would provide explanatory and predictive power to public relations research (Kuhn, 1970). What is needed is a willingness to go beyond the confines of the current social sciences viewpoint and look to the life sciences for answers. What is needed is a willingness to consider that evolutionary theory, with its emphasis on social relationships, may provide what public relations is seeking. Does the field of public relations not owe it to itself to at least consider using evolutionary theory as the framework for a new research agenda that might enlighten the discipline?

That research agenda could include the full range of research techniques, quantitative and qualitative, applied to the examination of research questions derived from evolutionary theory and directed to problems in public relations. These problems could include, among others, the management of relationships between organizations and groups, the relative efficacy of persuasion versus symmetry in approaches to communication, and the disparities between normative theories of behavior and actual human behavior. By using evolutionary theory to guide these explorations, the field of public relations could link its research to that of other fields already engaging in evolution-based research and, thus, expand both its knowledge base and its relevance. Scholars would benefit from the combined approach through increased collaboration and mutual recognition with scholars in other fields, and public relations research could gain the stature outside the field that it desires and deserves.

As Saad (2007) so eloquently pointed out in the conclusion of *The Evolutionary Bases of Consumption*, the article by the Ukrainian geneticist Theodosius

Dobzhansky – "Nothing in biology makes sense except in the light of evolution" (Dobzhansky, 1973) – has implications for other fields. Given that public relations is a human science, and given that humanity is unambiguously "biological," one might add, "Nothing in public relations makes sense except in the light of evolution."

★★★

The evolutionary basis for whistleblowing

The significance of whistleblowing to business and society demands the development of a research agenda in several disciplines, including public relations, journalism, organizational behavior, psychology, management, and ethics, to name a few. In part, the purpose of that agenda would be to investigate what factors, or motivations, could lead one to take a moral stance that, by most accounts, is frequently at odds with self-preservation. How does evolutionary theory explain whistleblowing? Are the whistleblower's actions a successful adaptive response to the environment? Five key concepts from evolutionary theory come to mind when considering whistleblowing: Machiavellian intelligence, cheater detection, cooperation, reciprocity, and reciprocal altruism.

One could label the wrongdoing on the part of organization members as a function of Machiavellian intelligence, the ability to manipulate others (Byrne & Whiten, 1997; Whiten & Byrne, 1997). Awareness by the whistleblower of manipulation on the part of organization members could be ascribed to cheater detection, the ability to know when one is being manipulated (Byrne & Whiten, 1988, 1997; Cosmides & Tooby, 1992; Whiten & Byrne, 1997). If left at that level, evolution has a great deal to say about whistleblowing in terms of those two concepts, but the nature of whistleblowing extends beyond cheating and the awareness of cheating. Whistleblowing involves taking action that may cause harm to oneself but that may benefit another, a concept often characterized as altruism, or reciprocal altruism (Trivers, 1971). Why, then, when the whistleblower knows that the potential consequences of his or her act may be deleterious, does he or she choose to act anyway?

Evolutionists are divided on that answer. As previously stated, Darwin (1979/1859) did not initially propose that changes in species were solely attributable to natural selection. Applying that lack of definitiveness to altruism, one side believes that evolution is transmitted exclusively through the genes of individual members of a species, and that being related fosters a willingness to sacrifice oneself for a relative to the degree to which one's own gene pool will be perpetuated (Hamilton, 1964). This concept is labeled "inclusive fitness" (or kin selection). Examinations of cooperation (Orbell et al., 2004) and heroism in war (Smirnov et al., 2007) appear to support kin selection. Moving beyond kin selection, reciprocal altruism [which Trivers sometimes called "altruism" and which may also be called "indirect reciprocity," a reputation for altruism and cooperative behavior (E.O. Wilson, 2012, in Marsh, 2018, p. 465)], is the willingness to endure some level of harm oneself for someone not closely, or at all, related, with the expenditure on the part of the benefactor generally less than the benefit to the recipient (Trivers, 1971). This act on the part of the benefactor also results in benefit to the benefactor and not, as some have suggested, a benefit to the group. Finally, reciprocal altruism extended to distant or non-kin assumes a level of recurring interaction whereby the possibility of repayment is maximized by the expectation of future opportunities (Trivers, 1971).

The other camp favors group selection, or multilevel selection. This is the theory that evolution favors traits that benefit the group, rather than the individual. This camp views group selection as Darwin's original viewpoint and kin selection as a competing theory (D. S. Wilson, 2009a) that allowed "altruism to be interpreted as a *form of self-interest*" (D. S. Wilson, 2009b, p. 1). For at least some proponents of group selection, the discussion is settled. "Selfishness beats altruism within groups. Altruistic groups beat selfish groups. Everything else is commentary" (D. S. Wilson, 2009a, p. 2).

Much like the arguments between empiricists and postmodernists referenced previously, the argument about kin selection/reciprocal altruism versus group selection rages on among evolutionists. Both sides have learned and worthy advocates. Both sides make compelling arguments for their perspectives. However, for the purposes of this book, the arguments of Hamilton (1964) and Trivers (1971) prevail. Reciprocal altruism is accepted as the underlying motivation for blowing the whistle, and the concept of the "Golden Handcuffs," an example of cooperation and reciprocity, as well as Machiavellian self-interest, is proposed as the underlying motivation for not blowing the whistle.

The Golden Handcuffs

The term "Golden Handcuffs" is a fairly well-known concept in several disciplines. Both management and public relations refer to the term, although it is fair to say the concept originated in management. In management, the term refers to a variety of employee benefits. These may include salary, insurance, fringe benefits, and pension plans (Capelli, 2000; Goldfarb, 2009; Morse, Hall, & Lake, 1997). As one author noted: "Golden handcuff agreements indeed tie an executive to the company, but the reward can be substantial and may even include a share of ownership" (Goldfarb, 2009, p. 1). In this view, stock ownership is only one possible benefit among many.

Other management scholars narrowly define Golden Handcuffs solely as employee stock ownership plans that reward longevity with the organization (Sengupta, Whitfield, & McNabb, 2007). Their studies have found that companies with employee stock ownership plans perform better than those that do not have some form of employee stock ownership. Although the reasons for that improved performance have been less clear, there is some indication that the improved performance can be attributed to increased employee commitment to the organization. "One explanation of the potential role of share ownership in promoting firm performance is that workers owning capital in their firms become more committed to its goals and values" (Sengupta et al., 2007,

p. 1509). Other explanations for improved firm performance include increased satisfaction leading to increased "organizational commitment, job satisfaction and organizational citizenship behavior (Pierce, 1991; Van Dyne and Pierce, 2004)," a concept collectively referred to as the "golden path" (Sengupta et al., 2007, p. 1509).

The Sengupta et al. (2007) study of business performance, which used results from an extensive British employment survey ($N = 28,323$), found a positive relationship between commitment to the organization and high pay, age (50 and older), and Asian ethnicity. However, it did not find that increased organizational performance was due to increased employee commitment. Instead, it found that increased performance was due to lower turnover among employees. This resulted in higher levels of competence among those employees who remained. Regardless of the mechanism, Sengupta (2007) found that companies that use Golden Handcuff rewards for employees outperform those that do not (Sengupta, 2007).

In public relations literature, the term "Golden Handcuffs" refers to high salaries, extensive benefits, and the power that goes with higher-level positions. The Golden Handcuffs concept also may have ethical implications for public relations managers. "The pressures of organizational compliance and corresponding material and social benefits that accrue to public relations managers in the dominant coalition may render doing the right thing even more difficult" (Berger, 2005, p. 14). What public relations and communications executives knew about wrongdoing, what they did with that knowledge, how their actions affected them, and how the actions of their employers toward them affected their relationships with their employers are key questions that prompted the development of this book. The first attempts to answer those questions resulted in a series of published and unpublished efforts (Greenwood 2007, March, 2008, May, 2009, August, 2010, 2011, 2012, August, 2013, March, 2013, May, 2013, June, 2014, April, 2014, May, 2014, August, 2015, 2015, April, 2016, 2017, April, 2020, forthcoming, Greenwood & Kahle, 2007, June). The answers to those questions, based on quantitative data from *this study*, make the argument for elevating the concept of the Golden Handcuffs to the theory of the Golden Handcuffs as a middle-range theory under the metatheory evolutionary theory. Although not agreeing with Greenwood's (2010) proposal to use evolutionary theory as the metatheory for public relations, Marsh (2013), nevertheless, supported the utility of a metatheory in representing more than one paradigm:

> This article does not use the terms metatheory and paradigm interchangeably. In addition to being "theory about theory" (Vogt, 1999, p. 174), a metatheory establishes "basic assumptions" (Leeper, 2001, p. 93) about a discipline or disciplines; a metatheory should provide a means of "conceptualizing [a discipline's] thought" (Greenwood, 2010, p. 456). The related but narrower concept of a paradigm, taken from Kuhn (1970), denotes "a widely accepted definition and central organizing principle" (Hutton, 2001, p. 205). A metatheory, thus, conceivably could inform different and competing paradigms.
>
> (Marsh, 2013, p. 426)

The next chapter, Chapter 2, explores the history of whistleblowing in the United States, the legal protections enacted for whistleblowers, and the whistleblowers who helped bring that legislation about.

Notes

1 From "Evolutionary Theory: The Missing Link for Conceptualizing Public Relations," by C. A. Greenwood, 2010, *Journal of Public Relations Research, 22*(4), pp. 456–476. Copyright 2010 by Taylor & Francis Ltd, www.tandfonline.com. Reprinted with permission.
2 See also Grunig, J. E. and Grunig, 1992, and Grunig, L. A., Grunig, and Dozier, 2002.

References

Aldrich, H. E. (1999). *Organizations evolving.* London: Sage.

Aldrich, H. E., & Ruef, M. (2006). *Organizations evolving* (2nd ed.). Thousand Oaks, CA: Sage.

Almaney, A. (1974). Communication and the systems theory of organization. *Journal of Business Communication, 12*(1), 35–43.

Axelrod, R. M. (1984). *The evolution of cooperation.* New York: Basic Books.

Barkow, J. H., Cosmides, L., & Tooby, J. (Eds.). (1992). *The adapted mind: Evolutionary psychology and the generation of culture.* New York: Oxford University Press.

Baum, J. A. C., & Singh, J. V. (Eds.). (1994). *Evolutionary dynamics of organizations.* New York: Oxford University Press.

Berger, B. K. (2005). Power over, power with, and power to relations: Critical reflections on public relations, the dominant coalition, and activism. *Journal of Public Relations Research, 17*(1), 5–28.

Bertalanffy, L. v. (1951). Problems of general systems theory. *Human Biology, 23*(4), 302–312. Retrieved from http://www.jstor.org/stable/41448003

Bertalanffy, L. v. (1968). *General system theory: Foundations, development, applications.* New York: Braziller.

Botan, C. H. (1989). Theory development in PR. In C. H. Botan & V. Hazleton, Jr. (Eds.), *Public relations theory* (pp. 99–110). Hillsdale, NJ: Lawrence Erlbaum Associates.

Botan, C. H. (1993). Introduction to the paradigm struggle in public relations. *Public Relations Review, 19*(2), 107–110.

Botan, C. H., & Hazleton, V., Jr. (Eds.). (1989). *Public relations theory.* Hillsdale, NJ: Lawrence Erlbaum Associates.

Botan, C. H., & Hazleton, V. (2006a). Public relations in a new age. In C. H. Botan & V. Hazleton (Eds.), *Public relations theory II* (pp. 1–20). Mahwah, NJ: Lawrence Erlbaum Associates.

Botan, C. H., & Hazleton, V. (Eds.). (2006b). *Public relations theory II.* Mahwah, NJ: Lawrence Erlbaum Associates.

Boulding, K. E. (1956). General systems theory: The skeleton of science. *Management Science, 2*(3), 197–208.

Buss, D. M. (1991). Evolutionary personality psychology. *Annual Review of Psychology, 42*, 459–491.

Byrne, R. W., & Whiten, A. (1988). *Machiavellian intelligence: Social expertise and the evolution of intellect in monkeys, apes, and humans.* Oxford, UK: Clarendon Press.

Byrne, R. W., & Whiten, A. (1997). Machiavellian intelligence. In A. Whiten & R. W. Byrne (Eds.), *Machiavellian intelligence II: Extensions and evaluations* (pp. 1–23). Cambridge, UK: Cambridge University Press.

Capelli, P. (2000). A market-driven approach to retaining talent. *Harvard Business Review, 78*(1), 103–111.

Cheney, G., & Christensen, L. T. (2001). Public relations as contested terrain: A critical response. In R. L. Heath (Ed.), *The handbook of public relations* (pp. 167–182). Thousand Oaks, CA: Sage.

Coombs, W. T. (2001). Interpersonal communications and public relations. In R. L. Heath (Ed.), *The handbook of public relations* (pp. 105–114). Thousand Oaks, CA: Sage.

Cords, M. (1997). Friendships, alliances, reciprocity and repair. In A. Whiten & R. W. Byrne (Eds.), *Machiavellian intelligence II: Extensions and evaluations* (pp. 24–49). Cambridge, UK: Cambridge University Press.

Cosmides, L., & Tooby, J. (1992). Cognitive adaptation for social change. In J. H. Barkow, L. Cosmides, & J. Tooby (Eds.), *The adapted mind: Evolutionary psychology and the generation of culture* (pp. 163–228). New York: Oxford University Press.

Cosmides, L., Tooby, J., & Barkow, J. H. (1992). Introduction: Evolutionary psychology and conceptual integration. In J. H. Barkow, L. Cosmides, & J. Tooby (Eds.), *The adapted mind: Evolutionary psychology and the generation of culture* (pp. 3–18). New York: Oxford University Press.

Cropp, F., & Pincus, J. D. (2001). The mystery of public relations: Unraveling its past, unmasking its future. In R. L. Heath (Ed.), *The handbook of public relations* (pp. 189–203). Thousand Oaks, CA: Sage.

Curtin, P. A., & Gaither, T. K. (2005). Privileging identity, difference, and power: The circuit of culture as a basis for public relations theory. *Journal of Public Relations Research, 17*(2), 91–115.

Cutlip, S. M., Center, A. H., & Broom, G. M. (1985). *Effective public relations* (6th ed.). Englewood Cliffs, NJ: Prentice-Hall.

Cutlip, S. M., Center, A. H., & Broom, G. M. (1994). *Effective public relations.* Englewood Cliffs, NJ: Prentice-Hall.

Darwin, C. (1871). *The descent of man, and selection in relation to sex.* London: J. Murray.

Darwin, C. (1979/1859). *On the origin of species.* New York: Gramercy Books.

Dennett, D. C. (1995). *Darwin's dangerous idea: Evolution and the meanings of life.* New York: Simon & Schuster.

de Santis, M. D. (2021). Misconceptions about historical sciences in evolutionary biology. *Evolutionary Biology, 48*(1), 94–99. https://doi.org/10.1007/s11692-020-09526-6

Dobzhansky, T. (1973). Nothing in biology makes sense except in the light of evolution. *The American Biology Teacher, 35*(March), 125–129.

Fessler, D. M. T., & Haley, K. J. (2003). The strategy of affect: Emotions in human cooperation. In P. Hammerstein (Ed.), *Genetic and cultural evolution of cooperation* (pp. 7–36). Cambridge, MA: MIT Press.

Field, A. J. (2004). *Altruistically inclined? The behavioral sciences, evolutionary theory, and the origins of reciprocity.* Ann Arbor, MI: University of Michigan Press.

Frith, C. D. (2007). The social brain? *Philosophical Transactions: Biological Sciences Social Intelligence: From Brain to Culture, 362*(1480), 671–678.

Gee, H., Howlett, R., & Campbell, P. (2009, January). 15 evolutionary gems. *Nature, 2009.* Retrieved from www.nature.com/evolutiongems

Gibson, M. A., & Lawson, D. W. (2015). Applying evolutionary anthropology. *Evolutionary Anthropology, 24*(1), 3–14. https://doi.org/10.1002/evan.21432

Gigerenzer, G. (1997). The modulatory of social intelligence. In A. Whiten & R. W. Byrne (Eds.), *Machiavellian intelligence II: Extensions and evaluations* (pp. 264–288). Cambridge, UK: Cambridge University Press.

Goldfarb, A. (2009). "Golden Handcuffs" can hold key to locking up top executives. *Fenton Report* (March 22, 2009). Retrieved from www.fentonreport.com/2009/03/22/entrepreneurs/%E2%80%9Cgolden-handcuffs%E2%80%9D-can-hold-key-to-locking-up-top-executives/684

Gower, K. K. (2006). Public relations research at the cross-roads. *Journal of Public Relations Research, 18*, 177–190.

Greenwood, C. A. (2007, March). *Evolutionary theory: The missing link for Public Relations.* Unpublished manuscript.

Greenwood, C. A. (2008, May). *Evolutionary theory: The missing link for public relations.* Paper presented at the Annual Meeting of the International Communication Association, Montreal, Canada.

Greenwood, C. A. (2009, August). *Whistleblowing in public relations: Call for a research agenda.* Poster presented at the Association for Education in Journalism and Mass Communication Annual Conference. Boston, MA.

Greenwood, C. A. (2010). Evolutionary theory: The missing link for conceptualizing public relations. *Journal of Public Relations Research, 22*(4), 456–476. https://doi.org/10.1080/10627261003801438

Greenwood, C. A. (2011). *Killing the messenger: A survey of public relations practitioners and organizational response to whistleblowing after Sarbanes-Oxley.* Doctoral dissertation. University of Oregon, Eugene, OR. Retrieved from ProQuest Dissertations & Theses (UMI No. 907550960).

Greenwood, C. A. (2012, August). *Whistleblowing in the Fortune 1000: Ethical dilemma or role responsibility?* Paper presented at the Association for Education in Journalism and Mass Communication Annual Conference, Chicago, IL.

Greenwood, C. A. (2013, March). *Whistleblowing in government: What whistleblowers and reporters say about it.* Paper presented at the Association for Education in Journalism and Mass Communication Midwinter Conference, Norman, OK

Greenwood, C. A. (2013, May). *What public relations practitioners do and what whistleblowers want.* Presentation at the PRSA/GA Annual Conference. Atlanta, GA.

Greenwood, C. A. (2013, June). *Whistleblowing in the Fortune 1000: What did public relations practitioners tell us?* Poster presented at the International Communication Association Conference. London, UK.

Greenwood, C. A. (2014, April). *Whistleblowing as an act of communication: What ethical choices do communicators face?* Panel presentation at the Eastern Communication Association Annual Meeting, Providence, RI.

Greenwood, C. A. (2014, May). *Whistleblowing in government: What whistleblowers say about it.* Paper presented at the International Communication Association Annual Conference, Seattle, WA.

Greenwood, C. A. (2014, August). *Whistleblowing in government as free expression: Are government whistleblowers traitors, heroes, or loyal employees trying to do the right thing?* Panel presentation at the Association for Education in Journalism and Mass Communication Annual Conference. Montreal, Canada.

Greenwood, C. A. (2015). Whistleblowing in the *Fortune 1000*: What practitioners told us about wrongdoing in corporations in a pilot study. *Public Relations Review, 41*(4), 490–500. https://doi.org/10.1016/j.pubrev.2015.07.005

Greenwood, C. A. (2015, April). *Whistleblowing in a national laboratory: Do whistleblower protections apply to federal contractors, and how is national security compromised when they don't?* Panel presentation at the Eastern Communication Association Annual Conference. Philadelphia, PA

Greenwood, C. A. (2016). Golden Handcuffs in the Fortune 1000? An employee-organization relationship survey of public relations executives and practitioners in the largest companies. *Communication Research Reports, 33*(3), 269–274. https://doi.org/10.1080/08824096.2016.1186624

Greenwood, C. A. (2017, April). *Whistleblowing: Can E&C programs induce reporting and reduce retaliation?* Presentation at the Ethics and Compliance Initiative Annual Conference. Washington, DC.

Greenwood, C. A. (2020). "I was just doing my job!" Evolution, corruption, and public relations in interviews with government whistleblowers. *PARTECIPAZIONE E CONFLITTO, 13*(2), 1042–1061. https://doi.org/10.1285/i20356609v13i2p1042

Greenwood, C. A. (forthcoming). Secrets, sources, whistleblowers, and leakers: Journalism in the Digital Age. [Review of the book *Journalism After Snowden: The Future of the Free Press in the Surveillance State*, E. Bell & T. Owen [Eds.]]. *Communication Booknotes Quarterly, 52*(1).

Greenwood, C. A., & Kahle, L. R. (2007, June). *Toward an evolutionary theory of marketing: Evolution and branding*. Proceedings of the Advertising & Consumer Psychology Conference, Santa Monica, CA. Retrieved from www.myscp.org/pdf/ACP%202007%20Proceedings.pdf

Grunig, J. E. (1975). A multi-systems theory of organizational communication. *Communication Research, 2*(2), 99–136.

Grunig, J. E. (1989). Symmetrical presuppositions as a framework for public relations theory. In C. H. Botan & V. Hazleton, Jr. (Eds.), *Public relations theory* (pp. 17–44). Hillsdale, NJ: Lawrence Erlbaum Associates.

Grunig, J. E. (Ed.). (1992). *Excellence in public relations and communication management*. Hillsdale, NJ: Lawrence Erlbaum Associates.

Grunig, J. E. (1993). Image and substance: From symbolic to behavioral relationships. *Public Relations Review, 19*(2), 121–139.

Grunig, J. E. (2001). Two-way symmetrical public relations: Past, present, and future. In R. L. Heath & G. Vasquez (Eds.), *The handbook of public relations* (pp. 11–30). Thousand Oaks, CA: Sage.

Grunig, J. E., & Grunig, L. A. (1992). Models of public relations and communication. In J. E. Grunig (Ed.), *Excellence in public relations and communication management* (pp. 285–325). Hillsdale, NJ: Lawrence Erlbaum Associates.

Grunig, J. E., & Grunig, L. A. (2000). Public relations in strategic management and strategic management of public relations: Theory and evidence from the IABC Excellence project. *Journalism Studies, 1*(2), 303–321.

Grunig, J. E., & Grunig, L. A. (2008). Excellence theory in public relations: Past, present, and future. In A. Zerfass, B. van Ruler, & K. Sriramesh (Eds.), *Public relations research: European and international perspectives* (pp. 327–347). Weisbaden, Germany: VS Verlag für Sozialwissenschaften.

Grunig, J. E., Grunig, L. A., & Dozier, D. M. (2006). The excellence theory. In C. H. Botan & V. Hazleton (Eds.), *Public relations theory II* (pp. 21–62). Mahwah, NJ: Lawrence Erlbaum Associates.

Grunig, J. E., & Grunig, L. S. (1986). Application of general system theory to public relations: Review of a program of research. *Public Relations Review, 12*(3), 54.

Grunig, J. E., & Huang, Y.-H. (2000). From organizational effectiveness to relationship indicators: Antecedents of relationships, public relations strategies, and relationship outcomes. In J. A. Ledingham & S. D. Bruning (Eds.), *Public relations as relationship management: A relational approach to the study and practice of public relations* (pp. 23–54). Mahwah, NJ: Lawrence Erlbaum Associates.

Grunig, J. E., & Kim, J.-N. (2021). 15 The four models of public relations and their research legacy. In C. Valentini (Ed.), Public Relations (pp. 277–312). Boston: De Gruyter Mouton. Retrieved from https://doi.org/10.1515/9783110554250-015.

Grunig, J. E., & White, J. (1992). The effect of worldviews on public relations theory and practice. In J. E. Grunig, D. M. Dozier, W. P. Ehling, L. A. Grunig, F. C. Repper, & J. White (Eds.), *Excellence in public relations and communication management* (pp. 31–64). Hillsdale, NJ: Lawrence Erlbaum Associates.

Grunig, L. A., Grunig, J. E., & Dozier, D. M. (2002). *Excellent public relations and effective organizations: A study of communication management in three countries.* Mahwah, NJ: Lawrence Erlbaum Associates.

Hamilton, W. D. (1964). The genetical evolution of social behaviour. I and II. *Journal of Theoretical Biology, 7*(1), 1–52.

Hammerstein, P. (2003). *Genetic and cultural evolution of cooperation.* Cambridge, MA: MIT Press.

Harcourt, A. H., & de Waal, F. B. M. (1992). *Coalitions and alliances in humans and other animals.* Oxford, UK: Oxford University Press.

Hickson, M., III. (1973). The open systems model: Auditing the effectiveness of organizational communication. *Journal of Business Communication, 10*(3), 7–14.

Holtzhausen, D. R. (2000). Postmodern values in public relations. *Journal of Public Relations Research, 12*(1), 93–114.

Holtzhausen, D. R., & Roberts, G. F. (2008). *An investigation into the role of image repair theory in strategic conflict management.* Paper presented at the meeting of the International Communication Association, Montreal, Canada.

Holtzhausen, D. R., & Voto, R. (2002). Resistance from the margins: The postmodern public relations practitioner as organizational activist. *Journal of Public Relations Research, 14*(1), 57–84.

Hon, L. C., & Grunig, J. E. (1999). *Guidelines for measuring relationships in public relations* (pp. 40). Retrieved from http://painepublishing.com/wp-content/uploads/2013/10/Guidelines_Measuring_Relationships.pdf

Huang, Y.-H. (1997). *Public relations strategies, relational outcomes, and conflict management strategies.* (Doctoral dissertation), University of Maryland, College Park, MD. Retrieved from ProQuest Dissertations Publishing 9816477

Humphrey, N. (1976). The social function of intellect. In P. P. G. Bateson & R. A. Hinge (Eds.), *Growing points in ethology* (pp. 303–317). Oxford, UK: Cambridge University Press.

Humphrey, N. (1988). The social function of intellect. In R. W. Byrne & A. Whiten (Eds.), *Machiavellian intelligence: Social expertise and the evolution of intellect in monkeys, apes and humans* (pp. 13–26). Oxford, UK: Oxford University Press.

Hutton, J. G. (2001). Defining the relationship between public relations and marketing. In R. L. Heath (Ed.), *The handbook of public relations* (pp. 205–214). Thousand Oaks, CA: Sage.

Kahle, L. R. (1984). *Attitudes and social adaptation: A person-situation interaction approach.* Oxford, UK: Pergamon Press.

Kelly, K. S. (2001). Stewardship: The fifth step in the public relations process. In R. L. Heath (Ed.), *Handbook of public relations* (pp. 279–289). Thousand Oaks, CA: Sage Publications.

Kuhn, T. S. (1970). *The structure of scientific revolutions.* Chicago, IL: University of Chicago Press.

Ledingham, J. A., & Bruning, S. D. (2000). *Public relations as relationship management: A relational approach to the study and practice of public relations.* Mahwah, NJ: Lawrence Erlbaum Associates.

Leeper, R. (2001). In search of a metatheory for public relations: An argument for communitarianism. In R. L. Heath (Ed.), *The handbook of public relations* (pp. 93–104). Thousand Oaks, CA: Sage.

Marsh, C. (2013). Social harmony paradigms and natural selection: Darwin, Kropotkin, and the metatheory of mutual aid. *Journal of Public Relations Research, 25*(5), 426–441. http://doi.org/10.1080/1062726X.2013.795861

Marsh, C. (2018). Indirect reciprocity and reputation management: Interdisciplinary findings from evolutionary biology and economics. *Public Relations Review, 44*(4), 463–470. https://doi.org/10.1016/j.pubrev.2018.04.002

McKie, D. (2001). Updating public relations: "New science," research paradigms, and uneven developments. In R. L. Heath (Ed.), *The handbook of public relations* (pp. 75–92). Thousand Oaks, CA: Sage.

Merton, R. K. (1967). *On theoretical sociology: Five essays, old and new.* New York: The Free Press.

Meyer, A. D. (1991). What is strategy's distinctive competence? *Journal of Management, 17*(4), 821–833.

Miller, G. F. (2000). *The mating mind: How sexual choice shaped the evolution of human nature.* New York: Doubleday.

Miller, G. R. (1989). Persuasion and public relations: Two "Ps" in a pod. In C. H. Botan & V. Hazleton Jr. (Eds.), *Public relations theory* (pp. 45–66). Hillsdale, NJ: Lawrence Erlbaum Associates.

Miller, K. S. (2000). U.S. public relations history: Knowledge and limitations. In M. E. Roloff & G. D. Paulson (Eds.), *Communication Yearbook* (Vol. 23, pp. 381–420). London: Sage.

Moloney, K. (2006). *Rethinking public relations: PR, propaganda, and democracy* (2nd ed. ed.). New York: Routledge Taylor & Francis Group.

Morse, C. T., Hall, W. E., & Lake, B. J. (1997). More than Golden Handcuffs. *Journal of Accountancy, 184*(5), 37–42.

Murphy, P. (1991). The limits of symmetry: A game theory approach to symmetric and asymmetric public relations. In L. A. Grunig & J. E. Grunig (Eds.), *Public relations research annual* (Vol. 3, pp. 115–131). Hillsdale, NJ: Lawrence Erlbaum Associates.

Murphy, P. (1996). Chaos theory as a model for managing issues and crises. *Public Relations Review, 22*(2), 95.

Murphy, P. (2000). Symmetry, contingency, complexity: Accommodating uncertainty in public relations theory. *Public Relations Review, 26*(4), 447–462.

Murphy, P. (2007). Coping with an uncertain world: The relationship between excellence and complexity theories. In E. L. Toth (Ed.), *The future of excellence in public relations and communication management* (pp. 119–134). Mahwah, NJ: Lawrence Erlbaum Associates, Inc.

Nelson, R. R., & Winter, S. G. (1982). *An evolutionary theory of economic change.* Cambridge, MA: Harvard University Press.

Nettle, D., Gibson, M. A., Lawson, D. W., & Sear, R. (2013). Human behavioral ecology: current research and future prospects. *Behavioral Ecology, 24*(5), 1031–1040. https://doi.org/10.1093/beheco/ars222

Nothhaft, H. (2016). A framework for strategic communication research: A call for synthesis and consilience. *International Journal of Strategic Communication, 10*(2), 69–86. http://doi.org/10.1080/1553118X.2015.1124277

Nothhaft, H. (2017). Disagreement about the therapy, Not the diagnosis: A reply to the rejoinders. *International Journal of Strategic Communication, 11*(3), 189–193. Retrieved from https://doi.org/10.1080/1553118X.2017.1318884

Orbell, J., Morikawa, T., Hartwig, J., Hanley, J., & Allen, N. (2004). "Machiavellian" intelligence as a basis for the evolution of cooperative dispositions. *American Political Science Review, 98*(1).

Pasadeos, Y., Renfro, R. B., & Hanily, M. L. (1999). Influential authors and works of the public relations scholarly literature: A network of recent research. *Journal of Public Relations Research, 11*(1), 29.

PriceWaterhouseCoopers. (2018). *2018 Global Economic Crime and Fraud Survey: US perspectives.* Retrieved from https://www.pwc.com/us/en/services/consulting/cybersecurity-privacy-forensics/library/global-economic-fraud-survey.html

Prior-Miller, M. (1989). Four major social scientific theories and their value to the public relations researcher. In C. H. Botan & J. Hazleton, V. (Eds.), *Public relations theory* (pp. 67–81). Hillsdale, NJ: Lawrence Erlbaum Associates.

Saad, G. (2004). Applying evolutionary psychology in understanding the representation of women in advertisements. *Psychology & Marketing, 21*(8), 593–612.

Saad, G. (2006a). Applying Darwinian principles in designing effective intervention strategies: The case of sun tanning. *Psychology & Marketing, 23*(7), 617–638.

Saad, G. (2006b). Applying evolutionary psychology in understanding the Darwinian roots of consumption phenomena. *Managerial and Decision Economics, 27,* 189–201.

Saad, G. (2007). *The evolutionary bases of consumption.* Mahwah, NJ: Lawrence Erlbaum Associates.

Saad, G., & Gill, T. (2000). Applications of evolutionary psychology in marketing. *Psychology & Marketing, 17*(12).

Safina, C. (2009). Darwinism must die so that evolution may live. *The New York Times* (February 10, 2009). Retrieved from http://www.nytimes.com/2009/02/10/science/10essa.html?th&emc=th

Sallot, L. M., Lyon, L. J., Acosta-Alzuru, C., & Jones, K. O. (2008). From aardvark to zebra redux: An analysis of theory development in public relations academic journals into the 21st century. In T. L. Hansen-Horn & B. Neff, Dostal (Eds.), *Public relations: From theory to practice* (pp. 343–387). Boston, MA: Pearson Allyn & Bacon.

Seiffert-Brockmann, J. (2018). Evolutionary psychology: A framework for strategic communication research. *International Journal of Strategic Communication, 12*(4), 417–432. https://doi.org/10.1080/1553118X.2018.1490291

Sengupta, S., Whitfield, K., & McNabb, B. (2007). Employee share ownership and performance: Golden path or Golden Handcuffs? *International Journal of Human Resource Management, 18*(8), 1507–1538.

Singh, J. V. (Ed.) (1990). *Organizational evolution.* Newbury Park, CA: Sage.

Smirnov, O., Arrow, H., Kennett, D., & Orbell, J. (2007). Ancestral war and the evolutionary origins of "heroism". *Journal of Politics, 69*(4), 927–940.

Stroh, U. (2007). An alternative postmodern approach to corporate communication strategy. In E. L. Toth (Ed.), *The future of excellence in public relations and communication management* (pp. 199–220). Mahwah, NJ: Lawrence Erlbaum Associates.

Trivers, R. (1971). The evolution of reciprocal altruism. *Quarterly Review of Biology, 46*(March), 35–57.

Trivers, R. (1985). *Social evolution.* Menlo Park, CA: Benjamin/Cummings.

Tucker, R. K. (1971). General systems theory application to the design of speech communication courses. *Speech Teacher, 20*(3), 159–166.

Verčič, D., & Grunig, J. E. (2000). The origins of public relations theory in economics and strategic management. In D. Moss, D. Vercic, & G. Warnaby (Eds.), *Perspectives on public relations research* (pp. 9–58). London: Routledge Taylor & Francis Group.

Volk, S. C. (2016). A systematic review of 40 years of public relations evaluation and measurement research: Looking into the past, the present, and future. *Public Relations Review, 42*(5), 962–977. https://doi.org/10.1016/j.pubrev.2016.07.003

Wade, N. (2009). Darwin, ahead of his time, is still influential. *The New York Times* (February 10, 2009). Retrieved from http://nytimes.com/2009/02/10/science/10evoluton.html?_r=1&th=&em=th&pagew

Weaver, A. J., & Wilson, B. J. (2009). The role of graphic and sanitized violence in the enjoyment of television dramas. *Human Communication Research, 35*(3), 442–463.

Whewell, W. (1840). *Aphorisms concerning ideas, science & the language of science.* London: Harrison & co., printers.

Whiten, A., & Byrne, R. W. (1988). The Machiavellian intelligence hypotheses: Editorial. In R. W. Byrne & A. Whiten (Eds.), *Machiavellian intelligence: Social expertise and the evolution of intellect in monkeys, apes, and humans.* Oxford, UK: Clarendon Press.

Whiten, A., & Byrne, R. W. (1997). *Machiavellian intelligence II: Extensions and evaluations.* Cambridge, UK: Cambridge University Press.

Wilson, D. S. (2009a). Truth and reconciliation for group selection II: The original problem. *The Huffington Post* (January 1, 2009). Retrieved from www.huffingtonpost.com/david-sloan-wilson/truth-and-reconciliation_b_154660.html

Wilson, D. S. (2009b). Truth and reconciliation for group selection XIII: Hamilton speaks. *The Huffington Post* (May 21, 2009). Retrieved from www.huffingtonpost.com/david-sloan-wilson/truth-and-reconciliation_b_206248.html

Wilson, E. O. (1975). *Sociobiology: The new synthesis.* Cambridge, MA: Harvard University Press.

Wilson, E. O. (1998). *Consilience: The unity of knowledge.* New York: Knopf.

2 The history of whistleblowing in the United States

Definition of whistleblowing

The concept of whistleblowing and the definition of who is a whistleblower, what type of activity is reported by a whistleblower, and to whom the activity is reported have undergone subtle revisions over time as research has been conducted in the public and private sectors and as laws in the United States and around the world have changed. For example, some researchers consider reporting to an internal authority a political action and not whistleblowing (Near & Miceli, 1987). Others view providing anonymous information to outside entities, such as the media, as leaking and not whistleblowing (Fasterling & Lewis, 2014), while still others think leaking is a form of whistleblowing: "Leaking is the unauthorized disclosure of information. It can be a method of whistleblowing, typically without the leaker's identify being revealed" (Martin, 2014, p. 516). Some think the definition of whistleblower should include organizational outsiders as well as insiders (Culiberg & Mihelič, 2017). Still others view reporting by those outside an organization as bell-ringing (Miceli, Dreyfus, & Near, 2014). This study uses the definition of whistleblowing that requires the whistleblower *to be a current or former employee, that requires the information to be about wrongdoing or potential wrongdoing by the employer, and that requires the notification to be made in an attempt to stop wrongdoing to an entity, internal or external, that has the ability to stop the wrongdoing.* However, the determination of who is and who is not a whistleblower is not always easy to determine; how the whistleblower reports and to whom, under what laws or regulations, in what manner and timeframe, and to what purpose are all components of whistleblowing. In some cases, that determination may be up to public opinion, administrative rule, the courts, or the long view of history.

Federal definitions of wrongdoing, whistleblowing, retaliation, and protection from retaliation

The *Civil Service Reform Act of 1978* (CSRA) [5 U.S.C. § 1101 (1978)] encouraged federal employees "to expose fraud, waste and mismanagement" (Merit Systems Protection Board, 1981, p. 8), and it promised those who did

DOI: 10.4324/9781315231891-3

protection from retaliation. The CSRA created the U.S. Merit Systems Protection Board (MSPB) to offer that protection by tracking trends in wrongdoing, whistleblowing, and retaliation, and by adjudicating whistleblower allegations of retaliation (See Appendix D). As part of its tracking mandate, the MSPB administered three longitudinal, stratified, random sample surveys to 39,000 federal employees in 1980, 1983, and 1992 (Merit Systems Protection Board, 1981, 1984, 1993). The purpose of the surveys was to identify trends in illegal and wasteful activity observed by federal employees, their reporting (or lack of reporting) of those activities, and the level of retaliation they experienced for reporting the activities. Subsequent federal research and evaluation added to the picture of federal employee whistleblowing (Merit Systems Protection Board, 2001, 2010a, 2010b, 2011a, 2011b, 2014), but the first three surveys established the nomenclature of, and approach to, whistleblowing research that would carry forward into other fields.

Wrongdoing

The characterization of wrongdoing in the 1981 MSPB report was "Fraud, waste, and mismanagement" (Merit Systems Protection Board, 1981, p. 1). The types of potential wrongdoing delineated in the survey were employee(s) stealing federal funds; employee(s) stealing federal property; employee(s) accepting bribes or kickbacks; waste of federal funds caused by ineligible people (or organizations) receiving funds, goods, or services; waste of federal funds caused by buying deficient goods or services; waste of federal funds caused by a badly managed federal program; employee(s) abusing his/her official position to obtain substantial personal services or favors; employee(s) giving unfair advantage to a particular contractor, consultant or vendor (for example, because of personal ties or family connections, or with the intent of being employed by that contractor later on); employee(s) tolerating a situation which poses a danger to public health or safety; employee(s) commiting [sic] a serious violation of federal law or regulation other than those described above (Merit Systems Protection Board, 1981, Appendix B, p. 4).

The characterization of wrongdoing in the 1984 report was "Fraud, waste, and abuse" (Merit Systems Protection Board, 1984, p. 5), and the list of wrongdoing was the same as that listed in 1981 with the exception that "employee(s)" was removed from the beginning of each activity and "organizations" was removed from "ineligible people (or organizations) receiving funds, goods, or services" (Merit Systems Protection Board, 1984, Appendix C, p. 4). The characterization remained "Fraud, waste, and abuse" in the 1993 report (Merit Systems Protection Board, 1993, p. 1), and the list of wrongdoing remained the same as that listed in 1984 (Merit Systems Protection Board, 1993, Appendix A, p. 6). However, in 2011, the MSPB defined "wrongdoing" as any one of a number of types of misconduct specified in the United States Code: "a violation of any law, rule, or regulation, or gross mismanagement, a gross waste of funds, an abuse of authority, or a substantial and specific danger to public health or safety may be referred to as 'wrongdoing'" (Merit Systems Protection Board, 2011a, p. 1). The 2010 survey was identical to the 1992 survey with the exception of the addition of the words "substantial and specific" preceding "danger to public health or safety" (Merit Systems Protection Board, 2011a, p. 29).

Whistleblowing

The MSPB used the term "whistleblowing" in its first two reports to characterize the delivery of information about wrongdoing to a particular entity (Merit Systems Protection Board, 1981, 1984). However, in its 1993 and 2011 reports (Merit Systems Protection Board, 1993, 2011a), it used the term "reporting." "Because our 1992 survey used the term 'report' to describe the act of telling others about wrongdoing, we opted to use that term for the 2010 survey as well" (Merit Systems Protection Board, 2011a, p. 2).

Respondents were asked if they had reported misconduct to one or more of the following entities:

> Co-workers, immediate supervisor, someone above my immediate supervisor, personnel office, the Office of the Inspector General or the IG 'Hot Line' within the agency,[1] a union representative, the Special Counsel within the Merit Systems Protection Board, the General Accounting Office, a member of Congress, or a member of the news media.
>
> (Merit Systems Protection Board, 1981, Appendix B, p. 5)

Reporting to co-workers was captured in the survey but excluded from the tally of whistleblowing activity because co-workers had no power to stop the wrongdoing, and reporting to them did not constitute whistleblowing under the law (Merit Systems Protection Board, 1981).

Retaliation

Types of retaliation, also called "reprisals," were listed in each of the MSPB surveys and changed only slightly over time. The 1980 survey listed nine types of reprisals:

> Poor performance appraisal; Denial of promotion; Denial of opportunity for training; Assigned less desirable or less important duties in my current job; Transfer or reassignment to a different job with less desirable duties; Reassignment to a different geographic location; Suspension from your job; Grade level demotion; [and] "Other."
>
> (Merit Systems Protection Board, 1981, Appendix B, p. 7)

The 1983 survey listed the same nine types of reprisals (Merit Systems Protection Board, 1984, Appendix D, p. 7). The 1992 survey listed five additional items: "Denial of award," "Fired from my job," "Shunned by coworkers or managers," "Verbal harassment or intimidation," and "Required to take a fitness-for-duty exam" (Merit Systems Protection Board, 1993, p. 45). The 2010 survey repeated the 14 types of reprisals listed in the 1992 survey (Merit Systems Protection Board, 2011a, p. 33).

Protection from retaliation

Protection for the whistleblower depended on the circumstances. "Not all reports of wrongdoing are protected disclosures, and not all unpleasant reactions by the agency constitute retaliation as defined by the law" (Merit Systems Protection Board, 2011a, p. 1). The use of "reporting" was not condoned by the court system when it came to whistleblowing protection:

> However, when it comes to protecting whistleblowers, the Federal Circuit has held that it is disclosures that are protected, not reports . . . "[w]hen an employee reports or states that there has been misconduct by a wrongdoer to the wrongdoer, the employee is not making a 'disclosure' of misconduct" and the Whistleblower Protection Act will not apply. This is because "the term "disclosure" means to reveal something that was hidden and not known."
> (Merit Systems Protection Board, 2011a, p. 2)

The MSPB also found it significant that the Whistleblower Protection Act (WPA) used the term "disclosure" and not a more general word "such as 'report' or 'state'" (2011a, p. 2). Although the federal definition of whistleblowing encompassed internal and external reporting, the court ruled that whistleblowing was not protected if the employee reported the violation to the violator. That makes a review of the laws governing whistleblowing imperative, with the further caveat that judicial interpretations are also relevant. A list of some of the laws impacting whistleblowing follows.

Whistleblowing in the United States

Federal laws

False Claims Act of 1863

The federal government sanctioned whistleblowing for the first time during the Civil War. The *False Claims Act of 1863* [12 U.S.C. § 696 (1863)], also called the "Lincoln Law," was enacted as a way to prevent private suppliers from defrauding the Union Army with inferior goods (Lumm, 2010). The FCA encouraged private citizens to report fraud in federal contracting by filing qui tam lawsuits on behalf of the federal government and themselves. Qui tam is Latin for "he who brings an action for the king as well as for himself" (The False Claims Act Legal Center, 2008). The law allowed the reporter, also called a "relator," to collect 50% of the amount the government recovered.

The concept of qui tam was imported from English law. Qui tam was falling out of favor in England about the time it was instituted in the United States due to abuses by professional informers, who made their living by bringing qui tam lawsuits (Beck, 2000). Abuse of qui tam in the United States came to light during World War II, when an informer filed a claim based on information gathered by the federal government in a fraud action and was rewarded under the FCA (Beck, 2000). As a result, Congress attempted to repeal the qui tam aspect of the act in 1942, but the Supreme Court upheld it. In 1943, Congress reduced the amount of the award from 50% to 25% (or 10% if the government sued) and disallowed claims based on information the government already had (Lumm, 2010).

The 1958 Code of Ethics for Government Service

It was almost 100 years before the federal government again passed whistle-blowing legislation. The next legislation focused on how federal employees should conduct themselves. The 1958 *Code of Ethics for Government Service* [72 Stat. B12 (1958)] listed the responsibilities of federal employees. These included:

> "Put loyalty to the highest moral principles above loyalty to persons, party, or Government department"; "Uphold the Constitution, laws, and legal regulations of the United States and of all governments therein and never be a party to their evasion"; "Never discriminate unfairly by the dispensing of special favors or privileges to anyone, whether for remuneration or not; and never accept, for himself or his family, favors or benefits under circumstances which might be construed by reasonable persons as influencing the performance of his governmental duties"; "Never use any information coming to him confidentially in the performance of governmental duties as a means for making private profit"; and "Expose corruption wherever discovered"; and "Uphold these principles, ever conscious that public office is a public trust."
>
> (*Code of Ethics for Government Service*, 72 Stat. B12, 1958)

The Freedom of Information Act of 1966

The next decade saw two major actions that benefited whistleblowers, one in the legislative arena and one in the judicial arena. The first was the *Freedom of Information Act of 1966* [5 U.S.C. § 552 (1966)], which "established government documents as public records" and gave whistleblowers "a statutory justification for exposing misconduct" on the basis of "the public's right to know" (Merit Systems Protection Board, 1993, p. 33). "It was the result of an eleven-year public relations program educating most of the press and the Congress and much of the public on the dangers of government secrecy" (Archibald, 1979, p. 315). However, the news media argued that the act had three problems: It did not require government to create documents; there was no requirement that documents be provided in a timely manner; and anyone who requested the information could receive it, including the news outlet's competitors (Archibald, 1979). As evidence of its importance, Congress amended the act ten times in the next five decades (Department of Justice Guide to the Freedom of Information Act, 2013).

The Nixon years

The changing of political parties at the federal level, which involved the election of a Republican president after two Democratic presidents, set the stage for the enactment of retaliatory federal personnel policies and contributed to the next major whistleblowing protection in the federal government, the CSRA. Richard M. Nixon, who served as vice president under Republican President of the United States Dwight D. Eisenhower for two terms during the 1950s, was elected the 37th President of the United States in 1968. He succeeded Lyndon B. Johnson, a Democrat, who had assumed the presidency after the assassination of President John F. Kennedy. Johnson had served a full term of his own before deciding not to run for a second full term. Nixon reportedly believed that federal agencies were top-heavy with Democrats who had been put in place in the last days of the Johnson administration and who would thwart his policies (U.S. Senate Committee on Governmental Affairs, 1978).

To deal with this perceived threat, the Nixon White House developed one of the most extensively documented processes of retaliation within the U.S. government, which eventually was codified in a personnel training manual called by some the "May Manual" (U.S. House of Representatives Subcommittee on Manpower and Civil Service of the Committee on Post Office and Civil Services, 1976) and by others the "Malek Manual" (U.S. Senate Committee on Governmental Affairs, 1978). At the time, Alan May was acknowledged as the only author of the manual, "though others have suspected he had help in the preparation" (U.S. House of Representatives Subcommittee on Manpower and Civil Service of the Committee on Post Office and Civil Services, 1976, p. 160). The manual instructed political appointees at the highest levels in the Nixon administration on ways to subvert the federal civil service system by firing existing federal employees and replacing them with political appointees (U.S. Senate Committee on the Judiciary, 1986). It showed Nixon-appointees in federal agencies how to fire civil service employees "without violating civil service rules" and also "served as a Watergate catalyst for civil service reform" (U.S. Senate Committee on the Judiciary, 1986, p. 123). Fred Malek, former special assistant to the president and later deputy director of the Office of Management and Budget (Rosenwald, 2008), denied any role in authoring the document (Malek, 2008).

Federal whistleblowers in the Nixon era

Daniel Ellsberg

In 1967, Daniel Ellsberg, an employee of the RAND Corporation and an advisor to the Nixon administration with a doctorate in economics from Harvard University, was given access to the "Top Secret McNamara study of *U.S. Decision-making in Vietnam, 1945–68*," which chronicled past and present U.S. policies in Vietnam (Ellsberg, 2018b). In reading the 7,000-page document, Ellsberg became concerned about those policies and the apparent intent to escalate the war under the Nixon administration. In 1969, he began copying the document and giving it to Senator J. William Fulbright, chair of the Senate Foreign Relations Committee, who he hoped would use it to effect a change in policy that would shorten the war (Ellsberg, 2018b). By 1971, when Fulbright had not yet released the document or acted on it, Ellsberg gave copies of the report to media outlets: first, the *New York Times*, then the *Washington Post* and numerous other newspapers (Ellsberg, 2018a). Despite court injunctions to repress publication, the *Times* and the *Post*, as well as other newspapers, published portions of the "Pentagon Papers," as the report became known. When the issue of injunctions to prevent publication was brought before the U.S. Supreme Court, it quickly ruled [*New York Times Co. v. United States*, 403 U.S. 713 (1971)] that the government could not execute prior restraint to prevent the newspapers from publishing the document (Spitzer, 2019). For his role in providing the top secret documents to the media, the U.S. government indicted Daniel Ellsberg on 12 felony counts (Ellsberg, 2018b).

The public outcry from publication of the Pentagon Papers, as well as President Nixon's concern that Ellsberg was about to release secret documents showing Nixon's plans to escalate the Vietnam War, including plans for nuclear war, upset the president (Krogh, 2007). Nixon authorized his operatives (the "White House plumbers") to burglarize the office of Ellsberg's psychiatrist, Dr. Lewis Fielding, under the auspices of national security to find information to discredit Ellsberg (Krogh, 2007). FBI documents discussed the possible role of the Central Intelligence Agency (CIA) in assisting E. Howard Hunt, one of the plumbers, in the Fielding break (Federal Bureau of Investigation, 1974). This break-in received little media attention, but it led to a subsequent burglary of the Democratic National Committee headquarters at the Watergate Hotel, to the White House cover-up of that event, and, eventually, to Nixon's resignation (Krogh, 2007), which took place on August 8, 1974. The government dismissed the felony counts against Daniel Ellsberg due to the illegal actions by the Nixon White House (Ellsberg, 2018b).

A. Ernest Fitzgerald

A. Ernest Fitzgerald was a Defense Department employee who revealed cost overruns in defense contracting in 1968 under President Lyndon B. Johnson and whose retaliation by the Pentagon ultimately played a role in the passage of the CSRA (Glazer & Glazer, 1989; Merit Systems Protection Board, 1993). He was a high-level "Pentagon financial analyst who exposed the $2 billion cost overrun in the production of the C5A cargo plane" (Bredemier, 1979). He "was dismissed in January 1970, in what the Pentagon said was a reduction in force" (Bredemier, 1979). Through a four-year administrative process with the Civil Service Commission, Fitzgerald eventually won reinstatement to his former job and $80,000 in back pay. However, he maintained that "the new job was in no way equivalent to the job he held at the time of his C5A disclosures" (Bredemier, 1979).

W. Mark Felt

One of the most famous figures during the Watergate scandal and one of the most enduring examples of whistleblowing in history was the whistleblower referred to as "Deep Throat." "Deep Throat" also was the name of a well-known pornographic movie of the day (D'Amato, 2006), but in this context it also referred to the concept of "deep background," in which a reporter grants anonymity to his or her source (The Watergate Story Part 4: Deep Throat Revealed, 2005). Deep Throat's leaks about the Watergate break-in to *Washington Post* reporters Bob Woodward and Carl Bernstein prompted the *Post's* investigation of the affair (Von Drehle, 2005) and eventually led to Richard Nixon's resignation as president. Deep Throat was viewed as a hero until he came forward in 2005 as W. Mark Felt, deputy director of the FBI at the time of Watergate (O'Connor, 2005). That information led to speculation that he had been motivated not by altruism but by revenge for having been passed over as successor to J. Edgar Hoover (The Watergate Story Part 4: Deep Throat Revealed, 2005).

Bernstein and Woodward's book, *All the President's Men* (Bernstein & Woodward, 1974), portrayed Deep Throat as a major, but not the only, source of information about Watergate and the inner workings of the Nixon White House. However, the movie version romanticized the cloak-and-dagger aspect of the relationship Woodward had with his source, and that made Deep Throat a household name and the personification of whistleblowing (The Watergate Story Part 4: Deep Throat Revealed, 2005). In 2005, Felt revealed himself as Deep Throat to his attorney, who published the scoop in *Vanity Fair* (O'Connor, 2005) ahead of Woodward's book about the relationship, *The Secret Man: The Story of Watergate's Deep Throat* (Woodward, 2005). In 2017, Peter Landesman promoted Felt as the true hero of Watergate in the movie *Mark Felt: The Man Who Brought Down the White House* (Butan, Scott, Landesman, & MadRiver, 2017). "I find Felt's story more interesting [than Bernstein and Woodward's] because Felt's the one – he wasn't just doing his job, he [*sic*] was sacrificing his own life" (Reilly, 2017). The fact that numerous people benefited from Felt's actions, while neither Felt nor his family ever did, would seem to underscore Landesman's claim that Felt was an unsung hero.

John W. Dean III

White House Counsel to President Richard Nixon, John W. Dean III, "was deeply involved in Watergate" (Gerald R. Ford Library and Museum, 2020). President Richard Nixon appointed Dean to document and help cover up the Watergate break-in (Gerald R. Ford Library and Museum, 2020). Media coverage about the event was limited at the time, and Nixon won reelection in 1972. In 1973, Dean testified before the Senate Watergate Committee and charged Nixon with participating in the Watergate cover-up. Nixon fired Dean for testifying. However, the Senate's investigations led to the disclosure of the White House tapes, which confirmed Nixon's role in the cover-up and eventually led to his resignation (The Watergate Story Part 2: The government investigates, 2008; The Watergate Story: John Dean, 2008). Dean "pleaded guilty of conspiring to obstruct justice, [and was] sentenced to 1 to 4 years in prison" (The heavy toll of Watergate, 1975). After credit for time served, he served four months of his sentence (Gerald R. Ford Library and Museum, 2020).

Karen Silkwood

Karen Silkwood was an employee of a federal contactor, the Kerr-McGee plutonium plant in Crescent, Oklahoma, when she died in an automobile crash on November 23, 1974. At the time, Kerr-McGee was under contract to the federal Atomic Energy Commission (AEC) "to produce fuel rods for the government's experimental fast-breeder reactor" (Kohn, 1977).

> She was also an activist who was critical of plant safety. During the week prior to her death, Silkwood was reportedly gathering evidence for the Union to support her claim that Kerr-McGee was negligent in maintaining plant safety, and at the same time, was involved in a number of unexplained exposures to plutonium. The circumstances of her death have been the subject of great speculation.
>
> (Los Alamos National Laboratory, 1995, p. 252)

"The Oklahoma Highway Patrol called [her death] an accident, but Oil, Chemical and Atomic Workers International's investigation concluded another car deliberately forced her off the road" (Kohn, 1977). At the time of her death, Silkwood was reportedly on her way to give a newspaper reporter the results of her investigation into what she alleged were her employer's unsafe practices involving handling, leakage, and loss of plutonium (Kohn, 1977).

Silkwood's death fed speculation about murder and a cover-up. An autopsy was conducted by the Oklahoma State Medical Examiner with assistance from Los Alamos National Laboratory personnel (Los Alamos National Laboratory, 1995). The autopsy found plutonium in her system overall but at an acceptable level; high concentrations of plutonium in her gastrointestinal tract, from which investigators concluded that she had ingested plutonium recently; and a high dose of Quaaludes in her system when she died. The plant closed a year after her death, and her estate eventually won a settlement of $1.3 million (Los Alamos National Laboratory, 1995). This followed an initial federal jury award of $10.5 million (Curry & Wenske, 1979) that was attributed, in part, to representation of her estate by famed defense attorney Gerry Spence and his skill at storytelling (Meyer, 2002).

Federal laws after Watergate

Civil Service Reform Act of 1978

The CSRA was a reaction to the Nixon presidency and Watergate. In the 1970s, the U.S. House of Representatives investigated the federal personnel system and found that the Civil Service Commission, among other agencies, had abused the system by hiring political favorites for civil service positions (U.S. House of Representatives Subcommittee on Manpower and Civil Service of the Committee on Post Office and Civil Services, 1976). Two years later, Congress passed the CSRA [*Civil Service Reform Act of 1978* (1978)] and replaced the former Civil Service Commission with the Merit Systems Protection Board (MSPB). The CSRA encouraged whistleblowers to report fraud and abuse and promised them protections from retaliation for doing so. It charged the MSPB with enforcing those protections; tracking wrongdoing, whistleblowing, and retaliation in the federal government; and adjudicating allegations of retaliation brought by federal employees against their employers.

Inspector General Act of 1978

After four years of investigations into fraud and abuse in federal agencies that included establishing Offices of Inspector General in the Department of Health, Education, and Welfare in 1976 and the Department of Energy in 1977, Congress determined that a more comprehensive approach was needed (Muellenberg & Volzer, 1980). As a result, Congress passed the *Inspector General Act of 1978* [5 U.S.C. app. (1978)], which created 12 more Offices of Inspector General. The purpose of the act was "to conduct and supervise audits and investigations relating to programs and operations . . . [and] to prevent and detect fraud and abuse in, such programs and operations" [*Inspector General Act of 1978*, [5 U.S.C. app. (1978)]. The act was received as a positive step toward reducing fraud and abuse in the federal system. "The newest component of the federal government's fight against white-collar crime is the Office of the Inspector General" (Muellenberg & Volzer, 1980, p. 1049).

False Claims Amendments Act of 1986

Between 1978 and 1993, Congress enacted more than 25 laws to protect whistleblowers in various situations, among them the *False Claims Amendments Act of 1986* [31 U.S.C. § 3701 nt (1986)]. These amendments to the FCA arose in response to inflated contractor prices in the 1980s that generated significant media interest and public outrage (Lumm, 2010). The amendments increased penalties to wrongdoers, removed the requirement that the wrongdoing be intentional, granted "costs, expenses, and attorneys' fees as well as 15% to 25% of the proceeds of the litigation when the Justice Department intervenes, and 25% to 30% if the Justice Department does not," and removed the requirement that the information cannot have been known previously by the government (Beck, 2000, p. 6). The False Claims Amendments Act also added protection to whistleblowers, those working with them, and those assisting the government "in furtherance of a False Claims Act action" (Bernstein Liebhard LLP, 2018b). If found to have been retaliated against, "The whistleblower is entitled to reinstatement with seniority, double back pay, interest, special damages sustained as a result of discriminatory treatment, and attorneys' fees and costs" (Bernstein Liebhard LLP, 2018a), a reward that some consider a conflict of interest that puts whistleblowers at odds with the public good (Beck, 2000).

Whistleblower Protection Acts of 1989 and 1994

The *Whistleblower Protection Act of 1989* (WPA) [5 U.S.C. § 1201 nt 1989)] expanded on the CSRA by giving federal employees appeal rights for "previously nonappealable personnel actions, such as reassignments and ratings" (Merit Systems Protection Board, 1993, p. 34). Among the tactics that previously had been used against civil service employees were "lateral transfers, reorganizations to eliminate jobs, and offering less desirable jobs on the same grade level (p. 147, Clawson, *Washington Post*, December 1971)" (U.S. House of Representatives Subcommittee on Manpower and Civil Service of the Committee on Post Office and Civil Services, 1976). With the WPA, federal employees were allowed to report wrongdoing to anyone; they did not have to report internally within their own agency (Peffer, Bocheko, Del Valle, Osmani, Peyton, & Roman, 2015). However, the WPA was not inclusive – it did not cover employees involved in national security and government contractors – and it was not effective – government employees who brought claims under the law between 1989 and 2010 lost more than 75% of them (Peffer et al., 2015). The WPA Amendments of 1994 [*Whistleblower Protection Act Amendments of 1994*, 5 U.S.C. § 101 nt (1994)] added more protections for federal whistleblowers, but they still did not cover everything or everyone: "Congress amended the WPA in 1994 to enhance confidentiality of disclosures and extend WPA protections to employees of government corporations. These protections do not cover all federal employees, all reports of wrongdoing, or all possible acts of retaliation" (Near & Miceli, 2008, p. 264).

9/11 and the FBI

Coleen Rowley

Could Coleen Rowley and her colleagues in the FBI office in Minneapolis have prevented 9/11, the attacks on the World Trade Center and the Pentagon on September 11, 2001? They had reason to suspect that a major attack was imminent on U.S. soil, and they believed they had arrested one of the co-conspirators, Zacarias Moussaoui, in a plot involving using passenger planes to attack U.S. targets. They asked FBI headquarters for permission to examine Moussaoui's laptop, but they did not receive it (Hosenball & Isikoff, 2002). In May 2002 after the attacks, Rowley wrote a lengthy memo to FBI Director Robert S. Mueller III, who had assumed the position on September 4, 2001, one week before the deadly attacks, detailing what she felt was wrong with the FBI's response and what might have been averted. That memo was subsequently leaked to the media and resulted in her being called later to testify before the Senate Judiciary Committee, experiencing negative comments from fellow FBI members, and being named one of *Time*'s three "Persons of the Year" (Lacayo & Ripley, 2002; Ripley & Sieger, 2002).

"Administration officials say they could not have foreseen September 11. But in the years and months before, critical warnings may have gone unheeded" (Hirsh, Isikoff, Klaidman, Hosenball, Clift, Barry & . . . , & Dickey, 2002). *Time* reported on the memo in a cover story (Ratnesar & Weisskopf, 2002). *New York Times* columnist William Safire accused FBI Director Mueller of a cover-up (Safire, 2002). Mueller praised Rowley when they both testified before the Senate Judiciary Committee in 2002 and assured her she would not suffer retaliation (Eggen, Fainaru, & Washington Post Staff Writers, 2002). She remained at her post and retired from the FBI in 2005 (F.B.I. agent who wrote critical memo retires at 50, 2005).

Federal laws after 9/11

Notification and Federal Employee Antidiscrimination and Retaliation Act of 2002

The No FEAR Act [*Notification and Federal Employee Anti-Discrimination and Retaliation Act of 2002*, 5 U.S.C. § 2301 (2002)] imposed five new categories of requirements on federal employers. Agencies were financially provided additional protections to liable for discriminatory or retaliatory behavior. They were required to notify employees annually about their rights under employment discrimination and whistleblower protection laws. They were required to train employees at least every two years about their rights and remedies under antidiscrimination and whistleblower protection laws. They were required to report to Congress and other federal agencies about their efforts to improve compliance with employment discrimination and whistleblower protection laws, as well as complaints against the agency under those laws. Agencies were required to post statistical data about Equal Employment Opportunity (EEO) complaints quarterly on their websites.

Failure of federal whistleblower protections

Toward the end of the first decade of the twenty-first century, the Government Accountability Project (GAP), a nonprofit, government, and corporate watchdog and a whistleblower advocate, believed the WPA and its amendments weakened, rather than strengthened, protections for whistleblowers (Government Accountability Project, 2008a). "Since its passage in 1989, and through subsequent amendments passed in 1994 to strengthen the law, the Whistleblower Protection Act (WPA) has been eroded to the point that federal workers have virtually no protections from agency retaliation" (Government Accountability Project, 2008b). GAP placed the blame for this degradation of protections on decisions by the U.S. Court of Appeals for the Federal Circuit, the court assigned to hear whistleblower complaints. GAP argued that the court issued rulings that removed protections for many types of reporting of wrongdoing, including those made to fellow workers, management, and wrongdoers, as well as any that may be seen as part of one's job duties (Government Accountability Project, 2008b). For example, Justice Department attorney Jessalyn Radack was retaliated against for advising against interrogating the "American Taliban," John Walker Lindh (Leslie, 2003), and Justice Department attorney Thomas Tamm was retaliated against for blowing the whistle to the media about the George W. Bush administration's unauthorized government surveillance program against U.S. citizens (Isikoff, 2008).

Whistleblower Protections for Federal Employees

In 2010, the MSPB issued a "how-to" manual for federal employees who wanted to blow the whistle on wrongdoing in their federal agencies, *Whistleblower Protections for Federal Employees* (Merit Systems Protection Board, 2010b). The manual was specific about the types of wrongdoing that should be reported. It also specified to whom one should report in order to maintain whistleblower protection. Finally, it spelled out those circumstances in which the intended whistleblower might not be covered by federal whistleblowing law. Those specifics included:

> To qualify as a protected whistleblower, a Federal employee or applicant for employment must disclose: a violation of any law, rule, or regulation; gross mismanagement; a gross waste of funds; an abuse of authority; or a substantial and specific danger to public health or safety. However, this disclosure alone is not enough to obtain protection under the law. The individual also must: avoid using normal channels if the disclosure is in the course of the employee's duties; make the report to someone other than the wrongdoer; and suffer a personnel action, the agency's failure to take a personnel action, or the threat to take or not take a personnel action. Lastly, the employee must seek redress through the proper channels before filing an appeal with the U.S. Merit Systems Protection Board ("MSPB"). A potential whistleblower's failure to meet even one of these criteria will deprive the MSPB of jurisdiction, and render us unable to provide any redress in the absence of a different (non-whistleblowing) appeal right.
>
> (Merit Systems Protection Board, 2010b)

Whistleblower Protection Enhancement Act of 2012

Congress passed the *Whistleblower Protection Enhancement Act of 2012* (WPEA) [5 U.S.C. § 101 nt (2012)] to correct problems with the original WPA and its amendments (Zuckerman, 2012). The WPEA was intended to close many of the restrictions imposed by the judiciary. It provided more remedies against retaliation by agencies and the authority to hold managers accountable for retaliation. It expanded whistleblower protections to employees of another federal agency, the Transportation Security Administration. Finally, it required more communication to inform federal employees of their whistleblower rights by "mandat[ing] broader outreach to inform federal employees of their whistleblower rights" (Zuckerman, 2012).

Presidential Policy Directive (PPD-19)

Also in 2012, President Barack Obama signed the Presidential Policy Directive (PPD-19) (Obama, 2012). It gave whistleblower protections to the intelligence and national security fields not included in the WPEA, which was being deliberated in Congress at that time (Pavgi, 2012). It protected whistleblowers in covered agencies in the Intelligence Community from retaliation, and it allowed employees to blow the whistle without losing their security clearances. However, a note of caution was offered by Tom Devine, legal director for the GAP, a whistleblower advocate organization. "There are only false due process teeth on the horizon. . . . Regulations to enforce whistleblower rights will be written by the same agencies that routinely are the defendants in whistleblower retaliation lawsuits" (Pavgi, 2012, p. 1). That concern was echoed later (U.S. Senate Select Committee on Intelligence, 2017).

Corporate whistleblowers

Enron – Sherron Watkins

"It all began with Enron" (Brickey, 2003, p. 357). Sherron Watkins, vice president of corporate development at Enron and a certified public accountant, became an internal whistleblower in August 2001 when she outlined her concerns about "an elaborate accounting hoax" in an anonymous memo to Enron Chairman of the Board and Chief Executive Officer (CEO) Kenneth Lay (Brickey, 2003, p. 361). Watkins sent her memo via a new communication channel, a company suggestion box created by Lay to elicit and allay employee concerns following the unexpected resignation of CEO and Chief Operating Officer Jeff Skilling (Brickey, 2003; Wild, 2003). Shortly thereafter, Watkins met with Lay and recommended he disclose the accounting irregularities, issue a restatement of earnings, and try to regain the trust of investors (Brickey, 2003). She warned Lay not to use Enron's attorneys to investigate her allegations because they had authorized the existing processes and urged him to appoint an outside law firm.

Lay did not follow her advice. The subsequent report issued by Enron's legal counsel found no evidence of the irregularities Watkins had exposed. Her supervisor, Chief Financial Officer Andrew Fastow, retaliated against her by removing her from her office, taking away her laptop, reassigning her duties, and making plans to terminate her, an action that was never carried out (Brickey, 2003). Within a few months, however, the irregularities Watkins reported caused the company to collapse. "On October 16, 2001, Enron stunned Wall Street by announcing that it had a $618 million net loss for the third quarter and would reduce shareholder equity by $1.2 billion" (Brickey, 2003, p. 357).

Five years later, Lay was convicted of six counts of fraud and conspiracy and four counts of bank fraud, and he was sentenced to life in prison. Skilling was convicted of 18 counts of fraud and conspiracy and one count of insider trading, and he was sentenced to 24 years in prison. Lay died in July 2006, soon after his conviction; a judge later vacated his conviction on the grounds that death prevents an appeal (Murphy, K., 2006). Skilling's conviction was upheld on appeal, but his 24-year sentence was ordered revisited and the possibility was raised of a new trial based on evidence favorable to him that had not been presented to his defense attorneys (Norris, 2009). After several additional appeals, the judge who had originally sentenced Skilling to 24 years reduced his sentence to 14 years with a release date in 2019 (Wilbanks, 2013); he was released from prison in Alabama to a halfway house in August 2018 (Sixel, 2018).

WorldCom – Cynthia Cooper

At about the same time Enron's financial situation was imploding, another major corporate financial disaster was becoming public at WorldCom, the world's largest telecommunications company (Katz & Homer, 2008). In the course of her duties as vice president of internal audit, Cynthia Cooper uncovered accounting irregularities at WorldCom. The basis for WorldCom's problems appeared to have been the heavy debt incurred by WorldCom's acquisition of ailing telecom company MCI. Cooper encountered resistance from Chief Financial Officer Scott Sullivan, who asked her to delay the company's capital-expenditure audit, and from Controller David Meyers, who argued against the need for capital expenditure audits. She first reported her concerns to an external party, the corporation's auditing firm, Arthur Andersen. It was only after Arthur Andersen ignored her that she reported her findings to the audit committee of the board of directors (Katz & Homer, 2008).

Cooper, like Watkins, experienced retaliation. This included berating by Sullivan, accusations that her allegations were based on personal motives, legal maneuvers by the company, and the pressures of publicity (Schaal, 2008). In the end, the board fired Sullivan and publicized the fraud. The fact that Cooper reported to the board of directors, rather than to the CEO (as Watkins had), may have led to her success (Moberly, 2006). Cooper, Watkins, and Rowley were named *Time's* "Persons of the Year" (Lacayo & Ripley, 2002).

Corporate laws

Despite the extensive federal legislation enacted to prevent such actions, retaliation against whistleblowers continued to be seen by some as commonplace and institutionalized (Devine, 1997). Many of the retaliation tactics were documented in the previously mentioned federal personnel manual from the Nixon era (U.S. Senate Committee on Governmental Affairs, 1978). These included diverting attention from the whistleblower's message to the whistleblower, trying to discredit the whistleblower, starting a paper trail to document alleged whistleblower performance deficiencies, threatening the whistleblower, isolating the whistleblower, humiliating the whistleblower in front of peers, creating unreasonable work expectations that guarantee failure, prosecuting the whistleblower legally over manufactured charges, assaulting the whistleblower physically, eliminating the whistleblower's job, stalling the whistleblower's career, and blacklisting the whistleblower (Devine, 1997). Federal employees, in theory, had protection from retaliation for whistleblowing, although in practice those protections may have been nonexistent. Corporate employees, however, were without even those protections until widespread financial disasters among U.S. corporations prompted Congress to pass the Sarbanes–Oxley Act of 2002 to extend federal protections to corporate whistleblowers.

Public Company Accounting Reform and Investor Protection Act of 2002

EXPECTATIONS FOR SARBANES–OXLEY

As the Enron financial disaster began unfolding, Congress took action to reassure investors that corrective actions were in place to prevent a repeat of those events (Moberly, 2007). The legal ramification of Enron's collapse was the swift drafting of the Public Company Accounting Reform and Investor Protection Act of 2002[2] [*Sarbanes-Oxley Act of 2002*, 15 U.S.C. § 7201 nt (2002)], also known as Sarbanes–Oxley. Named for its two authors, Senator Paul Sarbanes (D-MD) and Representative Michael G. Oxley (R-OH), Sarbanes–Oxley was introduced to prevent the kinds of financial fraud that had toppled Enron. As Congress was working on Sarbanes–Oxley, WorldCom's situation was becoming public. "Just six months after Enron filed the largest bankruptcy case in U.S. history, WorldCom filed an even larger one" (Brickey, 2008, p. 626). Expectations for Sarbanes–Oxley were high among academics and advocates: [One advocate] called the law "the single most effective measure possible to prevent recurrences of the Enron debacle and similar threats to the nation's financial markets" (Moberly, 2007, p. 68).

PROVISIONS OF SARBANES-OXLEY

Sarbanes-Oxley contained six main provisions to prevent financial fraud. It created the Public Company Accounting Oversight Board. It made auditors of public companies more independent. It added regulations for corporate governance and responsibility, and it required more financial disclosure. It regulated conflicts of interest among securities analysts, and it added new crimes and increased penalties for existing crimes under the securities laws.

Among its provisions, Sarbanes-Oxley was the first legislation to require publicly traded companies to maintain a communication channel for employees to report financial irregularities (Moberly, 2006), as well as 12 other kinds of irregularities (Vaughn, 2005, p. 4). It mandated that boards of directors of corporations establish a communication channel that allowed anonymous reporting of corporate financial wrongdoing directly to outside directors on the audit committee of the board of directors (Moberly, 2006). In addition, it protected those employees from retaliation: "Employers may not 'discharge, demote, suspend, threaten, harass, or in any other manner discriminate' against whistleblowers" (Moberly, 2006, p. 1126) and made retaliation that harmed someone who gave information about a federal crime to law enforcement a felony (Brickey, 2003). It required corporations to adopt a code of ethics for senior financial officers, to disclose whether or not they had adopted a code of ethics, and to notify the Securities and Exchange Commission (SEC) of any change in or waiver of the code of ethics (Delikat & Phillips, 2011). It also required corporations' annual reports to contain "a report of management on the company's internal control over financial reporting" (Securities and Exchange Commission, 2003).

REALITY OF SARBANES-OXLEY

The high hopes some had for Sarbanes-Oxley were not realized in its early years. According to the U.S. Department of Labor's Occupational Safety and Health (OSHA), which administers Sarbanes-Oxley and 21 other federal whistleblower laws, only 2% of Sarbanes-Oxley whistleblowers who filed administrative claims through the third quarter of 2006 had valid claims, and another 13% reached a settlement. A subsequent study showed 3.6% of whistleblowers prevailing in OSHA's administrative process and another 6.5% of those who appealed the OSHA ruling to the Department of Labor won on appeal (Moberly, 2007). A study of OSHA filings ten years after the passage of Sarbanes-Oxley found that only ten additional cases were decided in favor of the whistleblower, for a 1.8% win factor for whistleblowers out of 1,260 total OSHA cases (Moberly, 2012). A 2005 survey attributed a decrease in whistleblowing, even with increased protections under Sarbanes-Oxley, to a culture that did not support whistleblowing, to concerns about the value of whistleblowing in stopping wrongdoing, and to the retaliation experienced by the one-in-eight employees who reported wrongdoing (Ethics Resource Center, 2007).

Fraud Enforcement and Recovery Act of 2009

The Fraud Enforcement and Recovery Act of 2009 (FERA) [*Fraud Enforcement and Recovery Act of 2009*, 18 U.S.C. § 1 nt (2009)] was intended to plug loopholes in the FCA that let "subcontractors and non-governmental entities" go unpunished for fraud, expand whistleblower protections, and widen the coverage of the FCA itself (Faunce, Crow, Nikolic, Morgan, & Frederick, 2014, p. 382). This move was lauded by some as a positive move to decrease fraud and increase whistleblower protections (Faunce et al., 2014). However, not everyone considered the expansion of coverage and protection in the best public interest. Some saw FERA as an onerous imposition of oversight "that virtually ensured that private organizations that engage in transactions with the federal government will become more embattled than ever by whistle-blowing citizens seeking large cash bounties for infractions real or perceived, intended or inadvertent, large or miniscule" (Lumm, 2010, p. 527). The argument was also made that the government's decision to intervene or not could affect the reduction of fraud, that the individual's decision to file could be affected by the government's decision to intervene or not and by the possibility that delaying the filing might increase the magnitude of the fraud and the dollar amount of the award (Depoorter & De Mot, 2006).

Dodd-Frank Wall Street Reform and Consumer Protection Act of 2010

EXPECTATIONS FOR DODD-FRANK

Within six years after Sarbanes-Oxley, the United States and the world were facing another crisis, this time in the financial industry (Scholes, 2011). The *Banking Act of 1933* [12 U.S.C. § 228 (1935)], which had been designed to prevent another financial crash like the one the United States saw in 1929 by imposing regulations, as well as guarantees against failure, had been slowly circumvented by the banking industry (Acharya, Cooley, Richardson, Sylla, & Walter, 2011). To make matters worse, diminished regulation allowed banks to create what has been called a "shadow" or "parallel" banking industry (Acharya, Cooley, Richardson, Sylla, et al., 2011, pp. 2–3). Financial institutions in the United States grew increasingly larger, both on the surface and through the shadow banking system, and they took on increasing risk. When they suddenly began to fail, the impact was catastrophic, both in this country and around the world: "The Dodd-Frank Act arose from anger and cries for retribution against Wall Street" (Scholes, 2011, p. xii). The crisis revealed fundamental weaknesses in the financial regulatory systems of the United States, the United Kingdom, and other European nations. Those weaknesses have made regulatory reforms an urgent priority (Wilmarth, 2011, p. 2). Other observers noted that the crimes for which Ken Lay and Jeffery Skilling of Enron had been sent to prison, essentially risky trading behaviors, were exactly the crimes that brought down Wall Street (Steffy, 2013; Wilbanks, 2013).

If Sarbanes-Oxley was considered the ultimate in whistleblowing protection legislation of its time, the Dodd-Frank Wall Street Reform and Consumer Protection Act of 2010 [*Dodd-Frank Act of 2010*, 12 U.S.C. § 5301 (2010)], also known as Dodd-Frank, eight years later, was considered even better. Dodd-Frank not only made the whistleblower protections in Sarbanes-Oxley and the FCA stronger but also made the financial rewards greater and the protections for whistleblowers stronger (Oswald & Zuckerman, 2010). "The Act is widely described as the most ambitious and far-reaching over-haul of financial regulation since the 1930s" (Acharya, Cooley, Richardson, Sylla, et al., 2011, p. 1). The expectation was that Dodd-Frank and other reforms would instigate a major market restructuring (Acharya, Cooley, Richardson, Sylla, et al., 2011). "At the end of the day, the Dodd-Frank Wall Street Reform and Consumer Protection Act of 2010 is the keystone of the financial reform structure in the United States and will be influential worldwide" (Acharya, Cooley, Richardson, & Walter, 2011, p. xviii).

PROVISIONS OF DODD-FRANK

Dodd-Frank included 16 areas of change for the financial industry, including requiring "the SEC to compensate whistleblowers, among other whistleblower protections" (Kaal, 2016, p. 2). The Act provided financial rewards for original information given to the SEC and the Commodity Futures Trading Commission. It increased protections under Sarbanes-Oxley and the FCA, and it established new retaliation protection for whistleblowers (Oswald & Zuckerman, 2010). It allowed the SEC to award whistleblowers 10–30% of any judgment the SEC recovers over $1 million and protected whistleblowers from retaliation if they have "reported externally to regulators" (Faunce et al., 2014, p. 399). It did not, however, allow whistleblowers to file their own lawsuits, as the FCA does.

REALITY OF DODD-FRANK

One scholar raised concerns about how the whistleblower protections and incentives of Dodd-Frank affect the Foreign Corrupt Practices Act (FCPA) [*Foreign Corrupt Practices Act of 1977*, 15 U.S.C. § 78a nt (1977)] and its impact on corporations shortly after the law was passed (Hansberry, 2012). The FCPA, passed in 1977, prohibits bribing foreign officials and upholds sufficient accounting standards. Between 2008 and 2011, the FCPA allowed the Department of Justice and the SEC to collect more than $3 billion in settlements from corporations. Corporations typically agreed to resolve the claims with the agencies rather than contest them due to legal restrictions and the cost of lawsuits. The concern was that the provisions of Dodd-Frank that provide whistleblower bounties (financial awards), anonymity, freedom to be a party to the wrongdoing, absent a conviction for the crime, would escalate the bounties and increase the impact on corporations (Hansberry, 2012).

DODD-FRANK AND THE FALSE CLAIMS ACT

In the 2016 fiscal year, the Department of Justice recovered more than $4.7 billion from FCA cases (U.S. Department of Justice, 2016). More than half of that came from the health-care industry, and more than one-third came from the financial industry. Almost two-thirds of the total, or $2.9 billion, resulted from successful qui tam lawsuits filed by whistleblowers. Under the FCA, whistleblowers receive up to 30% of the money the government recovers. Those successful claims resulted in whistleblowers receiving $519 million in 2016 (U.S. Department of Justice, 2016).

DODD-FRANK AND THE SEC

In 2016, the SEC reported an all-time high of 868 actions for financial wrongdoing and judgments of more than $4 billion levied against corporate interests. The SEC "whistleblower program awarded over $57 million to 13 whistleblowers in fiscal year 2016, which is more than in all previous years" (Securities and Exchange Commission, 2016a). This year's actions included the agency's second whistleblower retaliation case and the first-ever prosecution based solely on retaliation against a whistleblower under provisions of Dodd-Frank. An employee in good-standing who reported concerns about financial practices in a casino-gaming company internally and to the SEC was subsequently fired. Although the company did not agree to wrongdoing, it did agree to pay a $500,000 penalty (Securities and Exchange Commission, 2016b).

DODD-FRANK AND THE SUPREME COURT

In February 2018, the U.S. Supreme Court unanimously ruled that Dodd-Frank does not give whistleblower status and protection from retaliation to an employee who reports wrongdoing internally, rather than to the SEC [*Digital Realty Trust, Inc. v. Somers*, 583 U. S.___ (2018)]. In response, the SEC opened a two-year public comment period on new rules (Securities and Exchange Commission, 2018). Following that period, the SEC announced new rules clarifying who would be protected from retaliation:

> For purposes of retaliation protection, an individual is required to report information about possible securities laws violations to the Commission "in writing." As required by the Supreme Court's decision, to qualify for the retaliation protection under Section 21F, the individual must report to the Commission before experiencing the retaliation. (Securities and Exchange Commission, 2020a)

A month later, the SEC announced it had "paid a record $114 million to an anonymous whistleblower" (Egan, 2020). Chief of the Office of the Whistleblower Jane Norberg commended the whistleblower's actions. "After repeatedly reporting concerns internally, and despite personal and professional hardships, the whistleblower alerted the SEC and the other agency of the wrongdoing and provided substantial, ongoing assistance that proved critical to the success of the actions" (Securities and Exchange Commission, 2020b).

Are they whistleblowers?

Julian Assange and WikiLeaks

Australian Julian Assange founded WikiLeaks in 2006 as a website for publishing documents leaked from other sources. Some identified WikiLeaks as a legitimate new media news site (Bosua, Milton, Dreyfus, & Lederman, 2014) whose benefit of transparency outweighed the risk to any country's national security (Dreyfus, Lederman, Bosua, & Milton, 2011), while others, notably the U.S. government, disagreed (Department of Homeland Security and Office of the Director of National Intelligence, 2016). WikiLeaks played a role in publishing many of the recent disclosures of information hostile to U.S. interests, including Bradley Manning's release of classified military documents and the Russian government's release of Hilary Clinton's emails during the 2016 presidential campaign (Stack, Cumming-Bruce, & Kruhly, 2018).In 2016, the U.S. Intelligence Community issued a statement identifying Russia as the source of the hacked Clinton emails (Department of Homeland Security and Office of the Director of National Intelligence, 2016). The CIA named the Russians who hacked the Democratic National Committee's email servers and fed the information to WikiLeaks, but Assange denied that Russia was the source of the emails (Reuters, 2017).

Assange lived in the Ecuadorian Embassy in London for seven years from 2011 to 2019 rather than stand for extradition to Sweden, where he had been charged with sexually assaulting two women (Perez-Pena & Magra, 2018). Although Sweden dropped its extradition request in 2017, Assange remained in the embassy because he was also wanted by the British for jumping bail on the original arrest warrant in order to enter the embassy. That charge was upheld twice by the British government in early 2018 (Perez-Pena & Magra, 2018). In April 2019, the British police removed Assange from the embassy and put him in London's Belmarsh prison, awaiting extradition to the United States on "18 charges – 17 of which fall under the Espionage Act – around conspiracy to receive, obtaining and disclosing classified diplomatic and military documents" (Doherty & Remeikis, 2019). His hearing on the U.S. extradition request, which began in February 2020, was delayed initially because of the Covid-19 pandemic and more recently by technical difficulties when it resumed in September 2020 (Specia, 2020). On October 29, 2020, his sentencing hearing was announced for January 4, 2021 (Kraterou, 2020). At that hearing, a judge ruled that Assange could not be extradited to the U.S. due to his mental health condition (Quinn, 2021). The U.S. appealed that ruling in February 2021. "The appeal made clear that Joe Biden intends to have Assange stand trial on espionage- and hacking-related charges over WikiLeaks' publication of hundreds of thousands of US military and diplomatic documents" (Agence France-Presse in Washington, 2021).

Bradley/Chelsea Manning

Private First Class Bradley (later Chelsea) Manning was a U.S. Army intelligence analyst who was "convicted of stealing" hundreds of thousands of documents and videos from his employer and giving them to WikiLeaks, which published them in 2010 (Jarrett & Borger, 2017). He did not follow federal whistleblowing protocols; and, therefore, he was not covered by federal whistleblower protections (Merit Systems Protection Board, 2010b). Manning was subsequently tried and "found guilty on 20 out of 22 possible charges (including violating the US Espionage Act) . . . demoted from private first class to private and dishonorably discharged. . . . Manning, a transgender woman, was serving a 35-year sentence at Fort Leavenworth," Kansas, when former President Barack Obama commuted her sentence not long before he left office (Jarrett & Borger, 2017). Despite opposition from his own cabinet and Republicans, Obama ended what he considered an excessive sentence and an untenable position for a woman in a male facility (Jarrett & Borger, 2017).

Edward Snowden

Edward Snowden was a contract employee for the U.S. National Security Agency (NSA) for three months in 2013 (Edward Snowden Fast Facts, 2013). He took an undisclosed number of documents from his employer and released them to various media outlets, including the *Guardian*, the *Washington Post*, and the *New York Times*. The documents revealed the NSA's electronic surveillance of U.S. citizens, as well as foreign nationals (Williams & Toropin, 2017). Although he said he had attempted to raise his concerns about the legality of the surveillance internally with his employer, the NSA denied the allegations (Gellman, 2013). Snowden's exposure of the NSA's surveillance operations led to a public outcry over the extent of surveillance of private citizens by the U.S. government, revocation of his visa, and charges of espionage and felony theft by the U.S. government (Gellman, 2013). Snowden was granted asylum by Russia in 2013 and began living in Moscow. In spring 2017, Moscow extended his asylum until 2020 (Williams & Toropin, 2017). In 2020, he was "granted permanent residency rights to live in Russia in a step towards citizenship, according to Reuters" (Vallejo, 2020).

Daniel Ellsberg praised Manning and Snowden as whistleblowers who were justified in their disclosures (MacAskill, Snowden, & Ellsberg, 2018). Tarzie, a "blogger who writes about media, propaganda, and the intelligence community" (Tarzie 2017, p. 348), considered Snowden not only a whistleblower but also a plant of the intelligence community. Members of the House Permanent Select Committee on Intelligence reported, "Snowden was not a whistleblower" (U.S. House of Representatives Permanent Select Committee on Intelligence, 2016,

p. ii), and he shared the intelligence information he took with Russia. "The Committee further found no evidence that Snowden attempted to communicate concerns about the legality or morality of intelligence activities to any officials, senior or otherwise, during his time at either CIA or NSA" (U.S. House of Representatives Permanent Select Committee on Intelligence, 2016, p. 16).

Christopher Steele

Christopher Steele, a former British Intelligence Service (M.I.6) Russian expert, was hired to investigate then U.S. presidential candidate Donald Trump by the presidential campaign of Hillary Clinton and the Democratic National Committee (Mayer, 2018). Because of the nature of what he uncovered, Steele felt he had a duty to report those findings to authorities. He did so first to the U.S. FBI; when the FBI did not respond, he reported to the U.S. State Department; when the State Department did not respond, he reported to various media outlets in off-the-record meetings; and when that did not work, he reported to a former British official who had access to Senator John McCain. When Senator McCain took the dossier to FBI Director James Comey, Comey informed the senator that the FBI had had the document for months:

> On June 14, 2016, . . . the Washington Post broke the news that the Russians were believed to have hacked into the Democratic National Committee's e-mail system. . . . [T]hree days before the start of the Democratic National Convention in Philadelphia, WikiLeaks dumped twenty thousand stolen D.N.C. e-mails onto the Internet. The e-mails had been weaponized: what had seemed a passive form of spying was now "an active measure," in the parlance of espionage.
>
> (Mayer, 2018, pp. 9–10)

In early January 2017, U.S. intelligence heads, including Comey, briefed then-President Barack Obama, Vice President Joe Biden, and others about a report they were about to make public: "It contained the agencies' unanimous conclusion that, during the Presidential campaign, Russian President Vladimir Putin had directed a cyber campaign aimed at getting Trump elected" (Mayer, 2018, p. 16).

Christopher Wylie

Christopher Wylie, a British citizen, was a former founder of, and analyst with, the British company Cambridge Analytica, an organization funded by Robert Mercer, a U.S. billionaire, and headed by former Donald Trump advisor Steve Bannon, which acquired tens of millions of personal accounts from unsuspecting users of the internet platform Facebook (Rosenberg, Confessore, & Cadwalladr, 2018). According to Wylie (U.S. Senate Committee on the Judiciary, 2018), Cambridge Analytica used those accounts in conjunction with the Russian government to sway the U.S. electorate in the 2016 presidential election against presidential candidate Hillary Clinton and in favor of presidential candidate Donald Trump (Rosenberg et al., 2018). Wylie provided this information in an extremely public way to numerous media outlets. Facebook founder and CEO Mark Zuckerberg (Zuckerberg, 2021) faced media scrutiny and user outrage and was called to testify before two U.S. Congressional committees in April 2018 about Facebook's plans to guard against future inappropriate and possibly unlawful use of the data it collects (U.S. House of Representatives Committee on Commerce and Energy, 2018; U.S. Senate Committee on Commerce, Science, & Transportation and the Senate Committee on the Judiciary, 2018). Senator Amy Klobuchar (D-MN) demanded he tell the committee what Facebook "knew about the misuse of its data to target political advertising and manipulate voters" (Rosenberg & Frenkel, 2018).

The next chapter, Chapter 3, presents an overview of whistleblowing research in the United States by government, the field of management and other areas of academia, and health care.

Notes

1 See Inspector General Act of 1978.
2 S.2673 – 107th Congress (2001–2002)_ Public Company Accounting Reform and Investor Protection Act of 2002 _ Congress.gov _ Library of Congress

References

Acharya, V. V., Cooley, T. F., Richardson, M., & Walter, I. (2011). Preface. In V. V. Acharya, T. F. Cooley, M. Richardson, & I. Walter (Eds.), *Regulating Wall Street: The Dodd-Frank Act and the New Architecture of Global Finance* (pp. xvii–xviii). Hoboken, NJ: John Wiley & Sons, Inc.

Acharya, V. V., Cooley, T. F., Richardson, M., Sylla, R., & Walter, I. (2011). Prologue: A bird's-eye view: The Dodd-Frank Wall Street Reform and Consumer Protection Act. In V. V. Acharya, T. F. Cooley, M. Richardson, & I. Walter (Eds.), *Regulating Wall Street: The Dodd-Frank Act and the New Architecture of Global Finance* (pp. 1–32). Hoboken, NJ: John Wiley & Sons, Inc.

Acharya, V. V., Cooley, T. F., Richardson, M., & Walter, I. (Eds.). (2011). *Regulating Wall Street: The Dodd-Frank Act and the new architecture of global finance.* Hoboken, NJ: John Wiley & Sons, Inc.

Agence France-Presse in Washington. (2021). US government appeals UK ruling against Julian Assange's extradition. *The Guardian* (Feb 12, 2021). Retrieved from https://www.theguardian.com/media/2021/feb/12/us-government-appeals-uk-ruling-against-julian-assanges-extradition-joe-biden-wikileaks

Archibald, S. J. (1979). The freedom of information act revisited. *Public Administration Review, 39*(4), 311–318. https://doi.org/10.2307/976206

Banking Act of 1935, 12 U.S.C. § 228 (1935).

Beck, J. R. (2000). The False Claims Act and the English eradication of qui tam legislation. *North Carolina Law Review, 78*, 539.

Bernstein, C., & Woodward, B. (1974). *All the President's men.* New York: Simon and Schuster.

Bernstein Liebhard LLP. (2018a). *False Claims Act and whistleblower employee protections anti-retaliation protections.* Retrieved from www.bernlieb.com/whistleblowers/FCA-Whistle-blower-Employee-Protections/index.html

Bernstein Liebhard LLP. (2018b). *History of the False Claims Act – The Whistleblower Act.* Retrieved from www.bernlieb.com/whistleblowers/History-Of-The-False-Claims-Act/index.html

Bosua, R., Milton, S., Dreyfus, S., & Lederman, R. (2014). Going public: Researching external whistleblowing in a new media age. In A. J. Brown, D. Lewis, R. E. Moberly, & W. Vandekerckhove (Eds.), *International handbook of whistleblowing research* (pp. 250–272). Cheltenham, UK: Edward Elgar Publishing Limited.

Bredemier, K. (1979). Tapes show Nixon role in firing of Ernest Fitzgerald. *The Washington Post* (March 7, 1979). Retrieved from https://www.washingtonpost.com/archive/politics/1979/03/07/tapes-show-nixon-role-in-firing-of-ernest-fitzgerald/048cd88e-60e5-498d-a8e2-e3b39461356b/?utm_term=.dac5c4cd35e0

Brickey, K. F. (2003). F. Hodge O'Neal Corporate and Securities Law Symposium: After the Sarbanes-Oxley Act: The future disclosure system: From Enron to Worldcom and Beyond: Life and crime after Sarbanes-Oxley. *Washington University Law Quarterly, 81*, 357–402.

Brickey, K. F. (2008). From boardroom to courtroom to newsroom: The media and the corporate governance scandals. *Journal of Corporation Law, 33*(3), 625–663.

Butan, M., Scott, R., Landesman, P., & MadRiver. (2017). *Mark felt: The man who brought down the White House* [Video/DVD]. Culver City, CA: Sony Pictures Classics.

Civil Service Reform Act of 1978, 5 U.S.C. § 1101 (1978).

Code of Ethics for Government Service, 72 Stat. B12 (1958).

Culiberg, B., & Mihelič, K. K. (2017). The evolution of whistleblowing studies: A critical review and research agenda. *Journal of Business Ethics, 146*(4), 787–803. https://doi.org/10.1007/s10551-016-3237-0

Curry, B., & Wenske, P. (1979). Silkwood family awarded $10.5 million in damages. *The Washington Post* (May 19, 1979). Retrieved from www.washingtonpost.com

D'Amato, A. (2006). Porn up, rape down. *Original Law Review, 2*(3), 91–100.

Delikat, M., & Phillips, R. B. (2011). *Corporate whistleblowing in the Sarbanes-Oxley/Dodd-Frank era* (2nd ed.). New York: Practising Law Institute.

Department of Homeland Security and Office of the Director of National Intelligence. (2016). *Joint statement from the Department of Homeland Security and Office of the Director of National Intelligence on Election Security* [Press release]. Retrieved from Joint Statement from the Department Of Homeland Security and Office of the Director of National Intelligence on Election Security | Homeland Security (dhs.gov)

Department of Justice Guide to the Freedom of Information Act. (2013). Retrieved from https://www.justice.gov/sites/default/files/oip/legacy/2014/07/23/intro-july-19-2013.pdf

Depoorter, B., & De Mot, J. (2006). Whistle blowing: An economic analysis of the False Claims Act. *Supreme Court Economic Review, 14*(1), 135–162.

de Santis, M. D. (2021). Misconceptions about historical sciences in evolutionary biology. *Evolutionary Biology, 48*(1), 94–99. https://doi.org/10.1007/s11692-020-09526-6

Devine, T. (1997). *The whistleblower's survival guide: Courage without martyrdom.* Washington, DC: Fund for Constitutional Government.

Digital Realty Trust, Inc. v. Somers, 583 U. S.___ (2018).

Dodd-Frank Act of 2010, 12 U.S.C. § 5301 (2010).

Doherty, B., & Remeikis, A. (2019). Julian Assange's extradition fight could turn on reports he was spied on for CIA. *The Guardian (London)* (December 16, 2019). Retrieved from https://www.theguardian.com/media/2019/dec/17/julian-assanges-extradition-fight-could-turn-on-reports-he-was-spied-on-for-cia

Dreyfus, S., Lederman, R., Bosua, R., & Milton, S. (2011). Can we handle the truth? Whistleblowing to the media in the digital era. *Global Media Journal: Australian Edition, 5*, 1–6.

Edward Snowden Fast Facts. (2013). *CNN* (September 11, 2013). Retrieved from https://www.cnn.com/2013/09/11/us/edward-snowden-fast-facts/index.html

Egan, M. (2020). A government agency just paid a record $114 million to an anonymous whistleblower. *CNN* (October 23, 2020). Retrieved from https://www.cnn.com/2020/10/23/business/sec-record-whistleblower-award/index.html

Eggen, D., Fainaru, S., & Washington Post Staff Writers. (2002). FBI Whistle-Blower to Testify in Senate. *The Washington Post* (June 1, 2002). Retrieved from www.washingtonpost.com

Ellsberg, D. (2018a). *Daniel Ellsberg*. Retrieved from www.ellsberg.net/

Ellsberg, D. (2018b). *Extended biography*. Retrieved from www.ellsberg.net/bio/extended-biography/

Ethics Resource Center. (2007). *The 2007 national business ethics survey: An inside view of private sector ethics*. Retrieved from Arlington, VA: www.ethics.org/resource/2007-national-business-ethics-survey

The False Claims Act Legal Center. (2008). *What does "qui tam" mean?* (May 30, 2008). Retrieved from www.taf.org/faq.htm#q2

False Claims Act of 1863, 12 U.S.C. § 696 (1863)

False Claims Amendments Act of 1986, 31 U.S.C. § 3701 nt (1986).

Fasterling, B., & Lewis, D. (2014). Leaks, legislation and freedom of speech: How can the law effectively promote public-interest whistleblowing? *International Labour Review,* *153*(1), 71–92. https://doi.org/10.1111/j.1564-913X.2014.00197.x

Faunce, T., Crow, K., Nikolic, T., & Morgan, J., Frederick, M. (2014). Because they have evidence: Globalizing financial incentives for corporate fraud whistleblowers. In A. J. Brown, D. Lewis, R. E. Moberly, & W. Vandekerckhove (Eds.), *International handbook of whistleblowing* (pp. 381–404). Cheltenham, UK: Edward Elgar Publishing Limited.

F.B.I. agent who wrote critical memo retires at 50. (2005). *New York Times* (January 2, 2005), 16. Retrieved from https://search-proquest-com.ezproxy.lib.ou.edu/docview/92870014?accountid=12964

Federal Bureau of Investigation. (1974). *Watergate (Summary) Part 01 of 02.* (139–4089). Retrieved from *https://vault.fbi.gov/watergate/watergate-summary-part-01-of-02/view.*

Foreign Corrupt Practices Act of 1977, 15 U.S.C. § 78a nt (1977).

Fraud Enforcement and Recovery Act of 2009, 18 U.S.C. § 1 nt (2009).

Freedom of Information Act of 1966, 5 U.S.C. § 552 (1966).

Gellman, B. (2013). Edward Snowden, after months of NSA revelations, says his mission's accomplished. *The Washington Post* (December 23, 2013). Retrieved from https://www.washingtonpost.com/

Gerald R. Ford Library and Museum. (2020). The Watergate Files. Retrieved from https://www.fordlibrarymuseum.gov/museum/exhibits/watergate_files/content.php?section=2&page=b&person=2

Glazer, M. P., & Glazer, P. M. (1989). *The whistleblowers: Exposing corruption in government and industry*. New York: Basic Books, Inc.

Government Accountability Project. (2008a). *S. 494 – H.R. 1317: Whistleblower Protection Act Amendments*. Retrieved from www.whistleblower.org/template/page.cfm?page_id=146

Government Accountability Project. (2008b). *Whistleblower Protection Act & Amendments*. Retrieved from http://web.archive.org/web/20080604135422/www.whistleblower.org/template/page.cfm?page_id=121

Guide to the Freedom of Information Act. (2013). Retrieved from https://www.justice.gov/sites/default/files/oip/legacy/2014/07/23/intro-july-19-2013.pdf

Hansberry, H. L. (2012). In spite of its good intentions, the Dodd–Frank Act has created an FCPA monster. *Journal of Criminal Law & Criminology*, *102*(1), 195–226.

The heavy toll of Watergate. (1975). *U.S. News & World Report*, (January 13, 1975), 16–20. Retrieved from https://advance-lexis-com.ezproxy.lib.ou.edu/api/document?collectio n=news&id=urn:contentItem:3SJ4-DTS0-000C-D54P-00000-00&context=1516831.

Hirsh, M., Isikoff, M., Klaidman, D., Hosenball, M., Clift, E., Barry, J., & . . ., & Dickey, C. (2002). What Went Wrong. *Newsweek, 139,* 28–36.

Hosenball, M., & Isikoff, M. (2002). Newsweek: FBI counterterrorism officials 'toned down' an agent's request for a warrant to search Moussaoui's computer, whistleblowing letter says. *PRNewswire* (May 26, 2002), 1. Retrieved from https://search-proquest-com. ezproxy.lib.ou.edu/docview/446796301?accountid=12964

Inspector General Act of 1978, 5 U.S.C. app. (1978).

Isikoff, M. (2008). The Fed Who Blew the Whistle. *Newsweek* (December 22, 2008). Retrieved from https://login.ezproxy.lib.ou.edu/login?url=https://www-proquest-com.ezproxy.lib. ou.edu/magazines/fed-who-blew-whistle/docview/214258835/se-2?accountid=12964

Jarrett, L., & Borger, G. (2017). Obama commutes sentence of Chelsea Manning. *CNN U.S.* (January 17, 2017). Retrieved from https://www.cnn.com/2017/01/17/politics/ chelsea-manning-sentence-commuted/index.html

Kaal, W. A. (2016). Dodd-Frank Act. In A. Farazmand (Ed.), *Global encyclopedia of public administration, public policy, and governance* (pp. 1–5). Switzerland: Springer International Publishing.

Katz, D. M., & Homer, J. (2008). WorldCom whistle-blower Cynthia Cooper. *CFO Magazine* (February 1, 2008), 38–40. Retrieved from http://www.cfo.com/article.cfm/10590507?f= search

Kohn, H. (1977). Karen Silkwood was right in plutonium scandal. *Rolling Stone* (October 20, 1977). Retrieved from https://www.rollingstone.com/culture/culture-news/karen-silk wood-was-right-in-plutonium-scandal-47908/

Kraterou, A. (2020). Julian Assange will learn on January 4 whether he will be sent to US to face hacking charges that could see him jailed for 175 years. *Daily Mail* (October 29, 2020). Retrieved from https://www.dailymail.co.uk/news/article-8894665/Julian-Assange-learn-January-4-sent-face-hacking-charges.html

Krogh, E. (2007). The break-in that history forgot. *The New York Times* (June 30, 2007). Retrieved from https://www.nytimes.com/2007/06/30/opinion/30krogh.html

Lacayo, R., & Ripley, A. (2002). Persons of The Year: The Whistleblowers. *Time, 160*(27). Retrieved from http://content.time.com/time/subscriber/article/0,33009,1003998,00.html

Leslie, G. (2003). Justice and the whistleblower. *News Media & the Law, 27*(3), 4–6.

Los Alamos National Laboratory. (1995). The Karen Silkwood Story. *Los Alamos Science, 23,* 252–255. Retrieved from PBS Frontline website: www.pbs.org/wgbh/pages/frontline/ shows/reaction/interact/silkwood.html

Lumm, D. C. (2010). The 2009 "Clarifications" to the False Claims Act of 1863: The all-purpose antifraud statute with the fun qui tam twist. *Wake Forest Law Review, 45.*

MacAskill, E., Snowden, E., & Ellsberg, D. (2018). 'Is whistleblowing worth prison or a life in exile?': Edward Snowden talks to Daniel Ellsberg. *The Guardian* (January 16, 2018). Retrieved from https://www.theguardian.com/world/2018/jan/16/is-whistleblowing-worth-prison-or-a-life-in-exile-edward-snowden-talks-to-daniel-ellsberg?CMP=share_btn_link

Malek, F. (2008). The truth about the "Malek Manual". *Fred Malek Blog* (March 6, 2008). Retrieved from http://www.fredmalekblog.com/2008/03/06/the-truth-about-the-% E2%80%9Cmalek-manual%E2%80%9D/

Martin, B. (2014). Research that whistleblowers want – and what they need. In A. J. Brown, D. Lewis, R. E. Moberly, & W. Vandekerckhove (Eds.), *International handbook of whistle-blowing* (pp. 497–521). Cheltenham, UK: Edward Elgar Publishing Limited.

Mayer, J. (2018). Christopher Steele, the man behind the Trump dossier. *The New Yorker* (March 12, 2018). Retrieved from www.newyorker.com/magazine/2018/03/12/ christopher-steele-the-man-behind-the-trump-dossier

Merit Systems Protection Board. (1981). *Whistleblowing and the federal employee: Blowing the whistle on fraud, waste, and mismanagement—who does it and what happens.* Washington, DC: MSPB.

Merit Systems Protection Board. (1984). *Blowing the whistle in the federal government: A Comparative analysis of 1980 and 1983 survey findings.* Washington, DC: MSPB.

Merit Systems Protection Board. (1993). *Whistleblowing in the federal government: An update.* Washington, DC: MSPB.

Merit Systems Protection Board. (2001). *Questions & answers about Whistleblower appeals.* Washington, DC: MSPB.

Merit Systems Protection Board. (2010a). *Prohibited personnel practices a study retrospective.* Washington, DC: MSPB.

Merit Systems Protection Board. (2010b). *Whistleblower protections for federal employees.* Washington, DC: MSPB.

Merit Systems Protection Board. (2011a). *Blowing the Whistle: Barriers to Federal Employees Making Disclosures* Washington, DC: MSPB.

Merit Systems Protection Board. (2011b). *Prohibited Personnel Practices: Employee Perceptions.* Washington, DC: MSPB.

Merit Systems Protection Board. (2014). *Current projects, planned projects, and proposed research topics for 2015–2018.* Washington, DC: MSPB.

Meyer, P. N. (2002). Making the narrative move: Observations based upon reading Gerry Spence's closing argument in the Estate of Karen Silkwood v. Kerr-Mcgee, Inc. *Clinical Law Review, 9*(1), 229–292.

Miceli, M., Dreyfus, S., & Near, J. (2014). Outsider 'whistleblowers': Conceptualizing and distinguishing 'bell-ringing' behavior. In A. J. Brown, D. Lewis, R. E. Moberly, & W. Vandekerckhove (Eds.), *International handbook on Whistleblower research* (pp. 71–94). Cheltenham, UK: Edward Elgar Publishing Limited.

Miller, G. R. (1989). Persuasion and public relations: Two "Ps" in a pod. In C. H. Botan & V. Hazleton Jr. (Eds.), *Public relations theory* (pp. 45–66). Hillsdale, NJ: Lawrence Erlbaum Associates.

Moberly, R. E. (2006). Sarbanes-Oxley's structural model to encourage corporate whistleblowers. *Brigham Young Law Review, 2006*(5), 1107–1180.

Moberly, R. E. (2007). Unfulfilled expectations: An empirical analysis of why Sarbanes-Oxley whistleblowers rarely win. *William and Mary Law Review, 49*, 65–156.

Moberly, R. E. (2012). Sarbanes-Oxley's whistleblower provisions: Ten years later. *South Carolina Law Review, 64*(1), 1–54.

Muellenberg, K. W., & Volzer, H. J. (1980). Inspector general act of 1978. *Temple Law Quarterly, 53*(4), 1049–1066.

Murphy, K. (2006). Judge Throws Out Kenneth Lay's Conviction *The New York Times,* (October 18, 2006). Retrieved from https://www.nytimes.com/2006/10/18/business/ 18enron.html?smid=em-share

Near, J. P., & Miceli, M. P. (1987). Whistle-blower in organizations: Dissidents or reformers? In L. L. Cummings & B. W. Staw (Eds.), *Research in organizational behavior* (pp. 321–368). Greenwich, CT: JAI Press.

Near, J. P., & Miceli, M. P. (2008). Wrongdoing, whistle-blowing, and retaliation in the U.S. Government: What have researchers learned from the Merit Systems Protection Board

(MSPB) survey results? *Review of Public Personnel Administration, 28*(3), 263–281. https://doi.org10.1177/0734371x08319153

New York Times Co. v. United States, 403 U.S. 713 (1971).

Norris, F. (2009). Could Skilling get a new trial? *The New York Times* (January 6, 2009). Retrieved from http://norris.blogs.nytimes.com/2009/01/06/could-skilling-get-a-new-trial/?pagemode=print

Notification and Federal Employee Anti-Discrimination and Retaliation Act of 2002, 5 U.S.C. § 2301 (2002).

Obama, B. (2012). *Presidential Policy Directive 19 (PPD-19) Protecting Whistleblowers with Access to Classified Information*. Retrieved from https://fas.org/irp/offdocs/ppd/ppd-19.pdf.

O'Connor, J. D. (2005). I'm the guy they called Deep Throat. *Vanity Fair*, 86–133.

Oswald, R. S., & Zuckerman, J. (2010). Whistleblower provisions of the Dodd-Frank Act. *The Employment Law Group*. Retrieved from https://www.employmentlawgroup.com/in-the-news/articles/whistleblower-provisions-dodd-frank-act/

Pavgi, K. (2012). Obama expands whistleblower protections to cover intelligence agencies. *Government Executive* (October 11, 2012). Retrieved from Factiva website: https://www.govexec.com/oversight/2012/10/obama-expands-whistleblower-protections-cover-intelligence-agencies/58728/

Peffer, S. L., Bocheko, A., Del Valle, R. E., Osmani, A., Peyton, S., & Roman, E. (2015). Whistle where you work? The ineffectiveness of the federal Whistleblower Protection Act of 1989 and the promise of the Whistleblower Protection Enhancement Act of 2012. *Review of Public Personnel Administration, 35*(1), 70–81. https://doi.org10.1177/0734371X13508414

Perez-Pena, R., & Magra, I. (2018). Julian Assange's arrest warrant is again upheld by U.K. Judge. *The New York Times* (February 13, 2018). Retrieved from https://www.nytimes.com/2018/02/13/world/europe/julian-assange-uk-warrant.html

Quinn, B. (2021). Julian Assange cannot be extradited to US, British judge rules. *The Guardian* (January 4, 2021). Retrieved from https://www.theguardian.com/media/2021/jan/04/julian-assange-cannot-be-extradited-to-us-british-judge-rules

Ratnesar, R., & Weisskopf, M. (2002). How the FBI blew the case. *Time, 159*(22).

Reilly, K. (2017). The true story about the new movie about Watergate and Deep Throat. *Time*. Retrieved from http://time.com/4969472/mark-felt-deep-throat-movie-fact-check/

Reuters. (2017). U.S. Intelligence Report Identifies Russians Who Gave DNC Emails to Wikileaks. *Time* (January 5, 2017). Retrieved from http://time.com/4625301/cia-russia-wikileaks-dnc-hacking/

Ripley, A., & Sieger, M. (2002). The special agent [Persons of the year]. *Time, 160*(271), 28–34. Retrieved from http://content.time.com/time/subscriber/article/0,33009,1003988,00.html

Rosenberg, M., Confessore, N., & Cadwalladr, C. (2018). How Trump Consultants Exploited the Facebook Data of Millions. *The New York Times* (March 17, 2018). Retrieved from https://www.nytimes.com/2018/03/17/us/politics/cambridge-analytica-trump-campaign.html

Rosenberg, M., & Frenkel, S. (2018). Facebook's role in data misuse sets off storms on two continents. *The New York Times* (March 18, 2018). Retrieved from https://www.nytimes.com/2018/03/18/us/cambridge-analytica-facebook-privacy-data.html

Rosenwald, M. S. (2008). Brokering power in business and politics. *Washington Post* (April 21, 2008). Retrieved from http://www.washingtonpost.com/wp-dyn/content/article/2008/04/20/AR2008042001564.html

Safire, W. (2002). The Rowley memo. *The New York Times (1923-Current File)* (May 27, 2002), A17. Retrieved from https://search-proquest-com.ezproxy.lib.ou.edu/docview/9 2229373?accountid=12964

Sarbanes-Oxley Act of 2002, 15 U.S.C. § 7201 nt (2002).

Schaal, D. (2008). Days in the life of a whistleblower. *The CRO Blog*. Retrieved from www.thecro.com/node/648

Scholes, M. S. (2011). Foreword. In V. V. Acharya, T. F. Cooley, M. Richardson, & I. Walter (Eds.), *Regulating Wall Street: The Dodd-Frank Act and the New Architecture of Global Finance* (pp. xi–xvi). Hoboken, NJ: John Wiley & Sons, Inc.

Securities and Exchange Commission Final rule: Management's report on internal control over financial reporting and certification of disclosure in Exchange Act periodic reports, 17 CFR PARTS 210, 228, 229, 240, 249, 270 and 274 (2003).

Securities and Exchange Commission. (2016a). *SEC announces enforcement results for FY 2016* [Press release]. Retrieved from www.sec.gov/news/pressrelease/2016-212.html

Securities and Exchange Commission. (2016b). *SEC: Casino-gaming company retaliated against whistleblower* [Press release]. Retrieved from www.sec.gov/news/pressrelease/2016-204.html

Securities and Exchange Commission. (2018). *SEC proposes whistleblower rule amendments* [Press release]. Retrieved from www.sec.gov/news/press-release/2018-120

Securities and Exchange Commission. (2020a). *SEC adds clarity, efficiency and transparency to its successful Whistleblower award program* [Press release]. Retrieved from https://www.sec.gov/news/press-release/2020-219

Securities and Exchange Commission. (2020b). *SEC issues record $114 million Whistleblower award* [Press release]. Retrieved from https://www.sec.gov/news/press-release/2020-266

Securities and Exchange Commission. (2020c). *SEC awards over $10 million to Whistleblower* [Press release]. Retrieved from https://www.sec.gov/news/press-release/2020-270

Sixel, L. M. (2018). Former Enron CEO Jeff Skilling out of prison, sent to halfway house. *Houston Chronicle* (August 31, 2018). Retrieved from https://www.chron.com/business/energy/article/Skilling-out-of-prison-sent-to-halfway-house-in-13194674.php

Specia, M. (2020). At Assange's Extradition Hearing, Troubled Tech Takes Center Stage. *The New York Times* (September 16, 2020). Retrieved from https://www.nytimes.com/2020/09/16/world/europe/assange-extradition-hearing.html?searchResultPosition=1

Spitzer, E. (2019). New York Times Co. v. US: Supreme Court Case, Arguments, Impact. (November 8, 2019). Retrieved from thoughtco.com/new-york-times-co-v-u-s-4771900

Stack, L., Cumming-Bruce, N., & Kruhly, M. (2018). Julian Assange: A legal history. *The New York Times* (February 13, 2018). Retrieved from https://www.nytimes.com/interactive/2019/world/julian-assange-wikileaks.html?mtrref=undefined&gwh=1F41BB0052 C5B3D7F98C87160622CEE2&gwt=regi&assetType=REGIWALL

Steffy, L. (2013). An end to the Enron saga. *Forbes* (June 21, 2013). Retrieved from https://www.forbes.com/sites/lorensteffy/2013/06/21/an-end-to-the-enron-saga/#1368dbfd163d

Tarzie. (2017). Edward Snowden, Frenemy of the State. *American Journal of Economics and Sociology,* 76(2), 348–380. https://doi.org10.1111/ajes.12179

U.S. Department of Justice. (2016). *Justice Department recovers over $4.7 billion from False Claims Act cases in fiscal year 2016* [Press release]. Retrieved from www.justice.gov/opa/pr/justice-department-recovers-over-47-billion-false-claims-act-cases-fiscal-year-2016

U.S. House of Representatives Permanent Select Committee on Intelligence. (2016). *(U) Review of the Unauthorized Disclosures of Former National Security Agency Contractor Edward Snowden.* (114 H. Rpt. 891). Washington, DC: G.P.O. Retrieved from https://www.govinfo.gov/app/details/CRPT-114hrpt891/CRPT-114hrpt891.

U.S. House of Representative Permanent Select Committee on Intelligence. (2019). House Intelligence Committee Releases Whistleblower Complaint, [Press release]. Retrieved from https://intelligence.house.gov/news/documentsingle.aspx?DocumentID=708

U.S. House of Representatives Committee on Commerce and Energy. (2018). *Facebook: Transparency and Use of Consumer Data.* (Committee Print No. 30-956). Washington, DC: G.P.O. Retrieved from https://www.govinfo.gov/content/pkg/CHRG-115hhrg30956/pdf/CHRG-115hhrg30956.pdf.

U.S. House of Representatives Subcommittee on Manpower and Civil Service of the Committee on Post Office and Civil Services. (1976). *Final report on violations and abuses of merit principles in Federal employment, together with minority views, 94th Cong., 2nd* (Committee Print No. 94-28). Washington, DC: G.P.O.

U.S. Senate Committee on Governmental Affairs. (1978). *The Whistleblowers: A Report on Federal employees who disclose acts of governmental waste, abuse, and corruption.* (CMP-1978-SGA-0004). Washington, DC: G.P.O.

U.S. Senate Committee on the Judiciary. (1986). *Confirmation hearings on appointments to the Federal Judiciary and the Department of Defense (testimony of Robert M. Tobias).* (S. Hrg. 99-141/Pt. 2). Washington, DC: G.P.O.

U.S. Senate Committee on the Judiciary. (2018). *Hearing on Cambridge Analytica and Future of Data Privacy (Testimony of Christopher Wylie).* Washington, DC: U.S. Senate Retrieved from https://www.judiciary.senate.gov/meetings/cambridge-analytica-and-the-future-of-data-privacy

U.S. Senate Select Committee on Intelligence. (2017). *Nomination of Christopher Sharpley to be the Inspector General of the Central Intelligence Agency.* (S. HRG. 115–303). Washington, DC: G.P.O. Retrieved from https://www.govinfo.gov/content/pkg/CHRG-115shrg27396/pdf/CHRG-115shrg27396.pdf.

U.S. Senate Committee on Commerce, Science, and Transportation and the Senate Committee on the Judiciary. (2018). *Facebook, Social Media Privacy, and the Use and Abuse of Data.* (Serial No. J-115-40). Retrieved from https://www.govinfo.gov/content/pkg/CHRG-115shrg37801/pdf/CHRG-115shrg37801.pdf.\

Vallejo, J. (2020). Whistleblower Edward Snowden granted permanent residency in Russia, reports say. *The Independent* (October 22, 2020). Retrieved from https://www.independent.co.uk/news/world/americas/edward-snowden-cia-nsa-surveillance-whistleblower-russia-asylum-residency-b1234646.html

Vaughn, R. G. (2005). America's first comprehensive statute protecting corporate whistleblowers. *Administrative Law Review, 57*(1), 1–105.

Von Drehle, D. (2005). FBI's no. 2 was 'Deep Throat': Mark Felt ends 30-year mystery of The Post's Watergate source. *The Washington Post* (June 1, 2005). Retrieved from http://www.washingtonpost.com

The Watergate Story: John Dean. (2008). *The Washington Post.* Retrieved from www.washingtonpost.com/wp-srv/politics/special/watergate/dean.html

The Watergate Story Part 2: The government investigates. (2008). *The Washington Post.* Retrieved from http://www.washingtonpost.com/wp-srv/politics/special/watergate/part2.html

The Watergate Story Part 4: Deep Throat Revealed. (2005). *The Washington Post* (June 1, 2005). Retrieved from https://www.washingtonpost.com/wp-srv/politics/special/watergate/part4.html

Whistleblower Protection Act Amendments of 1994, 5 U.S.C. § 101 nt (1994).

Whistleblower Protection Act of 1989, 5 U.S.C. § 1201 nt (1989).

Whistleblower Protection Enhancement Act of 2012, 5 U.S.C. § 101 nt (2012).

Wilbanks, C. (2013). Ex-Enron CEO Jeff Skilling to leave prison early. *CBS News* (June 21, 2013). Retrieved from CBS News website: https://www.cbsnews.com/news/ex-enron-ceo-jeff-skilling-to-leave-prison-early/

Wild, D. (2003). Profile: Sherron Watkins, Enron whistleblower. *Accountancy Age* (December 18, 2003). Retrieved from https://www.accountancyage.com/2003/12/18/profile-sherron-watkins-enron-whistleblower/

Williams, J., & Toropin, K. (2017). Russia extends Edward Snowden's asylum to 2020. *CNN U.S.* (January 1, 2017). Retrieved from https://www.cnn.com/2017/01/18/europe/russia-snowden-asylum-extension/index.html

Wilmarth, J., & Arthur, E. (2011). The Dodd-Frank Act: A flawed and inadequate response to the Too-Big-to-Fail problem. *Oregon Law Review*, *89*(951), 97.

Woodward, B. (2005). *The secret man: The story of Watergate's "Deep Throat"*. New York: Simon & Schuster.

Zuckerberg, M. (2021). *Mark Zuckerberg*. Retrieved from https://m.facebook.com/zuck

Zuckerman, J. (2012). Congress strengthens whistleblower protections for federal employees. *ABA LEL Flash* (November-December 2012). Retrieved from https://www.zuckermanlaw.com/wp-content/uploads/2019/01/Whistleblower-Protection-Enhancement-Act.pdf

3 Whistleblowing research in government, management, and law in the United States

Introduction to whistleblowing research in the United States

This chapter presents an overview of whistleblowing research in government, management, and law in the United States. As noted, the impetus for whistleblowing research in the United States was the federal government's three large-scale studies of whistleblowing by federal employees following Watergate. The size and availability of those datasets enticed management researchers to initiate the first nongovernmental analyses of the federal data (Miceli, Rehg, Near, & Ryan, 1999). Subsequently, communication and journalism scholars addressed some aspects of whistleblowing (see Chapter 5). However, public relations scholars ignored the topic until the mid-2000s and then touched on it only as one rarely used aspect of dissent (Berger & Reber, 2006).

Federal whistleblowing research: the data

The majority of research conducted on whistleblowing appears in management literature, and much of the early management literature on whistleblowing was based on the surveys conducted on federal employees in 1980, 1983, and 1992 by the MSPB. As part of its mandate to enforce the whistleblower protections, the MSPB administered three surveys to a total of 39,000 federal employees over a period of 12 years (Merit Systems Protection Board, 1981, 1984, 1993). The purpose of the surveys was to identify trends in illegal and wasteful activity observed by federal employees, their reporting (or lack of reporting) of those activities, and the level of retaliation they experienced for reporting the activities. Subsequent federal research and evaluation added to the picture of federal employee whistleblowing (Merit Systems Protection Board, 2001, 2010a, 2010b, 2011a, 2011b, 2014), but the first three surveys were instrumental in launching the academic investigation into whistleblowing:

> The existence of these three data sets provides social scientists a unique opportunity to consider the effects of a human resource policy initiative on a large number of employees in a number of large organizations regarding a particular question that has both theoretical and social-policy importance.

DOI: 10.4324/9781315231891-4

It is rare that the opportunity to examine a social phenomenon such as whistle-blowing over time is presented.

(Miceli et al., 1999, p. 148)

This chapter explores the findings in those surveys, as reported by the MSPB.

Merit Systems Protection Board 1981 survey

In 1980, the MSPB sent 13,000 surveys to randomly selected federal employees from 15 major federal organizations and received 8,600 responses for a response rate of 66% (Merit Systems Protection Board, 1981, p. 148). About 45% said they had seen at least one instance of illegal or wasteful activity during the past year, but only 30% reported it.[1] Of those who reported, 20% said they had suffered threats of reprisals or reprisals (retaliation or the threat of retaliation),[2] and the rest did not report because they felt nothing would be done (53%) or were afraid of reprisals (19%). Knowing the organization would correct the wrongdoing was the primary (81%) factor that federal employees said would encourage them to report wrongdoing.

Merit Systems Protection Board 1984 survey

In 1983, the MSPB sent its second survey to 7,563 randomly selected federal employees from the entire executive branch of government and received 4,897 responses for a response rate of 64.7% (Merit Systems Protection Board, 1984). This time, only 25% said they had seen at least one instance of illegal or wasteful activity during the past year, but as in the 1980 survey only 30% reported it. Of those who reported, 23% said they had suffered reprisal,[3] which was slightly more than the 20% reported in 1980. Those who did not report either felt nothing would be done (70%) or were afraid of reprisal (37%) (Merit Systems Protection Board, 1984).

Merit Systems Protection Board 1993 survey

In 1992, the MSPB sent a third survey to 20,851 randomly selected federal employees from all agencies in the executive branch of government and achieved a response of 13,432 for a response rate of 64%. Results showed that awareness of illegal or wasteful activities had decreased again to 8%, and reporting had increased to 50%. Unfortunately, the number of employees who said they had been threatened with or suffered reprisal for reporting wrongdoing also increased to 38%.[4] "This is significantly higher than the 24 percent of reporting employees who said in the Board's 1983 survey that they had been threatened with or had experienced reprisal" (Merit Systems Protection Board, 1993, p. 19). The most common forms of reprisal in 1992 were "poor performance appraisals, shunning by coworkers or management, and verbal harassment or intimidation" (Merit Systems Protection Board, 1993, p. iii).

Merit Systems Protection Board 2011 survey

In 2010, the MSPB sent a fourth survey to more than 40,000 randomly selected federal employees from all agencies in the executive branch of government. Unfortunately, the number of responses and the response rate were not reported, and comparable statistics were not provided in 2011 for comparison with 1992. One finding was that awareness of wrongdoing had decreased to 11.1% as compared with its 1992 survey. The number who reported wrongdoing was slightly higher in 2010 than in 1992. The number who reported reprisals (retaliation or the threat of retaliation)[5] stayed about the same at 36.2% in 2010 versus 36.9% in 1992 (Merit Systems Protection Board, 2011a).

Management whistleblowing research: the theories

Academic definitions of whistleblowing as derived from the federal definition

The first characteristic of a whistleblower is that he or she must be a current or former employee of the organization in which he or she is blowing the whistle (Miceli & Near, 1984, p. 689). The second characteristic of a whistleblower is that he or she must report some type of negative activity, which was identified as "illegal or wasteful" in the first federal study (Merit Systems Protection Board, 1981, p. 2) and as "illegal, immoral, or illegitimate" in subsequent management studies (Miceli & Near, 1984, p. 689). The third characteristic of a whistleblower is that he or she must report "to persons or organizations who may be able to affect action" (Miceli & Near, 1984, p. 689). This implies that the recipient of the report may be someone inside or outside the organization. For that reason, whistleblowers are characterized as either internal or external, depending on the location of the channels they use and to whom they report wrongdoing (Miceli & Near, 1984). The definition of whistleblowing used by most researchers (Miceli, Near, & Dworkin, 2008) is "the disclosure by organization members (former or current) of illegal, immoral, or illegitimate practices under the control of their employers, to persons or organizations that may be able to effect action" (Near & Miceli, 1985, p. 4). *This study* defines whistleblowing as disclosure of a private corporation's illegal, wasteful, or unethical practices by a current or former employee to persons or organizations inside or outside the corporation that may be able to effect action.

Theories

As noted, the majority of research conducted on whistleblowing appears in the management literature. A search on the term "whistleblowing" in the database Business Source Elite on February 3, 2020, yielded 2,602 results on a variety of topics from various fields. Although the topic has clearly resonated in the management discipline, much of that research depends on, or owes its origins to, the U.S. government's early studies (Merit Systems Protection Board, 1981,

1984, 1993). Management scholars used those large datasets to conduct more statistically sophisticated analyses than the government had and to test hypotheses drawn from theory (Near & Miceli, 2008). The idea that no overall theory guides whistleblowing research (Culiberg & Mihelič, 2017) is illustrated by the variety of theories used to understand whistleblowing, its motivations, and its repercussions.

These theories include organizational response and legitimacy (Parmerlee, Near, & Jensen, 1982); theory of principled organizational dissent (Graham, 1986; Perry, 1992); expectancy theory (Miceli & Near, 1984); power theory and justice theory (Near, Dworkin, & Miceli, 1993); deviance theory and justice theory (Miceli & Near, 1997); theory of emotion, theory of upward deviance, theory of organizational justice, theory of stress, theory of coping, and social optimism theory (Cortina & Magley, 2003); theory of minority influence and bases of power theory (Rehg, Miceli, Near, & Van Scotter, 2004); social role theory, status characteristics theory, institution theory, justice theory, and social contract theory (Rehg, Miceli, Near, & Van Scotter, 2008); theory of reasoned action (Richardson, Wang, & Hall, 2012); path dependence theory (Pittroff, 2015); prospect theory and social identity theory (Boo, Terence Bu-Peow, & Shankar, 2016); and theory of planned behavior (Alleyne, Hudaib, & Haniffa, 2018), to name a few. These theories are varied and, in most cases, conflicting or inconclusive. However, a number of researchers, including this author, have turned to a theory from management to explain at least some of whistleblowing's variables. Resource dependence perspective (RDP) – alone or in conjunction with other theories – has been used extensively by management scholars (Mesmer-Magnus & Viswesvaran, 2005; Miceli & Near, 1985; 1994; Miceli et al., 1999; Near et al., 1993; Near & Miceli, 1986; 1996; Rehg et al., 2004; Miceli & Near, 2002).

RDP argues that organizations are dependent on their environments for resources (Pfeffer & Salancik, 1978, 2003). Those resources include materials, financing, information, transportation, and workforce. Those resources are controlled by other actors who make demands on the organization. Management's handling of those demands will determine the effectiveness and, therefore, the survival of the organization (Pfeffer & Salancik, 2003). The demands of internal actors (i.e., employees, including whistleblowers) and management's handling of their demands are the focus of much of the whistleblowing research in management literature (Miceli et al., 2008).

RDP has three conceptual bases: (1) social context is important; (2) strategy can be effective in reducing obstacles; and (3) power matters more than economic efficiency (Pfeffer & Salancik, 2003). The ways in which organizations are dependent upon their environments for resources occur within a social context. The dependencies between organizations and those who hold the resources they need "are often reciprocal and sometimes indirect" (Pfeffer & Salancik, 2003, p. xii), but they occur within social structures. When businesses stop thinking only about products and customers and begin to recognize the environment within which they operate, the strategies to overcome obstacles within the environment become more important (Pfeffer & Salancik, 2003, p. xii). Those strategies include developing relationships with those with whom one's organization has ties or linkages, which provide information about other organizations, provide a "channel for communication" (Pfeffer & Salancik, 2003, p. 144) with those organizations, develop support for one's own organization, and provide legitimacy for one's own organization.

RDP focuses on the power relationships between organizations and other actors within their environments, including the interest groups from which organizations draw resources internally and externally. "The idea that power was important for understanding organization, as contrasted, for instance, with rationality or efficiency, was yet another way in which resource dependence ideas represented somewhat of a shift in focus for organization studies" (Pfeffer & Salancik, 2003, p. xiii). Power is a function of an organization's relationships, and external relationships affect internal relationships. Those individuals or groups within organizations that provide stability, control key relationships, and acquire resources are more powerful than those that cannot perform those functions because they play a key role in helping the organization remain viable (Pfeffer & Salancik, 2003). In terms of whistleblowing, the whistleblower's power was found, in some cases, to be negatively related to retaliation; organizational dependence on wrongdoing was positively related to retaliation; retaliation was negatively related to the relationship of the whistleblower to his or her direct supervisor; and retaliation and organizational dependence on wrongdoing were both related to external reporting (Rehg et al., 2004).

Methods used in whistleblowing research

Whistleblowing is a sensitive topic for individuals and for organizations, which makes research on whistleblowing difficult to conduct (Rehg, 1998). The methods used to examine the phenomenon of whistleblowing have included virtually all forms of research design. Those have included field experiments, quasi-experiments eliciting projected reactions to hypothetical situations, in-depth case studies, legal case studies, longitudinal nonexperimental field surveys, and meta-analysis (Miceli et al., 2008). However, much of the research on whistleblowing has used surveys of employees about their experience with whistleblowing or in blowing the whistle, and most of that survey research has been based on the first three surveys conducted by the MSPB. Management scholars who analyzed those three studies considered eight specific variables, plus demographic data (Near, Ryan, & Miceli, 1995). The variables were *incidence of wrongdoing* (the number who observed one or more of ten types of wrongdoing); *incidence of whistleblowing* (the number who reported serious wrongdoing divided by the number who observed wrongdoing); *incidence of identified whistleblowing* (assuming only whistleblowers who were identified could experience retaliation); *incidence of retaliation* (the number of identified whistleblowers who reported retaliation divided by the number of whistleblowers); *comprehensiveness of retaliation* (the number of incidents of retaliation experienced by the respondent); *lack of support from management, supervisors, and/ or co-workers*; *seriousness of wrongdoing* (dollar value or frequency); *use of internal or external whistleblowing channels*; and *demographic data*: race, gender, education, organizational tenure, job tenure, pay grade, job classification, supervisory position, and most recent performance rating (Near et al., 1995, p. 370).

Predictors of wrongdoing, whistleblowing, and retaliation

The broad categories of investigation into whistleblowing have included predictors of wrongdoing, predictors of whistleblowing, and predictors of organizational response to whistleblowing (Miceli et al., 2008).[6]

Wrongdoing

Predictors of wrongdoing have been difficult to quantify. "The variance in employees, organizations, wrongdoing reported, and recipients of complaints makes it difficult to predict when wrongdoing will occur" (Rehg, 1998, p. 121). The federal researchers did not draw predictions about wrongdoing from the studies, but they did characterize the types of wrongdoing reported in each study. They found that the waste of federal funds through badly managed programs and the waste of federal funds from improper purchasing were the most frequently cited categories of wrongdoing in all three years (Merit Systems Protection Board, 1981, 1984, 1993). Illegal or wasteful activities costing more than $1,000 were cited by 52% of those who saw wrongdoing in 1981 (Merit Systems Protection Board, 1981, p. 1), by 46% in 1983, and by 44% in 1993 (Merit Systems Protection Board, 1993, p. 7).

Whistleblowing

Predictors of whistleblowing have been identified at various times as attributes of the individual, such as personality, demographics, and job situation; attributes of the wrongdoing, such as seriousness, type, power or status of the wrongdoer, and support of the supervisor; and attributes of the organization, such as organizational climate or supportiveness, and industry type (Miceli & Near, 1988; Miceli et al., 1999, 2008; Near & Miceli, 1996). Predictors of organizational response to whistleblowing have been identified as "characteristics of the whistleblower and the job situation" (Miceli et al., 2008, p. 105) and "situational characteristics related to the wrongdoing and whistle-blowing" (Miceli et al., 2008, p. 109). These include attributes of the wrongdoer (Miceli & Near, 1988; Miceli, Near, & Schwenk, 1991; Near & Miceli, 1996), attributes of the wrongdoing (seriousness and type), whistleblowing channels, interpersonal interactions, and characteristics of the social setting, such as organizational climate or culture and "societal, country, or cultural variables" (Miceli et al., 2008, p. 122).

An early management study using the Merit Systems Protection Board (1981) data found that organizational dependence on wrongdoing as a resource, as measured by numerous actions of wrongdoing and threats of retaliation, resulted in organizational resistance to change and a propensity toward retaliation (Miceli & Near, 1985). The threat of retaliation increased external reporting:

> Whistleblowers went "inside" when the wrongdoing was at odds with other operations and the climate was less retaliatory; they went outside when the opposite conditions were present. Thus, resource dependence theory seems to be very useful in predicting both whether and *to whom* one would blow the whistle.
>
> (Miceli & Near, 1985, p. 540)

The study also found that whistleblowing was more likely to occur when the observer had hard evidence of wrongdoing; it increased with the seriousness of the wrongdoing; and it increased if the whistleblower was affected by the wrongdoing. Miceli and Near were the first to quantify the number of communication methods used to tell employees about the communication channels available for whistleblowing and to quantify employees' awareness of those channels, but neither the number of communication channels nor awareness of the channels appeared to affect the decision to blow the whistle (Miceli & Near, 1985).

In a further examination of whistleblowing using the model of principled organization dissent (i.e., organizational response could be approval or punishment, or issue resolution), Perry (1992) found organizations responded with increasing hostility as the power of the whistleblower increased. Hostility toward the whistleblower increased but resolution improved when the dominant coalition was involved in the wrongdoing. This may have been because hostility forced the whistleblower to report externally; the greater the change required of an organization, the less likely it was to change. Finally, change was more likely when there was an investigation of the whistleblower's claims by an outside group (Perry, 1992).

Additional research on the 1980 MSPB data found significant distinctions between whistleblowers and two other groups: those who do not observe wrongdoing (nonobservers) and those who observe wrongdoing but do not report it (inactive observers) (Miceli & Near, 1984). Nonobservers were more likely to expect protection from retaliation, less likely to be motivated by problem resolution, and less likely to support financial rewards. Inactive observers tended to be highly educated, low-paid supervisors. "It therefore is speculated that inactive observers are likely to be young, high potential, low seniority employees. They seem to be the 'fast-trackers'" (Miceli & Near, 1984, p. 699).

Whistleblowers had higher levels of pay and education than nonobservers and inactive observers, but internal and external whistleblowers differed on those categories. Internal whistleblowers were "more likely to be highly educated supervisors" and external whistleblowers had "higher pay levels in combination with lower education levels and . . . [were] less likely to be in supervisory positions" (Miceli & Near, 1984, p. 696–697). Whistleblowers as a whole believed more strongly than nonobservers and inactive observers that whistleblowing was a positive action. However, researchers found no greater fear of retaliation among inactive observers than among whistleblowers, leaving open the question of why employees who observe wrongdoing do or do not report it (Miceli & Near, 1984). One answer was found in a study of private sector, first-level managers who were administered the 1980 MSPB survey. This research found that managers were more likely to blow the whistle internally when they were confident their bosses would not retaliate (Keenan, 1988).

An analysis of the 1983 MSPB data found that individuals would blow the whistle to benefit the larger group if it benefited themselves as well (Miceli & Near, 1988). In this case, whistleblowing was more likely to occur when observers were male professionals who had been in their positions a long time, who had positive reactions to their work, who had been recognized recently for good performance, and who were working in larger work groups in organizations known for responsiveness to complaints (Miceli & Near, 1988). Miceli and Near found that organizational responsiveness could be demonstrated by publicizing "through employee newsletters or posters, how problems were solved as a result of the reports" (Miceli & Near, 1988, p. 278) and by making ethical behavior a part of performance reviews and compensation plans. A more recent study of whistleblowing cases that had gone to court found that allegations of violations of discrimination laws, sexual harassment claims, safety concerns and refusal to participate in illegal activities were predictors of a favorable outcome to the employee (Lopez, Lavan, & Katz, 2013).

Role-prescribed whistleblowing

In 1986, management researchers administered a survey to members of a national organization made up of directors of internal auditing, a group for whom some forms of internal whistleblowing were role-prescribed (Miceli et al., 1991). "About 90% of those who observed wrongdoing reported it." Those who did not report wrongdoing saw themselves as "relatively poor performers . . . [earning] somewhat lower salaries than persons who report wrongdoing" (Miceli et al., 1991, p. 126). They also did not report wrongdoing when reporting was not required morally, when reporting was not required by the job, when other observers witnessed the event, and when they saw the organization as bureaucratic. Observers of wrongdoing reported it when they viewed the wrongdoing as harmful to co-workers or the public, when it involved theft, when the wrongdoers were low-level employees, and when there were few observers (Miceli et al., 1991).

Whistleblowers versus inactive observers

A review of whistleblowing literature in the 1990s created a profile of whistleblowers that was different from people who observed wrongdoing but did not blow the whistle. Those non-reporters were identified as inactive observers.

Whistleblowers were found to be older males who were highly educated, higher-ranking, and better paid than inactive observers. They also were more likely than inactive observers to be in a position that required reporting wrongdoing (i.e., having role responsibility for reporting) (Near & Miceli, 1996). "In some studies, whistle-blowers are more satisfied and committed than inactive observers and perceive the organization to be more just" (Near & Miceli, 1996, p. 511).

Whistleblowing versus intent to blow

INTERNAL AUDITORS

In contrast to the high percentage of whistleblowing by internal auditors (Miceli et al., 1991), a meta-analysis of whistleblowing literature found a distinction between reported intent to blow the whistle and actual reported whistleblowing. For example, role prescription for whistleblowing, such as is found with internal auditors, predicted intent to blow the whistle, but it did not predict actual whistleblowing.

> This finding is unexpected, as one would expect that the organization creates and staffs internal 'watchdog' positions to facilitate whistleblowing on unsanctioned practices (e.g., Miceli, Near, & Schwenk, 1991; Near & Miceli, 1996). . . . Regardless, our data suggest that having a role-related responsibility to blow the whistle may not be sufficient to ensure whistle-blowing action.
>
> (Mesmer-Magnus & Viswesvaran, 2005, p. 290)

MBA STUDENTS IN NIGHT SCHOOL

In an attempt to determine whether financial rewards or anonymity in reporting is more effective in increasing the intent to report wrongdoing, researchers compared two recent pieces of legislation with differing requirements. The mandated whistleblowing channel provision of Sarbanes-Oxley offers anonymity, while the bounty provisions of Dodd-Frank require being identified as the source of the report. They surveyed 97 part-time MBA students in night school because they felt those students were more likely to have more work experience (hence, their enrollment in night school) and thus more experience with questionable behavior in the workplace. They found that the availability of an anonymous reporting channel had no effect on people's intent to report wrongdoing. However, having a bounty or financial reward made individuals more willing to report those questionable acts (Pope & Lee, 2013).

Whistleblowing effectiveness

Two additional analyses of the internal auditor data measured the effectiveness of whistleblowing. Effectiveness in whistleblowing was defined as getting the organization to stop wrongdoing (Near & Miceli, 1990; Perry, 1992). Both studies used RDP to explain the situational variables that predicted success. These included reporting an activity that co-workers saw as wrong, such as theft, and holding a position of power within the organization. Additional variables that predicted success included not going outside the organization, not reporting to the head of the organization or the manager over the employee doing wrong, not having been retaliated against, and not reporting a wrongdoing on which the organization depends, as evidenced by how long the wrongdoing had been occurring (Near & Miceli, 1990; Perry, 1992).

Retaliation

Several aspects of whistleblowing, such as retaliation, have captured the attention of researchers, even though some argue that retaliation has been reported infrequently (Near & Miceli, 1996). Retaliation is a complex phenomenon, but understanding why retaliation occurs is necessary to preventing its occurrence, and preventing its occurrence may be one way to encourage whistleblowing. "Whistle-blowing represents an influence attempt in which organization member(s) try to persuade other members to cease wrongdoing; sometimes they fail; sometimes they succeed; sometimes they suffer reprisal" (Rehg et al., 2008, p. 221). Researchers have suggested that an organization has several possible responses to whistleblowing. These include cessation or continuation of the wrongdoing, as well as rewarding the whistleblower, treating the whistleblower as before, or retaliating against the whistleblower (Miceli & Near, 1992).

Stages of retaliation

Four progressive stages of organizational retaliation have been identified (O'Day, 1974) and used in management literature to analyze retaliation (Parmerlee et al., 1982). The first stage is nullification, in which the complaint is diminished. The second stage is isolation, in which the complainant is diminished. The third stage is defamation of character, in which the complaint is resolved through character assassination of the complainant. The fourth stage is expulsion, in which the complainant is ejected from the organization (O'Day, 1974).

Predictors of retaliation

The management literature has identified several predictors of how an organization responds to whistleblowing (Miceli & Near, 1992). These include characteristics of the whistleblower, characteristics of the wrongdoing, characteristics of the organization, and the dependence of the organization on the wrongdoing, the wrongdoer, the whistleblower, and the person who receives the complaint. Whistleblower characteristics include credibility and loyalty. Wrongdoing characteristics include seriousness of wrongdoing (e.g., dollar amount or frequency) and type of wrongdoing, which includes individual wrongdoing (e.g., employee or executive theft or embezzlement) and corporate-level wrongdoing (e.g., erroneous financial reporting and regulatory breaches). Method of reporting includes various avenues for internal and/or external reporting. Organizational characteristics include types of retaliation, lack of support from management, and seriousness of the wrongdoing (Miceli & Near, 1992).

THE CIVIL SERVICE REFORM ACT OF 1978 – IMPACT ON RETALIATION

Management researchers who studied the longitudinal data from the three federal studies (1980, 1983, and 1992) predicted that enactment of the CSRA, the federal whistleblower protection law, would have several positive impacts on whistleblowing, including reducing wrongdoing, increasing whistleblowing, increasing identified whistleblowing, and reducing retaliation for identified whistleblowing (Near et al., 1995). Using RDP, they predicted that an organization that was dependent on wrongdoing, as evidenced by the seriousness of the wrongdoing, would be reluctant to change and would retaliate against whistleblowers, and that whistleblowers who had low power in the organization would experience retaliation. What they found was that the incidence of observed wrongdoing decreased by half in each subsequent study; the number of reports of wrongdoing increased by a third in each study; the number of identified whistleblowers decreased slightly in each study; and the incidents of retaliation doubled from the first study to the last. Several variables predicted retaliation in one or two of the studies, but only two variables predicted retaliation in all three studies: lack of supervisor support and lack of management support. Using external channels predicted retaliation in the 1980 and 1982 studies, and seriousness of wrongdoing predicted retaliation in the 1980 study (Near et al., 1995).

In a later review of the government data, researchers predicted that the CSRA whistleblower protections would have positive results in four areas. They predicted the CSRA would result in "(1) less wrongdoing, (2) more whistle-blowing when wrongdoing occurred, (3) more identified (vs. anonymous) whistle-blowers, and (4) less retaliation) (Miceli et al., 1999). Unfortunately, results were mixed" (Near & Miceli, 2008, p. 271). What the researchers found, as predicted, was a decrease in (observed) wrongdoing. They also found an increase in whistleblowing. However, contrary to predictions, they found no reduction in fears of retaliation, and they found an actual increase in retaliation (Near & Miceli, 2008, p. 271).

LACK OF SUPERVISOR/MANAGEMENT SUPPORT AND SERIOUSNESS OF WRONGDOING

Predictors of retaliation have varied over time with different studies, but lack of supervisor and management support and seriousness of wrongdoing have predicted retaliation in several studies through advanced statistical testing (Mesmer-Magnus & Viswesvaran, 2005; Near et al., 1995; Rehg et al., 2004, 2008; Miceli et al., 2008). Using multiple regression analysis, Near et al. (1995) found that seriousness of wrongdoing (defined as dollar amount and frequency) predicted retaliation in the 1980 federal study, but it did not predict retaliation in the 1983 and 1992 federal studies. However, hierarchical multiple regression of the same data in 1999 found that seriousness of wrongdoing predicted retaliation in 1983 only (Miceli et al., 1999; Near & Miceli, 2008). A meta-analysis of whistleblowing research (Mesmer-Magnus & Viswesvaran, 2005) found seriousness of wrongdoing and frequency of wrongdoing predicted retaliation. However, the authors did not define seriousness of wrongdoing.

In one study, Rehg (1998) found seriousness of wrongdoing, defined as frequency and dollar amount, only partially supported as a predictor of retaliation, but Rehg later found seriousness of wrongdoing, defined this time as "materiality, entrenchment, harm to multiple constituents," a predictor of retaliation (Rehg et al., 2004, p. E5). Seriousness of wrongdoing (measured as materiality and frequency) has also been linked to the organization's dependence on the wrongdoing (Miceli et al., 2008).

> Seriousness of wrongdoing can be gauged by its entrenchment or long-term nature, its materiality, and its perceived harm to multiple constituencies. "Materiality," as defined by accountants, is wrongdoing that is "sufficiently important to influence decisions made by reasonable users of financial statements," measured "by both the dollar amount and, the nature of the item" (Whittington et al., 1992, p. 47). Cost and frequency of wrongdoing, a similar measure, predicted retaliation in some studies (Lee et al. 2004, Parmerlee, Near, & Jensen, 1982), but not others.
>
> (Rehg et al., 2008, p. 225)

In the 1992 MSPB survey, those who lacked co-worker support, those who were of a race other than white, and those who had poor performance ratings were more likely to have experienced retaliation (Near et al., 1995). Co-worker support and race did not predict retaliation in some studies but did in others (Rehg et al., 2008).

GENDER

Gender was not a variable in the 1980 MSPB survey and not reported in the final survey in 1992. As a result, no comparisons were drawn. Subsequent studies also failed to find support for gender as a predictor of retaliation. That changed when a purposive census of employees of a military base returned a large enough response to justify the use of structural equation modeling (Rehg et al., 2008, p. 223). That study found that women were significantly more likely than men to experience retaliation.

DEPENDENCE ON WRONGDOING AND POWER

Researchers continue to evaluate the impact of the interaction between organizational dependence on wrongdoing, the power of the wrongdoer, and the power of the whistleblower on retaliation. One study found that the more an organization depends on the wrongdoing, the greater the retaliation against the whistleblower (Rehg et al., 2004). However, that retaliation lessens with the whistleblower's power, which was identified in the study as supervisory status and role prescription (Rehg et al., 2004). The study also found that an organization's dependence on wrongdoing is positively associated with the whistleblower's use of external channels to report the wrongdoing (Rehg et al., 2004). A more recent analysis placed more emphasis on the organization's dependence on the wrongdoing or the wrongdoer.

> We believe that the whistle-blower's power must be considered in the context of the relative power of the wrongdoer and the dependence of the organization on continuation of the wrongdoing. Where the organization depends heavily on the wrongdoer or the wrongdoing itself, even a whistle-blower with high status may not have sufficient relative power to escape retaliation.
>
> (Miceli et al., 2008, p. 104)

RELATIONSHIPS WITH MANAGEMENT

The relationship between the whistleblower and his or her direct supervisor and the relationship between the whistleblower and management are two other variables affecting both whistleblowing and retaliation. As noted previously, lack of supervisor support and lack of top management support were the only two variables that consistently predicted retaliation across all three federal studies. Supporting this view is a study in which lack of management support and age predicted retaliation among women who filed employment-related sex discrimination complaints (Parmerlee et al., 1982).

Not surprisingly, researchers have found that retaliation against the whistleblower leads to negative feelings about the relationship with the direct supervisor (Rehg et al., 2004). However, there is evidence to suggest that a positive relationship with the direct supervisor can lessen the amount of whistleblowing. "Specifically, supervisor support seems to increase the likelihood that an observer of wrongdoing will intend to blow the whistle, but to decrease actual whistleblowing behavior (e.g., Near and Miceli, 1986)" (Mesmer-Magnus & Viswesvaran, 2005, p. 291). The researchers hypothesized that a supportive relationship with one's supervisor might increase the intent of an observer of wrongdoing to blow the whistle because of having confidence in organizational support but that actual whistleblowing might be deterred because of unwillingness to place the supportive supervisor in an untenable position (Mesmer-Magnus & Viswesvaran, 2005). However, a recent survey of public accountants in Barbados found that high organizational support for whistleblowing positively influenced actual internal reporting (Alleyne et al., 2018).

Types of retaliation

Retaliation can be formal, something inflicted by the organization officially, or informal, something inflicted below the radar by co-workers, superiors, or subordinates without official organizational sanction; or, it can be both (Rehg, 1998). Dual-mode retaliation has been found to be the most frequent type of retaliation, and in that type of retaliation, "the supervisor's lack of support has the strongest effect of any variable" (Rehg, 1998, p. 112). This finding has implications both for the management of relationships within organizations and for legislation relating to whistleblower protections: "Both formal and informal types of retaliation occur, and legislation against retaliation cannot prevent informal retaliation" (Rehg, 1998, pp. 121–122). What has been apparent in many of the studies identified thus far has been the role of relationships both in the decision to report wrongdoing and in the results to the whistleblower.

Corruption

Three conditions must be met for corruption to become institutionalized in an organization: (1) the initial corrupt act; (2) incorporation of the corrupt act into the structures and routines (policies and procedures) of the organization; and (3) initiating new organizational members into the corrupt practices) (Ashforth & Anand, 2003). The corrupt act may be based on a number of possible rationales, but most initial corrupt acts represent either an immoral or an amoral decision, and that decision is typically made by the leader of the organization (Ashforth & Anand, 2003). In arguing for business ethics courses in college, Sherron S. Watkins, a former vice president at Enron, echoes Ashforth and Anand (2003) in recalling the lessons of that company's failure:

> Enron employees made the wrong choices, choosing unethical paths, but all of them (at least nearly all of them), never thought they were breaking the law, they did not intend to break the law (for the most part, white collar criminals rarely intend to break the law). They rationalized their behavior. Ethical choices as an adult are masked. Of course if asked to do something wrong, we'd all say NO. But if that choice is disguised, and presented in a positive manner, all the psychological tests from Yale's Milgram shock test of the 60s, to Stanford's prison experiment in the early 70s, show that ninety percent of us will to choose to act unethically, even extremely unethically.
>
> This is the reason I believe so strongly that universities must require ethics as a core curriculum in all business degrees. The complaint that one cannot teach or mold values at the college level is irrelevant; that is not the point. We must teach ethics so that our business graduates will not freeze like a deer-in-the-headlights when unexpectedly faced with an

ethical challenge. The frozen-in-fear reaction will result in the same consequences as the deer, but not taking action, the ethical challenge leaves you as road kill. You have "gone along" with it, just by not doing anything. [Sherron Watkins in Arbogast (2013), p. x]

Sarah Chayes, "a former NPR reporter and special adviser to the Chairman of the Joint Chiefs of Staff . . . [and] a senior associate in the Democracy and Rule of Law Program and the South Asia Program at the Carnegie Endowment" (Dille, 2016, Summer) presents a global concern. She argues that corruption on a governmental, or state, level is virtually endemic worldwide; she offers structural suggestions for minimizing corruption at every level of government; and she concludes with the recommendation that U.S. citizens rewrite the U.S. Constitution along the lines of the failed Icelandic constitutional initiative that followed the global financial crisis of 2008 (Chayes, 2015).

Ethics surveys

The national component of the Ethics and Compliance Initiative's 2018 Global Business Ethics Survey™, The State of Ethics & Compliance in the Workplace, found that observed wrongdoing in the United States had decreased 8% since the last survey in 2013 to 47% and reporting of wrongdoing had increased by 23% over 2013 to 69% (Ethics & Compliance Initiative, 2018). However, the types of observed wrongdoing remained static, and of that 63% was done by management and 67% was repeated wrongdoing. Of those who reported wrongdoing, 44% suffered retaliation, a 100% increase over 2013. The reported wrongdoing with the highest rates of retaliation included "accepting gifts/payoffs and bribery of elected officials" (83%), "improper political contributions" (62%), and "retaliation against a reporter" (56%), and 72% of those who experienced retaliation for reporting wrongdoing said the retaliation happened "within three weeks of their initial report" (Ethics & Compliance Initiative, 2018, p. 9).

> The single biggest influence on employee conduct is culture. **In strong cultures, wrongdoing is significantly reduced**. Yet only one in five employees indicate that their company has such an environment. This status remains largely unchanged over the past decade. Furthermore, in 2017, 40% of employees believed that their company has a weak or weak-leaning ethical culture; a trend that has not notably changed since 2000.
> (Ethics & Compliance Initiative, 2018, p. 10, emphasis in original)

The 2018 Edelman Trust Barometer, which surveys 28 markets globally, saw virtually no change worldwide on the four sectors surveyed (nongovernmental organizations (NGOs), business, government, and the media) (Edelman, 2018). However, the survey saw a significant decline in trust (37%) within the United States and a significant rise in trust (27%) in China. The greatest drop in trust in the United States was among better-informed respondents. On a global scale, 20 out of 28 markets fall within the category of "distruster" (Edelman, 2018, p. 4), but certain segments of the population, authority figures such as technical experts, academics, journalists, and CEOs, rated higher in trust. Globally, 72% of respondents trusted their employers (Edelman, 2018).

Health care

A regional medical clinic discovered that a popular diet drug combination, fen-phen, was implicated in heart valve disease. The clinic partnered with a much larger organization to blow the whistle on the manufacturer. Their goal was to stop physicians from prescribing the two drugs together (Johnson, Sellnow, Seeger, Barrett, & Hasbargen, 2004). They argued that the definition of whistleblower should be expanded to include those external to the organization because some industries are so interconnected. They also argued for the use of the ethic of significant choice (i.e., the dissemination of all available information in order for the public to make informed choices) as the rationale for whistleblowing and the ethical basis for dealing with health-related issues (Johnson et al., 2004).

Intelligence industry and the impact of "the Snowden revelations"

The impact of Edward Snowden is being assessed in various quarters in addition to government intelligence and legal sectors. The "Snowden revelations," as his disclosures have been called, have prompted a new wave of academic research. In fact, the current interest in whistleblowing has been attributed directly to his actions:

> The many processes and discussions triggered by "the Snowden revelations" are also reflected by the growing body of academic literature that has emerged since the first disclosures in summer 2013. This literature can be roughly grouped into four research streams, each focusing on a different aspect of the manifold issues at stake in the post-Snowden environment.
>
> (Pohle & Van Audenhove, 2017, p. 2)

Those four areas include "an analytical interest in surveillance and its societal repercussions . . . public reaction to the NSA revelations . . . civil disobedience in general and whistleblowing in particular . . . national and global Internet policy" (Pohle & Van Audenhove, 2017, p. 3). The impact of Snowden's unauthorized distribution of classified U.S. documents on the intelligence community, journalism, law, and internet policy has been explored by a variety of other authors, including Bell and Owen (Bell & Owen, 2017). The missing voice in that discussion, as the editors noted, was the federal government (Greenwood, forthcoming); however, one former government official who contributed to the book decried the lack of journalistic integrity in the willingness of news outlets to publish illegally obtained information that could compromise national security (Bradbury, 2017).[7]

The next chapter, Chapter 4, presents an overview of whistleblowing around the world. It offers observations from published literature that describe the public support, or lack thereof, of whistleblowing in different countries, and it explores laws enacted to protect whistleblowers.

Notes

1 Percentages differ from one federal report to another. This study presents the percentages and assertions of statistical significance published in the original government documents in this section and those published in Miceli et al. (1999) for comparison purposes later in this book (see Chapter 7, Table 7.4).
2 See Chapter 2 for list of reprisals.
3 The 1983 survey contained the same nine types of reprisals as the 1980 survey.
4 The 1992 survey added five types of reprisals to the prior list; see Chapter 2.
5 The 2010 federal survey followed the 1993 survey in listing 14 types of reprisal; see Chapter 2.
6 Analyses reported from cited journals are statistically valid; specifics are not reported due to space considerations.
7 See Chapter 5 for a discussion of Snowden's impact on Journalism.

References

Alleyne, P., Hudaib, M., & Haniffa, R. (2018). The moderating role of perceived organisational support in breaking the silence of public accountants. *Journal of Business Ethics, 147*(3), 509–527. https://doi.org/10.1007/s10551-015-2946-0

Arbogast, S. V. (2013). *Resisting corporate corruption: Cases in practical ethics from Enron through the financial crisis* (2nd ed.). Hoboken, NJ: Wiley-Scrivener.

Ashforth, B. E., & Anand, V. (2003). The normalization of corruption in organizations. In R. M. Kramer & B. M. Staw (Eds.), Research in organizational behavior: An annual series of analytical essays and critical reviews. In R. M. Kramer & B. M. Staw (Series Eds.), *Research in organizational behavior* (vol. 25, pp. 1–52). Oxford, UK: Elsevier. https://doi.org/10.1016/S0191-3085(03)25001-2.

Bell, E., & Owen, T. (Eds.). (2017). *Journalism after Snowden: The future of the free press in the surveillance state*. New York: Columbia University Press.

Berger, B. K., & Reber, B. H. (2006). *Gaining influence in public relations: The role of resistance in practice*. Mahwah, NJ: Lawrence Erlbaum Associates.

Boo, E. f., Terence Bu-Peow, N., & Shankar, P. G. (2016). Effects of incentive scheme and working relationship on whistle-blowing in an audit setting. *Auditing: A Journal of Practice & Theory, 35*(4), 23–38. https://doi.org10.2308/ajpt-51485

Bradbury, S. G. (2017). National security and the "New Yellow Press". In E. Bell & T. Owen (Eds.), *Journalism after Snowden* (pp. 172–185). New York: Columbia University Press.

Chayes, S. (2015). *Thieves of state: Why corruption threatens global security*. New York: W. W. Norton.

Cortina, L. M., & Magley, V. J. (2003). Raising voice, risking retaliation: Events following interpersonal mistreatment in the workplace. *Journal of Occupational Health Psychology, 8*(4), 247–265.

Culiberg, B., & Mihelič, K. K. (2017). The evolution of whistleblowing studies: A critical review and research agenda. *Journal of Business Ethics, 146*(4), 787–803. https://doi.org/10.1007/s10551-016-3237-0

Dille, B. (2016, Summer). [Review of the book *Thieves of state: Why corruption threatens global security*. By Sarah Chayes. New York: W.W. Norton & Company, 2015]. *Journal of Strategic Security, 9*(2), 129–132.

Dodd-Frank Act of 2010, 12, U.S.C. § 5301 (2010).

Edelman. (2018). *2018 Edelman Trust Barometer*. Retrieved from www.edelman.com/trust-barometer/.

Ethics & Compliance Initiative. (2018). *The state of ethics & compliance in the workplace* (978-1-5323-7114-1). Retrieved from https://www.ethics.org/knowledge-center/2018-gbes-2/

Graham, J. W. (1986). Principled organizational dissent: A theoretical essay. *Research in Organizational Behavior, 8*, 1–52. Retrieved from https://psycnet.apa.org/record/1988-12437-001

Greenwood, C. A. (forthcoming). Secrets, sources, whistleblowers, and leakers: Journalism in the Digital Age. [Review of the book *Journalism After Snowden: The Future of the Free Press in the Surveillance State*, E. Bell & T. Owen [Eds.]]. *Communication Booknotes Quarterly*.

Johnson, C. E., Sellnow, T. L., Seeger, M. W., Barrett, M. S., & Hasbargen, K. C. (2004). Blowing the whistle on Fen-Phen *Journal of Business Communication, 11*(4), 350–369. https://doi.org/10.1177/0021943604265608

Keenan, J. P. (1988, August). *Communication climate, whistle-blowing, and the first-level manager: A preliminary study*. Paper presented at the Annual Meeting of the Academy of Management, Anaheim, CA.

Lopez, Y. P., Lavan, H., & Katz, M. (2013). Whistleblowing in organizations: A logit analysis of litigated cases. *Journal of Workplace Rights, 17*(3/4), 283–302. https://doi.org/10.2190/WR.17.3-4.c

Merit Systems Protection Board. (1981). *Whistleblowing and the federal employee: Blowing the whistle on fraud, waste, and mismanagement—who does it and what happens*. Washington, DC: MSPB.

Merit Systems Protection Board. (1984). *Blowing the Whistle in the federal government: A comparative analysis of 1980 and 1983 survey findings*. Washington, DC: MSPB.

Merit Systems Protection Board. (1993). *Whistleblowing in the federal government: An update*. Washington, DC: MSPB.

Merit Systems Protection Board. (2001). *Questions & answers about Whistleblower appeals*. Washington, DC: MSPB.

Merit Systems Protection Board. (2010a). *Prohibited personnel practices a study retrospective*. Washington, DC: MSPB.

Merit Systems Protection Board. (2010b). *Whistleblower protections for federal employees*. Washington, DC: MSPB.

Merit Systems Protection Board. (2011a). *Blowing the Whistle: Barriers to federal employees making disclosures*. Washington, DC: MSPB.

Merit Systems Protection Board. (2011b). *Prohibited personnel practices: Employee perceptions*. Washington, DC: MSPB.

Merit Systems Protection Board. (2014). *Current projects, planned projects, and proposed research topics for 2015–2018*. Washington, DC: MSPB.

Mesmer-Magnus, J. R., & Viswesvaran, C. (2005). Whistleblowing in organizations: An examination of correlates of whistleblowing intentions, actions, and retaliation. *Journal of Business Ethics, 62*, 277–297.

Miceli, M. P., & Near, J. P. (1984). The relationships among beliefs, organizational position, and whistle-blowing status: A discriminant analysis. *Academy of Management Journal, 27*(4), 687–705.

Miceli, M. P., & Near, J. P. (1985). Characteristics of organizational climate and perceived wrongdoing associated with whistle-blowing decisions. *Personnel Psychology, 38*, 525–544.

Miceli, M. P., & Near, J. P. (1988). Individual and situational correlates of whistle-blowing. *Personnel Psychology, 41*, 267–281.

Miceli, M. P., & Near, J. P. (1992). *Blowing the whistle: The organizational and legal implications for companies and employees.* New York: Lexington Books.

Miceli, M. P., & Near, J. P. (1994). Relationships among value congruence, perceived victimization, and retaliation against whistle-blowers. *Journal of Management, 20*(4), 773–794.

Miceli, M. P., & Near, J. P. (1997). Whistle-blowing as antisocial behavior. In R. A. Giacalone & J. Greenberg (Eds.), *Antisocial behavior in organizations* (pp. 130–149). Thousand Oaks, CA: SAGE Publications, Inc.

Miceli, M. P., & Near, J. P. (2002). What makes whistle-blowers effective? Three field studies. *Human Relations, 55*(4), 455–479.

Miceli, M. P., Near, J. P., & Dworkin, T. M. (2008). *Whistle-blowing in organizations.* New York: Routledge Taylor & Francis Group.

Miceli, M. P., Near, J. P., & Schwenk, C. R. (1991). Who blows the whistle and why? *Industrial and Labor Relations Review, 45*(1), 113–130.

Miceli, M. P., Rehg, M. T., Near, J. P., & Ryan, K. C. (1999). Can laws protect whistle-blowers?: Results of a naturally occurring field experiment. *Work and Occupations, 26*(1), 129–151. https://doi.org/10.1177/0730888499026001007

Near, J. P., Dworkin, T. M., & Miceli, M. P. (1993). Explaining the whistle-blowing process: Suggestions from power theory and justice theory. *Organization Science, 4*(3), 393–411.

Near, J. P., & Miceli, M. P. (1985). Organizational dissidence: The case of whistle-blowing. *Journal of Business Ethics, 4*, 1–16.

Near, J. P., & Miceli, M. P. (1986). Retaliation against whistle blowers: Predictors and effects. *Journal of Applied Psychology, 71*(1), 137–145.

Near, J. P., & Miceli, M. P. (1990, August). *When whistleblowing succeeds: Predictors of effective whistleblowing.* Paper presented at the Annual Meeting of the Academy of Management, San Francisco.

Near, J. P., & Miceli, M. P. (1996). Whistle-blowing: Myth and reality. *Journal of Management, 22*(3), 507.

Near, J. P., & Miceli, M. P. (2008). Wrongdoing, whistle-blowing, and retaliation in the U.S. government: What have researchers learned from the Merit Systems Protection Board (MSPB) survey results? *Review of Public Personnel Administration, 28*(3), 263–281. https://doi.org10.1177/0734371x08319153

Near, J. P., Ryan, K. C., & Miceli, M. P. (1995, August). *Results of a human resource management "experiment": Whistle-blowing in the federal bureaucracy, 1980–1992.* Paper presented at the Annual Meeting of the Academy of Management, Vancouver, BC.

O'Day, R. (1974). Intimidation rituals: Reactions to reform. *The Journal of Applied Behavioral Science, 10*(3), 373–386.

Parmerlee, M. A., Near, J. P., & Jensen, T. C. (1982). Correlates of whistle-blowers' perceptions of organizational retaliation. *Administrative Science Quarterly, 27*, 17–34.

Perry, J. L. (1992). *The consequences of speaking out: processes of hostility and issue resolution involving federal whistleblowers Vol. 8. Best papers proceedings – Academy of Management* (pp. 311–315). Retrieved from https://doi.org/10.5465/AMBPP.1992.17516059

Pfeffer, J., & Salancik, G. (1978). *The external control of organizations: A resource dependence perspective.* New York: Harper Row, Publishers.

Pfeffer, J., & Salancik, G. (2003). *The external control of organizations: A resource dependence perspective.* Stanford, CA: Stanford University Press.

Pittroff, E. (2015). Whistle-blowing regulation in different corporate governance systems: An analysis of the regulation approaches from the view of path dependence theory. *Journal* of *Management and Governance, 20,* 703–727. Retrieved from https://doi.org/10.1007/s10997-015-9311-7

Pohle, J., & Van Audenhove, L. (2017). Post-Snowden Internet policy: Between public outrage, resistance and policy change. *Media and Communication, 5*(1), 1–6. https://doi.org/10.17645/mac.v5i1.932

Pope, K. R., & Lee, C.-C. (2013). Could the Dodd-Frank Wall Street Reform and Consumer Protection Act of 2010 be helpful in reforming corporate America? An investigation on financial bounties and whistle-blowing behaviors in the private sector. *Journal of Business Ethics, 112*(4), 597–607.

Rehg, M. T. (1998). *An examination of the retaliation process against whistleblowers: A study of federal government employees.* Doctoral dissertation. Indiana University, Bloomington, IN.

Rehg, M. T., Miceli, M. P., Near, J. P., & Van Scotter, J. R. (2004, August). *Predicting retaliation against whistle-blowers: Outcomes of power relationships within organizations.* Paper presented at the Academy of Management, New Orleans, LA.

Rehg, M. T., Miceli, M. P., Near, J. P., & Van Scotter, J. R. (2008). Antecedents and outcomes of retaliation against whistleblowers: Gender differences and power relationships. *Organization Science, 19*(2), 221–240.

Richardson, B. K., Wang, Z., & Hall, C. A. (2012). Blowing the whistle against Greek hazing: The Theory of Reasoned Action as a framework for reporting intentions. *Communication Studies, 63*(2), 172–193. https://doi.org10.1080/10510974.2011.624396

4 Whistleblowing around the globe

Whistleblowing laws around the globe

Whistleblowing is not universally accepted

Whistleblowing is not accepted as a positive action worldwide. Different cultures place a different value, or lack of value, on reporting wrongdoing, with some saying that English-speaking countries, led by the United States, place the highest value on whistleblowing (Vandekerckhove, Uys, Rehg, & Brown, 2014). For example, in Uganda, reporting wrongdoing is considered disloyal; Brazil has no word for whistleblowing; Germans have a negative attitude toward whistleblowing because of Hitler's legacy and the Chinese have a negative attitude toward it because of the Cultural Revolution, both of which encouraged reporting one's family and neighbors to authorities. "Jewish law simply prohibits whistleblowing, as one is not allowed to be a 'talebearer'" (Vandekerckhove et al., 2014, pp. 39–40). Despite these cultural differences, attempts have been made in certain areas, such as Israel, to promote whistleblowing as a prosocial activity. In addition, considerable legislation and research are occurring in those countries with ties to Great Britain and the United States (Vandekerckhove et al., 2014).

United Kingdom of Great Britain and Northern Ireland

Employment Rights Act 1996 and Public Interest Disclosure Act 1998

The two primary laws that address whistleblowing in the United Kingdom are the Employment Rights Act 1996 (ERA) and the Public Interest Disclosure Act 1998 (PIDA 1998) (Skivenes & Trygstad, 2014).[1] Although some rights to disclose wrongdoing existed under the ERA, "Workers have never had a general right to disclose information about their employment" (Lewis, 2001, p. 10). The PIDA 1998 was enacted expressly "to protect individuals who make certain disclosures of information in the public interest" in either the public or private sector (Lewis, Devine, & Harpur, 2014, p. 359). The PIDA 1998 modified the ERA to identify the types of wrongdoing that constitute "a qualifying disclosure" for protection as a whistleblower:

DOI: 10.4324/9781315231891-5

A "qualifying disclosure" is (ERA 1996, section 43B(1)):
Any disclosure of information which includes one or more of the following:

(i)   A criminal offense;
(ii) a failure to comply with any legal obligation;
(iii) a miscarriage of justice;
(iv) danger to the health and safety of any individual [i.e., not necessarily a worker];
(v)   damage to the environment;
(vi) the deliberate concealment of information tending to show any of the matters listed above.

(Cf. Lewis and Trygstad, 2009)

The UK definition combines a wide definition of wrongdoing with a criterion that an act causes harm, for example to the environment.

(Skivenes & Trygstad, 2014, p. 99)

In reviewing the third edition of *Whistleblowing Law and Practice* (Lewis, Bowers, Fodder, & Mitchell, 2017), Lewis (2018) notes that changes to Part IVA Employment Rights Act 1996 [by the Enterprise and Regulatory Reform Act 2013 (Ashton, 2015)] reflect the movement from the former common law standard of "good faith" to one of "public interest" as a criterion for "qualifying disclosure," and also include more specific sanctions for retaliation against a whistleblower (Lewis, 2018, p. 165). In addition, courts have ruled on the nature of disclosure, causation for termination, and the definition of "worker" for purposes of "detriment or dismissal suffered after making a protected disclosure" (Lewis, 2018, p. 165). The PIDA includes specific provisions for whistleblowers who report externally under certain circumstances.

The PIDA in particular protects workers engaged in external reporting, when the workers have reasonable belief that evidence would be destroyed or hidden when disclosures are made to employers; or when workers have reasonable belief that they would be subject to retaliations by employers when disclosures are made to the latter; or when the employers have not acted to investigate or address the wrongdoing.

(Yeoh, 2013, p. 222)

A more recent law, the UK Bribery Act 2010, encourages businesses to establish mechanisms for internal reporting to address corruption, but it does not offer any provisions for protection of whistleblowers or recommendation about the kind of mechanisms businesses need to implement (Yeoh, 2013).

A recent court decision, *Chesterton Global and another v. Nurmohamed*, has clarified the term "in the public interest" (Court rules small groups can bring whistleblowing claims, 2017). Perhaps most importantly, the court decided that the public interest may involve relatively small groups. This case involved a real estate (estate) agent who alleged managers were deliberately underestimating the commissions of a group of approximately 100 agents in order to give the agents' commissions to shareholders of the firm.

> The public interest test introduced to whistleblowing law in 2013 was intended to prevent workers using whistleblowing laws to make personal grievances about their contracts, and placed the onus on employees to prove their disclosure was made in the public interest. . . . The changes introduced in 2013 failed to define what "in the public interest" meant.
> (Court rules small groups can bring whistleblowing claims, 2017)

The ruling also indicated that the whistleblower's standing in the community would lend weight to the whistleblower's claim, as would the type of wrongdoing that was being alleged (Court rules small groups can bring whistleblowing claims, 2017).

Australia

Whistleblowing protection in Australia began in the 1990s with state laws instituted to protect public sector employees in response to highly publicized fraud and corruption, and with the expectation that existing legislation would be adequate to protect whistleblowers (Brown, Meyer, Wheeler, & Zuckerman, 2014). Now, Australia employs elements of both the U.S. and the U.K. systems in its whistleblowing protection, including a federal law protecting workers' employment rights, a federal law offering specific whistleblower protection, state laws protecting public sector workers, and protection for corporate employees (Lewis, Devine, et al., 2014). The federal Fair Work Act 2009 (Cth) protects workers' rights broadly, while the federal Public Interest Disclosure Act 2013 (Cth) added whistleblowing protection; however, those protections generally only cover public sector employees who report internally to a specific recipient on matters in the public interest (Lewis, Devine, et al., 2014). Private sector employees are covered by the Corporations Act 2001, which is similar to Sarbanes-Oxley but which has not been an effective remedy for whistleblowers. Unfortunately, for a variety of reasons, Australia's whistleblowing laws have not been particularly well-known, well-used, or beneficial; in terms of suits for damages under state laws, "There is no known case of a successful outcome" (Lewis, Devine, et al., 2014, p. 365).

Canada

"Despite Canada's international reputations as a leader in equality rights and protection of the individual, successive governments have denied protection for whistleblowers" (Lewis, Devine, et al., 2014, p. 372). Canada's Public Servants Disclosure Protection Act of 2005 effectively reduced Canadians' access to civil remedies and restricted them to administrative remedies, available only to certain categories of public workers, that is based on secrecy and the abrogation of free speech rights. "The law does not cover corporate workers or government employees in military or national security fields and has a 60-day statute of limitations for filing reprisal claims (FAIR 2012)" (Lewis, Devine, et al., 2014, p. 372).

> While the determination of whistleblowing limitations is essential to ensure a fair, secure and open society, the Canadian legal framework is uncertain and unclear. Without knowing the criteria of protection, their rights, obligations and the risks involved to their safety, informed people will not disclose.
>
> (Martin-Bariteau & Newman, 2018, p. 1)

European Union and Norway

Whistleblowing laws in Europe vary widely and are, in many cases, works-in-progress, with some asserting that the U.K.'s PIDA sets the standard to which other countries should aspire (Ashton, 2015, p. 398), while others, including the European Union (EU), are promoting the U.S. FCA as a model, at least for global corporate whistleblowing laws (Faunce, Crow, Nikolic, Morgan, & Frederick, 2014). The Council of Europe has called for members "to develop a robust national framework that facilitates and protects whistleblowers. . . . Four EU member states have advanced whistleblower protection laws including the United Kingdom (UK), Luxembourg, Romania and Slovenia" (Soon & Manning, 2017). Italy has an anti-corruption law (Law No. 190/2012), but it "still lacks a legislative and institutional framework for regulating whistleblowing processes" (Ciasullo, Cosimato, & Palumbo, 2017, p. 172). France has whistleblowing legislation that protects workers in public and private employment but which applies only to "corruption, such as fiscal of financial matters, accounting or suspected bribery offenses" (Skivenes & Trygstad, 2014, p. 101), and in Germany, "Whistleblowers' rights to report have been based on the freedom of expression and civic rights in German court decisions" (Fasterling, 2014, p. 335), but "Germany has failed to fulfill [the] requirement" of the "Group of Twenty (G20), who determined that every member state must implement whistle-blower protection by the end of 2012" (Pittroff, 2015, p. 704) Outside the EU, Norway is considered to have some of the broadest protections for whistleblowers by way of the Norwegian Working Environment Act 2005, which makes it illegal to harass a worker in the public or private sector and under which "both co-workers and managers have an *obligation* to blow the whistle if they detect harassment" (Skivenes & Trygstad, 2014, p. 96).

Global whistleblowing research: the public sector

United Kingdom

Public Interest Disclosure Act of 1998

"With the Public Interest Disclosure Act of 1998 (PIDA) the United Kingdom established an approach that protects whistle-blowers, dependent on several conditions. External whistle-blowers are virtually unprotected if the organization has implemented a whistle-blowing system (Schmidt 2005)" (Pittroff, 2015, p. 715). A study of public sector whistleblowing in Great Britain 12 years after the PIDA was enacted found that more than half of the 25% of employees who were aware of wrongdoing were not willing to report it (Yeoh, 2014). "It would appear that the PIDA only provided wavering protection to whistleblowers as it failed to directly challenge the anti-whistleblowing culture" (Yeoh, 2014, p. 466).

Scotland

Chinese and Scottish students in Scotland and intent to blow

Researchers interested in assessing the potential impact of cultural differences on the acceptance of whistleblowing surveyed two groups of students: a group of 47 Chinese students recently arrived in the UK and a group of 47 students from the UK. Both groups were students at the University of Glasgow, Scotland. They found that the Chinese students were less willing to blow the whistle than the UK students. The researchers attributed this reluctance to cultural differences. However, they also found that both groups were equally unwilling to blow the whistle when the perceived personal costs of whistleblowing were high (Cheng, Karim, & Lin, 2015).

Italy

Italian National Health Service

An Italian study identified managers as the key to institutionalizing whistleblowing in the health sector (Ciasullo et al., 2017). The study analyzed the barriers to implementing mandated whistleblowing processes in three Italian National Health Service (INHS) organizations. It found that managers were instrumental in establishing an environment in which employees were willing to blow the whistle. It also determined that managers were essential in creating sufficient commitment to the organization by employees to interest them in blowing the whistle. "Whistleblowing effectiveness is strictly related to managerial ability to build a sense of safeness and commitment towards the organization" (Ciasullo et al., 2017, p. 179).

Australia

Assange and WikiLeaks

Australia was forced to grapple with how to deal with one of its own citizens, Julian Assange, and his invention, WikiLeaks, within the laws of Australia and its understanding of whistleblowing. The initial view was that Assange had broken the law, but that proved not to be the case (Brown, 2011). WikiLeaks was accepted as a new media form, and laws were passed at the state and federal level that extended the concept of journalist and publishing to include WikiLeaks. The new platform raised questions about whether or not it is always possible to know in advance what is or is not in the public interest, a key determinant in whistleblowing protection in Australia, and who is authorized to make that determination. "Faced with the challenges of this era, conflicting responses have reinforced the need to maintain a long-term vision about the role of public whistleblowing in ensuring integrity in government" (Brown, 2011, p. 7).

Support at work

The government of Australia conducted a nationwide survey of public sector workers along the lines of the MSPB studies through a random sample of more than 7,500 government employees in 118 agencies, case studies of 15 government agencies, 92 personal interviews, and a review of whistleblowing documentation from 175 agencies (Brown et al., 2014). The survey found that "71 per cent of respondents . . . observed serious wrongdoing, and 28 per cent . . . reported (Brown, Mazurski and Olsen 2008, p. 38)" (Lewis, Brown, & Moberly, 2014, p. 16). The study found a wide variance in reporting wrongdoing and retaliation across agencies (Brown et al., 2014). It also found that whistleblowers needed more protection, that slightly more than half of the agencies had mechanisms for supporting whistleblowers, and that only 11 % had formal procedures for whistleblowing (Brown et al., 2014).

Multi-country meta-analysis

A meta-analysis was undertaken by management scholars of six massive studies of government workers over three countries and several decades (Miceli & Near, 2013). The study included the Australian government's extensive survey of agencies (Lewis, Brown, et al., 2014), the first three U.S. Merit System Protection Board studies (Merit Systems Protection Board, 1981, 1984, 1993), and two Norwegian studies (Miceli & Near, 2013). The meta-analysis found a widespread awareness of wrongdoing across those three countries over a wide timespan and a fairly high level of whistleblowing. The level of retaliation against whistleblowers was considered high, although it was not more than 50%. The exception was Norway, which supported whistleblowing (Miceli & Near, 2013).

South Africa and the Republic of Mauritius

A recent study of public employees in two former British colonies documented the history of corruption in both countries and multiple variables that affect whistleblowing intent. The countries under review were South Africa, which had supported apartheid (segregation of minorities) until the election of Nelson Mandela in 1994, and Mauritius, the island nation off the coast of southeast Africa that has become a global financial center. However, despite South Africa's past, the study found that public officials from South Africa were more willing than those from Mauritius to report wrongdoing:

> In South Africa, the Protected Disclosures Act No. 26 of 2000 makes provision for the protection of employees who make a disclosure in good faith and in accordance with the procedure prescribed by the employer. Whistle-blower protection was originally part of the Open Democracy Bill. Based on the comparative experiences of Australia and the United Kingdom, it became a free-standing law to give it greater recognition and promotion (Chene, 2009, p. 9).
>
> (Pillay, Ramphul, Dorasamy, & Meyer, 2018, p. 206)

Unfortunately, few lawsuits have been filed in South Africa using the PDA. This may indicate a lack of trust in implementation of the law, and/or a reliance on external authorities to police corruption now that the law is in place.

In Mauritius, the government has tried to fight corruption by establishing two new entities, the Independent Commission Against Corruption (ICAC) and the Financial Intelligence Unit. Unfortunately, again, reports of wrongdoing are not as numerous as those in South Africa. Public officials in both countries show some willingness to report wrongdoing. However, the number of variables that impact disclosure and the cultural differences among countries can impact disclosure. "Disclosure management tools need to match individual, institutional, and country context variables" (Pillay et al., 2018, p. 209).

Global whistleblowing research in the private sector

Governance structures: voice and exit

Pittroff (2015) argues that history, laws, and cultures divide private sector institutions into two types of corporate governance structures: voice culture and exit culture. Voice culture is stakeholder-focused (including employees) and bank-financed. Exit culture is shareholder-focused and market-financed. He further defines them geographically:

> Corporate governance systems are generally divided into two special extremes . . . the Continental-European system (voice system) and the Anglo-American system (exit) system . . . Australia, South Africa and United Kingdom just as much belong to the Anglo-American system as

the United States of America. Moreover, South Korea and Taiwan can be classified in the Continental-European system as well as Germany (La Porta et al. 1998).

(Pittroff, 2015, p. 710)

In voice culture, employees have a greater stake in the organization, more loyalty to it, and more willingness to report wrongdoing internally, while in exit cultures, employees have a lesser stake in the organization, less loyalty to it, more willingness to exit if they have power (higher-level positions), and more incentive to remain and be bribed into silence if they have less power (lower-level positions). To be effective in stopping wrongdoing, regulations must be tailored to the particular culture (Pittroff, 2015).

Great Britain

Finance sector

A recent Reuters report claimed the climate for whistleblowing in Great Britain had deteriorated and corporate whistleblowing claims had decreased by 40% since 2014 (Reuters Staff, 2017). The efforts in spring 2017 by Jes Staley, the CEO of Barclays, a British banking institution since 1690, to discover the identity of a whistleblower created a stir in the country. "Michael Potts, managing partner at Byrne and Partners, said although there was now more robust protection for whistleblowers, the statistics showed Britain was nevertheless becoming 'increasingly hostile' for those who alerted others to potential wrongdoing" (Reuters Staff, 2017). The conclusion was that corporate whistleblowers in the finance industry in particular needed more protection and more support from upper management (Reuters Staff, 2017). This was in contrast to a recent industry report that cited 94% compliance with new British financial industry requirements, the FCA/PRA Senior Managers Regime Whistleblowing Rules designed to facilitate internal whistleblowing (Foose, 2017).

Food industry sector

A conceptual study of whistleblowing and food crime in Great Britain proposed a model for preventing crime and minimizing the need for whistleblowing. The model was based on two theories of attitudes and behaviors:

In previous research, the theory of planned behaviour (TPB) see Fishbein and Ajzen (1975), Ajzen and Fishbein (1980) and the theory of reasoned action (TRA) see Ajzen (1985, 1991) have been used to study how attitudes and subjective norms affects an individual's behaviour towards food handling, consumption and purchase (Bianchi and Mortimer, 2015;

Irianto, 2015; Mullan et al., 2015), but not whistleblowing specifically in the food sector.

(Soon & Manning, 2017, p. 2632)

The study provided managers with a list of actions that would improve the workplace based on specific strategies, including commitment to employees and communicating the organizational culture. The goal was to "encourage and build a loyal and committed workforce" (Soon & Manning, 2017, p. 2644).

Australia

CPAs and intent to blow

A study of 2,000 Australian Certified Practising Accountants (CPAs; 1,000 males and 1,000 females) found that intent to blow the whistle was impacted by the threat of retaliation, age, and gender (Liyanarachchi & Adler, 2011). Early in their careers, 25–34-year-old, male accountants were more likely to blow the whistle than female accountants in the face of both weak and strong retaliation threats. In mid-career, 35–44-year-old, both genders were equally likely to blow the whistle in the face of strong retaliation, although women were less likely than men to blow the whistle in the face of weak retaliation. However, in the 45 and over age group, men were more likely than women to blow the whistle as the threat of retaliation increased (Liyanarachchi & Adler, 2011).

Whistleblowers as journalistic sources

An analysis of whistleblowing in British newspapers from 1997 to 2009 found that journalists rely on whistleblowers, hold them in high regard as sources, and portray them in heroic terms as champions against wrongdoing as long as the whistleblowers' stories fit pre-existing journalist storytelling needs; it also found that whistleblowers need more protection than is currently provided (Wahl-Jorgensen & Hunt, 2012). A study of sports journalists' interactions with whistleblowers found that the only factor that predicted interaction with whistleblowers was their "length of time at a newspaper" (Reed, 2015, October, p. 145). A news article from *Media Asia* shortly after the release of NSA documents by Snowden via WikiLeaks in 2013 chronicled the state of Asian countries' protections for whistleblowers (Mazumdar, 2013). "In China, journalist-whistleblowers routinely report power abuses of officials on the Internet . . . Weibo, the Chinese version of the Twitter . . . [is] a serious challenge to Beijing's control of information" (Mazumdar, 2013, p. 200). Mazumdar (2013) also found that South Korea and Japan have whistleblower protections, while other parts of Asia, including India and the

Philippines, pose real dangers to whistleblowers (Lewis & Vandekerckhove, 2018; Mazumdar, 2013).

The next chapter, Chapter 5, reviews whistleblowing research in communication, journalism, and public relations in the United States.

Note

1 This study does not address the impact of Brexit on whistleblowing laws.

References

Ashton, J. (2015). 15 Years of whistleblowing protection under the Public Interest Disclosure Act 1998: Are we still shooting the messenger? *Industrial Law Journal, 44*(1), 29.

Brown, A. J. (2011). Weeding out WikiLeaks (and why it won't work): Legislative recognition of public whistleblowing in Australia. *Global Media Journal: Australian Edition, 5*(1), 1–11.

Brown, A. J., Meyer, D. P., Wheeler, C., & Zuckerman, J. (2014). Whistleblower support in practice: Towards an integrated research model. In A. J. Brown, D. Lewis, R. E. Moberly, & W. Vandekerckhove (Eds.), *International handbook on whistleblowing research* (pp. 457–494). Cheltenham, UK: Edward Elgar Publishing Limited.

Cheng, X., Karim, K. E., & Lin, K. J. (2015). A cross-cultural comparison of whistleblowing perceptions. *Management and Decision Making, 14*(1), 15–31.

Ciasullo, M. V., Cosimato, S., & Palumbo, R. (2017). Improving health care quality: the implementation of whistleblowing. *The TQM Journal, 29*(1), 167–183. https://doi.org/10.1108/tqm-06-2016-0051

Court rules small groups can bring whistleblowing claims. (2017). *People Management* (August 2017), 14. Retrieved from https://issuu.com/peoplemgt/docs/pm_aug17_web

Fasterling, B. (2014). Whistleblower protection: A comparative law perspective. In A. J. Brown, D. Lewis, R. E. Moberly, & W. Vandekerckhove (Eds.), *International handbook on whistleblowing research* (pp. 331–349). Cheltenham, UK: Edward Elgar Publishing Limited.

Faunce, T., Crow, K., Nikolic, T., Morgan, J., & Frederick, M. (2014). Because they have evidence: Globalizing financial incentives for corporate fraud whistleblowers. In A. J. Brown, D. Lewis, R. E. Moberly, & W. Vandekerckhove (Eds.), *International handbook of whistleblowing* (pp. 381–404). Cheltenham, UK: Edward Elgar Publishing Limited.

Foose, A. (2017). UK Financial Services Whistleblowing Regulation Survey. *Benchmark. NAVEX Global: Lake Oswego, OR*. Retrieved from https://www.navexglobal.com/en-us/file-download-canonical?file=/uk-financial-services-whistleblowing-regulation-report-emea.pdf&file-name=uk-financial-services-whistleblowing-regulation-report-emea.pdf

Lewis, D. (Ed.). (2001). *Whistleblowing at work*. London: The Athlone Press.

Lewis, D. (2018). Book reviews: Lewis, Bowers, Fodder and Mitchell, Whistleblowing: Law and Practice. [Review of the book *Whistleblowing: Law and Practice* by J. Lewis, J. Bowers QC, M. Fodder and J. Mitchell]. *Industrial Law Journal, 47*(1), 165.

Lewis, D., Brown, A. J., & Moberly, R. E. (2014). Whistleblowing, its importance and the state of the research. In A. J. Brown, D. Lewis, R. E. Moberly, & W. Vandekerckhove (Eds.), *International handbook on whistleblowing research*. Cheltenham, UK: Edward Elgar Publishing Limited.

Lewis, D., Devine, T., & Harpur, P. (2014). The key to protection: Civil and employment law remedies. In A. J. Brown, D. Lewis, R. E. Moberly, & W. Vandekerckhove (Eds.),

International handbook on whistleblowing research (pp. 350–380). Cheltenham, UK: Edward Elgar Publishing Limited.

Lewis, D., & Vandekerckhove, W. (2018). Trade unions and the whistleblowing process in the UK: An opportunity for strategic expansion? *Journal of Business Ethics, 148*(4), 835–845. https://doi.org/10.1007/s10551-016-3015-z

Lewis, J., Bowers QC, J., Fodder, M., & Mitchell, J. (2017). *Whistleblowing: Law and Practice* (Third ed.). Oxford, UK: Oxford University Press.

Liyanarachchi, G. A., & Adler, R. (2011). Accountants' whistle-blowing intentions: The impact of retaliation, age, and gender. *Australian Accounting Review, 21*(2), 167–182. https://doi.org/10.1111/j.1835-2561.2011.00134.x

Martin-Bariteau, F., & Newman, V. (2018). *Lancer une alerte au Canada: une synthèse des connaissances (Whistleblowing in Canada: A Knowledge Synthesis)*. Elsevier SSRN. Retrieved from https://ssrn.com/abstract=3112688

Mazumdar, S. (2013). Whistleblowers: More threatened than threatening? *Media Asia, 40*(3), 198–203. https://doi.org/10.1080/01296612.2013.11689966

Merit Systems Protection Board. (1981). *Whistleblowing and the Federal Employee: Blowing the whistle on fraud, waste, and mismanagement – who does it and what happens.* Washington, DC: MSPB.

Merit Systems Protection Board. (1984). *Blowing the whistle in the Federal government: A comparative analysis of 1980 and 1983 survey findings.* Washington, DC: MSPB.

Merit Systems Protection Board. (1993). *Whistleblowing in the Federal government: An update.* Washington, DC: MSPB.

Miceli, M. P., & Near, J. P. (2013). An international comparison of the incidence of public sector whistle-blowing and the prediction of retaliation: Australia, Norway, and the US. *Australian Journal of Public Administration, 72*(4), 433–446. https://doi.org/10.1111/1467-8500.12040

Pillay, S., Ramphul, N., Dorasamy, N., & Meyer, D. (2018). Predictors of whistle-blowing intentions: An analysis of multi-level variables. *Administration & Society, 50*(2), 186–216. https://doi.org/10.1177/0095399715581621

Pittroff, E. (2015). Whistle-blowing regulation in different corporate governance systems: An analysis of the regulation approaches from the view of path dependence theory. *Journal of Management and Governance, 20*, 703–727. https://doi.org/10.1007/s10997-015-9311-7

Reed, S. (2015, October). *Calling a Foul.* Paper presented at the Annual International Conference on Journalism & Mass Communications, Singapore. Article retrieved from http://libraries.ou.edu/access.aspx?url=http://search.ebscohost.com/login.aspx?direct=true&db=cms&AN=112931819&site=ehost-live

Reuters Staff. (2017). Britain remains hostile to whistleblowers, statistics show. *Reuters* (November 21, 2017). Retrieved from https://www.reuters.com/article/britain-whistleblowing/britain-remains-hostile-to-whistleblowers-statistics-show-idUSL8N1NR4R9

Skivenes, M., & Trygstad, S. C. (2014). Wrongdoing: Definitions, identification and categorizations. In A. J. Brown, D. Lewis, R. E. Moberly, & W. Vandekerckhove (Eds.), *International handbook on whistleblowing research.* Cheltenham, UK: Edward Elgar Publishing Limited.

Soon, J. M., & Manning, L. (2017). Whistleblowing as a countermeasure strategy against food crime. *British Food Journal, 119*(12), 2630–2652. https://doi.org/10.1108/BFJ-01-2017-0001

Vandekerckhove, W., Uys, T., Rehg, M. T., & Brown, A. J. (2014). Understandings of whistleblowing: Dilemmas of societal culture. In A. J. Brown, D. Lewis, R. E. Moberly, & W. Vandekerckhove (Eds.), *International handbook on whistleblowing research* (pp. 37–70). Cheltenham, UK: Edward Elgar Publishing Limited.

Wahl-Jorgensen, K., & Hunt, J. (2012). Journalism, accountability and the possibilities for structural critique: A case study of coverage of whistleblowing. *Journalism, 13*(4), 399–416. https://doi.org/10.1177/1464884912439135

Yeoh, P. (2013). Whistle-blowing laws in the UK. *Business Law Review, 34*(6), 218–224.

Yeoh, P. (2014). Whistleblowing: motivations, corporate self-regulation, and the law. *International Journal of Law and Management, 56*(6), 459–474. Retrieved from https://doi.org/10.1108/IJLMA-06-2013-0027

Yeoh, P. (2015). Whistleblowing laws: Before and after Sarbanes-Oxley. *International Journal of Disclosure and Governance, 12*(3), 254–273. http://doi.org/10.1057/jdg.2014.5

5 Whistleblowing research in communication, journalism, and public relations in the United States

Whistleblowing research in communication

A few scholars in both business and communication have identified whistle-blowing as an act of communication (Keenan, 1988; King, 1997; Richardson, 2005; Richardson & McGlynn, 2007; McGlynn & Richardson, 2014; Richardson, Wang, & Hall, 2012). "Although studies have examined whistleblowing primarily from an organizational behavior perspective, the process of revealing a wrongdoing is a communication phenomenon" (King, 1997, p. 419). In fact, communication has been called a fundamental aspect of whistleblowing (Richardson, 2005). However, communication scholars have not taken up the topic of whistleblowing to the degree business scholars have done. An early call by business scholars to "examine the role of organizational communications in affecting whistle-blowing decisions" (Miceli & Near, 1985, p. 359) had gone relatively unheeded, with little research conducted by communication scholars on the communication aspect of whistleblowing (Richardson & McGlynn, 2007) until fairly recently.

Whistleblowing as communication

In the studies that have addressed whistleblowing as a function of communication, areas of interest have included upward communication (Eisenberg & Witten, 1987; Keenan, 1988; King, 1997; McGlynn & Richardson, 2014), organizational climate (Keenan, 1988; Miceli & Near, 1985), interpersonal closeness (King, 1997; Mesmer-Magnus & Viswesvaran, 2005), communication channels (Miceli & Near, 1985), discourse analysis (Tholander, 2011), rhetoric (Chu, 2016), and social support and tainting (McGlynn & Richardson, 2014). Theories have included stakeholder theory, organizational structure and social influence processes (Richardson, 2005), and narrative identity theory (Gravley, Richardson, & Allison Jr., 2015). Not all areas will be discussed in this book. However, a few of the more recurring areas will be explored. The hope is that future researchers will take up where this discussion ends.

DOI: 10.4324/9781315231891-6

Upward communication

Upward communication is communication that originates within lower ranks and is transmitted to higher ranks within an organization. Whistleblowing, by its nature, is upward communication of bad news or "bad information" (King, 1997, p. 422), and that type of communication is less likely to be reported than good news (Glauser, 1984; King, 1997). "When communicating with superiors, subordinates deviate from openness to protect self-interests; messages directed upward in organizations are 'largely edited, cautious, and inaccurate' (Krone, 1985, p. 9)" (Eisenberg & Witten, 1987, pp. 420–421). Upward communication also has been found to have a positive effect on performance.

> Research on upward communication in organizations indicates that openness, trust, and receptivity tend to have beneficial effects in terms of organizational performance although one needs to be cautious in inferring direct relationships exist between the two (Eisenberg and Witten, 1987; Jablin, 1985; Glausser, 1982).
>
> (Keenan, 1988, p. 247)

Organizational climate

Organizational climate has been found to affect whistleblowing decisions (Miceli & Near, 1985). It is defined as organizational dependence on wrongdoing, perceived potential for retaliation to the whistleblower, and encouragement of whistleblowing through internal and external communication. Although both whistleblowers and those who saw wrongdoing but did not report it were found to have encountered the same organizational climate, those who did not report said they were not aware of channels for reporting wrongdoing (Miceli & Near, 1985).

The finding that whistleblowers are more likely to work in organizations known for their responsiveness to complaints (Miceli & Near, 1988) also was found in a study of organizational communication climate. Keenan (1988) administered the 1980 MSPB survey to first-level managers and found them more likely to blow the whistle internally when they were confident their bosses would not retaliate (Keenan, 1988). Using Gibb's (1961) typology of supportive or defensive organizational climate, Keenan (1988) found "a high supportive and low defensive organization climate is a major factor in influencing the decision of first-level managers to blow the whistle or not" (Keenan, 1988, p. 250).

Interpersonal closeness

Interpersonal closeness between the wrongdoer and the observer of the wrongdoing has been found to have a negative correlation with whistleblowing. An employee is less likely to report wrongdoing by someone with whom he or she has a close interpersonal relationship than wrongdoing by someone with whom he or she does not have that relationship (King, 1997). As noted earlier, it has been found that a positive relationship between an employee and a supervisor does not lead to more whistleblowing. There is a difference between the intent to blow the whistle and the act of whistleblowing; that difference is related to support from the would-be whistleblower's supervisor; and that support from the supervisor equates to a greater intent to blow the whistle but to less actual whistleblowing (Mesmer-Magnus & Viswesvaran, 2005).

Communication channels

Communication channels have been shown to play an important role in whistleblowing. However, the research has been conducted within a management framework and not a communication one. Observers of wrongdoing who did not report the wrongdoing cited a lack of awareness of communication channels for whistleblowing as a reason for not reporting (Miceli & Near, 1985). In addressing the lack of whistleblowing in certain instances by role-prescribed whistleblowers (internal auditors), researchers recommended that organizations communicate to employees those instances in which whistleblowing is appropriate. They also recommended organizations engage employees in "participation and two-way communication" with the organization in order to encourage whistleblowing (Miceli, Near, & Schwenk, 1991, p. 126).

Rhetoric, discourse analysis, and narrative identity theory

A rhetorician questioned why his discipline has ignored the burgeoning research in whistleblowing and makes the case that the concept of parrhesia, or speaking without fear, should be considered as a corollary to whistleblowing in rhetorical studies (Chu, 2016). A case study of whistleblowing among British junior high school students during a group self-assessment demonstrated the animosity that whistleblowing can bring upon the dissident (Tholander, 2011). Interviews with whistleblowers in the Texas Public School System used narrative identity theory to show the impact of whistleblowing on whistleblowers' "identities, lived narratives, and experiences with retaliation initiated by whistle-blowing" (Gravley et al., 2015, p. 194).

Whistleblowing and journalism

Whistleblowers as sources

Importance to journalism

Sources, which are often anonymous, are viewed by some journalists as the lifeblood of reporting. "As a practical matter, news media – whatever their sense of social mission, their standards, their technological savvy and market health, their legal shields or constitutional privileges – depend, first and foremost, on their sources" (Wasserman, 2017, p. 72). He argued, "Disruptive sources challenge and defy the routines of normal journalism" (Wasserman, 2017, p. 73). He defended such disruptive sources as Daniel Ellsberg, Julian Assange and WikiLeaks, Chelsea/Bradley Manning, and Edward Snowden as performing a public service for which they were punished, while the news outlets that published their information were not. He argued that they and other sources should not bear the burden of disclosing information that news outlets felt was sufficiently in the public interest to publish with impunity (Wasserman, 2017).

New York Times, Snowden, and British intelligence

As one of the journalists who published some of the leaked Snowden material, Jill Abramson, managing editor at the time and later executive editor of the *New York Times*, worked with the *Guardian* to publish part of Snowden's material related to the British intelligence service (Abramson, 2017). She considered getting the material from the *Guardian* a scoop and publishing it as a protected activity under the First Amendment. "Given the massive intrusion of the government's snooping, I viewed the Snowden materials as even more consequential than the Pentagon Papers" (Abramson, 2017, p. 30). Nevertheless, the *Times* held the material "for more than a year, in part because of such national security concerns" (Abramson, 2017, p. 31), and she and her colleagues were extremely cautious in working with it. "A tiny group worked in a windowless storage room that was kept under security surveillance. Cell phones, which can be uses as eavesdropping devices by the NSA [National Security Agency] were not allowed in the room" (Abramson, 2017, p. 30). Although the delay allowed the *Guardian* and *Washington Post* to scoop the *Times* with other material from Snowden, the *Times* weighed "the concerns of the government against the press's duty to inform the public" before publishing (Abramson, 2017, p. 32).[1]

A voice on the other side of this discussion decried the leaking of classified and top-secret information to the media. Steven G. Bradbury, an attorney, served as head of the Justice Department's Office of Legal Counsel during the George W. Bush administration and frequently briefed the executive branch of government on national security and foreign affairs. His views reflect that role:

> Professional news organizations are critical to the health of a mature democratic republic. But the professionalism of news reporting today is under great stress in this age of the Internet. Established media outlets compete for attention against social networks, weblogs, and Wikis sites – sometimes by rushing to publish sensationalist news articles that skirt the important ethical and editorial standards developed over decades by traditional journalism.
>
> (Bradbury, 2017, p. 172)

He opposed the media's treatment of the leaks from Edward Snowden and Bradley Manning who, with the help of Glenn Greenwald (of the *Guardian*), and Julian Assange and WikiLeaks, published significant portions of the material they took. He felt the media outlets that published them mischaracterized the nature of the documents and endangered the United States' national security: "The code of journalistic standards seems to have broken down" (Bradbury, 2017, p. 177).

Whistleblowing research in public relations

Whistleblowing has been studied widely in virtually every discipline – except public relations. A search for whistleblowing in Academic Search Premier on April 19, 2018, yielded 2,015 citations, while the identical search on the same date in Communication Source yielded 89 citations. A search for whistleblowing on April 27, 2018, in *Public Relations Review* found only the author's article (Greenwood, 2015), and the same search on April 27, 2018, in the *Journal of Public Relations Research* found no whistleblowing articles. Clearly, articles may be included in more than one database. However, the discrepancy between the number of whistleblowing articles in the business and academic databases, on the one hand, and the communication database, on the other, is stark, and the lack of articles on whistleblowing and public relations in the primary public relations journals is baffling.

Research in communication and, to some extent, journalism touched on whistleblowing, but public relations scholars ignored the topic until the early 2000s. Then, they touched on it only as a metaphor for a critical public relations perspective (Moloney, 2006, 2008, November) or as one rarely used aspect of practitioner dissent (Berger, 2005; Berger & Reber, 2006; Kang & Berger, 2010; Kang, Berger, & Shin, 2012). Research focused on whistleblowing in public relations began 12 years ago (Greenwood, 2009, August, 2011, 2012, August, 2013, March, 2013, May, 2013, June, 2014, April, 2014, May, 2014, August, 2015, 2015, April, 2016, 2017, April, 2020, forthcoming); and one subsequent study looked at the possible role for public relations in the implementation of the Sarbanes-Oxley mandates (Pompper, 2014). The research cited here is an effort to rectify the gap in research on whistleblowing in public relations.

Codes of conduct

As noted, whistleblowing in the field of public relations had not been studied directly prior to the studies reported here. Several possible reasons for this lack of research effort come to mind. One obstacle could be the origin of the field of public relations as a support function for management's viewpoint (Broom, Casey, & Ritchey, 1997; Dozier & Grunig, 1992; J. E. Grunig & Grunig, 2000, 2008; J. E. Grunig & Hunt, 1984; Lauzen & Dozier, 1992; Greenwood, 2010; Skinner & Shanklin, 1978). Another reason could be the proliferation of codes of ethics developed by professional organizations that attempt to guide the conduct of members (Holtzhausen, 2015; Kim & Ki, 2014; Kruckeberg, 1989, 1993; Meyer & Leonard, 2014; Roth, Hunt, Stavropoulos, & Babik,

1996; Watson, 2014; Yang, Taylor, & Saffer, 2016) in lieu of any public relations licensing structure but which may constrain practitioners from engaging in behavior that could be construed as unprofessional. For example, the Code of Ethics for the Public Relations Society of America, the largest public relations professional organization in the United States, lists loyalty to one's client or organization as one of its professional values: "We are faithful to those we represent, while honoring our obligation to serve the public interest," and advocacy for one's client as another: "We serve the public interest by acting as responsible advocates for those we represent" (Public Relations Society of America, 2008, p. 11). Taken together, those two statements are somewhat redundant, but they clearly put the client ahead of the public. They also would seem to discourage any attempt to report wrongdoing.

"Secrets and lies"

The attitude of the public relations industry toward whistleblowers, leakers, and others who step outside the boundaries of official corporate reporting generally has been negative. In 2003, the managing editor of the flagship magazine for the PRSA, the industry's primary trade organization, asked industry leaders if "the age-old tactic of attempting to root out the culprit" [who leaked information about the company] was "the right strategy" (Stateman, 2003, p. 36).

> Leaks continued to be a source of consternation for organizations and the government last year. Putting aside whistleblowers, who are to be championed for their courage . . . unauthorized leaks typically cause harm. According to several professionals interviewed for this article, leaks of this nature serve only to buttress the ego of the person who divulges the information.
>
> (Stateman, 2003, p. 36)

Gil Schwartz, then-executive vice president of communications for CBS Television, was clear on his view of leakers. "There have been losers who have wanted to leak stuff throughout the history of time. They're called spies. There are always going to be disaffected, shallow, dishonest, creepy people who are going to do this" (Stateman, 2003, p. 37).

Whistleblowing as dissent

While Schwartz complimented whistleblowers, only recently has whistleblowing been explored in the field of public relations, and then only as one of several approaches public relations practitioners use to gain power and exert influence in their organizations (Berger & Reber, 2006). These researchers identified three types of strategies public relations practitioners use to gain power and exert influence: advocacy, dissent, and activism. They called sanctioned influence tactics "Alpha strategies." These included the traditional approaches of public relations: rational arguments, coalition and alliance-building, assertiveness and persistence, inspiration, and personal appeals, among others. "Advocacy is accepted or sanctioned as a form of influence so long as it is seen to be in the interests of the organization and its objectives and is institutionalized within the office or position of the advocate" (Berger & Reber, 2006, p. 56).

They called unsanctioned influence tactics dissent tactics or "Omega approaches." These included leaking information, starting rumors, and whistleblowing, among other tactics. Dissent ran the gamut from relatively harmless complaining among colleagues "to whistle-blowing, one of the most extreme forms of dissent" (Berger & Reber, 2006, p. 58). Activist tactics encompassed sanctioned and unsanctioned forms of dissent, including "compliance hot lines and governance committees . . . leaking information, alerting stakeholders, and whistle-blowing" (Berger & Reber, 2006, p. 162). Although the types of activities reported by public relations professionals varied among the studies based on differences in terminology and methodology, the findings showed the majority of public relations professionals opposed using unsanctioned influence tactics. In three different studies, "Fewer than one in five professionals in each study reported using such approaches" (Berger & Reber, 2006, p. 165).

They argued that public relations executives who know about wrongdoing in an organization could choose to bring bad news to management directly and make a case for proper behavior, or they could use dissent tactics. However, dissent tactics were not the choice of most practitioners; only 4% of them said they would blow the whistle if the activity were illegal and only 1% of them said they would use hot lines and audit committees (Berger & Reber, 2006). "The vast majority of professionals in our studies said that whistle-blowing was not the right thing to do under virtually any circumstances" (Berger & Reber, 2006, p. 166), and 73.8% said they "would never employ . . . tactics such as whistle-blowing" (p. 49). That finding was tempered, however, by a small but vocal group who said such tactics were precisely what was needed in certain circumstances, which led the authors to propose that "public relations professionals hold strong but polar feelings about the appropriateness of whistle-blowing" (Berger & Reber, 2006, p. 166). A later study upheld those findings, with more than 75% of practitioners reporting they had never leaked information) (Kang & Berger, 2010).

Public relations roles

> Good public relations has been called the corporate conscience – an indispensable attribute of modern and progressive business.
>
> (Hill, 1958, in Bowen, Heath, & Lee, 2006, p. 12)

Despite the apparent unwillingness of public relations practitioners to engage in whistleblowing, public relations roles research provides the foundation for viewing whistleblowing as a role-prescribed function of public relations. In public relations roles research, two of the functions that distinguish the public relations manager from the public relations technician are involvement in man-agement decision-making and informing management about issues (Dozier, 1992). One of the long-standing goals of public relations practitioners has been to gain a seat at the management table in order to participate in management decision-making (Berger & Reber, 2006, p. 5). One of the ways in which public relations managers and practitioners accomplish that goal is by acting as boundary spanners who scan the environment (an area defined by the orga-nization as external to organizational boundaries), identify issues of concern to management, and raise those issues within the internal dominant coalition (White & Dozier, 1992).

Counselor to management

As part of this boundary spanner function, public relations practitioners are expected to bring bad external news to management (Berger & Reber, 2006), and nothing precludes the public relations manager from bringing bad internal news to management, as well. Jason Vines, former vice president of corporate communications for Chrysler, appears to be referencing bringing internal bad news to management (why else would the emperor have no clothes?) when he argues for having public relations report to the CEO:

> You almost have to be the CEO's alter ego. . . . Once the relationship is developed, you can almost replace one another because you're thinking along the same lines all the time. . . . You have to have the guts to tell the CEO when he's naked and to be able to say it without fear of retribution.
> (Cobb, 2008, p. 6)

Despite the fact that public relations choose overwhelmingly not to engage in external whistleblowing, almost a quarter report using ethical advocacy to argue for correct behavior on the part of the organization (Berger & Reber, 2006). The use of ethical advocacy implies that practitioners are aware of some real or potential issue or behavior that requires them to make an ethical argu-ment, and the act of making that argument inside the organization may fall within the definition of whistleblowing. "Whistle-blowing represents an influ-ence attempt in which organization member(s) try to persuade other members to cease wrongdoing" (Rehg, Miceli, Near, & Van Scotter, 2008, p. 221).

Public relations practitioners are in a unique position to critique their orga-nization's actions and motives, a role that some argue they should undertake more vigorously (Bowen et al., 2006; L. A. Grunig, Grunig, & Dozier, 2002; Holtzhausen, 2000; Holtzhausen & Voto, 2002). Although polarized about the role of ethical advisor to management (Bowen, 2008), many public rela-tions practitioners consider this one of their most important roles (Bowen et al, 2006). If accepted, the tasks of keeping management informed and acting as ethical advisor to management open the door to viewing whistleblowing as a role-prescribed function of the public relations manager. From the perspective of public relations as a management role, from the perspective of public relations as a boundary spanning function, and from the perspective of public relations as ethical counsel, the public relations function can be viewed as encompassing role-prescribed whistleblowing, just as internal auditing does. The door to doing so already has been opened in the United States by the Sarbanes-Oxley requirement for publicly traded corporations to develop whistleblowing communication channels, the implications of which for public relations were first explored by Greenwood (2010).

In order to avoid the types of internal practices that created the need for Sarbanes-Oxley, scholars from various disciplines have called on organizations to publicize their whistleblowing channels. This has occurred in the legal profession: "Corporations could disclose information regarding their whistleblower system. For example, corporations might publicize the structure of their whistleblower disclosure model in order to advise shareholders and employees of the extent of their system" (Moberly, 2006, p. 1111). It has also occurred in management:

> Results of the study indicate that, of all the variables examined, organizational propensity as assessed through knowledge and information to report wrongdoing as well as organization encouragement of [reporting] wrongdoing is the single most powerful influence on the likelihood of blowing the whistle on less serious fraud.
>
> (Keenan, 2000, pp. 212–213)

Sarbanes-Oxley focuses primarily on corporate governance (Meintjes & Grobler, 2014); however, it also offers a potential new role for public relations in corporate governance. This role has not been implemented explicitly in the United States, but it has been implemented elsewhere. One recent example is the King Reports on Governance for South Africa. The 2009 report (King III) positions public relations practitioners as counselors to management on corporate governance by developing corporate strategy, giving advice to senior management, and managing crisis communication (Meintjes & Grobler, 2014).

Another potential role for public relations in corporate governance is through the Sarbanes-Oxley requirement that corporate management state its responsibility for having an adequate internal structure for financial reporting and assess the effectiveness of the structure in the annual report [*Sarbanes-Oxley Act of 2002*, 15 U.S.C. § 7201 nt (2002)]. Those who prepare corporate quarterly and annual reports are well aware of the requirements placed on those documents by the SEC (Laskin, 2018). However, those requirements have increased in the wake of the passage of Section 404 of Sarbanes-Oxley [*Sarbanes-Oxley Act of 2002*, 15 U.S.C. § 7201 nt (2002)]. "Because the reporting requirements for SOX [Sarbanes-Oxley] 404 are a result of Congressional action following corporate failures, the language used by firms to address material [having a financial impact] weaknesses in internal control is a relatively new type of corporate communication" (Erickson, Weber, & Segovia, 2011, p. 215). Coordination among the communication, legal, and finance departments has always been necessary to ensure that communication is legally sound and comprehensible. However, the need for that coordination has increased following Sarbanes-Oxley:

> Strong interprofessional collaboration must be maintained within organizations because CEOs and CFOs rely on information provided by corporate communicators, finance officers, and legal counselors. Each of these three functions is integrally related to SOX [Sarbanes-Oxley] compliance and effective communication is essential across internal reporting processes.
> (Pompper, 2014, p. 133)

Counselors-turned-whistleblowers – or not?

As noted previously, whistleblowing has become a topic of discussion, as well as a point of contention, in the discussion of ethical public relations roles and responsibilities within the trade literature for at least the past 12 years. Many former Washington insiders have come forward to reveal the inner workings of the institutions in which they have been employed, which has blurred the lines between whistleblowing and possibly heart-felt, possibly financially inspired, intentions without meeting the definition of whistleblowing.

McClellan, Stephanopoulos, Clinton, Wolff, and Comey

Former White House Press Secretary Scott McClellan's book about the George W. Bush White House, *What Happened: Inside the Bush White House and Washington's Culture of Deception* (McClellan, 2008), was an exposé by a former political insider (Susskind, 2004; Clarke, 2004; Stephanopoulos, 1999). McClellan, who was press secretary to President George W. Bush from 2003 to 2006, claimed he was misled by Bush about the build-up to the Iraq war and other matters of policy, and his book was an attempt to bring about change in Washington, DC (Bowman, 2008). However, McClellan satisfied only two of the three factors required for a whistleblowing designation: he was a former employee of the organization on which he was reporting, and he accused his former employer of wrongdoing; on the other hand, he did not take his message to an entity in a position to correct the wrongdoing, and his intent in publishing a book was at least partially for monetary gain.[2] McClellan was not a whistleblower.

One factor in the McClellan case that parallels actual whistleblowers' cases was the depiction of him by the administration as a "'disgruntled' former administration employee" (Bowman, 2008). Although seemingly a routine denial in a typical "he said, she said" scenario, this statement illustrates the threat of retaliation – in this case, denigration – faced by those who expose wrongdoing through book sales, as well as by actual whistleblowers. McClellan, as a public relations practitioner, may have acted in a way that some would see as counter to the code of ethics of the PRSA. One of the core principles of the PRSA code, safeguarding confidences, states: "Client trust requires appropriate protection of confidential and private information" (Public Relations Society of America, 2008). That possible aversion to external exposure of confidential information by public relations practitioners is supported by research into public relations influence-gaining practices (Berger, 2005; Berger & Reber, 2006; Kang & Berger, 2010); and by research into the views about whistleblowing held by corporate public relations and communications executives.

Another memoir by an individual formerly in political life with public relations responsibilities, *All Too Human: A Political Education* by George Stephanopoulos (Stephanopoulos, 1999), recounted his time in the White House as a senior advisor on politics and public relations to former President Bill Clinton. Former Secretary of State and presidential candidate Hillary Rodham Clinton's recounting of her campaign for the presidency, *What Happened* (Clinton, 2017), was a detailed memoir of her campaign for the presidency, including allegations of her opponent's possible involvement with a foreign power to sway the election that echoed what she said repeatedly on the campaign trail; nevertheless, Clinton was not a whistleblower. Michael Wolff, whose exposé *Fire and Fury: Inside the Trump White House* (Wolff, 2018) offered a harsh critique of the president and the White House, was a reporter who gained access to the White House and, presumably, wrote about what he heard. Wolff was not a whistleblower. Former FBI Director James Comey alleged allegations of wrongdoing by his former employer in his book, *A Higher Loyalty: Truth, Lies, and Leadership* (Comey, 2018). Comey was an employee of the U.S. Justice Department who was fired after delivering bad news to management – in his case, the President of the United States – and according to Comey, for refusing to express loyalty to Mr. Trump. He subsequently wrote about his experience, which earned him the standard designation for dismissed employees, including whistleblowers: "disgruntled former employee." Comey was not a whistleblower.[3]

Relationships in public relations

The management literature holds numerous references to the role of relationships in whistleblowing and retaliation, but management theory, including RDP, is not well-equipped to deal with relationships. In fact, one review of whistleblowing research from its inception by the three leading whistleblowing scholars contained only one indexed reference to relationships, and that was a reference to differing values placed on relationships by women and men (Miceli et al., 2008). Public relations, on the other hand, deals directly with relationships (J. E. Grunig & Huang, 2000; Ledingham & Bruning, 2000). The concept of relationships has become a major focus of public relations theory and research over the past several decades (Sallot, Lyon, Acosta-Alzuru, & Jones,

2008; S.-U. Yang, 2007). Because of this focus on relationships, public relations may offer the key to understanding how relationships with one's organization affects whistleblowing through one tool public relations has developed to study relationships and their management – organization–public relationships.

This study uses the Hon and Grunig (1999) model, which employs four relationship quality outcomes (trust, control mutuality, commitment, and satisfaction) and two relationship types (communal and exchange) (J. E. Grunig & Huang, 2000; Hon & Grunig, 1999; Huang, 1997). Relationship quality outcomes are defined as trust, which is the confidence in, and the willingness to be open to, another party; satisfaction, which is the result of a cost-benefit analysis that favors the relationship; commitment, which is a willingness to spend time on the relationship; and control mutuality, which is a sense that power is shared appropriately in the relationship (J. E. Grunig & Huang, 2000; Hon & Grunig, 1999). Together, "trust, control mutuality, relational satisfaction, and relational commitment have been used extensively by scholars to evaluate the quality of an organization's relationships with its publics" (Ni, 2007, p. 54). Relationship types include exchange relationships, in which there is an expected trade of benefits, and communal relationships, in which a benefit is extended but from which no reciprocal benefit is anticipated (Hon & Grunig, 1999). Exchange relationships have been identified as the norm for human interaction that has been hardwired by evolution (Greenwood, 2010), while communal relationships have been identified as the higher order of relationships and the type to which public relations should aspire (Hon & Grunig, 1999).

In studying relationships, scholars have found differing effects for relationship quality outcomes. For example, trust and commitment were "key predictors of attitude and behavioral intentions for members of a public who have strong relationships" (Ki, 2006, p. 163), while satisfaction had the strongest effect on attitude and behavioral intentions in a study of university students (Ki & Hon, 2007). Employees' trust in their organization was increased by positive interpersonal communication by managers (Jo & Shim, 2005); trust and satisfaction were negatively associated with asymmetrical communication from an organization (H.-S. Kim, 2007); and trust also was found to be "key to understanding the relationship development process in crisis communication" (Huang, 2008, p. 319). In attempting to explain these divergent results, scholars have noted that the Hon and Grunig (1999) measure appears to measure both interpersonal dimensions and organizational dimensions, at least when dealing with relationships between employees and organizations (Gallicano, Curtin, & Matthews, 2012; Greenwood, 2016; Jo, Hon, & Brunner, 2004; Ni, 2007, 2009). For example, in a study of Chinese employees and public relations managers, Ni (2007) found that trust has an interpersonal dimension (trust in a supervisor) and an organization dimension (trust in the organization), while in a study of millennial generation public relations practitioners (those born in 1982 and later), researchers found that trust, control mutuality, and commitment all may have interpersonal and organizational dimensions (Gallicano et al., 2012).

Evolutionary theory and whistleblowing research in public relations

This study proposes using evolutionary theory to understand whistleblowing in public relations. Evolution has been mentioned previously in public relations literature (e.g. Cutlip & Center, 1952; J. E. Grunig & Grunig, 2008), or used, again, as the basis for a critical perspective of public relations (Moloney, 2006, 2008), but research that applied the principles of evolutionary theory to public relations began in early 2007 (Greenwood, 2007, March, 2008, May, 2010, 2011, 2012, August, 2013, March, 2013, June, 2015, 2016, 2017, April, 2020; Greenwood & Kahle, 2007, June). Additionally, the body of research that explored ways in which evolutionary theory could be used to understand whistleblowing, including some mentioned earlier, began shortly after (Greenwood, 2011, 2012, August, 2013, March, 2013, June, 2014, August, 2015, 2016, 2017, April, 2020). Given that no theory has been found to address all aspects of whistleblowing, *this study* evaluates theories and literary traditions from several sources: biology, evolutionary biology, and evolutionary psychology; RDP from management; and organization-public relationships and relationship management theory from public relations. The goal is to provide greater understanding of the topic of whistleblowing in public relations and the application of evolutionary theory to whistleblowing.

The next chapter, Chapter 6, presents the questions *this study* tries to answer, offers hypotheses about those questions, outlines the theories used, and explains the method used.

Notes

1 See Chapter 3 for a discussion of the research areas enjoined since the release of the Snowden material.

2 The potential for monetary gain from legally sanctioned whistleblowing has been an element since the *False Claims Act of 1863* [12 U.S.C. § 696 (1863)], the *Securities Exchange Act of 1934* [15 U.S.C. § 78a (1934)], the *False Claims Amendments Act of 1986* [31 U.S.C. § 3701 nt (1986)], the Public Company Accounting Reform and Investor Protection Act of 2002 [*Sarbanes-Oxley Act of 2002*, 15 U.S.C. § 7201 nt (2002)], the No FEAR Act of 2002 [*Notification and Federal Employee Anti-Discrimination and Retaliation Act of 2002*, 5 U.S.C. § 2301] and the Dodd-Frank Wall Street Reform and Consumer Protection Act of 2010 [*Dodd-Frank Act of 2010*, 12 U.S.C. § 5301 (2010)]. The difference between publishing a memoir and whistleblowing can be a fine line. However, in addition to the argument that a book author has not revealed an employer's wrongdoing to an entity that can do something about it, the memoir is an individual action unrelated to legally proscribed whistleblowing avenues; the memoir might be undertaken solely for monetary value; and the memoir, in some cases, legitimately could be considered "sour grapes."

3 Numerous additional tell-all books about the Donald J. Trump presidency have been published recently, and more are in the pipeline.

References

Abramson, J. (2017). In defense of leaks. In E. Bell & T. Owen (Eds.), *Journalism after Snowden* (pp. 29–33). New York: Columbia University Press.

Berger, B. K. (2005). Power over, power with, and power to relations: Critical reflections on public relations, the dominant coalition, and activism. *Journal of Public Relations Research, 17*(1), 5–28.

Berger, B. K., & Reber, B. H. (2006). *Gaining influence in public relations: The role of resistance in practice.* Mahwah, NJ: Lawrence Erlbaum Associates.

Bowen, S. A. (2008). A state of neglect: Public relations as "corporate conscience" or ethics counsel. *Journal of Public Relations Research, 20*(3), 271–296. https://doi.org/10.1080/10627260801962749

Bowen, S. A., Heath, R. L., & Lee, J. (2006, June). *An international study of ethical roles and counsel in the public relations function.* Paper presented at the International Communication Association Annual Conference, Dresden, Germany.

Bowman, M. (2008). Former White House press secretary defends tell-all book. *Voice of America News* (May 28, 2008). Retrieved from https://www.voanews.com/a/a-13-2008-05-29-voa15/401785.html

Bradbury, S. G. (2017). National security and the "New Yellow Press". In E. Bell & T. Owen (Eds.), *Journalism after Snowden* (pp. 172–185). New York: Columbia University Press.

Broom, G. M., Casey, S., & Ritchey, J. (1997). Toward a concept and theory of organization-public relationships. *Journal of Public Relations Research, 9*(2), 83–98.

Chu, A. (2016). In tradition of speaking fearlessly: Locating a rhetoric of whistleblowing in the Parrhēsiastic dialectic. *Advances in the History of Rhetoric, 19*(3), 231–250. https://doi.org/10.1080/15362426.2016.1232206

Clarke, R. A. (2004). *Against all enemies: Inside America's war on terror.* New York: Free Press.

Clinton, H. R. (2017). *What happened* (1st ed.). New York: Simon & Schuster.

Cobb, C. (2008). Driving public relations: Chrysler moves PR under the HR umbrella, spurs debate about where PR reports. *Strategist, 14*(3), 6–11.

Comey, J. (2018). *A higher loyalty: Truth, lies, and leadership.* New York: Flat Iron Books.

Cutlip, S. M., & Center, A. H. (1952). *Effective public relations: Pathways to public favor.* New York: Prentice-Hall, Inc.

Dodd-Frank Act of 2010, 12 U.S.C. § 5301 (2010).

Dozier, D. A. (1992). The organizational roles of communications and public relations practitioners. In J. E. Grunig, D. A. Dozier, W. P. Ehling, L. A. Grunig, F. C. Repper, & J. White (Eds.), *Excellence in public relations and communication management* (pp. 327–355). Hillsdale, NJ: Lawrence Erlbaum Associates.

Dozier, D. A., & Grunig, L. A. (1992). The organization of the public relations function. In J. E. Grunig (Ed.), *Excellence in public relations and communication management* (pp. 395–417). Hillsdale, NJ: Lawrence Erlbaum Associates.

Eisenberg, E. M. & Witten, M. G. (1987). Reconsidering openness in organizational communication. *The Academy of Management Review, 12*(3), 418–426.

Erickson, S. L., Weber, M., & Segovia, J. (2011). Using communication theory to analyze corporate reporting strategies. *Journal of Business Communication, 48*(2), 207–223. https://doi.org/10.1177/0021943611399728

The False Claims Act Legal Center. (2008). *What does "qui tam" mean?* (May 30, 2008). Retrieved from http://www.taf.org/faq.htm#q2

False Claims Act of 1863, 12 U.S.C. § 696 (1863).

False Claims Amendments Act of 1986, 31 U.S.C. § 3701 nt (1986).

Fraud Enforcement and Recovery Act of 2009, 18 U.S.C. § 1 nt (2009).

Gallicano, T. D., Curtin, P., & Matthews, K. (2012). I love what I do, but . . . A relationship management survey of millennial generation public relations agency employees. *Journal of Public Relations Research, 24*(3), 222–242. https://doi.org/10.1080/1062726x.2012.671986

Gibb, J. R. (1961). Defensive communication. *Journal of Communication, XI*(3), 141–148.

Glauser, M. J. (1984). Upward information flow in organizations: Review and conceptual analysis. *Human Relations, 37*(8), 613–643. https://doi.org/10.1177/001872678403700804

Gravley, D., Richardson, B. K., & Allison Jr., J. M. (2015). Navigating the "Abyss": A narrative analysis of whistle-blowing, retaliation, and identity within Texas Public School Systems. *Management Communication Quarterly, 29*(2), 171–197. https://doi.org/10.1177/0893318914567666

Greenwood, C. A. (2007, March). *Evolutionary theory: The missing link for public relations.* Unpublished manuscript.

Greenwood, C. A. (2008, May). *Evolutionary theory: The missing link for public relations.* Paper presented at the Annual Meeting of the International Communication Association, Montreal, Can.

Greenwood, C. A. (2009, August). *Whistleblowing in public relations: Call for a research agenda.* Poster presented at the Association for Education in Journalism and Mass Communication Annual Conference. Boston, MA.

Greenwood, C. A. (2010). Evolutionary theory: The missing link for conceptualizing public relations. *Journal of Public Relations Research, 22*(4), 456–476. https://doi.org/10.1080/10627261003801438

Greenwood, C. A. (2011). *Killing the messenger: A survey of public relations practitioners and organizational response to whistleblowing after Sarbanes-Oxley.* (Doctoral dissertation), University of Oregon, Eugene, Oregon. Retrieved from ProQuest Dissertations & Theses (UMI No. 907550960)

Greenwood, C. A. (2012, August). *Whistleblowing in the Fortune 1000: Ethical dilemma or role responsibility?* Paper presented at the Association for Education in Journalism and Mass Communication Annual Conference, Chicago, IL.

Greenwood, C. A. (2013, March). *Whistleblowing in government: What whistleblowers and reporters say about it.* Paper presented at the Association for Education in Journalism and Mass Communication Midwinter Conference, Norman, OK.

Greenwood, C. A. (2013, May). *What public relations practitioners do and what whistleblowers want.* Presentation at the PRSA/GA Annual Conference, Atlanta, GA.

Greenwood, C. A. (2013, June). *Whistleblowing in the Fortune 1000: What did public relations practitioners tell us?* Poster presented at the International Communication Association Conference. London, UK.

Greenwood, C. A. (2014, April). *Whistleblowing as an act of communication: What ethical choices do communicators face?* Panel presentation at the Eastern Communication Association Annual Meeting, Providence, RI.

Greenwood, C. A. (2014, May). *Whistleblowing in government: What whistleblowers say about it.* Paper presented at the International Communication Association Annual Conference, Seattle, WA.

Greenwood, C. A. (2014, August). Whistleblowing in Government as Free Expression: Are Government Whistleblowers Traitors, Heroes, or Loyal Employees Trying to Do the Right Thing? Panel presentation at the Association for Education in Journalism and Mass Communication Annual Conference. Montreal, Can.

Greenwood, C. A. (2015). Whistleblowing in the *Fortune 1000*: What practitioners told us about wrongdoing in corporations in a pilot study. *Public Relations Review, 41*(4), 490–500. https://doi.org/10.1016/j.pubrev.2015.07.005

Greenwood, C. A. (2015, April). *Whistleblowing in a national laboratory: Do whistleblower protections apply to federal contractors, and how is national security compromised when they don't?* Panel presentation at the Eastern Communication Association Annual Conference. Philadelphia, PA.

Greenwood, C. A. (2016). Golden Handcuffs in the Fortune 1000? An employee-organization relationship survey of public relations executives and practitioners in the largest companies. *Communication Research Reports, 33*(3), 269–274. http://doi.org/10.1080/08 824096.2016.1186624

Greenwood, C. A. (2017, April). *Whistleblowing: Can E&C programs induce reporting and reduce retaliation?* Presentation at the Ethics and Compliance Initiative Annual Conference. Washington, DC.

Greenwood, C. A. (2020). "I was just doing my job!" Evolution, corruption, and public relations in interviews with government whistleblowers. *PARTECIPAZIONE E CONFLITTO, 13*(2), 1042–1061. https://doi.org/10.1285/i20356609v13i2p1042

Greenwood, C. A. (forthcoming). Secrets, sources, whistleblowers, and leakers: Journalism in the Digital Age. [Review of the book *Journalism after Snowden: The future of the free press in the surveillance state*, E. Bell & T. Owen (Eds.)]. *Communication Booknotes Quarterly.*

Greenwood, C. A., & Kahle, L. R. (2007, June). *Toward an evolutionary theory of marketing: Evolution and branding.* Proceedings of the Advertising & Consumer Psychology Conference, Santa Monica, CA. Retrieved from www.myscp.org/pdf/ACP%202007%20 Proceedings.pdf

Grunig, J. E., & Grunig, L. A. (2000). Public relations in strategic management and strategic management of public relations: Theory and evidence from the IABC Excellence project. *Journalism Studies, 1*(2), 303–321.

Grunig, J. E., & Grunig, L. A. (2008). Excellence theory in public relations: Past, present, and future. In A. Zerfass, B. van Ruler, & K. Sriramesh (Eds.), *Public relations research: European and international perspectives* (pp. 327–347). Weisbaden, Germany: VS Verlag für Sozialwissenschaften.

Grunig, J. E., & Huang, Y.-H. (2000). From organizational effectiveness to relationship indicators: Antecedents of relationships, public relations strategies, and relationship outcomes. In J. A. Ledingham & S. D. Bruning (Eds.), *Public relations as relationship management: A relational approach to the study and practice of public relations* (pp. 23–54). Mahwah, NJ: Lawrence Erlbaum Associates.

Grunig, J. E., & Hunt, T. (1984). *Managing public relations.* New York: Holt, Rinehart and Winston.

Grunig, L. A., Grunig, J. E., & Dozier, D. M. (2002). *Excellent public relations and effective organizations: A study of communication management in three countries.* Mahwah, NJ: Lawrence Erlbaum Associates.

Holtzhausen, D. R. (2000). Postmodern values in public relations. *Journal of Public Relations Research, 12*(1), 93–114.

Holtzhausen, D. R. (2015). The unethical consequences of professional communication codes of ethics: A postmodern analysis of ethical decision-making in communication practice. *Public Relations Review, 41*(5), 769–776. https://doi.org/10.1016/j.pubrev.2015. 06.008

Holtzhausen, D. R., & Voto, R. (2002). Resistance from the margins: The postmodern public relations practitioner as organizational activist. *Journal of Public Relations Research, 14*(1), 57–84.

Hon, L. C., & Grunig, J. E. (1999). *Guidelines for measuring relationships in public relations* (pp. 40). Retrieved from http://painepublishing.com/wp-content/uploads/2013/10/Guidelines_ Measuring_Relationships.pdf

Huang, Y.-H. (1997). *Public relations strategies, relational outcomes, and conflict management strategies.* Doctoral dissertation. University of Maryland, College Park, MD. Retrieved from ProQuest Dissertations Publishing 9816477

Huang, Y.-H. (2008). Trust and relational commitment in corporate crises: The effects of crisis communicative strategy and form of crisis response. *Journal of Public Relations Research, 20,* 297–327. https://doi.org/10.1080/10627260801962830

Jo, S., Hon, L. C., & Brunner, B. R. (2004). Organization-public relationships: Measurement validation in a university setting. *Journal of Communication Management, 9*(1), 14–27.

Jo, S., & Shim, S. W. (2005). Paradigm shift of employee communication: The effect of management communication on trusting relationships. *Public Relations Review, 31*(2), 277–280.

Kang, J.-A., & Berger, B. K. (2010). The influence of organizational conditions on public relations practitioners' dissent. *Journal of Communication Management, 14*(4), 368–387. https://doi.org/10.1108/13632541011090464

Kang, J.-A., Berger, B. K., & Shin, H. (2012). Comparative study of American and Korean practitioners' dissent with perceived unethical management decisions. *Public Relations Review, 38,* 147–149. https://doi.org/10.1016/j.pubrev.2011.12.006

Keenan, J. P. (1988, August). *Communication climate, whistle-blowing, and the first-level manager: A preliminary study.* Paper presented at the Annual Meeting of the Academy of Management, Anaheim, CA.

Keenan, J. P. (2000). Blowing the whistle on less serious forms of fraud: A study of executives and managers. *Employee Responsibilities and Rights Journal, 12*(4), 199–217.

Ki, E.-J. (2006). *Linkages among relationship maintenance strategies, relationship quality outcomes, attitude, and behavioral intentions.* Doctoral dissertation. University of Florida, Gainesville.

Ki, E.-J., & Hon, L. C. (2007). Testing the linkages among the organization-public relationship and attitude and behavioral intentions. *Journal of Public Relations Research, 19*(1), 1–23.

Kim, H.-S. (2007). A multilevel study of antecedents and a mediator of employee-organization relationships. *Journal of Public Relations Research, 19*(2), 167–197.

Kim, S.-Y., & Ki, E.-J. (2014). An exploratory study of ethics codes of professional public relations associations: Proposing modified universal codes of ethics in public relations. *Journal of Mass Media Ethics, 29*(4), 238–257. https://doi.org/10.1080/08900523.2014.946602

King, G. (1997). The effects of interpersonal closeness and issue seriousness on blowing the whistle. *The Journal of Business Communication, 34*(4), 419–436.

Kruckeberg, D. (1989). The need for an international code of ethics. *Public Relations Review, 15*(2), 6–18. https://doi.org/10.1016/S0363-8111(89)80050-5

Kruckeberg, D. (1993). Universal ethics code: Both possible and feasible. *Public Relations Review, 19*(1), 21–31. https://doi.org/10.1016/0363-8111(93)90027-A

Laskin, A. V. (2018). The narrative strategies of winners and losers: Analyzing annual reports of publicly traded corporations. *International Journal of Business Communication, 55*(3), 338–356. https://doi.org/10.1177/2329488418780221

Lauzen, M. M., & Dozier, D. M. (1992). The missing link: The public relations manager role as mediator of organizational environments and power consequences for the function. *Journal of Public Relations Research, 4*(4), 205–220.

Ledingham, J. A., & Bruning, S. D. (2000). *Public relations as relationship management: A relational approach to the study and practice of public relations.* Mahwah, NJ: Lawrence Erlbaum Associates.

McClellan, S. (2008). *What happened: Inside the Bush White House and Washington's culture of deception.* New York: Public Affairs.

McGlynn, J., & Richardson, B. K. (2014). Private support, public alienation: Whistle-Blowers and the paradox of Social Support. *Western Journal of Communication, 78*(2), 213–237. https://doi.org/10.1080/10570314.2013.807436

Meintjes, C., & Grobler, A. F. (2014). Do public relations professionals understand corporate governance issues well enough to advise companies on stakeholder relationship management? *Public Relations Review, 40*(2), 161–170. https://doi.org/10.1016/j.pubrev.2013.10.003

Mesmer-Magnus, J. R., & Viswesvaran, C. (2005). Whistleblowing in organizations: An examination of correlates of whistleblowing intentions, actions, and retaliation. *Journal of Business Ethics, 62*, 277–297.

Meyer, A. L., & Leonard, A. (2014). Are we there yet? En route to professionalism. *Public Relations Review, 40*(2), 375–386. https://doi.org/10.1016/j.pubrev.2013.11.012

Miceli, M. P., & Near, J. P. (1985). Characteristics of organizational climate and perceived wrongdoing associated with whistle-blowing decisions. *Personnel Psychology, 38*, 525–544.

Miceli, M. P., & Near, J. P. (1988). Individual and situational correlates of whistle-blowing. *Personnel Psychology, 41*, 267–281.

Miceli, M. P., Near, J. P., & Dworkin, T. M. (2008). *Whistle-blowing in organizations*. New York: Routledge Taylor & Francis Group.

Miceli, M. P., Near, J. P., & Schwenk, C. R. (1991). Who blows the whistle and why? *Industrial and Labor Relations Review, 45*(1), 113–130.

Moberly, R. E. (2006). Sarbanes-Oxley's structural model to encourage corporate whistle-blowers. *Brigham Young Law Review, 2006*(5), 1107–1180.

Moloney, K. (2006). *Rethinking public relations: PR, propaganda, and democracy* (2nd ed.). New York: Routledge Taylor & Francis Group.

Moloney, K. (2008, November). *Trouble making and whistleblowing*. Paper presented at the Institute of Communication Ethics, London College of Communications, London. Retrieved from http://eprints.bournemouth.ac.uk/7996/1/Trouble_making_231108.pdf

Ni, L. (2007). Refined understanding of perspectives on employee-organization relationships. *Journal of Communication Management, 11*(1), 53–70.

Ni, L. (2009). Strategic role of relationship building: Perceived links between employee-organization relationships and globalization strategies. *Journal of Public Relations Research, 21*(1), 100–120.

Pompper, D. (2014). The Sarbanes-Oxley Act: Impact, processes, and roles for strategic communication. *International Journal of Strategic Communication, 8*(3), 130–145. https://doi.org/10.1080/1553118X.2014.905476

Public Relations Society of America. (2008). *Public Relations Society of America Member Code of Ethics 2000*. Retrieved from www.prsa.org/aboutUs/ethics/preamble_en.html

Rehg, M. T., Miceli, M. P., Near, J. P., & Van Scotter, J. R. (2008). Antecedents and outcomes of retaliation against whistleblowers: Gender differences and power relationships. *Organization Science, 19*(2), 221–240.

Richardson, B. K. (2005, May). *Expanding whistle-blowing scholarship: How stakeholder theory, organizational structure, and social influence processes can inform whistle-blowing research*. Paper presented at the International Communication Association Annual Conference, New York.

Richardson, B. K., & McGlynn, J. (2007, May). *Gendered retaliation, irrationality, and structured isolation: Whistle-blowing in the collegiate sports industry as gendered process*. Paper presented at the International Communication Association Annual Conference, San Francisco.

Richardson, B. K., Wang, Z., & Hall, C. A. (2012). Blowing the whistle against Greek hazing: The theory of reasoned action as a framework for reporting intentions. *Communication Studies, 63*(2), 172–193. https://doi.org10.1080/10510974.2011.624396

Roth, N. L., Hunt, T., Stavropoulos, M., & Babik, K. (1996). Can't we all just get along: Cultural variables in codes of ethics. *Public Relations Review, 22*(2), 151–161. https://doi.org/10.1016/S0363-8111(96)90004-1

Sallot, L. M., Lyon, L. J., Acosta-Alzuru, C., & Jones, K. O. (2008). From aardvark to zebra redux: An analysis of theory development in public relations academic journals into the 21st century. In T. L. Hansen-Horn & B. Neff Dostal (Eds.), *Public relations: From theory to practice* (pp. 343–387). Boston, MA: Pearson Allyn & Bacon.

Sarbanes-Oxley Act of 2002, 15 U.S.C. § 7201 nt (2002).

Securities Exchange Act of 1934, 15 U.S.C. 78a (1934).

Skinner, R. W., & Shanklin, W. L. (1978). The changing role of public relations in business firms. *Public Relations Review, 4*(2), 40–45. http://doi.org/10.1016/S0363-8111(78)80005-8

Stateman, A. (2003). Secrets and lies: How good communication prevents leaks. *The Strategist, 9*, 36–39.

Stephanopoulos, G. (1999). *All too human: A political education*. Boston, MA: Little, Brown.

Susskind, R. (2004). *The price of loyalty: George W. Bush, the White House, and the education of Paul O'Neill*. New York: Simon & Schuster Paperbacks.

Tholander, M. (2011). Mundane whistleblowing: Social drama in assessment talk. *Discourse Studies, 13*(1), 69–92.

Wasserman, E. (2017). Safeguarding the news in the era of disruptive sources. *Journal of Media Ethics, 32*(2), 27–85. https://doi.org/10.1080/23736992.2017.1294020

Watson, T. (2014). IPRA Code of Athens – The first international code of public relations ethics: Its development and implementation since 1965. *Public Relations Review, 40*(4), 707–714. https://doi.org/10.1016/j.pubrev.2013.11.018

White, J., & Dozier, D. A. (1992). Public relations and management decision making. In J. E. Grunig (Ed.), *Excellence in public relations and communication management*. Hillsdale, NJ: Lawrence Erlbaum Associates.

Wolff, M. (2018). *Fire and fury: Inside the Trump White House* (1st ed.). New York: Henry Holt and Company.

Yang, A., Taylor, M., & Saffer, A. J. (2016). Ethical convergence, divergence or communitas? An examination of public relations and journalism codes of ethics. *Public Relations Review, 42*(1), 146–160. https://doi.org/10.1016/j.pubrev.2015.08.001

Yang, S.-U. (2007). An integrated model for organization-public relational outcomes, organizational reputation, and their antecedents. *Journal of Public Relations Research, 19*(2), 91–121.

6 Whistleblowing in public relations study

The questions

This study included a census of the highest-ranking public relations executives possible in the *Fortune 1000* corporations and a random sample of public relations and communications executives in a surrogate for the *Wilshire 5000*. Together, the recipients worked in the largest U.S. corporations. Because public relations and communication executives could be expected to have a role, and in some cases an oversight role, in the communication function in most organizations, these executives could be expected to have had a role in the developing and/or publicizing the anonymous communication channel for whistleblowing mandated by the *Sarbanes-Oxley Act of 2002* [15 U.S.C. § 7201 nt (2002)]. However, no research has been conducted on the role of public relations in developing and/or publicizing those Sarbanes-Oxley channels, or on the use of those channels by public relations practitioners. This finding led to:

> *Research Question 1:* Have public relations executives helped develop and/ or publicize Sarbanes-Oxley whistleblowing channels?

The Excellence study has linked the communication manager role as part of, or at least reporting to, the dominant coalition (J. E. Grunig, 1992; L. A. Grunig, Grunig, & Dozier, 2002), and whistleblowing research at times has linked higher job levels to whistleblowing (Mesmer-Magnus & Viswesvaran, 2005). Because of their oversight over the boundary spanning function of awareness of environmental hazards (Berger & Reber, 2006), public relations executives of large corporations are more likely than most employees to know about wrongdoing within their organizations (Cobb, 2008). It has been found that bad news, in general, is less likely to be reported upward than good news (King, 1997), and federal studies on whistleblowing have found that only one-third (Merit Systems Protection Board, 1981, 1984) to one half (Merit Systems Protection Board, 1993) of those who see wrongdoing report it. In addition, the limited amount of research that has been conducted on whistleblowing in public relations has shown that public relations practitioners are divided on the

DOI: 10.4324/9781315231891-7

use of dissent tactics such as whistleblowing, with three-quarters saying they would never use such tactics (Berger & Reber, 2006). These findings led to:

Research Question 2: Have public relations executives blown the whistle?

The only study of role-prescribed whistleblowers thus far, a national study of internal auditors, found that they have a high incidence of whistleblowing but that they also make individual determinations about when and how to blow the whistle (Miceli, Near, & Schwenk, 1991). In their role as advisors to senior management, public relations executives also are in a position that might be viewed as role-prescribed in terms of bringing information about wrongdoing to upper management. However, research has shown that public relations practitioners are deeply divided on the role of public relations practitioners as ethical counsel to management. Some consider it their responsibility, and others do not. These divided findings regarding public relations' ethical role within organizations led to:

Research Question 3: Do public relations executives think it is their job to blow the whistle?

Communication channels have been found to play a major role in several aspects of whistleblowing, including the decision to blow the whistle, the choice of channels for blowing the whistle, and the impact of the channel chosen on retaliation for whistleblowing. Research has shown that those who see wrongdoing are more likely to blow the whistle internally if the organizational climate supports reporting of wrongdoing, if the organization makes reporting channels available to report wrongdoing, and if the organization publicizes those channels to employees (Keenan, 2000; Miceli & Near, 1985). Those who see wrongdoing but do not blow the whistle say they were not aware of whistleblowing channels. Whistleblowers use external channels to blow the whistle when the organizational climate causes them to fear retaliation, and most external whistleblowers have blown the whistle internally first. Previous studies have shown employees are more likely to blow the whistle when the organization encourages whistle blowing and communicates with employees about internal and external whistleblowing channels, which led to:

Research Question 4: What channels have public relations executives used to blow the whistle?

Internal auditors reported that they favored internal channels slightly over external channels (Miceli et al., 1991). However, given the reluctance of public relations professionals to use dissent channels that include whistleblowing, or internal channels such as hot lines and audit committees (Berger & Reber,

2006), and given the theory that suggests public relations practitioners serve as advisers to, if not members of, the dominant coalition of decision-makers (Berger, 2005; Berger & Reber, 2006; Bowen, 2008; J. E. Grunig, 1992; L. A. Grunig et al., 2002), Hypothesis 1 can be stated as:

> *Hypothesis 1*: Public relations executives will use the chain of command more often than they use Sarbanes-Oxley channels.

Although prior research found "The majority of whistleblowers restrict their disclosures to persons within the organization, rather than to external sources" (Miethe, 1999, p. 219), predicting how public relations and communications executives would react to a new reporting mechanism (e.g., an anonymous tip line) was difficult. Personal observation in a *Fortune* 500 company uncovered little evidence for an inclination to use such a line. The experience of Sherron Watkins, who reported irregularities to Enron CEO Kenneth Lay through an anonymous suggestion box, and shortly after to Lay directly, also seemed a cautionary tale for upper management. She experienced retaliation. Prior research indicated that most upper-echelon public relations professionals opposed whistleblowing under any circumstances, but a few would leak information or use internal hot lines or tip lines in extreme situations (Berger & Reber, 2006). This conflicting data led to *Hypothesis 2*.

> *Hypothesis 2*: Public relations executives will use external channels more often than they use Sarbanes-Oxley channels.

The amount of retaliation experienced by whistleblowers to date has been unclear (Miceli et al., 2008). Reports of retaliation in the federal studies ranged from 20% to 37% of those who reported whistleblowing and were identified. However, public relations professionals report that they rarely blow the whistle (Berger & Reber, 2006). Therefore, no conclusions can be drawn about the instance of retaliation for public relations whistleblowers. This lack of information led to:

> *Research Question 5*: How have public relations executive been treated by their employers?

Power appears to confer some protection to whistleblowers. Whistleblowers with power, as measured by supervisory status, position, gender, race, education, years with company, job tenure (years in position), and job performance, report less retaliation than those without power (Rehg, Miceli, Near, & Van Scotter, 2004). Good job performance, in particular, was found to protect from retaliation (Mesmer-Magnus & Viswesvaran, 2005, p. 280). Despite Perry's (1992) study of federal whistleblowers, which found that power did not confer protection from retaliation after whistleblowing, this study relied on previously cited management studies to formulate its proposition that power confers protection. This led to:

Hypothesis 3: Power (as measured by supervisory status, position, gender, race, education, tenure, and job performance) protects from retaliation.

However, an organization's dependence on wrongdoing may reduce the protection of power for the whistleblower. Dependence on wrongdoing has been measured by seriousness of wrongdoing, defined as dollar amount and frequency, and duration of the wrongdoing. Seriousness of wrongdoing alone has been a predictor of retaliation in several studies, including the 1980 and 1983 federal studies (Merit Systems Protection Board, 1981, 1984). The 1981 report characterized seriousness of wrongdoing as wrongdoing "perceived either to involve substantial amounts of money or to occur on a more or less regular basis" (Merit Systems Protection Board, 1981, p. 10). A meta-analysis of whistleblowing research found seriousness of wrongdoing and frequency of wrongdoing (reported as separate items) predicted retaliation (Mesmer-Magnus & Viswesvaran, 2005). This led to:

Hypothesis 4: Power will not protect if the wrongdoing is serious.

The use of external reporting channels has been a predictor of retaliation in a management study (Near, Ryan, & Miceli, 1995), a study of federal whistleblowers, and two of the three federal studies (Merit Systems Protection Board, 1981, 1984). This led to:

Hypothesis 5: External reporting results in more retaliation than internal reporting.

Lack of supervisor support and lack of management support have predicted retaliation through various federal and management studies (Miceli & Near, 1992; Near et al., 1995). This led to:

Hypothesis 6: Those who report retaliation report greater lack of supervisor support and management support.

This study employed the Hon and Grunig (1999) relationship quality outcomes measure (trust, control mutuality, commitment, and satisfaction) to answer research questions and hypotheses about how relationships affect whistleblowing and retaliation and to measure the relationships between public relations executives who have blown the whistle and their organizations. Furthermore, it uses the shorter version of that instrument because the completion rate for that version is higher than the completion rate for the longer instrument (Hon & Grunig, 1999).

In public relations studies using Hon and Grunig's measure, trust and commitment were the strongest predictors of attitude and behavioral intention when the relationship was strong (Ki, 2006), while satisfaction was the strongest predictor of attitude and behavioral intention with university students (Ki & Hon, 2007). As noted previously, asymmetrical communication, a category which could include retaliation for whistleblowing, has been shown to reduce employee trust and satisfaction (Kim, 2007), while positive communication from the supervisor increases trust in the organization (Jo & Shim, 2005). This led to:

> *Research Question 6:* Has retaliation affected public relations executives' relationships with their employers?

In addition, management research has found that whistleblowers who suffer retaliation have more negative relationships with their direct supervisors than those who do not suffer retaliation (Rehg et al., 2004). This study did not survey respondents on their relationships with their direct supervisors. However, numerous researchers have noted the linkage between interpersonal relationships and organizational relationships (J. E. Grunig & Huang, 2000; L. A. Grunig, Grunig, & Ehling, 1992; Hon & Grunig, 1999; Ledingham & Bruning, 1998). Therefore:

> *Hypothesis 7:* Those who report retaliation report more negative relationships with their employers.

One additional variable has been found to predict retaliation: gender. Rehg, Miceli, Near, and Van Scotter's (2008) study of a military base contained enough responses to uncover this effect. Those findings led to:

> *Research Question 7:* Do females experience more retaliation than males?

The theories

This study tested evolutionary theory, RDP, and relationship management theory in the form of organization-public relationships. The questions and hypotheses reflect the content of the federal questionnaires and the analyses of those federal studies by management scholars using RDP, among other theories. Evolutionary theory was not the driving force behind their formulation, but the manifestations of evolutionary theory are clearly evident in the questionnaire and its analyses, in the tenets of RDP, and in the work by public relations scholars on organization-public relationships. They are also behind the premise that the concept of the Golden Handcuffs is a prime motivator of attitudes and behaviors among public relations executives who encountered wrongdoing in their organizations. Therefore, the *post hoc* assignment of variables in resource dependence and organization-public relationships to evolutionary concepts is relevant.

Evolutionary theory is not as well-known to management scholars as RDP or to public relations and communications scholars as organization-public relationships. In this analysis, key concepts of evolutionary theory are equated with key concepts of RDP and organization-public relationships. Rephrasing these concepts in an evolutionary framework may help the field of public relations understand those evolutionary concepts. Doing so may also prove a bridge for applying those concepts in public relations and communications theory and practice. The goal of this study is to identify support for the establishment of evolutionary theory as the metatheory for public relations and communication and to support raising the Golden Handcuffs from a concept to a mid-level theory (see Chapter 1).

Evolutionary theory suggests that humans have developed large brains quickly, from an evolutionary perspective, through social intelligence (Humphrey, 1976, 1988). Social intelligence has allowed us to live in groups, recognize others, remember interactions with others, mislead others, know when we have misled, and cooperate with others (Byrne & Whiten, 1997). The ability to mislead others is known as "Machiavellian intelligence," and the ability to know when one is being manipulated is known as "cheater detection" (Cosmides & Tooby, 1992), although Byrne and Whiten (Byrne & Whiten, 1997) argue that Machiavellian intelligence incorporates both capabilities. In prior whistleblowing research, an individual's awareness of wrongdoing has been a surrogate for measuring the level of wrongdoing in the environment. For that reason, Machiavellian intelligence is operationalized with cheater detection as two sides of the same coin: incidence of wrongdoing (misleading or manipulating others), which is represented by awareness of wrongdoing (cheater detection) by individuals in groups or organizations.

Also operationalized are four sometimes overlapping evolutionary concepts (inclusive fitness, cooperation, reciprocity, and reciprocal altruism) as one of two relationship types: exchange or communal. Evolutionary biology suggests that primates and other species may choose to aid others at a cost to themselves if the recipient is a close relative, a state known as "kin selection" or "inclusive fitness" (Hamilton, 1964) "Cooperation" involves activities that benefit both parties (Trivers, 1971), a state which could include the benefits of higher rank known as the "Golden Handcuffs." Reciprocity involves trading favors for possible future benefit (Cords, 1997). The study operationalized inclusive fitness, cooperation, and reciprocity as exchange relationship type. Reciprocal altruism involves giving something that is of more value to the recipient than it is to the benefactor (Trivers, 1971). It is operationalized as communal relationships.

In Hon and Grunig (Hon & Grunig, 1999), communal relationships are defined as relationships maintained without consideration of potential return by the recipient; they are acknowledged to be normative, or aspirational (Hon & Grunig, 1999). Although the basis for communal relationships in social psychology was described as a romantic or familial relationship (Clark & Mills,

1979), whether or not communal relationships are altruistic has been a topic of discussion:

> Clark and Mills (1993), who developed the concept of communal relationships, pointed out that communal relationships are not completely altruistic. People achieve broader goals from communal relationships with their families, friends, and acquaintances. Organizations, likewise, benefit by building a reputation for being concerned about communal relationships and encounter less opposition and more support over the long term from their publics.
>
> (J. E. Grunig, 2000, p. 42)

Altruism (separate from reciprocal altruism) has several manifestations. One is heroism, which is sacrificing oneself for the benefit of others, as in war (Smirnov, Arrow, Kennett, & Orbell, 2007, p. 927), and another is "psychological altruism: The existence of ultimate desires concerning the well-being of others" (Schulz, 2011, p. 252), to name two. Both present altruism as an ultimate explanation for behavior.

An ultimate explanation for behavior explains why the behavior is integral to natural selection, while a proximate explanation for behavior explains how the behavior provides an advantage to natural selection (Scott-Phillips, Dickins, & West, 2011). Ultimate explanations are grounded in biology, and proximate explanations are often grounded in social science. The identification of altruism as a mental state in psychology is an example of a proximate explanation presented as an ultimate explanation in part because altruism has different meanings in the biological and social sciences (Scott-Phillips et al., 2011). The distinction between ultimate and proximate explanations for behavior places altruism at the heart of one of the major controversies in evolutionary theory: whether natural selection operates at the level of the individual (Darwin, 1979/1859); at the level of the gene (Dawkins, 1976; Dennett, 1995; Scott-Phillips et al., 2011); or at the level of the group, that is, group selection (Wexler, 1981; Wilson & Sober, 1994). Given the ongoing debate over altruism in the evolutionary community, as noted, and the questions raised about relationship types in the public relations community (Shen, 2017), altruism is not operationalized in this research.

This study answers the call for research into the role of evolutionary theory on relationships between public relations and communications executives and their employers through the potential impact of the Golden Handcuffs (Greenwood, 2010, 2011, 2015, 2016, 2020). This research further operationalizes the Golden Handcuffs as the power variables[1] and allows for testing the impact of those variables[2] on awareness of wrongdoing, reporting wrongdoing (whistleblowing), and the level of retaliation experienced after blowing the whistle. It also allows for using the organization-public relationship scale to examine the impact of awareness of wrongdoing, whistleblowing, and retaliation for whistleblowing on those relationships, which has not been studied previously.[3] Prior research with resource dependence theory suggests that employees with power would be more important to an organization and, therefore, protected from retaliation for whistleblowing. Operationalization of this construct is the effect of the power variables on retaliation (see *Hypothesis 3*). The exception to protection for those with power is thought to be blowing the whistle on serious wrongdoing (i.e., wrongdoing on which the organization depends or wrongdoing that harms oneself, co-workers, or the organization). Operationalization of this construct is the effect of seriousness of wrongdoing on retaliation (see *Hypothesis 4*). In prior studies, reporting externally increased retaliation. Whistleblowing and external whistleblowing, in particular, could be viewed as an extension of cheater detection that violates social or group bonds or norms in a way that brings harm to the group. Operationalization of this concept is the effect of external whistleblowing on retaliation (see *Hypothesis 5*). The same concept (cheater detection), followed by whistleblowing (violation of group norms) which is then followed by punishment for the whistleblowing, could be seen as a special case of exchange relationship (i.e., inclusive fitness, cooperation, and reciprocity). In this scenario, the organization's Machiavellian actions are detected and seen as cheating by the individual, and the individual's actions (i.e., whistleblowing) are seen as Machiavellian by the organization and met with punishment (i.e., retaliation). The reaction to punishment by the individual is a rejection of the extension of kin selection to the organization, an unwillingness to cooperate, an invoking of reciprocity (i.e., tit for tat), and an unwillingness to engage in reciprocal altruism, all of which result in negative feelings toward the organization. The operationalization of this concept is the impact of retaliation on relationships with one's own organization, as measured by the Hon and Grunig (1999) short scale (see *Hypothesis 7*).[4]

The expectations

In this study, the expectation is that power leads to awareness of wrongdoing, whistleblowing, and protection from retaliation. Awareness of wrongdoing leads to whistleblowing and/or negative relationships with one's employer. Whistleblowing leads to retaliation and/or negative relationships with one's employer. Public relations and communications executives will use internal chain-of-command channels more often than they use internal Sarbanes-Oxley channels, and they will use external channels more often than they use internal Sarbanes-Oxley channels. In this study, external channels include, in addition to the media, Inspectors General and Congress. The use of external channels results in more retaliation, and retaliation results in greater lack of managerial support and more negative relationships with the organization. The exceptions to the protection from retaliation that power bestows are in the cases of reporting serious wrongdoing and in reporting externally.

The method

The populations for the study consisted of a 61-question internet survey emailed to two separate-but-related target populations between February and

December of 2010[5] and March and December of 2012.[6] As noted, the first survey, the *Fortune 1000*, was an attempted census of the highest-ranking public relations executive in each of the publicly traded companies listed on CNN's Money Magazine *Fortune 1000* list in 2009.[7] Intended recipients were public relations and communications executive officers with stated public relations responsibilities, or vice presidents of public relations, corporate communications, marketing, sales, and finance and administration with public relations responsibilities, identified from an international, commercial business database[8] and corporate websites.[9] The second survey, an approximation of the *Wilshire 5000*, was sent to a random sample of the same population plus vice presidents of public affairs, investor relations, or advertising from U.S. corporations with more than $1.7 billion in annual revenues (turnover) available in the same commercial database in 2012.[10]

Survey error

The *Fortune 1000* survey addressed coverage error by developing a census of the target population by adding the use of a commercial business database. The *Wilshire 5000* survey addressed coverage error by using the commercial business database to query more companies with added search terms. The *Fortune 1000* survey addressed sampling error by augmenting the initial list of public relations executives with increasingly lower levels of employees drawn from the database in an attempt to achieve a sample that was representative of the target population. The *Wilshire 5000* survey addressed sampling error by drawing a random sample from the larger population derived from the commercial business database. Both surveys addressed construct validity by using validated survey instruments: the first federal questionnaire (Merit Systems Protection Board, 1981), adapted for a corporate audience, and the relationship management scale (Hon & Grunig, 1999), validated by numerous public relations researchers (Ki, 2006; Lee & Kee, 2017). The *Fortune 1000* survey addressed nonresponse error by increasing the response rate with the five university-allowed email contacts (Dillman, 2000), testing subject lines, cleaning and replacing bounce backs, moving the survey from one hosted internet platform to one that claimed a higher response rate, and developing new contacts. The *Wilshire 5000* survey used a random sample drawn from a larger population with an expanded list of potential job titles and departments. Measurement error remained a concern for both surveys because of the sensitive nature and negative connotation of whistleblowing (Groves et al., 2004; Krumpal, 2013) and the unintended introduction of instrument error into one part of the *Fortune 1000* survey.[11]

Response rate

In the *Fortune 1000* survey, five email contacts were sent with encrypted internet survey links to 2,243 executives and practitioners who appeared to have responsibility for, or involvement with, public relations, and 80 responses, complete and partial, were received for a response rate of 3.5% (Greenwood, 2011, 2015). In the *Wilshire 5000* survey, a random sample of 40,162 names of public relations and communications executives and practitioners who appeared to have responsibility for, or involvement with, public relations and communication was drawn from the commercial database and duplicate names from the *Fortune 1000* list removed, leaving a sampling frame of 40,162 names. From that, a random sample of 38,100 names was drawn. After cleaning the list further, five email contacts with encrypted links to internet surveys were sent to 38,084 executives and practitioners, and 158 responses, complete and partial, were received for a response rate of .0042%. The distribution of combined surveys totaled to 40,327 public relations and communications executives and practitioners working in the largest U.S. companies and received 238 responses, complete and partial, for a response rate of .006%.

What follows is a report of the results of the combined survey data and the statistical analyses conducted. Despite the obvious difficulty of accessing this target population, the lack of an accessible sampling frame, and the small response rate, the findings may be instructive. However, a word of caution: They also may only suggest trends and areas for future research. Clearly, more research is needed with this population.[12]

The adapted questionnaire

The questionnaire was adapted from the first federal whistleblowing questionnaire (Merit Systems Protection Board, 1981) for a corporate audience and consisted of five sections, described later.[13]

Section I gathered new descriptive data on corporations' compliance with the Sarbanes-Oxley mandate to create a whistleblowing channel to the audit committee of the board of directors and the role, if any, that public relations had in developing and/or publicizing the channel.

Section II introduced the concept of whistleblowing by asking respondents to focus on their knowledge of wrongdoing and whistleblowing by public relations executives *other than themselves in a different organization*. The intent was to increase knowledge about whistleblowing in public relations and communications in a non-threatening manner and to decrease measurement error due to bias and variance. The section ended with an open-ended question soliciting comment about the topic.

Section III mirrored Survey Section II but was directed toward the respondents' *own knowledge of wrongdoing and whistleblowing activities in their current organization*. The section ended with an open-ended question soliciting comment about the topic.

Section IV asked respondents to characterize their *relationship with their current organization* using a validated 26-question scale (Hon & Grunig, 1999) presented in random order (Ki & Hon, 2007) with a five-point Likert scale (Yang, 2007; Gallicano et al., 2012).

Section V asked for demographic information (gender, age group, education, and race) and employment characteristics (organizational tenure, job tenure, salary range, status as the top-ranking public relations or communication executive, reporting relationship to chief executive officer, department in the organization, supervisory status, most recent performance evaluation, and external reporting of wrongdoing).

Measures

Whistleblowing research traditionally analyzed four variables at the *corporate*[14] level (incidence of wrongdoing, incidence of whistleblowing, incidence of identified whistleblowing, and incidence of retaliation) and three variables at the *individual* level (seriousness of wrongdoing, lack of support from management, supervisor, and/or co-worker, and comprehensiveness of retaliation), as well as demographic and employment characteristics (gender, race, education, salary, job status (professional or nonprofessional), job tenure (time in position), job performance, and external whistleblowing channels).

For employment characteristics in this study, supervision for professional job position (professional or nonprofessional) was substituted, and age, years employed, reporting relationship to the CEO, status as top-ranking public relations or communications executive, and department were added. A retaliation scale encompassing six items from reward to retaliation to replace comprehensiveness of retaliation was added. Finally, awareness of wrongdoing, whistleblowing, and retaliation for a third party were added to assess the impact of those three states, if any, on respondents' relationships with their employers.

Unit of analysis: the corporation (or environment)

Incidence of wrongdoing was the number of respondents who knew of wrongdoing in their own organization divided by the total number of respondents to this question (see Chapter 7, Table 7.3).[15] *Incidence of whistleblowing* was the number of respondents who blew the whistle divided by the number of respondents who were aware of wrongdoing in their own organization.[16] *Incidence of identified whistleblowing* was the number of respondents who were identified as whistleblowers divided by the number of respondents to this question.[17] *Incidence of role-prescribed whistleblowing* was the number of respondents who said blowing the whistle was a part of their job divided by the number of respondents who blew the whistle.[18] *Incidence of retaliation*[19] was the number of identified whistleblowers who reported lack of support and/or retaliation divided by the number of respondents to this question.[20]

Unit of analysis: the individual

Seriousness of wrongdoing[21] represented dollar volume of the wrongdoing or frequency of occurrence. Incidents involving less than $1,000 or occurring rarely were "Least serious"; incidents involving $1,000 to $99,999 or occasionally were "Somewhat serious"; and incidents involving $100,000 or more or frequently were "Most serious." *Lack of support*[22] from one's co-workers, lack of support from one's supervisor, and lack of support from someone above one's supervisor were elements of the retaliation scale (see *retaliation*). Previously, *comprehensiveness of retaliation* calculated the number of types of retaliation experienced by identified whistleblowers; it was the dependent variable. *This study* did not enumerate types of retaliation, and it used a new variable, *retaliation*, as the dependent variable. This study introduced a new, six-item *retaliation* scale: "I was rewarded"; "Nothing happened to me"; "My co-workers were unhappy with me"; "My supervisor was unhappy with me"; "Someone above my supervisor was unhappy with me"; and "I experienced retaliation." In addition to demographic and employment characteristics requested by prior studies (1) age; (2) gender; (3) race; (4) level of education; (5) length of time in position; (6) salary; (7) supervision; (8) most recent performance appraisal; and (9) use of external whistleblowing channels, *this study* added (10) length of time employed by the company; (11) position as top-ranking public relations or communications executive; (12) reporting relationship to the CEO; and (13) department in the organization.

Scale reliability

As with previous researchers (e.g., Gallicano et al., 2012) this study used the short versions of the relationship quality outcomes and relationship type scales to measure organization-public relationships (Hon & Grunig, 1999). These include "control mutuality," meaning "the degree to which parties agree on who has the rightful power to influence one another"; trust, meaning "one party's level of confidence in and willingness to open oneself to the other person"; satisfaction, meaning "the extent to which each party feels favorably toward the other because positive expectations about the relationship are reinforced . . . [and] the benefits outweigh the costs"; commitment, meaning "the extent to which each party believes and feels the relationship is worth spending energy to maintain and promote"; communal relationship, in which "both parties provide benefits to the other because they are concerned for the welfare of the other – even when they get nothing in return"; and exchange relationship, in which "one party gives benefits to the other only because the other has provided benefits in the past or is expected to do so in the future" (Hon & Grunig, 1999, p. 3). Cronbach's (1951) coefficient alpha was used to measure internal reliability (consistency) for the relationship management scale.[23] Cronbach's alpha for the overall scale was .877, when .700 is "acceptable" (Hair et al., 1998). All individual scale items except the exchange scale were acceptable at above the .700 level (trust, α = .896; control mutuality, α = .798; commitment, α = .878; satisfaction, α = .883; and communal relationship, α = .817). The exchange scale was questionable with α = .599. The fourth item in the exchange scale, "This organization takes care of people who are likely to reward the organization," had a low item correlation ($r = .04$), and removing it would have increased scale reliability to an acceptable level ($\alpha = .800$). However, the four items in the exchange scale were retained for purposes of comparison with other studies. A new six-item scale to assess retaliation ($\alpha = .176$) was retained, even though a four-item scale had a higher reliability ($\alpha = .840$), because the six-item scale captured the range of possible outcomes of whistleblowing, and the four-item scale would have further reduced the sample for that question.

Statistical analysis

The data once cleaned were submitted for statistical analysis by the SPSS 24 statistical package. The following is based on reported frequencies, descriptive statistics, chi-squares, correlations, simple regressions, hierarchical regressions, logistic regressions, and multivariate analysis of variance (MANOVA) as appropriate for the research question or hypothesis being analyzed. Statistical significance was set at $\alpha \leq .05$ (i.e., the amount of error in the statistical tests used did not exceed 5% for all statistical tests unless otherwise indicated).

Comparison of this study with the three federal studies

One way of evaluating results from this study is to compare those results with prior results from comparable prior studies. Unfortunately, at the time this study was conducted, there were few corporate studies of whistleblowing. For that reason, the results of this study are compared with the findings from the three federal employee whistleblowing surveys that had been examined extensively by management scholars (Miceli et al., 1999) and with the findings from the 2010 federal survey (Merit Systems Protection Board, 1981). See Chapters 2 and 3 for detailed discussion of those surveys.

The next chapter, Chapter 7, presents the results of *this study*.

Notes

1 Age, gender, race, education, years employed, years in position, salary, rank, reporting relationship to the CEO, supervisory status, and job performance.
2 In this study, race was a constant.
3 Retaliation has been associated with positive or negative relationships with one's immediate supervisor and management, but those studies did not use the organization-public relationship scale.
4 Hypothesis 6 was not measured due to the small sample size for retaliation.
5 The Institutional Review Board at the University of Oregon approved this study.
6 The Institutional Review Board at Middle Tennessee State University approved this study.
7 Two companies had merged, making the *Fortune 1000* the *Fortune 999*.
8 Contact information was accessed through the University of Oregon's subscription to Mint Global, an international, commercial business contact database owned by Bureau Van Dijk of Brussels, Belgium, and through more than 500 corporate websites.
9 The low initial response rate to the first distribution led the author to contact professionals in three public relations organizations about distributing the first survey to their

members. Two organizations chose not to participate, in part, due to concerns about the sensitive nature of the topic, the length of the survey, and/or lack of relevance to the organization's mission. The author chose not to pursue the third organization because of conflicts between its research approval process and the restrictions of the Institutional Review Board at her organization. Prior to distributing the second survey, an approximation of the *Wilshire 5000*, the author completed the research review process for the third organization. Unfortunately, that organization declined to field the survey.

10 Bureau Van Dijk gave the author short-term access to its Mint U.S. database.

11 Moving the *Fortune 1000* survey from one internet platform to another introduced measurement error when multiple choice answers about Sarbanes-Oxley publicity, whistleblowing channels, and retaliation were mistakenly coded for single response rather than multiple response. This issue was corrected in the *Wilshire 5000* survey. Approximately 60% of respondents to the *Fortune 1000* survey, which was 25% of respondents to the combined survey, were not able to use the full range of possible responses for those questions. As a result, responses to the Sarbanes-Oxley publicity channel questions were not reported, and responses to the use of whistleblowing channels and retaliation scale questions may have been underreported.

12 Surveys of this population often suffer small response rates due to the duties associated with executives. Such requests, even after multiple requests for participation, are often ignored due to pressing daily business problems. As noted earlier, too, the research objective of understanding whistleblowing may have been too controversial for many corporate executives.

13 See Appendix A for recruitment emails, consent form, and survey. More detail on data collection is available from the author.

14 Management scholars who analyzed the federal data used the term, "firm," to refer to the federal agency surveyed.

15 Miceli, Rehg, Near, and Ryan (1999) calculated *Incidence of wrongdoing* by dividing the number of respondents who knew of wrongdoing in their own organization by the total number of respondents from the same organization.

16 *Incidence of whistleblowing* was calculated the same way in both studies.

17 Miceli et al. (1999) calculated *Incidence of identified whistleblowing* by dividing the number of respondents who were identified as whistleblowers by the number of whistleblowers. The number of respondents who said they were whistleblowers was not consistent from one question to another in *this study*.

18 Miceli et al. (1999) calculated *Incidence of role-prescribed whistleblowing* by dividing the number of respondents who said blowing the whistle was a part of their job by the number of whistleblowers.

19 Retaliation, called "reprisal" in the MSPB studies, was the last item in an eight-item response that began with, "I was *not* identified as the source of the report," and concluded with, "I received an actual reprisal for having reported the problem" (Merit Systems Protection Board, 1981, p. 6, Appendix B). The next question asked respondents to identify one or more of nine categories of retaliation they had experienced in the past 12 months. In *this study*, retaliation was part of a six-item response: "I was rewarded; Nothing happened; My co-workers were unhappy with me; My supervisor was unhappy with me; Someone above my supervisor was unhappy with me; and "I experienced retaliation." Responses to this item made up the retaliation scale. Respondents to one or more of the last four items were considered to have experienced retaliation.

20 Miceli et al. (1999) calculated *Incidence of retaliation* by dividing the number of identified whistleblowers who reported one or more of nine types of retaliation by the number of whistleblowers.

21 Seriousness of Wrongdoing was introduced by the federal government (Merit Systems Protection Board, 1981) and reported later in management literature (Miceli et al., 1999). The MSPB studies reported Seriousness of Wrongdoing as the percentage of employees who reported wrongdoing involving "more than $1,000 in Federal funds

or property" (Merit Systems Protection Board, 1981, p. 1) and introduced the practice of using the frequency of the activity as a surrogate for the dollar amount when the dollar amount was unknown. That report also introduced an error into the calculations. Although the text stated that serious wrongdoing involved "more than $1,000" in federal funds, the questionnaire listed the response options as "Less than $100, $100 to $999, $1,000 to $100,000," and "More than $100,000" (Merit Systems Protection Board, 1981, p. 4, Appendix B). That characterization continued in the 1984 report (Merit Systems Protection Board, 1984, p. 5) but was corrected in the 1993 report (Merit Systems Protection Board, 1993). Miceli et al. (1999) reported this percentage for all three federal studies, but they used a different standard to calculate the lower range than that used in the federal studies. Miceli et al. (1999) appeared to count $1,000 twice. "A code of 1 is given to wrongdoing involving $1,000 or less regardless of frequency. Wrongdoings involving $1,000 to $99,999 are coded as 2 regardless of frequency. Cases of wrongdoing exceeding $100,000 – regardless of frequency – are codes as 3. For other wrongdoings . . . seriousness is coded according to frequency (1 = rare to 3 = frequent)" (Miceli et al., 1999, p. 139). The three federal studies also provided data for wrongdoing that involved more than $100,000. Later management studies calculated the dollar amount of the wrongdoing, sometimes referred to as "material wrongdoing" (Rehg, Miceli, Near, & Van Scotter, 2004) or "materiality" (Near & Miceli, 1996) when known, and when the dollar amount was not known, used frequency of occurrence of wrongdoing as a surrogate for the dollar amount (Rehg et al., 2004).

22 Lack of support, as reported in management studies, included lack of support from one's co-workers, lack of support from one's supervisor, and/or lack of support from someone above one's supervisor. Lack of support from supervisors and management were predictors of retaliation in the federal studies "Significant predictors at all three time periods [(Merit Systems Protection Board, 1981, 1984, 1993)] include top management lack of support and supervisor lack of support" (Miceli et al., 1999, p. 144).

23 Reliability is the "extent to which a variable or set of variables is consistent in what it is intended to measure" (Hair, Anderson, Tatham, & Black, 1998, p. 90).

References

Berger, B. K. (2005). Power over, power with, and power to relations: Critical reflections on public relations, the dominant coalition, and activism. *Journal of Public Relations Research*, *17*(1), 5–28.

Berger, B. K., & Reber, B. H. (2006). *Gaining influence in public relations: The role of resistance in practice.* Mahwah, NJ: Lawrence Erlbaum Associates.

Bowen, S. A. (2008). A state of neglect: Public relations as "corporate conscience" or ethics counsel. *Journal of Public Relations Research*, *20*, 271–296.

Byrne, R. W., & Whiten, A. (1997). Machiavellian intelligence. In A. Whiten & R. W. Byrne (Eds.), *Machiavellian intelligence II: Extensions and evaluations* (pp. 1–23). Cambridge, UK: Cambridge University Press.

Clark, M. S., & Mills, J. (1979). Interpersonal attraction in exchange and communal relationships. *Journal of Personality and Social Psychology, 37*(1), 12–24. https://doi.org/10.1037/0022-3514.37.1.12

Cobb, C. (2008). Driving public relations: Chrysler moves PR under the HR umbrella, spurs debate about where PR reports. *Strategist, 14*(3), 6–11.

Cords, M. (1997). Friendships, alliances, reciprocity and repair. In A. Whiten & R. W. Byrne (Eds.), *Machiavellian intelligence II: Extensions and evaluations* (pp. 24–49). Cambridge, UK: Cambridge University Press.

Cosmides, L., & Tooby, J. (1992). Cognitive adaptation for social change. In J. H. Barkow, L. Cosmides, & J. Tooby (Eds.), *The adapted mind: Evolutionary psychology and the generation of culture* (pp. 163–228). New York: Oxford University Press.

Cronbach, L. J. (1951). Coefficient alpha and the internal structure of tests. *Psychometrika, 16*(3), 297–334. https://doi.org/10.1007/BF02310555

Darwin, C. (1979/1859). *On the origin of species.* New York: Gramercy Books.

Dawkins, R. (1976). *The selfish gene:* New York: Oxford University Press.

Dennett, D. C. (1995). *Darwin's dangerous idea: Evolution and the meanings of life.* New York: Simon & Schuster.

Digital Realty Trust, Inc. v. Somers, 583 U. S.___ (2018).

Dillman, D. A. (2000). *Mail and Internet surveys: The tailored design method* (2nd ed.). New York: Wiley.

Gallicano, T. D., Curtin, P., & Matthews, K. (2012). I Love What I Do, But…A Relationship Management Survey of Millennial Generation Public Relations Agency Employees. *Journal of Public Relations Research, 24*(3), 222–242. https://doi.org/10.1080/10627 26X.2012.671986

Greenwood, C. A. (2010). Evolutionary theory: The missing link for conceptualizing public relations. *Journal of Public Relations Research, 22*(4), 456–476. https://doi.org/10.1080/10627261003801438

Greenwood, C. A. (2011). *Killing the messenger: A survey of public relations practitioners and organizational response to whistleblowing after Sarbanes-Oxley.* Doctoral dissertation., University of Oregon, Eugene, OR. ProQuest Dissertations & Theses (UMI No. 907550960).

Greenwood, C. A. (2015). Whistleblowing in the *Fortune 1000*: What practitioners told us about wrongdoing in corporations in a pilot study. *Public Relations Review,* (41), 490–500. https://doi.org/10.1016/j.pubrev.2015.07.005

Greenwood, C. A. (2016). Golden Handcuffs in the Fortune 1000? An employee-organization relationship survey of public relations executives and practitioners in the largest companies. *Communication Research Reports, 33*(3), 269–274. http://doi.org/10.10 80/08824096.2016.1186624

Greenwood, C. A. (2020). "I was just doing my job!" Evolution, corruption, and public relations in interviews with government whistleblowers. *PARTECIPAZIONE E CONFLITTO, 13*(2), 1042–1061. https://doi.org/10.1285/i20356609v13i2p1042

Groves, R. M., Fowler, F. J., Couper, M. P., Lepkowski, J. M., Singer, E., & Tourangeau, R. (2004). *Survey methodology.* Hoboken, NJ: Wiley.

Grunig, J. E. (Ed.) (1992). *Excellence in public relations and communication management.* Hillsdale, NJ: Lawrence Erlbaum Associates.

Grunig, J. E. (2000). Collectivism, collaboration, and societal corporatism as core professional values in public relations. *Journal of Public Relations Research, 12*(1), 23–48.

Grunig, J. E., & Huang, Y.-H. (2000). From organizational effectiveness to relationship indicators: Antecedents of relationships, public relations strategies, and relationship outcomes. In J. A. Ledingham & S. D. Bruning (Eds.), *Public relations as relationship management: A relational approach to the study and practice of public relations* (pp. 23–54). Mahwah, NJ: Lawrence Erlbaum Associates.

Grunig, L. A., Grunig, J. E., & Dozier, D. M. (2002). *Excellent public relations and effective organizations: A study of communication management in three countries.* Mahwah, NJ: Lawrence Erlbaum Associates.

Grunig, L. A., Grunig, J. E., & Ehling, W. P. (1992). What is an effective organization? In J. E. Grunig (Ed.), *Excellence in public relations and communication management* (pp. 65–90). Hillsdale, NJ: Lawrence Erlbaum Associates.

Hair, J. F., Jr., Anderson, R. E., Tatham, R. L., & Black, W. C. (1998). *Multivariate data analysis* (5th ed.). Upper Saddle River, NJ: Prentice Hall.

Hamilton, W. D. (1964). The genetical evolution of social behaviour. I and II. *Journal of Theoretical Biology, 7*(1), 1–52.

Hon, L. C., & Grunig, J. E. (1999). *Guidelines for measuring relationships in public relations.* Gainesville, FL: The Institute for Public Relations, Commission on PR Measurement and Evaluation.

Humphrey, N. (1976). The social function of intellect. In P. P. G. Bateson & R. A. Hinge (Eds.), *Growing points in ethology* (pp. 303–317). Oxford, UK: Cambridge University Press.

Humphrey, N. (1988). The social function of intellect. In R. W. Byrne & A. Whiten (Eds.), *Machiavellian intelligence: Social expertise and the evolution of intellect in monkeys, apes and humans* (pp. 13–26). Oxford, UK: Oxford University Press.

Jo, S., & Shim, S. W. (2005). Paradigm shift of employee communication: The effect of management communication on trusting relationships. *Public Relations Review, 31*(2), 277–280.

Keenan, J. P. (2000). Blowing the whistle on less serious forms of fraud: A study of executives and managers. *Employee Responsibilities and Rights Journal, 12*(4), 199–217.

Ki, E.-J. (2006). *Linkages among relationship maintenance strategies, relationship quality outcomes, attitude, and behavioral intentions.* Doctoral dissertation, University of Florida, Gainesville, FL.

Ki, E.-J., & Hon, L. C. (2007). Reliability and validity of organization-public relationship measurement and linkages among relationship indicators in a membership organization. *Journalism & Mass Communication Quarterly, 84*(3), 419–438.

Kim, H.-S. (2007). A multilevel study of antecedents and a mediator of employee-organization relationships. *Journal of Public Relations Research, 19*(2), 167–197.

King, G. (1997). The effects of interpersonal closeness and issue seriousness on blowing the whistle. *The Journal of Business Communication, 34*(4), 419–436.

Krumpal, I. (2013). Determinants of social desirability bias in sensitive surveys: A literature review. *Quality & Quantity, 47*(4), 2025–2047. https://doi.org/10.1007/s11135-011-9640-9

Ledingham, J. A., & Bruning, S. D. (1998). Relationship management in public relations: Dimensions of an organization-public relationship. *Public Relations Review, 24*, 55–65.

Lee, S. T., & Kee, A. (2017). Testing an environmental framework for understanding public relations practitioners' orientation toward relationship management. *Journal of Public Relations Research, 29*(6), 259–276. https://doi.org/10.1080/1062726X.2017.1408465

Merit Systems Protection Board. (1981). *Whistleblowing and the federal employee: Blowing the whistle on fraud, waste, and mismanagement—who does it and what happens.* Washington, DC: MSPB.

Merit Systems Protection Board. (1984). *Blowing the whistle in the federal government: A comparative analysis of 1980 and 1983 survey findings.* Washington, DC: MSPB.

Merit Systems Protection Board. (1993). *Whistleblowing in the federal government: An update.* Washington, DC: MSPB.

Merit Systems Protection Board. (2011). *Blowing the whistle: Barriers to federal employees making disclosures.* Washington, DC: MSPB.

Mesmer-Magnus, J. R., & Viswesvaran, C. (2005). Whistleblowing in organizations: An examination of correlates of whistleblowing intentions, actions, and retaliation. *Journal of Business Ethics, 62*, 277–297.

Miceli, M. P., & Near, J. P. (1985). Characteristics of organizational climate and perceived wrongdoing associated with whistle-blowing decisions. *Personnel Psychology, 38*, 525–544.

Miceli, M. P., & Near, J. P. (1992). *Blowing the whistle: The organizational and legal implications for companies and employees.* New York: Lexington Books.

Miceli, M. P., Near, J. P., & Dworkin, T. M. (2008). *Whistle-blowing in organizations*. New York: Routledge Taylor & Francis Group.

Miceli, M. P., Near, J. P., & Schwenk, C. R. (1991). Who blows the whistle and why? *Industrial and Labor Relations Review, 45*(1), 113–130.

Miceli, M. P., Rehg, M. T., Near, J. P., & Ryan, K. C. (1999). Can laws protect whistle-blowers? Results of a naturally occurring field experiment. *Work and Occupations, 26*(1), 129–151. https://doi.org/10.1177/0730888499026001007

Miethe, T. D. (1999). *Whistleblowing at work: Tough choices in exposing fraud, waste, and abuse on the job*. Boulder, CO: Westview Press.

Near, J. P., & Miceli, M. P. (1996). Whistle-blowing: Myth and reality. *Journal of Management, 22*(3), 507.

Near, J. P., Ryan, K. C., & Miceli, M. P. (1995, August). *Results of a human resource management "experiment": Whistle-blowing in the federal bureaucracy, 1980–1992*. Paper presented at the Annual Meeting of the Academy of Management, Vancouver, BC.

Perry, J. L. (1992). The consequences of speaking out: processes of hostility and issue resolution involving federal whistleblowers. In *Best papers proceedings – Academy of management* (vol. 8, pp. 311–315). Las Vegas, NV. https://doi.org/10.5465/AMBPP.1992.17516059.

Rehg, M. T., Miceli, M. P., Near, J. P., & Van Scotter, J. R. (2004, August). *Predicting retaliation against whistle-blowers: Outcomes of power relationships within organizations*. Paper presented at the Academy of Management, New Orleans, LA.

Rehg, M. T., Miceli, M. P., Near, J. P., & Van Scotter, J. R. (2008). Antecedents and outcomes of retaliation against whistleblowers: Gender differences and power relationships. *Organization Science, 19*(2), 221–240.

Sarbanes-Oxley Act of 2002, 15 U.S.C. § 7201 nt (2002).

Schulz, A. (2011). Sober & Wilson's evolutionary arguments for psychological altruism: A reassessment. *Biology & Philosophy, 26*(2), 251–260. https://doi.org/10.1007/s10539-009-9179-5

Scott-Phillips, T. C., Dickins, T. E., & West, S. A. (2011). Evolutionary theory and the ultimate proximate distinction in the human behavioral sciences. *Perspectives on Psychological Science, 6*(1), 38–47. Retrieved from https://doi.org/10.1177/1745691610393528

Shen, H. (2017). Refining organization–public relationship quality measurement in student and employee sample. *Journalism and Mass Communication Quarterly, 94*(4), 994–1010. https://doi.org/10.1177/1077699016674186

Smirnov, O., Arrow, H., Kennett, D., & Orbell, J. (2007). Ancestral war and the evolutionary origins of "heroism". *Journal of Politics, 69*(4), 927–940.

Trivers, R. (1971). The evolution of reciprocal altruism. *Quarterly Review of Biology, 46*(March), 35–57.

Wexler, M. N. (1981). The Biology of Human Altruism. *Social Science, 56*(4), 195–203.

Wilson, D. S., & Sober, E. (1994). Reintroducing group selection to the human behavioral sciences. *Behavioral and Brain Sciences, 17*(4), 585–608. https://doi.org/10.1017/S0140525X00036104

Yang, S.-U. (2007). An integrated model for organization-public relational outcomes, organizational reputation, and their antecedents. *Journal of Public Relations Research, 19*(2), 91–121.

7 Whistleblowing in public relations findings

Results

Demographics

To better understand the study's sample, the sample demographics are first reported in Table 7.1.

Respondents

Based on responses to individual questions, most respondents were middle-aged ($M = 48.29$; $SD = 8.98$), white (92.8%) males (57.6%) with a four-year college degree (33.8%) only or a graduate or professional degree (41%) (see Table 7.1).

Almost two-thirds (61.2%) supervised others, and more than two-thirds (68.8%) were more than fully successful. Almost three-quarters (72.8%) were paid $100,000 or more, and one-fifth (19.7%) were paid $200,000 or more. More than one-third (37.1%) were the top-ranking public relations or communications executive in their department; three-fifths (59.6%) of the top-ranking public relations or communications executives were males; and more than two-fifths (41.6%) of the top-ranking executives were paid $200,000 or more. Nine (90%) of the ten who reported directly to the CEO were the top-ranking public relations or communications executives in their department, and all were identified in the *Fortune 1000* study. Almost half (44.2%) of top-ranking public relations or communications executives worked in corporate communications departments, and less than one-quarter (23.1%) worked in marketing departments. Less than one-tenth (7.7%) worked in public relations departments.

Insights

Respondents fit the model of middle-aged, well-educated, well-paid, white males. One-third were the top-ranking public relations or communications executive in their department, and three-fifths of those were males.

DOI: 10.4324/9781315231891-8

Table 7.1. Demographic and Employment Variables

Variables	Category	N	Min/ Max	Mean or %	SD	n	Min/ Max	Mean or %	SD
			All respondents				Top-ranking		
Respondents		238				52			
Gender		139				52			
	Male	80		57.6		31		59.6	
	Female	59		42.4		21		40.4	
Age		122	29/74	48.30	8.98	45	31/61	48.16	8.20
Age group	≤48	54		44.3		21		46.7	
	>48	68		55.7		24		53.3	
Education		139				52			
	Some college	9		6.5		1		1.9	
	Four-year college degree	47		33.8		18		34.6	
	Some graduate or professional school	26		18.7		10		19.2	
	Graduate or professional degree	57		41.0		23		44.2	
Race		138				52			
	American Indian/ Alaskan Native	1		0.7		1		1.9	
	Asian/Asian American	2		1.4		0		0.0	
	Black or African American	3		2.2		1		1.9	
	White, not Hispanic[a]	128		92.8		51		98.1	
	Hispanic/Latino	7		5.1		1		1.9	
	Other	1		0.7		0		0.0	
Years employed		128	.75/49	11.54	8.37	51	.75/49	11.68	10.08
Years in position		130	.75/25	5.14	4.27	51	.75/15	5.26	3.88
Employed	≤11.5	73		57.0		28		54.9	
	>11.5	55		43.0		23		45.1	
Position	≤5	91		70.0		35		68.6	
	>5	39		30.0		16		31.	
Salary		132				49			
	<$100,000	36		27.3		11		22.4	
	$100,000– $199,999	69		52.3		17		34.7	
	$200,000– $500,000	26		19.7		20		40.8	
	>$500,000	1		0.8		1		0.8	
Top-ranking		140				52			
	No	88		62.9					

(*Continued*)

Table 7.1 (Continued)

Variables	Category	All respondents				Top-ranking			
		N	Min/Max	Mean or %	SD	n	Min/Max	Mean or %	SD
	Yes					52		37.1	
CEO		140				52			
	Other	31		22.1		5		9.6	
	Report to someone who reports to someone who reports to CEO	54		38.6		12		23.1	
	Report to someone who reports to CEO	45		32.1		26		50.0	
	Report to CEO	10		7.1		9		17.3	
Department		148				52			
	Public relations	14		10.1		4		7.8	
	Corporate communications	43		30.9		23		44.2	
	Marketing	51		36.7		12		23.1	
	Finance/Admin.	3		2.2		2		3.9	
	Public Affairs[b]	1		0.7		1		1.9	
	Investor relations[b]	1		0.7		0		0	
	Advertising[b]	2		1.4		0		0	
	Sales[b]	9		6.5		4		7.7	
	Other	15		10.8		6		11.5	
Supervision		139				52			
	No	54		38.8		8		15.4	
	Yes	85		61.2		44		84.6	
Rating		138				51			
	Minimally successful	4		2.9		1		2.0	
	Fully successful	39		28.3		12		23.5	
	Exceeds fully successful	61		44.2		20		39.2	
	Outstanding	34		24.6		18		35.3	

[a] One identified as White, not Hispanic and Hispanic/Latino.
[b] Added to second study.

Post hoc *chi-square tests of independence for demographic and employment variables*

"The chi-square (χ^2) test of independence is used to examine the relationship between two discrete variables" (Tabachnick & Fidell, 2007, p. 58). *Post hoc* chi-square tests of independence examined differences between four variables (age group, rank, gender, and study) and the demographic and employment variables.

Post hoc chi-square tests of independence were conducted between age group (at or below mean, or above mean), rank, gender, and study (*Fortune 1000 and Wilshire 5000*) and the remaining demographic and employment variables.[1]

Age group

Post hoc chi-square tests of independence were significant between age group and years with the company, $\chi^2(1, 112) = 8.41$, $p = .004$,[2] and earning a salary of $100,000 or more, $\chi^2(1, 119) = 7.17$, $p = .007$.[3] Age group tended toward differences with years in current position, $\chi^2(1, 114) = 3.27$, $p = .070$), and earning a salary of $200,000 or more, $\chi^2(1, 119) = 3.19$, $p = .074$).

INSIGHTS

Older employees had been with the company longer than younger employees, and more older employees earned a salary of $100,000 or more. Older employees also may have been in their positions longer than younger employees, and more older employees may have earned $200,000 or more.

Rank

Post hoc chi-square tests of independence were significant between being a top-ranking public relations or communications executives and supervision, $\chi^2(1, 139) = 19.25$, $p < .001$,[4] reporting directly to the CEO, $\chi^2(1, 140) = 12.89$, $p < .001$,[5] and earning a salary of $200,000 or more, $\chi^2(1, 132) = 24.04$, $p < .001$.[6]

INSIGHTS

Top-ranking public relations or communications executives were more likely than others to supervise others, report directly to the CEO, and earn more than $200,000.

Gender

Chi-square tests of independence were significant between gender and age group, $\chi^2(1, 122) = 4.29$, $p = .038$,[7] and earning a salary of $100,000 or more, $\chi^2(1, 32) = 4.63$, $p = .031$.[8] Gender tended toward differences for years with the company, $\chi^2(1, 127) = 2.73$, $p = .099$, time in current position, $\chi^2(1, 129) = 3.691$, $p = .055$, and a beyond fully successful ("exemplary") performance rating, $\chi^2(1, 137) = 2.83$, $p = .093$.

INSIGHTS

Male respondents were older than female respondents, and more males than females earned $100,000 or more. Males may have been with the company and in their positions longer and may have earned a higher performance rating than females.

Study

Chi-square tests of independence were significant between study and being the top-ranking public relations or communications executive in the corporation, $\chi^2(1, 140) = 29.45$, $p < .001$,[9] supervision, $\chi^2(1, 139) = 11.98$, $p = .001$,[10] reporting directly to the CEO, $\chi^2(1, 140) = 16.15$, $p < .001$,[11] years with the company, $\chi^2(1, 128) = 4.13$, $p = .042$,[12] and earning \$200,000 or more, $\chi^2(1, 132) = 12.90$, $p < .001$.[13]

INSIGHTS

The *Fortune 1000* study had more top-ranking public relations or communications executives, more supervisors, more direct reports to the CEO, and more respondents paid \$200,000 or more than the *Wilshire 5000* study. The *Wilshire 5000* study had more long-time company employees than the *Fortune 1000* study.

> *Research Question 1:* Have public relations executives helped develop and/ or publicize Sarbanes–Oxley whistleblowing channels?

Sarbanes-Oxley whistleblowing channels

More than half (54.6%) of respondents worked for an organization that had an anonymous Sarbanes-Oxley whistleblowing channel that reported directly to the audit committee of the board of directors; one-tenth (10%) helped develop it; and one-third (34.2%) helped publicize it (see Table 7.2).[14]

Post hoc chi-square tests of independence for Sarbanes-Oxley involvement

Post hoc chi-square tests of independence examined differences in working for an organization with an anonymous whistleblowing channel, helping develop the anonymous whistleblowing channel, and helping publicize the anonymous whistleblowing channel and the demographic and employment variables.[15] The only significant difference was between age group and working for an organization with an anonymous whistleblowing channel, $\chi^2(1, 59) = 5.50$, $p = .019$.[16] Exemplary performance rating tended toward differences in participating in developing the anonymous channel, $\chi^2(1, 72) = .3.60$, $p = .056$, and publicizing it, $\chi^2(1, 60) = 3.14$, $p = .076$. Some graduate education also tended toward differences in helping develop the anonymous channel, $\chi^2(1, 77) = 3.55$, $p = .060$. There was not a significant difference for top-ranking public relations and communications professionals in working for an organization with an anonymous

Table 7.2 Descriptives and Frequencies for Involvement with Sarbanes-Oxley Anonymous Communication Channel

Variables	All respondents		Top-ranking	
	N	%	n	%
Anonymous channel	229		52	
No	39	17.0	10	19.2
Yes	125	54.6	40	76.9
Do not know	65	28.4	2	3.8
Develop channel	219		47	
No	136	62.1	35	74.5
Yes	22	10.0	12	25.5
Does not apply	61	25.6	0	0
Publicize channel	193		47	
No	75	38.9	17	36.2
Yes	66	34.2	29	61.7
Does not apply	52	26.9	1	2.1

whistleblowing channel $\chi^2(1, 69) = .117$, $p = .732$, developing it, $\chi^2(1, 73) = .612$, $p = .434$, or publicizing it, $\chi^2(1, 61) = .485$, $p = .486$.[17]

INSIGHTS

Age was the only variable significantly associated with the Sarbanes-Oxley whistleblowing channels. More older employees than younger employees worked for an organization with an anonymous whistleblowing channel. Rank played no role in working for an organization with an anonymous whistle-blowing channel, helping develop it, or helping publicize it.

Research Question 2: Have public relations executives blown the whistle?

The questionnaire

The questionnaire used in *this study* followed the 1980 federal questionnaire with modifications for a corporate population (see Appendix A). Responses addressed the corporate and individual level variables reported in Table 7.3 and answered research questions and hypotheses.

Corporate-level variables

INCIDENCE (AWARENESS) OF WRONGDOING

Incidence (awareness) of wrongdoing was 21% (see Table 7.3).[18]

Thirty-five (21%) of 167 respondents to that question out of 238 full and partial respondents to the survey were aware of wrongdoing in their own

Table 7.3 Whistleblowing Questions Frequencies

Variables	All respondents		Top-ranking	
	N	%	n	%
Other aware	196		52	
No	106	54.1	30	57.7
Yes	90	45.9	22	42.3
Other amount	82		22	
<$1,000	5	6.1	0	
$1,000–$49,999	5	6.1	1	4.5
$50,000–$99,999	6	7.3	3	13.6
$100,000–$500,000	10	12.2	3	13.6
>$500,000	10	12.2	2	9.1
Do not know	46	56.1	13	59.1
Other frequency	80		22	
Rarely	34	42.5	9	40.9
Occasionally	19	23.8	5	22.7
Frequently	7	8.8	3	13.6
Do not know	20	25.0	5	22.7
Other reported	75		19	
No	12	16.0	4	21.1
Yes	47	62.7	11	57.9
Do not know	16	21.3	4	21.1
Other's job	73		19	
No	41	56.2	12	63.2
Yes	12	16.4	3	15.8
Do not know	20	27.4	4	21.1
How other reported	68		19	
Internally: COC	25	36.8	8	42.1
Internally: Anon	22	32.4	4	21.1
Externally	1	1.5	0	
Do not know	28	41.2	8	42.1
Other identified	67		19	
No	22	32.8	9	47.4
Yes	12	17.9	2	10.5
Do not know	33	49.3	8	42.1
What happened to other	60		18	
Rewarded	1	1.7	1	5.6
Nothing	24	40.0	9	50.0
Co-workers unhappy	1	1.7	0	
Supervisor unhappy	4	6.7	2	11.1
Someone above supervisor unhappy	3	5.0	3	16.7
Retaliation	7	11.5	0	
Do not know	25	41.7	4	22.2
You aware	167		52	
No	132	79.0	38	73.1
Yes	35	21.0	14	26.9
Your dollar amount	35		14	
<$1,000	2	5.7		
$1,000–$49,999	6	17.1	2	14.3
$50,000–$99,999	5	14.3	2	14.3
$100,000–$500,000	10	28.6	5	35.7

	All respondents		Top-ranking	
>$500,000	1	2.9	0	
Do not know	11	31.4	5	35.7
Your frequency	35		13	
Rarely	11	31.4	4	30.8
Occasionally	14	40.0	5	38.5
Frequently	8	22.9	3	23.1
Do not know	2	5.7	1	7.7
You reported	35		14	
No	17	48.6	5	35.7
Yes	18	51.4	9	64.3
Your job	31		13	
No	28	90.3	12	92.3
Yes	3	9.7	1	7.7
How you reported	21		10	
Internal: COC	16	76.2	9	90.0
Internal: Anon	5	23.8	2	20.0
External	2	9.5	0	
You identified	24		11	
No	9	37.5	4	36.4
Yes	15	62.5	7	63.6
What happened to you	22		11	
Rewarded	0		0	
Nothing	12	54.5	7	63.6
Co-workers unhappy	4	18.2	1	9.1
Supervisor unhappy	6	27.3	2	18.2
Someone above supervisor unhappy	5	22.7	1	9.1
Retaliation	7	31.8	3	27.3

organization. Fourteen (40%) of those were top-ranking public relations and communications executives, which was 26.9% of top-ranking public relations and communications executives.

INSIGHTS

One-fifth of respondents were aware of wrongdoing in their own organizations. Two-fifths of those were top-ranking public relations and communications executives, but only one quarter of top-ranking public relations and communication executives were aware of wrongdoing in their own organizations.

Post hoc chi-square tests of independence for awareness of wrongdoing

Post hoc chi-square tests of independence between awareness of wrongdoing and the demographic and employment variables found no significance.[19]

INSIGHTS

Demographic and employment variables were not associated with awareness of wrongdoing in this analysis.

INCIDENCE OF WHISTLEBLOWING

Incidence of whistleblowing was 51.4%.[20] Eighteen of 35 respondents who were aware of wrongdoing in their own organization blew the whistle. Nine (50%) of those were top-ranking public relations or communications executives, which was two-thirds (64.3%) of top-ranking public relations or communications executives who were aware of wrongdoing but only 17.3% of top-ranking public relations or communications executives.

Post hoc chi-square tests of independence for whistleblowing

Post hoc chi-square tests of independence between whistleblowing and the demographic and employment variables found no significance.

INSIGHTS

Half of respondents who were aware of wrongdoing in their own organizations blew the whistle. Half of those were top-ranking public relations and communications executives, which was two-thirds of those who were aware of wrongdoing but less than one-fifth of top-ranking public relations and communications executives.

INCIDENCE OF IDENTIFIED WHISTLEBLOWING

Incidence of identified whistleblowing was 62.5%.[21] Of the 24 who responded to this question as whistleblowers, 15 were identified. Seven (46.3%) of the 15 were top-ranking public relations or communications executives, which was almost two-thirds (63.6%) of those who answered the question, more than three-quarters (77.8%) of top-ranking public relations or communications executives who blew the whistle, but slightly more than one-tenth (13.5%) of top-ranking public relations and communications executives.

INSIGHTS

Two-thirds of whistleblowers were identified; more than three-quarters of top-ranking public relations or communications executives who reported wrongdoing were identified; that represented slightly more than one-tenth of top-ranking public relations and communications executives.

> *Research Question 3:* Do public relations executives think it is their job to blow the whistle?

Public relations roles

INCIDENCE OF ROLE-PRESCRIBED WHISTLEBLOWING

Incidence of role-prescribed whistleblowing was 9.7%.[22] Three of the 18 respondents to this question said reporting wrongdoing was part of their job.

Of those, one (33.3%) was a top-ranking public relations or communications executive, which was 2% of top-ranking public relations or communications executives.

INSIGHTS

Overwhelmingly, public relations and communications executives did not consider whistleblowing part of their job. Only one of the three who considered whistleblowing part of their job was a top-ranking public relations or communications executive, which was a small fraction of top-ranking public relations or communications executives.

Research Question 4: What channels have public relations executives used to blow the whistle?

Internal or external?

HYPOTHESIS 1 AND HYPOTHESIS 2

Hypothesis 1, which said that public relations executives would use the chain-of-command more often than they would use Sarbanes-Oxley channels, was supported. A *post hoc* chi-square test of independence between chain-of-command and Sarbanes-Oxley channels was significant, $\chi^2(1, 21) = 4.738, p = .030$. *Hypothesis 2*, which said that public relations executives would use external channels more often than they would use Sarbanes-Oxley channels, was not supported. A *post hoc* chi-square test of independence between external channels and Sarbanes-Oxley channels was not significant, $\chi^2(1, 21) = .691, p = .406$.

INSIGHTS

Public relations and communications executives blew the whistle through the internal chain-of-command three times more often than through Sarbanes-Oxley anonymous whistleblowing channels, but they blew the whistle through Sarbanes-Oxley anonymous whistleblowing channels two-and-one-half times more often than through external channels.

Acceptance or retaliation?

INCIDENCE OF RETALIATION

Incidence of retaliation was 45%.[23] Of the 22 respondents to this question, ten reported lack of support and/or retaliation. Four (40%) were top-ranking public relations executives or communications executives, which was more than half (57.1%) of top-ranking public relations executives or communications executives who were identified and 7% of top-ranking public relations executives or communications executives.

INSIGHTS

More than two-fifths of all identified whistleblowers experienced retaliation. Two-fifths of those who responded to the question were top-ranking public relations and communications executives, which was more than half of identified top-ranking public relations and communications executives, but less than one-tenth of top-ranking public relations and communications executives.

Corporate-level variables compared with federal surveys

The following table compares results of the 2010/2012 Greenwood corporate survey for corporate-level variables with the management analysis) of the first three federal surveys using Z-scores (infrrr, 2020), otherwise known as the difference in proportions hypothesis test (see Table 7.4).

Incidence of wrongdoing (21%) in the 2010/2012 Greenwood corporate survey was significantly lower than that in the 1980 federal survey (45%) and

Table 7.4 Descriptive Statistics and Z-scores for Corporate Variables

Variables	MSPB 1980[a]	MSPB 1983[b]	MSPB 1992[c]	Greenwood 2010/2012
Respondents	8,296	4,427	13,432	238
Incidence of wrongdoing (%)	45	18	14	21
z-score difference vs. 1980				
z-score difference vs. 1983	4.24***[d]			
z-score difference vs. 1992	4.94***	0.77		
z-score difference vs. 2010–12	7.50***[d]	−0.94[d]	−2.21*[d]	
Incidence of whistleblowing (%)	26	40	48	51
z-score difference vs. 1980				
z-score difference vs. 1983	−1.79			
z-score difference vs. 1992	−2.91**	−1.14		
z-score difference vs. 2010–12	−2.95**[d]	−1.28[d]	−0.35[d]	
Incidence of identified whistleblowing (%)	74	60	55	63
z-score difference vs. 1980				
z-score difference vs. 1983	2.11*			
z-score difference vs. 1992	2.81**	0.72		
z-score difference vs. 2010–2012	1.10[e]	−0.29 [e]	−0.80 [e]	
Incidence of retaliation (%)	17	21	38	45
z-score difference vs. 1980				
z-score difference vs. 1983	−0.91			
z-score difference vs. 1992	−3.50***	−6.64**		
z-score difference vs. 2010–2012	−2.61**[e]	−2.18*[e]	−0.64 [e]	
No retaliation	52	46	37	55

Note: Adapted from "Can Laws Protect Whistle-Blowers? Results of a Naturally Occurring Field Experiment," by M. P. Miceli, M. Rehg, J. P. Near, & K. C. Ryan (1999), *Work and Occupations*, 26, p. 142. Copyright 1999 by Sage Publications, Inc. Adapted with permission. [a] MSPB (1981). [b] MSPB (1984). [c] MSPB (1993). [d] Results of difference in proportions tests. [e] Sample two size may be insufficient.

significantly higher than that in the 1992 (14%) study. Incidence of whistle-blowing in the 2010/2012 Greenwood corporate survey (51.4%) was significantly higher than that in the 1980 federal survey (26%). Incidence of identified whistleblowing in the 2010/2012 Greenwood corporate survey (62.5%) was not significantly different than in the 1980, 1983, or 1992 federal surveys. Incidence of retaliation in the 2010/2012 Greenwood corporate study (45%) was significantly higher than that in the 1980 (17%) and 1983 (21%) federal surveys.

Individual-level variables

EMPLOYMENT AND DEMOGRAPHIC VARIABLES

Percentages or means and standard deviations for employment and demographic variables are reported in Table 7.5.

SERIOUSNESS OF WRONGDOING

Seriousness of wrongdoing ($M = 2.33$, $SD = .650$) was a three-level scale made up of dollar volume or frequency of occurrence (see Table 7.5).

INSIGHTS

Of the 33 who reported personal awareness of dollar amount and/or frequency of wrongdoing, 30 (90.9%) reported incidents that were somewhat serious or most serious.

LACK OF SUPPORT

Three levels of lack of support were presented in Table 7.5, but they were not tested separately because they were included in the retaliation scale.

INSIGHTS

Lack of support was not tested because it was included in the retaliation scale.

Comprehensiveness of retaliation

Comprehensiveness of retaliation ($M = .80$, $SD = 1.26$) was presented here for comparison only.

Table 7.5 Means or Percentages and Standard Deviations for All Individual-Level Variables

	MSPB1980[a]		MSPB 1983[b]		MSPB 1992[c]		Greenwood 2010/2012	
	M /%	SD	M /%	SD	M /%	SD	M /%	SD
Respondents	640[d]		202[d]		353[d]		15[d]	
Retaliation							3.64[e, f]	1.89
Comprehensiveness of retaliation	.57[g]	1.52	.66[g]	1.56	.69[g]	1.32	.80[h]	1.26
Seriousness of wrongdoing	2.23[i]	.75	2.41[i]	.73	2.45[j]	.65	2.33[k]	.65
Lack of support:								
Management	26%		22%		38%		23%[l]	
Supervisor	24%		15%		34%		27%[l]	
Co-worker	8%		5%		21%		18%[l]	
Education	3.89	[m]	4.30	[m]	3.54	[m]	3.94[n]	1.01
Salary	2.96[o]	1.12	4.18[o]	.95	2.93[o]	.78	1.94[p]	.71
Professional job			.69	.46	.64	.48		
Supervisory job							61%	
Years employed							11.54	8.37
Years in position			3.11	1.04	2.62	.83	5.14	4.27
Report to CEO							2.24[q]	.88
Top-ranked PR							37%	
Job performance					4.02	.79	3.91	.80
Age							48.30	8.98
Female			9%		37%		42%	
Majority race			91%		82%		93%	
External reporting	16%		5%		22%		10%	

Note: Adapted from "Can Laws Protect Whistle-Blowers? Results of a Naturally Occurring Field Experiment," by M. P. Miceli, M. Rehg, J. P. Near, and K. C. Ryan (1999), *Work and Occupations*, 26, p. 143. Copyright 1999 by Sage Publications, Inc. Adapted with permission. [a] Merit Systems Protection Board (1981), 15 agencies. [b] MSPB (1984), executive branch. [c] MSPB (1993), entire federal government. [d] Identified whistleblowers. [e] All whistleblowers. [f] Five-point scale from Reward to Retaliation included management, supervisor, and co-worker lack of support; used in regressions. [g] Multiple types of retaliation. [h] Calculated for 15 identified whistleblowers; not used in regressions. [i] Five-point scale from No to >$100,000. [j] Five-point scale from <$100 to >$500,000. [k] Three-point scale: Least, Somewhat, Most. [l] Included in retaliation scale. [m] Missing from original study. [n] Some college, four-year degree, some graduate/professional school, graduate/professional degree. [o] Federal pay grades 1–15. [p] <$100,000, $100,000–$199,999, $200,000–$500,000, and >$500,000. [q] Other; I report to someone who reports to someone who reports to the CEO; I report to someone who reports to the CEO; I report to the CEO; I am the CEO.

INSIGHTS

Comprehensiveness of retaliation was not used in *this study* due to the low response rate for retaliation.

Retaliation

Retaliation ($M = 3.64$, $SD = 1.89$) was a six-item scale composed of 34 responses from 22 respondents to the question, "If you were identified as the source of the report, what happened to you?"[24] Retaliation replaced compre-hensiveness of retaliation as the dependent variable in the 2010/2012 Green-wood corporate study.

INSIGHTS

Forty-five percent experienced one or more of the last four items: lack of support from co-workers, supervisors, and/or upper management; and/or retaliation.

Relationship demographics

Public relations and communications executives had generally positive views of their relationships with their employers ($M = 3.77$, $SD = .86$) as shown in responses to the Hon and Grunig (1999) short relationship scales (see Table 7.6). Satisfaction had the highest score among the relationship quality outcomes ($M = 3.94$, $SD = .88$). Communal relationship type had the highest score of all items ($M = 4.06$, $SD = .86$), and exchange relationship type had the lowest ($M = 3.26$, $SD = .75$). All relationship quality outcomes and communal rela-tion type were strongly positively correlated with the exception of exchange type. Relationship types had a small negative correlation, $r(132) = -.23$, $p < .01$. The complete results from this study, compared with the results from a study of Millennials' relationships with their public relations employers (Gallicano et al., 2012), are presented in Appendix B.

INSIGHTS

Public relations and communications executives had positive views of their relationships with their employers, and relationship quality outcomes and com-munal relationship type were positively correlated. However, exchange and communal relationship types were negatively correlated with each other, with low levels of exchange relationship type associated with high levels of com-munal relationship type.

Table 7.6 Descriptive Statistics, Reliability, and Correlations for Relationships

	N	Alpha	M	SD	1	2	3	4	5	6
Trust	137	.90	3.75	.86	1					
Control mutuality	136	.80	3.75	.80	.835**	1				
Commitment	136	.88	3.82	.96	.838**	.768**	1			
Satisfaction	138	.88	3.94	.88	.882**	.802**	.860**	1		
Communal relationship	135	.82	4.06	.86	.778**	.808**	.726**	.758**	1	
Exchange relationship	136	.60	3.26	.75	-.014	-.033	.009	-.003	-.233**	1

Note: Adapted from "Engaged at work? An employee engagement model in public relations," by H. Shen, & H. Jiang (2019), *Journal of Public Relations Research*, 31:1-2, p. 40. Copyright 2019 by Taylor & Francis Ltd. Adapted with permission. * p < .05; ** p < .01.

Predictors of whistleblowing

What predicted awareness of wrongdoing?

RANK PREDICTED AWARENESS OF WRONGDOING

Simple regressions on the demographic and employment variables of age, years employed, and job tenure were not significant for awareness of wrongdoing.[25] However, a logistic regression found that being the top-ranking public relations or communications executive in one's organization was the strongest positive predictor ($z = 5.615$, $p = .018$) of awareness of wrongdoing (see Table 7.7).[26]

Top-ranking public relations and communications executives had 5.570 times higher odds of being aware of wrongdoing in their own organization than those who were not top-ranking public relations and communications executives.

INSIGHTS

Rank (i.e., being the top-ranking public relations or communications executive) was the strongest positive predictor of awareness of wrongdoing.

What predicted whistleblowing?

SERIOUSNESS OF WRONGDOING PREDICTED WHISTLEBLOWING

Logistic regressions on whistleblowing with seriousness of wrongdoing and other demographic and employment variables were not significant. However, a simple logistic regression with seriousness of wrongdoing on whistleblowing found that seriousness of wrongdoing was a significant predictor of whistleblowing ($z = 4.405$, $p = .036$), and it had four times higher odds of being associated with whistleblowing than less serious wrongdoing.[27]

Table 7.7 Logistic Regression Predictors of Awareness of Wrongdoing

Predictor	Aware[a]	
	OR[b]	95% CI[c]
Gender	.668	[.23, 1.97]
Age	.983	[.93, 1.04]
Education	1.618	[.94, 2.80]
Top-ranked PR	5.570*	[1.35, 23.06]
Supervision	.172**	[.05, .63]
Rating	.892	[.47, 1.71]
Report to CEO	.522	[.26, 1.07]

[a] Awareness of wrongdoing. [b] Odds Ratio [c] Confidence Interval. * $p < .05$; ** $p < .01$; two-tailed.

Table 7.8 Results of Regression Analyses for Retaliation: Standardized Regression Coefficients

	MSPB 1980	MSPB 1983	MSPB 1992	2010/2012
Size of agency	-.08*			
Seriousness of wrongdoing	.06	.13*	.09	-.38
Management lack of support	.18***	.33***	.29***	a
Supervisor lack of support	.26***	.40***	.16**	1.96**a
Co-worker lack of support	-.02	.08	.04	-1.58★a
Education	.10*	.14*	.04	2.33b
Salary	-.16***	-.04	-.06	-.33
Professional job status		-.04	.05	
Supervision				-.08
Job tenure (years in position)		-.10	-.03	.99*
Job performance (rating)			-.19***	.75*
Female (gender)		.08	-.05	.89*
Race (White, non-Hispanic)		-.12*	-.13*	c
Use of external channels	.12**		.15**	.87*
Adjusted R^2 (controls only)	.06	.00	.06	-.21
Total adjusted R^2	.19	.41	.27	.55
F value	20.1***	14.8***	12.0***	3.05
N whistleblowers				22d
N of identified whistleblowers	640	202	353	15
N of agencies	15	22	22	

Note: Adapted from "Can Laws Protect Whistle-Blowers? Results of a Naturally Occurring Field Experiment," by M. P. Miceli, M. Rehg, J. P. Near, and K. C. Ryan (1999), *Work and Occupations, 26,* p. 145. Copyright 1999 by Sage Publications, Inc. Adapted with permission. Federal studies calculated multiple types of retaliation; the Greenwood 2010/2012 retaliation scale included all responses to all items from the question: "If you were identified as the source of the report, what happened to you?" Miceli et al. (1999) conducted hierarchical multiple regressions on each of the federal studies: Merit Systems Protection Board (1981, 1984, 1993). Greenwood followed Miceli et al. (1999) with hierarchical multiple regressions on the retaliation scale. If no value is shown, the variable was not measured that year. [a] Variables included in retaliation scale. [b] Education approached significance, $p = .053$. [c] Race (White, Non-Hispanic) was a constant. [d] This is the number of whistleblowers used in most analyses.

* $p < .05$; ** $p < .01$; *** $p < .001$; two-tailed. 2010/2012: Pairwise deletion.

INSIGHTS

Seriousness of wrongdoing was the only positive predictor of whistleblowing.

Research Question 5: How have public relations executive been treated by their employers?

What predicted retaliation?

JOB TENURE, PERFORMANCE, GENDER, AND EXTERNAL REPORTING PREDICTED RETALIATION

A hierarchical multiple regression using pairwise deletion with the variables used in Miceli et al. (1999) found time in position (job tenure), performance rating, female gender, and external reporting were significant for retaliation (see Table 7.8).

Hypothesis 3, which predicted that power would protect from retaliation, was partially supported. The hierarchical multiple regression found that education, salary, and supervision, three elements of power, were not significant for retaliation, which suggests that some elements of power may protect from retaliation. However, time in position (job tenure), performance rating female gender, and external reporting predicted retaliation. Simple regressions on retaliation with each of the power variables found no significance. *Hypothesis 4*, which predicted that power would not protect if the wrongdoing was serious, was not supported. The hierarchical multiple regression and a simple regression with seriousness of wrongdoing on retaliation found no significance. Some elements of power appeared to protect whistleblowers, even when reporting serious wrongdoing. *Hypothesis 5*, which predicted that external reporting would result in more retaliation than internal reporting, was supported. The hierarchical multiple regression found that reporting externally was significant for retaliation. However, simple regressions on retaliation with reporting channels found no significance. *Hypothesis 6,* which predicted that retaliation would be associated with greater supervisor and management lack of support, was not tested. The hierarchical multiple regression found that lack of co-worker support and lack of supervisor support were significant for retaliation, but their significance must be attributed to their inclusion in the retaliation scale.

> *Research Question 7*: Do female public relations executives who blow the whistle experience more retaliation than male public relations executives?[28]

The hierarchical multiple regression found gender (coded for female) significant for retaliation in *this study*. A simple regression with gender on retaliation was not significant.

INSIGHTS

Women experienced more retaliation than men.

> *Research Question 6*: In what ways has retaliation for whistleblowing affected their relationships with their corporate employers?

Awareness of wrongdoing

Awareness of wrongdoing had a significant negative effect on trust, control mutuality, commitment, and satisfaction, the four relationship quality outcomes, and communal relationship type (Hon & Grunig, 1999) (see Table 7.9).

Awareness of wrongdoing had significant negative effects on trust,[29] control mutuality,[30] commitment,[31] satisfaction,[32] and communal relationship,[33] but only if the respondent was aware of wrongdoing in his or her own organization

Table 7.9 Results of Regression Analyses for Effects of Awareness of Wrongdoing, Whistleblowing, and Retaliation on Relationships: Unstandardized Regression Coefficients

Relationship variables	Trust		Control mutuality		Commitment	
	B	95% CI[b]	B	95% CI[b]	B	95% CI[b]
Awareness[a]						
Self	.13	[-.46, .71]	.32	[-.20, .85]	.44	[-.21, 1.09]
Other	.15	[-.18, .48]	.00	[-.30, .31]	.18	[-.19, .55]
Both	-.58**	[-.99, -.19]	-.71***	[-1.07, -.36]	-.63**	[-1.08, -.17]
Whistleblowing[c]						
Self	-2.53**	[-4.21, -.85]	-2.13*	[-3.76, -.49]	-2.78**	[-4.66, -.90]
Other	-1.20**	[-2.08, -.31]	-1.31**	[-2.17, -.45]	-1.36*	[-2.49, -.24]
Both	-1.14**	[-1.89, -.40]	-1.21**	[-1.93, -.48]	-1.36**	[-2.20, -.53]
Retaliation[d]						
Self	-.35**	[-.61, -.10]	-.36**	[-.61, -.12]	-.37*	[-.69, -.05]

Relationship variables	Satisfaction		Communal		Exchange	
	B	95% CI[b]	B	95% CI[b]	B	95% CI[b]
Awareness[a]						
Self	.28	[-.32, .87]	.14	[-.46, .74]	.40	[-.13, .92]
Other	.09	[-.26, .43]	-.05	[-.38, .28]	.07	[-.23, .37]
Both	-.63**	[-1.04, -.23]	-.80***	[-1.19, -.41]	.34	[-.02, 0.70]
Whistleblowing[c]						
Self	-2.87**	[-4.65, -1.09]	-3.14**	[-4.93, -1.34]	.69	[-.93, 2.30]
Other	-1.50**	[-2.43, -.56]	-1.70**	[-2.64, -.75]	.06	[-.79, .91]
Both	-1.25**	[-2.03, -.46]	-.72	[-1.52, -.80]	-.73*	[-1.45, -.14]
Retaliation[d]						
Self	-.42**	[-.69, -.14]	-.36*	[-.64, -.08]	-.09	[-.32, .14]

Note: Simple linear regression. [a] Awareness of wrongdoing: Self-awareness, Other awareness, Both awareness. [b] CI is confidence interval. [c] Whistleblowing: Self-report, Other report, Both report. [d] Retaliation: Retaliation against self. * $p < .05$; ** $p < .01$; *** $p < .001$; two-tailed.

and if the respondent was aware of wrongdoing in another organization as described by someone in that organization. Awareness of wrongdoing had no effect on exchange relationship type.

INSIGHTS

Awareness of wrongdoing had a significant negative effect on all four of the relationship quality outcomes and the communal relationship type, but only if the respondent was aware of wrongdoing in his or her own organization and aware of wrongdoing in another organization as described by someone in that organization.

Whistleblowing

Whistleblowing had significant negative effects on the four relationship quality outcomes and both relationship types.

Whistleblowing by the respondent, whistleblowing in another organization as described by someone in that organization, and whistleblowing by the respondent and whistleblowing in another organization as described by someone in that organization had significant negative effects on trust,[34] control mutuality,[35] commitment,[36] and satisfaction.[37] Whistleblowing by the respondent had a significant negative effect on communal relationship, and whistleblowing in another organization as described by someone in that organization had significant negative effects on communal relationship.[38] Whistleblowing by the respondent and whistleblowing in another organization as described by someone in that organization had a significant negative effect on exchange relationship type.[39]

INSIGHTS

Whistleblowing in all three categories had significant negative effects on trust, control mutuality, commitment, and satisfaction. Whistleblowing by the respondent and whistleblowing in another organization as described by someone in that organization had significant negative effects on communal relationship type. Whistleblowing by the respondent and whistleblowing in another organization as described by someone in that organization had a significant negative effect on exchange relationship type.

Retaliation

Retaliation had a significant negative effect on all relationship quality outcomes and communal relationship type.

Retaliation against the whistleblower had a significant negative effect on trust,[40] control mutuality,[41] commitment,[42] satisfaction,[43] and communal relationship type.[44] Retaliation did not have a significant effect on exchange relationship type.

Retaliation for whistleblowing had significant negative effects on the four relationship quality outcomes and communal relationship type, but it did not have a significant effect on exchange relationship type.

Hypothesis 7, which proposed that retaliation for whistleblowing would be associated with more negative relationships, was predominantly supported. Those who reported more retaliation for whistleblowing reported more negative relationships with their employers for trust, control mutuality, commitment, satisfaction, and communal relationship type than those who reported less retaliation. Exchange relationship type was not affected by retaliation.

Did any other variables influence relationships?

RANK INFLUENCED RELATIONSHIPS

Respondents in the *Fortune 1000* survey, which had twice as many top-ranking public relations or communications executives as the *Wilshire 5000* survey, were more positive (e.g. Trust ($M = 4.053$, $SD = .678$)) toward their relationships with their employers than those in the *Wilshire 5000* survey (Trust ($M = 3.540$, $SD = .911$)). Simple regressions on relationship quality outcomes and relationship types by study were *negatively* significant for all measures except exchange relationship type (see Table 7.10).

A one-way between-groups MANOVA on the combined study found that being the top-ranking public relations or communications executive was positively significant for relationship quality outcomes and relationship types overall, $F(6, 118) = 3.17$, $p = .006$; Wilks' lambda = .86; partial eta squared = .14. The only individual scale to reach statistical significance was control mutuality, $F(1, 123) = 13.62$, $p = .006$, partial eta squared = .10 (Pallant, 2005; Rehg, Miceli, Near, & Van Scotter, 2008).[45]

Table 7.10 Regressions on Relationship Scales with *Fortune 1000* and *Wilshire 5000* Studies Unstandardized Regression Coefficients

Relationship factors[a]	B	95% CI[b]
Trust	-.51***	[-.80–.23]
Control mutuality	-.64***	[-.89, -.38]
Commitment	-.47**	[-.80, -.15]
Satisfaction	-.50**	[-.79, -.21]
Communal	-.45**	[-.78, -.21]
Exchange	-.06	[-.32, .20]

Note: Simple linear regression. [a] Fortune had twice as many top-ranking public relations and communications executives as Wilshire. [b] CI is confidence interval. *$p < .05$; **$p < .01$; ***$p < .001$; two-tailed.

INSIGHTS

Top-ranking public relations and communications executives were significantly more positive toward their employers than other employees.

Summary

- *Post hoc* chi-square tests of independence examined differences between four variables (age group, rank, gender, and study) and the demographic and employment variables.

  - *Post hoc* chi-square tests of independence were significant between age group and time with the company and salary.

    - Older employees had been with the company longer than younger employees.
    - More older employees earned a salary of $100,000 or more.

  - *Post hoc* chi-square tests of independence were significant between being a top-ranking public relations or communications executive and supervision, reporting directly to the CEO, and earning a salary of $200,000 or more.

    - Top-ranking public relations and communications executives were more likely to supervise others.
    - Top-ranking public relations and communications executives were more likely to report directly to the CEO.
    - Top-ranking public relations and communications executives were more likely to earn a salary of $200,000 or more.

  - *Post hoc* chi-square tests of independence were significant between gender and age group and earning a salary a salary of $100,000 or more.

    - Male respondents were older than female respondents.
    - Male respondents were more likely to earn a salary of $100,000 or more.

  - *Post hoc* chi-square tests of independence were significant between study and being the top-ranking public relations or communications executive in the corporation, supervision, reporting directly to the CEO, years with the company, and earning a salary of $200,000 or more.

    - The *Fortune 1000* study had more top-ranking public relations or communications executives.
    - The *Fortune 1000* study had more supervisors.
    - The *Fortune 1000* study had more direct reports to the CEO.
    - The *Fortune 1000* study had more respondents who earned a salary $200,000 or more.

- The *Wilshire 5000* study had more long-time company employees.

- *Post hoc* chi-square tests of independence examined differences in working for an organization with an anonymous whistleblowing channel, helping develop the channel, and helping publicize the channel and the demographic and employment variables.
  - Age was the only variable significantly associated with the Sarbanes-Oxley whistleblowing channels.
  - More older employees than younger employees worked for an organization with an anonymous whistleblowing channel.

- *Post hoc* chi-square tests of independence between awareness of wrongdoing and the demographic and employment variables found no significance.
- *Post hoc* chi-square tests of independence between whistleblowing and the demographic and employment variables found no significance.
- A *post hoc* chi-square test of independence between chain-of-command and Sarbanes-Oxley channels was significant. *Hypothesis 1*, which said that public relations executives would use the chain-of-command more often than they would use Sarbanes-Oxley channels, was supported.
- A *post hoc* chi-square test of independence between external channels and Sarbanes-Oxley channels was not significant. *Hypothesis 2*, which said that public relations executives would use external channels more often than they would use Sarbanes-Oxley channels, was not supported.
- A logistic regression found that top-ranking public relations and communications executives were significantly more likely to be aware of wrongdoing than others.
- A logistic regression found that seriousness of wrongdoing predicted whistleblowing.
- The hierarchical multiple regression found that education, salary, and supervision, three elements of power, were not significant for retaliation, but four others (time in position (job tenure), performance rating female gender, and external reporting) were. *Hypothesis 3*, which predicted that power would protect from retaliation, was partially supported.
- The hierarchical multiple regression with seriousness of wrongdoing on retaliation was not significant. *Hypothesis 4*, which predicted that power would not protect if the wrongdoing was serious, was not supported.
- The hierarchical multiple regression found that reporting externally was significant for retaliation. *Hypothesis 5*, which predicted that external reporting would result in more retaliation than internal reporting, was supported.
- *Hypothesis 6*, which predicted that retaliation would be associated with greater supervisor and management lack of support, was not tested.
- Pearson correlations found that relationship quality outcomes and communal relationship type were positively correlated, and exchange and communal relationship types were negatively correlated.

- Simple regressions found that awareness of wrongdoing using three states of awareness (other aware, self-aware, and both aware) had a significant negative effect on all relationship quality outcomes and communal relationship type.
- Simple regressions using three states (other reported, self-reported, and both reported) found that whistleblowing had a significant negative effect on all relationship quality outcomes and both relationship types.
- Simple regressions found that personal experience of retaliation for whistleblowing had a significant negative effect on all relationship quality outcomes and communal relationship type. *Hypothesis 7*, which predicted that retaliation would have negative effects on relationships, was predominantly supported.
- Simple regressions found that differences in attitudes toward employers between the *Fortune 1000* study, with two-thirds of respondents in the top-ranking public relations or communications executive category, and the *Wilshire 5000* study, with one-third of respondents in the top-ranking public relations or communications executive category, were significantly negative for all relationship quality outcomes and communal relationship type.
- A one-way between-groups MANOVA on the combined study found that being the top-ranking public relations or communications executive was positively significant for relationship quality outcomes and relationship types overall.

The next chapter, Chapter 8, will discuss the implications of these findings for the Golden Handcuffs and the future of public relations.

Notes

1 Supervisory status, education (some graduate education or not, graduate degree or not), years employed (at or below mean, or above mean), years in current position (at or below mean, or above mean), reporting directly to the CEO, salary (at or above $100,000, and at or above $200,000), and performance rating (at or above "fully successful" and at or above "exceeds fully successful," or "exemplary").
2 A chi-square test of independence was conducted between age group (at or below the mean of 48 years or above 48 years) and years with the company (at or below the mean of 11.5 years or more than 11.5 years). All expected cell frequencies were greater than five. There was a statistically significant association between age group and years with the company, $\chi^2 (1, 112) = 8.41$, $p = .004$. There was a small positive association between age group and years with the company, $\varphi = .27$, $p = .004$. Thirty-two (71.1 5%) of respondents who had been with the company more than 11.5 years were from the older age group, which was 52.5% of the older age group.
3 A chi-square test of independence was conducted between age group (at or below the mean of 48 years or above 48 years) and earning a salary of $100,000 or more. All expected cell frequencies were greater than five. There was a statistically significant association between age group and earning a salary of $100,000 or more, $\chi^2(1, 119) = 7.17$, $p = .007$. There was a small positive association between age group and earning a salary of $100,000 or more, $\varphi = .25$, $p = .007$.

4 A chi-square test of independence was conducted between being a top-ranking public relations or communications executive and supervising others. All expected cell frequencies were greater than five. There was a statistically significant association between being a top-ranking public relations or communications executive and supervising others, $\chi^2(1, 139) = 19.25$, $p < .001$. There was a moderate positive association between being a top-ranking public relations or communications executive and supervising others, $\varphi = .37$, $p < .001$. Forty-four (51.8%) of those who supervised others were top-ranking public relations or communications executives, which was 84.6% of top-ranking public relations or communications executives.

5 A chi-square test of independence was conducted between being a top-ranking public relations or communications executive and reporting directly to the CEO. One expected cell frequency was less than five. There was a statistically significant association between being a top-ranking public relations or communications executive and reporting directly to the CEO, $\chi^2(1, 140) = 12.89$, $p < .001$. There was a moderate positive association between being a top-ranking public relations or communications executive and reporting directly to the CEO, $\varphi = .30$, $p < .001$. Nine (90%) of those reporting directly to the CEO were top-ranking public relations or communications executives, which was 17.3% of top-ranking public relations or communications executives.

6 A chi-square test of independence was conducted between being a top-ranking public relations or communications executive and earning a salary of $200,000 or more. All expected cell frequencies were greater than five. There was a statistically significant association between being a top-ranking public relations or communications executive and earning $200,000 or more, $\chi^2(1, 132) = 24.04$, $p < .001$. There was a moderate positive association between being a top-ranking public relations or communications executive and earning a salary of $200,000 or more, $\varphi = .43$, $p < .001$. Twenty-one (77.8 %) of those who earned $200,000 or more were top-ranking public relations or communications executives, which was 42.9% of top-ranking public relations or communications executives.

7 A chi-square test of independence was conducted between gender and age group (at or below the mean of 48 years or above 48 years). All expected cell frequencies were greater than five. There was a statistically significant association between gender and age group, $\chi^2(1, 122) = 4.29$, $p = .038$. There was a small negative association between gender and age group, $\varphi = -.19$, $p = .038$. Forty-three (63.2%) of those in the older age group were males, which was 64.2% of males.

8 A chi-square test of independence was conducted between gender and earning a salary of $100,000 or more. All expected cell frequencies were greater than five. There was a statistically significant association between gender and earning $100,000 or more, $\chi^2(1, 32) = 4.63$, $p = .031$. There was a small negative association between gender and earning a salary of $100,000 or more, $\varphi = -.19$, $p = .031$. Sixty (62.5%) of those earning $100,000 or more were males, which was 80.0% of males.

9 A chi-square test of independence was conducted between study and being the top-ranking public relations or communications executive in the corporation. All expected cell frequencies were greater than five. There was a statistically significant association between study and being the top-ranking public relations or communications executive in the corporation, $\chi^2(1, 140) = 29.45$, $p < .001$. There was a moderate negative association between study and being the top-ranking public relations or communications executive in the corporation, $\varphi = -.46$, $p < .001$. Thirty-six (69.2%) of top-ranking public relations or communications executives were identified in the *Fortune 1000* study, which was 64.3% of those in the *Fortune 1000* study.

10 A chi-square test of independence was conducted between study and supervising others. All expected cell frequencies were greater than five. There was a statistically significant association between study and supervising others, $\chi^2(1, 139) = 11.98$, $p = .001$. There was a moderate negative association between study and supervising others, $\varphi = -.29$,

$p = .001$. Forty-four (51.8%) of those who supervised others were identified in the *Fortune 1000* study, which was 78.6% of those in the *Fortune 1000* study.

11 A chi-square test of independence was conducted between study and reporting directly to the CEO. One expected cell frequency was less than five. There was a statistically significant association between study and reporting directly to the CEO, $\chi^2(1, 140) = 16.15$, $p < .001$. There was a moderate negative association between study and reporting directly to the CEO, $\varphi = .34$, $p < .001$. The 10 (100.0%) respondents who reported directly to the CEO were identified in the *Fortune 1000* study, which was 17.9% of those in the *Fortune 1000* study.

12 A chi-square test of independence was conducted between study and years employed by the company (11.5 years or less or more than 11.5 years). All expected cell frequencies were greater than five. There was a statistically significant association between study and years employed by the company, $\chi^2(1, 128) = 4.13$, $p = .042$. There was a small positive association between study and years employed by the company, $\varphi = .18$, $p = .042$. Thirty-seven (67.3%) of the respondents who had been employed by their company more than 11.5 years were identified in the *Wilshire 5000* study, which was 50.7% of those in the *Wilshire 5000* study.

13 A chi-square test of independence was conducted between study and earning $200,000 or more. All expected cell frequencies were greater than five. There was a statistically significant association between study and earning $200,000 or more, $\chi^2(1, 132) = 12.90$, $p < .001$. There was a moderate negative association between study and earning $200,000 or more, $\varphi = -.31$, $p < .001$. Nineteen (70.4%) of the respondents who earned $200,000 or more were identified in the *Fortune 1000* study, which was 35.8% of those in the *Fortune 1000* study.

14 One invitee declined to take the survey because he could not answer that question, and another declined because the organization's Sarbanes-Oxley channel did not go directly to the audit committee of the board of directors. Disagreement about how the Sarbanes-Oxley anonymous communication channel should be implemented and under what organizational structure is evident in the literature (Moberly, 2006).

15 Age group (at or below mean, or above mean), rank, gender, study (*Fortune 1000* and *Wilshire 5000*), supervisory status, education (some graduate education or not, graduate degree or not), years employed (at or below mean, or above mean), years in current position (at or below mean, or above mean), reporting directly to the CEO, salary (at or above $100,000, and at or above $200,000), and performance rating (at or above "fully successful" and at or above "exceeds fully successful," or "exemplary").

16 There was a moderate negative association between age group and working in an organization with an anonymous whistleblowing channel, $\varphi = -.31$, $p = .019$.

17 A chi-square test of independence was conducted between rank and working for an organization with an anonymous whistleblowing channel. One cell had an expected count less than five. There was not a statistically significant association between rank and working for an organization with an anonymous whistleblowing channel, $\chi^2(1, 69) = .117$, $p = .732$. A chi-square test of independence was conducted between rank and helping develop the anonymous whistleblowing channel. Two cells had an expected count less than five. There was not a statistically significant association between rank and helping develop the anonymous whistleblowing channel, $\chi^2(1, 73) = .612$, $p = .434$. A chi-square test of independence was conducted between rank and helping publicize the anonymous whistleblowing channel. All expected cell frequencies were greater than five. There was not a statistically significant association between rank and publicizing the anonymous whistleblowing channel, $\chi^2(1, 61) = .485$, $p = .486$.

18 This was the number (35) of respondents who were aware of wrongdoing divided by the total number of respondents to the question (167).

19 Awareness of wrongdoing was not significant for age, $\chi^2(1, 122) = .178$, $p = .673$, rank, $\chi^2(1, 140) = .765$, $p = .382$, gender, $\chi^2(1, 139) = .416$, $p = .519$, study, $\chi^2(1, 167) = .022$, $p = .883$, supervision, $\chi^2(1, 139) = 1.528$, $p = .216$, education (some graduate), $\chi^2(1,$

100) = .182, p = .670, education (graduate degree), $\chi^2(1, 100)$ = 1.072, p = .300, years employed, $\chi^2(1,128)$ = .018, p = .894, years in position, $\chi^2(1, 130)$ = .099, p = .753, reporting directly to the CEO, $\chi^2(1, 140)$ = .312, p = .577, salary at or above \$100,000, $\chi^2(1, 132)$ = 1.035, p = .309, salary at or above \$200,000, $\chi^2(1, 132)$ = .198, p = .657, performance rating at or above "Fully Successful," $\chi^2(1, 138)$ = .008, p = .931, or performance rating at or above "Beyond Fully Successful," (exemplary), $\chi^2(1, 138)$ = .201, p = .654.

20 This was the number (18) of respondents who blew the whistle divided by the number (35) of respondents who were aware of wrongdoing in their own organization.

21 This was the number (15) of identified whistleblower divided by the number (24) who responded to this question.

22 This was the number (3) of respondents who reported that blowing the whistle was a part of his or her job divided by the number (18) of respondents who blew the whistle.

23 This was the number (10) of identified whistleblowers who reported lack of support and/or retaliation divided by the number (22) of respondents to this question.

24 "I was rewarded;" "Nothing happened to me"; "My co-workers were unhappy with me;" "My supervisor was unhappy with me"; "Someone above my supervisor was unhappy with me"; and "I experienced retaliation."

25 "[M]ultiple regression . . . is a technique to assess the impact of a set of predictors on a dependent variable. . . . For multiple regression your dependent variable . . . needs to be a continuous variable. . . . Logistic regression allows you to test models to predict categorical outcomes with two or more categories. Your predictor (independent) variables can be either categorical or continuous, or a mix of both in the one model. . . . If your dependent variable has more than two categories, you will need to use the Multinomial Logistic set of procedures" (Pallant, 2005, p. 160). "When the problem involves a single independent variable, the statistical technique is called simple regression" (Hair et al., 1998, p. 149).

26 A logistic regression assessed the effects of seven variables (age, gender, education, rank, reporting relationship to the CEO, supervision, and last performance rating) on the likelihood that respondents were aware of wrongdoing in their own organizations. After assessing the linearity of the continuous variable (age) with respect to the logit of the dependent variable using the Box-Tidwell (1962) procedure, age was found to be linearly related to the logit of the dependent variable, awareness of wrongdoing. After removing two standardized residuals with values greater than 2.500 standard deviations from the model, the logistic regression model was statistically significant, $\chi^2(7)$=16.305, p=.022. It explained 21.0% (Nagelkerke R^2) of the variance in awareness and correctly classified 82.1% of cases. Sensitivity was 18.2%; specificity was 96.8%; positive predictive value was 66.9%; and negative predictive value was 97.9% (Laerd Statistics, 2017). Of the seven predictor variables, only rank was positively significantly associated with awareness of wrongdoing (z = 5.615, p = .018).

27 A test of the full model using seriousness of wrongdoing against a constant-only model was statistically reliable ($\chi^2(1, N = 32)$ = 5.301, p = .021). This indicated that seriousness of wrongdoing distinguished between those who blew the whistle and those who did not, and the Hosmer and Lemeshow test, ($\chi^2(1, N = 32)$ = .689, p = .406), was non-significant, as required. The model summary showed seriousness of wrongdoing explained 20.4 % (Nagelkerke R Square) of variability and correctly classified 65.6 % of cases (Laerd Statistics, 2020). In the model, seriousness of wrongdoing significantly positively predicted whistleblowing (z = 4.405, p = .036) and had 4.124 higher odds of being associated with whistleblowing than less serious wrongdoing.

28 Research Question 7 has been answered before Research Question 6 due to the length of Research Question 6 findings.

29 Awareness of wrongdoing also explained a significant proportion of variance in trust scores, R^2 = .09, $F(3, 133)$ = 4.13, p = .008.

30 Awareness of wrongdoing also explained a significant proportion of variance in control mutuality scores, $R^2 = .13$, $F(3, 132) = 6.71$, $p < .001$.
31 Awareness of wrongdoing also explained a significant proportion of variance in commitment scores, $R^2 = .09$, $F(3, 132) = 4.34$, $p = .006$.
32 Awareness of wrongdoing also explained a significant proportion of variance in satisfaction scores, $R^2 = .09$, $F(3, 134) = 4.41$, $p = .005$.
33 Awareness of wrongdoing also explained a significant proportion of variance in communal relationship scores, $R^2 = .12$, $F(3, 131) = 6.21$, $p < = .001$.
34 Whistleblowing also explained a significant proportion of variance in trust scores, $R^2 = .30$, $F(5,63) = 5.48$, $p < .001$.
35 Whistleblowing also explained a significant proportion of variance in control mutuality scores, $R^2 = .30$, $F(5, 61) = 5.20$, $p < .001$.
36 Whistleblowing also explained a significant proportion of variance in commitment scores, $R^2 = .30$, $F(5, 62) = 5.22$, $p < .001$.
37 Whistleblowing also explained a significant proportion of variance in satisfaction scores, $R^2 = .32$, $F(5, 62) = 5.90$, $p < .001$.
38 Whistleblowing also explained a significant proportion of variance in communal relationship scores, $R^2 = .31$, $F(5,60) = 5.44$, $p < .001$.
39 Whistleblowing had no effect on variance in exchange relationship type scores, $R^2 = .10$, $F(5, 63) = 1.40$, $p = .237$.
40 Retaliation also explained a significant proportion of variance in trust scores, $R^2 = .32$, $F(1, 18) = 8.43$, $p = .009$.
41 Retaliation also explained a significant proportion of variance in control mutuality scores, $R^2 = .34$, $F(1, 18) = 9.42$, $p = .007$.
42 Retaliation also explained a significant proportion of variance in commitment scores, $R^2 = .27$, $F(1, 16) = 5.90$, $p = .028$.
43 Retaliation also explained a significant proportion of variance in satisfaction scores, $R^2 = .36$, $F(1, 18) = 10.25$, $p = .005$.
44 Retaliation also explained a significant proportion of variance in communal scores, $R^2 = .28$, $F(1, 18) = 7.08$, $p = .016$.
45 A one-way between-groups multivariate analysis of variance was conducted to investigate rank differences in relationships with organizations. This used the six dependent variables were taken from the Hon and Grunig (1999) scales: trust, control mutuality, commitment, satisfaction, communal relationship type, and exchange relationship type. The independent variable was rank (being the top-ranking public relations or communications executive in an organization, or not). Preliminary assumption testing was conducted to check for normality, linearity, univariate and multivariate outliners, homogeneity of variance-covariance matrices, and multicollinearity, with no serious violations noted other than the multicollinearity found among several of the relationship scales (see Table 7.6) (Pallant, 2005, pp. 247–262). There was a statistically significant difference between ranking and non-ranking respondents, $F(6, 118) = 3.17$, $p = .006$; Wilks' lambda = .86; partial eta squared = .14. When the results for the dependent variables were considered separately, the only difference to reach statistical significance, using a Bonferroni adjusted alpha level of .008, was control mutuality, $F(1, 123) = 13.62$, $p = .006$, partial eta squared = .10.

References

Gallicano, T. D., Curtin, P., & Matthews, K. (2012). I Love What I Do, But…A Relationship Management Survey of Millennial Generation Public Relations Agency Employees. *Journal of Public Relations Research, 24*(3), 222–242. Retrieved from https://doi.org/10.1080/1062726X.2012.671986

Greenwood, C. A. (2015). Whistleblowing in the *Fortune 1000*: What practitioners told us about wrongdoing in corporations in a pilot study. *Public Relations Review*, (41), 490–500. Retrieved from https://doi.org/10.1016/j.pubrev.2015.07.005

Hair, J. F., Jr., Anderson, R. E., Tatham, R. L., & Black, W. C. (1998). *Multivariate data analysis* (5th ed.). Upper Saddle River, N. J.: Prentice Hall.

Hon, L. C., & Grunig, J. E. (1999). *Guidelines for measuring relationships in public relations* (p. 40). Retrieved from http://painepublishing.com/wp-content/uploads/2013/10/Guidelines_Measuring_Relationships.pdf

infrrr. (2020). *Difference in proportions hypothesis test calculator*. Retrieved from https://infrrr.com/proportions/difference-in-proportions-hypothesis-test-calculator

Laerd Statistics. (2017). *Binomial logistic regression using SPSS Statistics*. Statistical Tutorials and Software Guide. Retrieved from https://statistics.laerd.com/

Laerd Statistics. (2020). *Binomial logistic regression using SPSS Statistics*. Retrieved from https://statistics.laerd.com/premium/spss/blr/binomial-logistic-regression-in-spss.php

Merit Systems Protection Board. (1981). *Whistleblowing and the Federal Employee: Blowing the whistle on fraud, waste, and mismanagement—who does it and what happens*. Washington, DC: MSPB

Merit Systems Protection Board. (1984). *Blowing the Whistle in the Federal Government: A Comparative Analysis of 1980 and 1983 Survey Findings*. Washington, DC: MSPB.

Merit Systems Protection Board. (1993). *Whistleblowing in the Federal Government: An Update*. Washington, DC: MSPB.

Miceli, M. P., Rehg, M. T., Near, J. P., & Ryan, K. C. (1999). Can laws protect whistleblowers? Results of a naturally occurring field experiment. *Work and Occupations, 26*(1), 129–151. https://doi.org/10.1177/0730888499026001007

Moberly, R. E. (2006). Sarbanes-Oxley's structural model to encourage corporate whistleblowers. *Brigham Young Law Review, 2006*(5), 1107–1180.

Pallant, J. (2005). *SPSS survival manual* (2nd ed.). Chicago: Open University Press.

Rehg, M. T., Miceli, M. P., Near, J. P., & Van Scotter, J. R. (2008). Antecedents and outcomes of retaliation against whistleblowers: Gender differences and power relationships. *Organization Science, 19*(2), 221–240.

Shen, H., & Jiang, H. (2019). Engaged at work? An employee engagement model in public relations. *Journal of Public Relations Research, 31*(1–2), 32–49. https://doi.org/10.1080/1062726X.2019.1585855

Tabachnick, B. G., & Fidell, L. S. (2007). *Using multivariate statistics* (5th ed.). Boston, MA: Pearson.

8 Whistleblowing in public relations

Discussion

Response rate

Response rate was low

The response rate was the most significant limitation of *this study*. The response rate for the first survey (the *Fortune 1000*) was low (3.5%), but it was comparable to the rate (4.02%) reported by (Kang & Berger, 2010) in their random sample survey of the membership of the Public Relations Society of America, and it was within the anticipated 1–30% response rate for Internet surveys (Wimmer & Dominick, 2006). Expanding the population to communications executives and practitioners by way of an approximation of the *Wilshire 5000* might have increased the response rate to a respectable level. That did not happen, and the response rate for that survey was also low (.0043%). The response rate for *this study* (the combined surveys) was .006%. Despite the low response rate, the data provided a window into a rarely studied subset of public relations and communications executives: those who work for the largest corporations in the United States. The expanded window into that population could suggest trends and areas of interest for future research.

Respondents

Respondents represented target population

One-third of respondents in *this study* were the top-ranking public relations or communication executives in their organizations, which was the target population for the study. The demographic characteristics of the sample suggest it was representative of the target population, which was older, better educated, and higher-ranking white males (Berger, 2005; L. A. Grunig, Grunig, & Dozier, 2002; Near & Miceli, 1996). Comparing the demographic characteristics of the sample and the previously identified characteristics of the target population is an accepted method of addressing nonresponse error, which occurs when

DOI: 10.4324/9781315231891-9

respondents and nonrespondents differ (Dooley & Lindner, 2003). These findings confirm expectations that top-ranking public relations or communication executives were members of, or at least reported to, the dominant coalition (Aldrich & Herker, 1977; Aldrich & Ruef, 2006; Grunig, 1992; Grunig et al., 2002; J. White & Dozier, 1992).

Third-party questions introduced topic

Including questions about third-party knowledge of wrongdoing, whistleblowing, and retaliation allowed the respondent to consider the topic of whistleblowing in a less threatening manner before considering his or own personal knowledge of those topics. Although that aspect of the survey was criticized as introducing priming in a review of the federal studies (Rehg, 1998), the questionnaire followed the federal surveys against which *this study* was viewed. In addition, unlike a previously published article about whistleblowing in the *Fortune 1000* (Greenwood, 2015), the third-party responses in *this study* were used only to answer the questions about the impact of knowledge of wrongdoing, whistleblowing, and retaliation on relationship quality outcomes and relationship types, and then only to augment the small response for retaliation.

Open-ended responses provided context

Several respondents took advantage of the three open-ended questions (see Appendix A) to offer comments, including comments about the ethical values of their companies (see Appendix C). One commented, "By and large, ethical behavior rules. I have not witnessed any unethical actions." Another said, "We have signs posted in our buildings to make sure that team members understand how importanat [*sic*] of an issue ethics is." A third said, "Ethics and ethical behavior is a core value of our company. All employees are educated to report ethical violations immediately, either to their supervisors or to the compliance officer for their business unit." A fourth said, "I've worked in PR for 41 years for two Fortune 500 companies. Both had very ethical management." And a fifth said, "We have annual Code of Conduct training – all employees must participate".

> *Research Question 1:* Have public relations executives helped develop and/
> or publicize Sarbanes-Oxley whistleblowing channels?

Sarbanes-Oxley whistleblowing channels

AGE DETERMINED WHO WORKED FOR AN ORGANIZATION WITH A
SARBANES-OXLEY CHANNEL

This study was the first to attempt to identify who among public relations and communications executives worked in an organization with an internal, anonymous, Sarbanes-Oxley-mandated whistleblowing channel [*Sarbanes-Oxley Act of 2002*, 15 U.S.C. § 7201 nt (2002)] that allowed employees to report corporate financial wrongdoing directly to outside directors who sit on the audit committees of those boards, who had responsibility for the channel's development, and who had responsibility for publicizing it to employees. The results of *this study* showed that the only demographic or employment variable that was significant for determining any of these responsibilities was age: Older employees were significantly more likely than younger employees to work for such an organization. *This study* also found that older employees were significantly more likely to have worked for the company longer and to have achieved a higher salary level than younger employees. They also may have been in their positions longer and may have been more likely to earn $200,000 or more. Given that years with the company, time in position, and salary are among the power indicators in *this study*, their significance here may be that, as Cheney and Christensen (2001) discovered, longer-term employees identified more with the organization than shorter-term employees, and, as *this study* found, their higher standing in the organization may have placed them in a more likely position to be aware of the Sarbanes-Oxley whistleblowing channel.

Research Question 2: Have public relations executives blown the whistle?

Corporate-level variables

INCIDENCE (AWARENESS) OF WRONGDOING

Incidence of wrongdoing (21%) in the 2010/2012 Greenwood corporate survey was significantly lower than in the 1980 federal survey (45%) and significantly higher than in the 1992 federal survey (14%), but it was comparable to the awareness of wrongdoing (22%) in the *Fortune 1000* study (Greenwood, 2015). Management researchers proposed that the decline in the federal incidence of wrongdoing from 1980 to 1992 was due to the major reorganization of the federal civil service under the CSRA (Miceli, M. P., Rehg, M. T., Near, J. P., & Ryan, K. C., 1999), which specifically encouraged federal employees to report wrongdoing [*Civil Service Reform Act of 1978*, 5 U.S.C. § 1101 (1978)]. The level of wrongdoing in the federal government's 2010 survey (11%) was more than one-third less than that in 1992 (18%) (Merit Systems Protection Board, 2011a). The corollary argument involving the passage of the Public Company Accounting Reform and Investor Protection Act of 2002 (Sarbanes-Oxley) and the Dodd-Frank Wall Street Reform and Consumer Protection Act of 2010 [*Dodd-Frank Act of 2010*, 12 U.S.C. § 5301 (2010)] for corporate whistleblowers did not explain the low level of incidence of wrongdoing in the 2010/2012 Greenwood corporate study compared with three more recent business surveys. The 2009 PriceWaterhouseCoopers Global Economic Crime Survey found corporate fraud (i.e., wrongdoing) at 30%

(PriceWaterhouseCoopers, 2009), while two more recent surveys found it at 47% nationally (Ethics & Compliance Initiative, 2018), and at 45% worldwide (Ethics & Compliance Initiative, 2019).

The differences in survey results between the various studies could be, in part, the result of differences in the populations surveyed: The 2009 PriceWaterhouseCoopers survey used a global population (PriceWaterhouseCoopers, 2009); the 2018 Ethics & Compliance Initiative survey was directed nationally at 18-year-olds and older who worked at least half time for a company with at least two employees (Ethics & Compliance Initiative, 2018); and the 2019 Ethics & Compliance Initiative survey (Ethics & Compliance Initiative, 2019) did not report respondent characteristics. The federal surveys were administered across employment levels and agencies, while the 2010/2012 Greenwood corporate survey was directed at the top-ranking public relations and communications executives in the largest U.S. corporations. Respondents may have been more willing to respond honestly to a survey from a recognized business source than to a survey from an unknown academic; public relations and communications executives may not have been comfortable answering questions about whistleblowing, especially at work; and it is also possible that wrongdoing increased in the interval between the 2010/2012 Greenwood corporate survey and the 2018 and 2019 Ethics & Compliance Initiative surveys. However, the latter supposition is contradicted by the finding "that observed wrongdoing in the U.S. had decreased 8% since the last survey in 2013" (Ethics & Compliance Initiative, 2018).

INCIDENCE OF WHISTLEBLOWING

Incidence of whistleblowing in the 2010/2012 Greenwood corporate survey (51.4%) was significantly higher than in the 1980 federal survey (26%). However, it did not differ significantly from 1983 (40%), 1992 (48%), or 2010 (40%) (Merit Systems Protection Board, 2011a). Whistleblowing in these federal reports and the 2010/2012 Greenwood corporate study was lower than the 2018 Ethics and Compliance survey, which found whistleblowing nationwide at 69% among those who were aware of wrongdoing (Ethics & Compliance Initiative, 2018). As noted under incidence of wrongdoing, the difference between that finding and the 2010/2012 Greenwood corporate study finding could be the inclusion in the 2018 Ethics and Compliance survey of younger and lower ranking employees. Although by no means a given, this finding suggests that the laws that protect corporate whistleblowers (i.e., Sarbanes-Oxley and Dodd-Frank) may have reduced wrongdoing and increased whistleblowing.

INCIDENCE OF IDENTIFIED WHISTLEBLOWING

The incidence of identified whistleblowing in the 2010/2012 Greenwood corporate survey (63%) was not significantly different from the 1980 (74%), 1983 (60%), or 1992 (55%) federal studies, but it was higher than the 2010 MSPB survey (43%). The MSPB reported the drop in identified whistleblowing from

1992 to 2010 was a positive trend because "the ability of whistleblowers to protect their identity is important to them" (Merit Systems Protection Board, 2011a, p. 9). The fact that significantly more public relations and communications executives in *this study* chose to use the internal chain-of-command (a process designed to ensure identified whistleblowing) than the internal Sarbanes-Oxley anonymous whistleblowing channel may speak to the trust that population puts in its upper-level management, the efficacy of corporate legislation to protect whistleblowers, or the influence of the culture and training of public relations and communications executives.

> *Research Question 3:* Do public relations executives think it is their job to blow the whistle?

INCIDENCE OF ROLE-PRESCRIBED WHISTLEBLOWING

The almost total (more than 90%) rejection of the concept of role-prescribed whistleblowing in *this study* raised questions about how public relations and communications executives view their roles as advisers and counselors to management with regard to whistleblowing. Perhaps public relations and communications executives view reporting wrongdoing as an external activity and not something that occurs internally through the chain-of-command. Perhaps public relations and communications executives do not view reporting wrongdoing as part of their jobs because management does not direct them to do so. It also could be that public relations and communications executives do not operate with a knowledge of the broader definition of whistleblowing used in *this study*. Two responses to open-ended questions supported that supposition: "Involvement of PR people was BECAUSE of their role, not as the person observing or reporting" (see Appendix C.1.11), and "[R]emember, in this position we are involved in addressing and/or managing almost every incident of this nature" (see Appendix C.2.6).

> *Research Question 4:* What channels have public relations executives used to blow the whistle?

Respondents to *this study* blew the whistle almost exclusively through internal channels, both chain-of-command and the internal Sarbanes-Oxley anonymous whistleblowing channel. They used internal chain-of-command significantly more often than they used the internal Sarbanes-Oxley anonymous whistleblowing channel (which supported *Hypothesis 1*), but they used the internal Sarbanes-Oxley anonymous whistleblowing channel significantly more often than they reported externally (which did not support *Hypothesis 2*). The rationale for proposing that was the assumption they would trust an agency or Congress more than a new reporting channel and the finding that whistleblowers preferred external channels when the organization depended on the wrongdoing and when retaliation was likely (Mesmer-Magnus & Viswesvaran,

2005, p. 281; Miceli & Near, 1985). That prediction was not supported by the results from this survey. However, this proclivity to report internally should be revisited now that the recent U.S. Supreme Court ruling in *Digital Realty Trust, Inc. v. Somers* [583 U. S.___ (2018)] directs Dodd-Frank whistleblowers to take their cases externally to the SEC or lose their whistleblower protection under the law.

INCIDENCE OF RETALIATION

Incidence of retaliation in the 2010/2012 Greenwood corporate study (45%) was significantly higher than in the 1980 (17%) and 1983 (21%) federal surveys; however, it was comparable to the 1992 (38%) and 2010 (37%) federal studies (Merit Systems Protection Board, 2011a). The increase in retaliation in the 1992 federal study over the 1980 and 1983 federal studies was concerning to researchers because it was associated with an increase in anonymous whistle-blowing (Miceli et al., 1999). Corporate studies with larger populations than *this study* found similar retaliation results to the 2010/2012 Greenwood corpo-rate study. Nationally, corporate retaliation increased from 22% in 2013 to 44% in 2017 (Ethics & Compliance Initiative, 2018), but whistleblowing did not increase by that much. "While in past years of this research . . . reporting and retaliation rise and fall together . . . in 2017, retaliation rose significantly higher than reporting – a 100% increase as opposed to a 7% increase" (Ethics & Com-pliance Initiative, 2018, p. 9). The reasons offered for the increase in retaliation were the increase in pressure to compromise ethics as the stock market rose and a persistent lack of growth in the number of business organizations that demonstrated an ethical culture (Ethics & Compliance Initiative, 2018). The increase in retaliation may well account for the small number of respondents who admitted they were aware of wrongdoing (35), even though half (18) of those blew the whistle.

Individual-level variables

SERIOUSNESS OF WRONGDOING

Both *this study* and the most recent fraud report show that serious wrongdo-ing continues to exist in large U.S. corporations despite Sarbanes-Oxley's and Dodd-Frank's provisions to prevent fraud and encourage whistleblow-ing. In *this study*, 49% of incidents of wrongdoing were somewhat serious (involving $1,000–$100,000 or occurring occasionally), and 42% were most serious (involving more than $100,000 or occurring frequently). Concur-rently, PriceWaterhouseCoopers found that 27% of global fraud was valued at more than $500,000 (PriceWaterhouseCoopers, 2009); a more recent crime report found 53% of U.S. companies had experienced fraud; and 37% reported fraud at $1 million or more (PriceWaterhouseCoopers, 2018). The recent Supreme Court ruling [*Digital Realty Trust, Inc. v. Somers*, 583

U. S.___ (2018)] that removes whistleblower protections from those who do not report externally to the SEC and attempts by Congress to remove restrictions on small and medium-sized banks that were imposed as part of Dodd-Frank to prevent another financial crisis (Rappeport & Flitter, 2018) do not bode well for improving the corporate fraud climate. However, one positive sign was the SEC's recent decision to allow whistleblower protections to those who report internally as long as they report to the SEC before they experienced retaliation (Securities and Exchange Commission, 2020a).

LACK OF SUPPORT

Lack of support was not tested.

RETALIATION

In *this study*, the percentage of retaliation among identified whistleblowers was almost half (46%), but the number of those retaliated against was small (10). Of the 22 who responded, none were rewarded, and 12 experienced nothing. The remaining ten reported four incidents of lack of co-worker support, six incidents of lack of supervisor support, five incidents of lack of upper management support, and seven incidents of retaliation. Retaliation in the corporate studies looked at six types of wrongdoing and the percentage of respondents who experienced retaliation for reporting each. The latest report said 46% of those who reported sexual harassment were retaliated against; 44% of those who reported corruption were retaliated against; 43% of those who reported discrimination were retaliated against; 36% of those who reported conflicts of interest were retaliated against; 34% of those who reported abusive behaviors were retaliated against; and 30% of those who reported violations of health and/or safety regulations were retaliated against. "Retaliation comes in many forms, ranging from a decrease in work hours, providing unfavorable work assignment(s), and co-worker avoidance. Whether perception or reality, it is pertinent that an organization investigate all employee reports of retaliation" (Ethics & Compliance Initiative, 2019, p. 7).

Predictors of awareness of wrongdoing, whistleblowing, and retaliation

Predictors of awareness of wrongdoing: rank

"To report wrongdoing, respondents must first be aware of it" (Greenwood, 2015, p. 497). In that study, a logistic regression using first-person and third-person awareness of wrongdoing to compensate for a small sample found that gender (male) and rank predicted awareness of wrongdoing: "In other words, male, top-ranking public relations executives were more likely than other public relations executives to be aware of wrongdoing" (Greenwood, 2011, p. 128). In *this study*, however, a logistic regression with first-person awareness found that rank was the only variable that predicted awareness of wrongdoing. Top-ranking public relations or communications executives were significantly more likely to be aware of wrongdoing in their own organizations than other employees, which indicates a perk of rank that perhaps allows a heightened level of cheater detection. "[I]n my position, I am involved in responding to and addressing most significant incidents in this regard" (see Appendix C.2.6).

Predictors of whistleblowing: seriousness of wrongdoing

In prior research, numerous variables were associated with intent to blow the whistle (e.g., age, job level, ethical judgment, role responsibility, and approval of whistleblowing), while actual whistleblowing was associated with job level, sex, time in position, job satisfaction, and job performance (Mesmer-Magnus & Viswesvaran, 2005); lower pay, higher education, lower job performance, and minority race (Miceli et al., 1999); higher rank (Keenan, 2002; Merit Systems Protection Board, 1981); age (50–59), and gender (males) (Merit Systems Protection Board, 1984). Seriousness of wrongdoing (dollar amount and frequency) was associated with whistleblowing in the 1983 federal survey (Miceli et al., 1999) and in the meta-analysis (Mesmer-Magnus & Viswes-varan, 2005). In *this study*, seriousness of wrongdoing was the only variable that predicted whistleblowing. This finding supports the supposition that in the face of reciprocity among employees (what *this study* calls reciprocal altruism), "Wrongdoing that harms the organization and/or co-workers is more likely to be reported (especially using internal channels)" (Mesmer-Magnus & Viswes-varan, 2005, p. 281).

Predictors of retaliation: job tenure, performance, gender, and external reporting

In *this study*, a hierarchical multiple regression using the predictor variables from Miceli and Near (Miceli et al., 1999), plus additional variables unique to *this study* (supervisory job, reporting relationship to the CEO, rank, and years with company), found that time in position (job tenure), performance rating, female gender, and external reporting positively predicted retaliation. Of those, female gender and external reporting were also predictors of retaliation in one or more of the three federal studies (Miceli et al., 1999). Education, salary, and supervision were not significant for retaliation and may have offered protection from retaliation, and of the three, only salary was a predictor of retaliation in one or more of the three federal studies (Miceli et al., 1999). As a result, *Hypothesis 3*, which predicted that power would protect from retaliation, was only partially supported. Because some variables do appear to offer protection from retaliation, this raises questions about which variables actually represent power attributes.

The meta-analysis found that age (being older), value congruence, seriousness of wrongdoing, and use of an external channel were positively associated with retaliation, and supervisor support was negatively associated (Mesmer-Magnus & Viswesvaran, 2005). In *this study*, among those three variables only the use of an external channel was a predictor of retaliation. Reporting serious wrongdoing had no effect on retaliation, and it did not remove the protection from retaliation of education, salary, and supervision. *Hypothesis 4*, which predicted that power would not protect from retaliation if the wrongdoing was serious, was not supported. Power in the form of education, salary, and supervision did appear to protect from retaliation in the face of reporting serious wrongdoing, which raises questions about the role of those variables with regard to kin selection, cooperation, and reciprocity.

This study validated prior studies (Mesmer-Magnus & Viswesvaran, 2005; Miceli et al., 1999) that found the use of external channels predicted more retaliation than internal reporting. In *this study*, also, those who reported externally reported significantly more retaliation than those who did not. *Hypothesis 5*, which predicted that external reporting would result in more retaliation than internal reporting, was supported. In this situation, external reporting could be viewed as cheater detection that results in potential harm to the group (i.e., a violation of group norms) and, therefore, justifies retaliation. More research would be needed to identify what observations in biology might reflect this effect of perceived harm to the group resulting in retaliation against the individual by the group.

Prior analyses found management and supervisor lack of support significant for retaliation in various federal studies (Miceli et al., 1999). Supervisor lack of support alone was significant for retaliation in the meta-analysis of 26 datasets (Mesmer-Magnus & Viswesvaran, 2005). In *this study*, co-worker lack of support, supervisor lack of support, and management lack of support were significant in the hierarchical multiple regression, but only co-worker and supervisor lack of support were significant. However, that significance must be attributed to their inclusion in the retaliation scale. Therefore, *Hypothesis 6*, which predicted that retaliation would be associated with greater supervisor and management lack of support, was not tested.

> *Research Question 7*[1]: Do female public relations executives who blow the whistle experience more retaliation than male public relations executives?

As noted, in prior studies the effect of gender on retaliation typically was found only with large samples (Rehg, Miceli, Near, & Van Scotter, 2008). Gender was a predictor of whistleblowing but not a predictor of retaliation in the meta-analysis (Mesmer-Magnus & Viswesvaran, 2005). However, in the analysis of the three federal studies (Miceli et al., 1999) and in *this study*, hierarchical multiple regression found gender (coded for female) significant for retaliation. Female public relations and communications executives experienced more retaliation than male public relations and communications executives. These results indicate that female gender is not a power variable.

> *Research Question 6*: In what ways has retaliation for whistleblowing affected their relationships with their corporate employers?

Awareness of wrongdoing had a significant negative effect on the four relationship quality outcomes and communal relationship type but not on exchange relationship type. Whistleblowing had a significant negative effect on the four relationship quality outcomes and both relationship types. Retaliation had a significant negative effect on the four relationship quality outcomes and communal relationship type but not on exchange relationship type. Rank also influenced relationships positively. Top-ranking public relations and communications executives were significantly more positive toward their employers than other employees were.

What the future holds

Whistleblowers as defense against fraud

Given the crisis in the U.S. housing and financial industries in late 2008 and the worldwide economic crisis that created (Yeoh, 2013), the role of employees as the first line of defense in preventing financial and other types of fraud could be crucial. Both the federal government and Congress apparently believed that to be the case and encouraged whistleblowing as a form of communicating about wrongdoing before it became a crisis. Unfortunately, the "statutory rights" that protect U.S. employees are numerous and "highly fragmented" (Lewis, Devine, & Harpur, 2014, p. 352). For example, the U.S. Supreme Court's decision [*Digital Realty Trust, Inc. v. Somers*, 583 U. S.___ (2018)] that whistleblowers who reported internally but not to the SEC are not protected from retaliation as whistleblowers might have had a negative impact on the way potential corporate whistleblowers choose to report wrongdoing. However, subsequent SEC rule changes allowed individuals to be protected from retaliation and receive monetary awards even if they had reported internally, as long as they also reported to the SEC in writing before experiencing retaliation (Securities and Exchange Commission, 2020a), and these rule changes were followed not long afterward by a record award of $114 million to a whistleblower who had reported internally before reporting to the SEC (Egan, 2020).

The significance of Sarbanes-Oxley [*Sarbanes-Oxley Act of 2002*, 15 U.S.C. § 7201 nt (2002)] to public relations is that it mandates that publicly traded companies maintain a communication channel for whistleblowing that allows employees to report financial wrongdoing anonymously to the audit committee of their company's board of directors. Later interpretations have made that charge less prescriptive: "The structure of the channel can be fairly simple, such as designating an internal officer to receive such reports or setting up a 'hotline' for employees to call" (Moberly, 2006, p. 1109, footnote 1107). Given the responsibility public relations has for communications in many organizations, the role of public relations and communications in the internal whistleblowing process, or lack thereof, deserves examination. Researchers should determine who has responsibility for this mandated internal communication channel and how it works, and for the internal chain-of-command channels that public relations and communications executives frequently prefer to use.

Implications for public relations theory

Public relations role theory and Excellence theory did not appear to explain many of the study results. For example, top-ranking public relations and communications executives were more likely than anyone else to be aware of wrongdoing, but they did not report wrongdoing any more often than other employees. Public relations and communications executives, including those who worked in management and, presumably, were part of the dominant coalition, as well as those at lower levels in their organizations, overwhelmingly did not consider reporting wrongdoing as part of their jobs. They also all reported relationships with their employers that were significantly higher in the *Fortune 1000* study, which had more top-ranking public relations and communications executives than the *Wilshire 5000*, and top-ranking public relations and communications executives held significantly more positive relationships with their employers than other employees. Other theoretical approaches appear to be necessary, then, to account for these results.

Public relations roles or organizational turf

This study provides a different view of the traditional communication manager and technician roles, in which communication managers are primarily responsible for communication program results, communication policy, and counseling senior management; and communication technicians are primarily responsible for writing and producing communication materials (Dozier, 1992; L. A. Grunig et al., 2002; J. White & Dozier, 1992). In *this study*, public relations and communications executives reported operating more as technicians than as communication managers with regard to Sarbanes-Oxley implementation. Within the context of roles theory, helping to develop an organization's Sarbanes-Oxley whistleblowing channels would be an example of operating in the communication manager or executive role. Developing publicity to inform employees about the whistleblowing channel would be an example of operating in the technician role. The findings from *this study* suggest that the distinction between the communication manager role and the technician role may have been less pronounced in practice, at least with regard to whistleblowing, at the time these surveys were undertaken than was characterized by CEOs and communication managers in the Excellence study previously (L. A. Grunig et al., 2002).

Excellence theory and the dominant coalition

This finding also has implications for the role of communication managers as members of the dominant coalition. Excellence theory suggests that organizations that rely predominantly on negotiation and collaboration (i.e., two-way symmetrical communication), rather than persuasion and manipulation (i.e., two-way asymmetrical communication), in their practice of public relations will entrust higher-level communication functions to their public relations leaders and will be more likely to include those managers as members of the dominant coalition of decision-makers (L. A. Grunig et al., 2002). As one scholar noted: "The CEOs seem to believe that public relations has its greatest value when it fulfills the managerial role specified in the Excellence theory" (L. A. Grunig et al., 2002, p. 77). The finding that public relations and communications executives operate more as technicians than as communication managers on the topic of Sarbanes-Oxley implementation could mean that they are not part of the dominant coalition to the degree predicted by role theory and Excellence theory.

What role should public relations and communications play in Sarbanes-Oxley implementation?

Is Sarbanes-Oxley implementation a legal function?

Conversely, the finding may support the concept that Sarbanes-Oxley implementation may be perceived by organizations as a human resources or legal department function, rather than as a public relations and communications function. For example, the public relations and communications director of a national whistleblower support organization objected to the premise that public relations and communications should be involved in the development of the Sarbanes-Oxley whistleblowing channels. "The primary responsibility (by far) falls to the HR position, legal . . . and Executive Management. And I think that this, *in actuality*, is where it primarily is handled" (Personal communication, March 10–11, 2010, emphasis in original).

This perspective was supported by at least one member of the target population who declined to participate in the survey: "I was not involved in developing our Sarbanes-Oxley reporting strategy. In our organization this was all handled by our legal department."

The lack of public relations and communications involvement in the development of Sarbanes-Oxley whistleblowing channels lends support to prior research on the encroachment of legal departments into public relations decision-making (Fitzpatrick & Rubin, 1995); J. Lee, Jares, & Heath, 1999; Reber, Cropp, & Cameron, 2001). "The relationship between public relations practitioners and lawyers has been historically troublesome. . . . More than 30 years later, many believe this rift between the professions remains" (Reber et al., 2001, p. 187). As one public relations practitioner who is also an attorney phrased it: "Over the years, lawyers have seated themselves importantly at management's decision-making table while we have waited in an ante room for the news – so we could publicize it after the fact" (Corbin, 1997, p. 17). The ambivalent position occupied by corporate public relations personnel was echoed by a corporate vice president in another study: "Sometimes we're partners in decision making in the eyes of others: always we are technicians and wordsmiths, we prepare and deliver messages" (Berger, 2005, p. 14). The way in which public relations executives view themselves, and how they are viewed by the CEO, in terms of dominant coalition membership may not always coincide (Bowen, 2009).

Is Sarbanes-Oxley implementation a human resources function?

Scholars also cite human resources as another function that has encroached on public relations, and encroachment by the human resources and legal functions is thought to occur when the public relations manager lacks a vision of public relations as having a powerful role in the organization (Lauzen & Dozier, 1992). Although the Excellence study did not find many instances of the public relations function reporting to the human resources function (L. A. Grunig et al., 2002), the views previously expressed concerning the responsibility of human resources for employee communication raise questions about the relationship between human resources and public relations in the area of whistleblowing communication. That relationship has not been explored to the degree to which the relationship between public relations and legal departments has been explored, but such research could prove instructive.

Further research is needed about the use of whistleblowing channels

Future research needs to examine the channels used in whistleblowing. Reporting through chain-of-command channels could be a way for public relations and communications executives to gain access to, or retain access in, the dominant coalition. Research is needed to determine under what circumstances public relations and communications executives choose to use chain-of-command channels, anonymous whistleblowing channels, and external channels, and what those decisions mean for their relationships with their employers. This research could be conducted using interviews with public relations and communications executives who may not be identified as whistleblowers but who may have been in a position to report wrongdoing, or with those who have been identified as whistleblowers in media reports.

How should employers communicate about whistleblowing policies and channels?

IN-PERSON COMMUNICATION WAS FAVORED IN OTHER STUDIES

Keenan (2000) noted that organizations need to communicate their whistleblowing policies and procedures to employees. The communications director for the whistleblower protection group encouraged organizations to make whistleblowing information available on their websites (personal communication, March 10–11, 2010). White, Vanc, and Stafford (2010) noted that employees preferred in-person communication, and (Karanges, Johnston, Beatson, & Lings (2015) found that supervisor communication contributed to employee engagement. Lim and Greenwood (2017) found that using employee engagement strategies (e.g., meetings, workshops, and dialogue) was the most effective way to "[improve] employee recruitment and retention [and improve] employee morale, engagement and commitment" (Lim & Greenwood, 2017, p. 772). Taken together, those findings pointed to in-person communication from supervisor to employee as potentially the most effective method of publicizing whistleblowing policies and channels.

RESEARCHERS FIND FORMAL WHISTLEBLOWING CHANNELS
LESS EFFECTIVE THAN HOPED

Despite respondents to *this study* preferring the internal Sarbanes-Oxley anonymous whistleblowing channel to external channels, research indicates that organizations may not have been communicating these policies and procedures to the extent necessary to make the internal whistleblowing channels effective. The 2009 Global Economic Crime Survey from PriceWaterhouseCoopers (PriceWaterhouseCoopers, 2009) found that only 7% of fraud was found through formal whistleblowing channels. The study attributed part of that to inadequate publicity and lack of management support. In 2018, PriceWaterhouseCoopers found that only 6% of fraud in the United States was detected through the formal whistleblowing channels of whistleblowing hotlines (PriceWaterhouseCoopers, 2018). Taken together, these results suggest that current efforts to communicate to employees about internal whistleblowing channels are not sufficient to uncover significant amounts of wrongdoing.

ORGANIZATIONS RATE THEIR FORMAL WHISTLEBLOWING CHANNELS AS EFFECTIVE

In contrast, a worldwide study of ethics and compliance programs' policies and procedures (Penman, Fox, Snelling, & Stricker, 2018) showed that 67% of ethics and compliance programs included an "Anonymous (e.g., Hotline) Reporting Channel," and 63% of respondents rated their performance as "Good" or "Excellent" on "Whistleblowing Channels (e.g., Telephone, Web Intake, Open Door)." In addition, 57% of respondents rated "Whistleblower" as one of the "Most Commonly Managed Policies and Procedures." When asked to identify areas in which they felt a need to increase awareness of policies, only 12% listed "Improving the Effectiveness of Our Whistleblowing Channels or Investigation techniques" as their top priority. "Taking Actions to Prevent Retaliation against Employees" was the top priority for only 8%. Respondents seemed to believe they were performing more than adequately on whistleblower reporting channels (Penman et al., 2018).

Further research is needed about the responsibility for whistleblowing channels

In order to further the understanding of public relations and communications roles, additional research is needed to identify which departments handle Sarbanes-Oxley compliance issues, including developing and publicizing the anonymous communication channel for whistleblowers. Phone or mail surveys directed at human resources departments could identify the overall organizational structure within which Sarbanes–Oxley compliance is housed. The survey approach to human resources departments may avoid the emotion-laden issues of whistleblowing and could provide an increased response rate. In addition, Web sites, corporate annual reports, and SEC 10-K reports could be reviewed to identify whistleblowing channels. Of interest would be which companies discuss their anonymous whistleblowing channels, how those channels are constructed, and the ways in which those companies promote the channels.

Further research is needed about whistleblowing knowledge and understanding

Further research is needed among public relations and communications executives at all levels to determine how they define whistleblowing and how they view the role of public relations and communications regarding whistleblowing. How do they currently receive information about their organization's whistleblowing policies and channels; how would they like to receive such information; are current channels effective and if so by what metrics? How do they view their obligations to their employers, their profession, and society in terms of whistleblowing? Under what circumstances have they been, or would they be, willing to blow the whistle, and what channels have they used, or would they use, and why? Finally, what level of retaliation, if any, have they experienced for past acts of whistleblowing, and did retaliation prompt them to take further action?

Further research is needed about whistleblowing laws

Although legal issues have not been a major focus of public relations and communications practice or research in the past, they should be considered for the future. This is particularly important to public relations and communications because of the continuing impacts and requirements of whistleblowing laws. These include the impact of Sarbanes–Oxley [*Sarbanes-Oxley Act of 2002*, 15 U.S.C. § 7201 nt (2002)] and Dodd-Frank [*Dodd-Frank Act of 2010*, 12 U.S.C. § 5301 (2010)] on business nationally and internationally; the impact of *the Whistleblower Protection Act of 1989* [5 U.S.C. § 1201 nt (1989)], the *Whistleblower Protection Act Amendments of 1994* [5 U.S.C. § 101 nt (1994)] and the *Whistleblower Protection Enhancement Act of 2012* [5 U.S.C. § 101 nt (2012)] on the conduct of whistleblowing and public affairs in the federal government and the statutory protection from retaliation they promise whistleblowers; and the impact of the FCA on U.S. citizens as a whole. These laws, among others, make the legal impacts of whistleblowing of concern to public relations and communications in the private sector and to contractors in the private sector who contract to do business in the public sector. The laws deserve a closer look by public relations and communications executives with the assistance of the legal department. This, like SEC required filings, supports the concept of collaboration and cooperation.

This research could be conducted through surveys delivered to a broad spectrum of public relations and communications professionals at all organizational levels. Membership lists made available by public relations and communications organizations or commercial databases would help facilitate this research. *This study* demonstrates that survey research on this topic is difficult to conduct. Employee privacy concerns may continue to increase the difficulty for online survey research on this topic. It also should be noted that survey research has other limitations, including offering only a snapshot in time, lacking depth, and offering little context for the data derived.

Further qualitative research is needed in all areas

Future research should incorporate qualitative methods in addition to surveys in order to alleviate these concerns and provide a more complete understanding of whistleblowing. Given the problems this researcher encountered with *this study*, gathering this additional data through surveys could prove difficult. Personal interviews with whistleblowers who have been identified in the media and are willing to discuss their experiences may offer the only avenue to gain additional data. Qualitative research could more fully explore organizational culture and climate in terms of how supportive the organization is to whistleblowers and to what degree it encourages whistleblowing. Researchers have found that a supportive climate encourages the decision to blow the whistle internally (Keenan, 1988), that upper-level managers "perceive greater degrees of organizational encouragement of whistleblowing" (Keenan, 2002, p. 29), and that organizations can encourage whistleblowing through policies and procedures that promote whistleblowing and provide sanctions against retaliation for whistleblowing (Miceli, Near, & Dworkin, 2009).

Qualitative research could prove helpful in determining if public relations and communications executives were active in counseling senior management on Sarbanes-Oxley implementation. It also might identify the current, or potential, role for public relations and communications executives in the internal whistleblowing process. All of these topics would lend themselves to qualitative methods of inquiry and provide more complete data on organizational approaches. However, a word of caution is in order with regard to qualitative studies of whistleblowers. Qualitative interviews with government and government contractor whistleblowers found they were not in the least impressed with, or confident in assistance from, public relations/public affairs professionals with regard to whistleblowing:

> The role of public relations in the actions of these whistleblowers is easy to characterize: There was not one. None of the whistleblowers contacted public relations personnel, and no one indicated he or she would have done so. The predominant sentiment they expressed was that public relations

professionals were the "tool of management," that they were only interested in maintaining the image of the organization, and that any contact
with one would have had negative consequences for the whistleblower.

(Greenwood, 2020, pp. 1056–1057)

Whistleblowing as ethical obligation

A study of public relations and communications executives indicated they
placed a high value on ethical behavior (Lee & Cheng, 2011). However, the
current study found that more than 90% of public relations and communications executives do not believe reporting wrongdoing is part of their job duties.
The findings suggest that public relations and communications executives do
not believe that reporting wrongdoing is required of them. In other words, it is
not a role-prescribed function of public relations and communications. Some
might argue that a job duty is, by definition, prescribed by management and
that, in this case, management has not made reporting wrongdoing part of the
public relations and communications function at their organizations. Kang and
Berger (2010) found that the ethical practices of an organization's top management were instrumental in determining the ways in which employees chose to
deal with unethical organizational behavior.

A cross-disciplinary approach

Sarbanes-Oxley's bridge to corporate finance

Whistleblowing is a complex issue, much like "international trade, bribery and
corruption, emergency preparedness, and global outsourcing" (Hitt, Beamish,
Jackson, & Mathieu, 2007, p. 1395). Perhaps it could benefit from a cross-
disciplinary approach using multiple levels of theory, measurement, and analysis. Sarbanes-Oxley places an emphasis on mandated communication channels,
culturally supported whistleblowing, and codes of ethics for its executives. In
doing so, Sarbanes-Oxley has built a bridge between public relations and communications and corporate finance, for example, which should not be ignored.
The potential for other collaboration on investigations into whistleblowing
includes partnerships with management, marketing, psychology, sociology,
political science, and law, in addition to communication, organizational communication, and strategic communication.

Challenges to cross-disciplinary studies

THEORETICAL CHALLENGES

Challenges to cross-disciplinary studies are inherent in the ways in which different disciplines define terms, the units of analysis they employ, and the theories they use to understand data and phenomena. For example, public relations

and communications literature tends to promote normative theories, such as relationship management theory and Excellence theory, that describe how individuals and organizations should behave based on professional practice and ethical considerations. Management literature, on the other hand, tends to rely on descriptive theories that describe the nature of reality, such as the behavioral theory of the firm, which explains the decision-making process in terms of goals, expectations, and processes (Cyert & March, 1963). These two perspectives can be difficult to reconcile unless researchers are aware of the differences, delineate the scope of their research, define terms, and explain their theories in terms of origins and connectivity to the other discipline. The linkages between these theories and other theories in other disciplines could prove valuable to the disciplines involved if they were acknowledged and incorporated routinely into cross-disciplinary work.

UNIT OF ANALYSIS CHALLENGES

One area of concern in cross-disciplinary research is the unit of analysis that each study employs. Relationship management theory is intended to measure the relationship between the individual and the organization. However, the Hon and Grunig (1999) instrument contains questions taken from several disciplines, including interpersonal relationship, marketing, and management (J. E. Grunig & Huang, 2000). Given that it appears to measure at least some aspects of organization-public relationships at the interpersonal level, researchers need to determine at what level or levels each component of the Hon and Grunig (1999) scales is actually measuring relationships. It appears more work is needed to segregate those aspects of the relationship management scale that measure organization-level constructs from those that measure individual- or interpersonal-level constructs. Future studies could characterize findings as related to one or the other construct.

THREE DISCIPLINARY HERITAGES

One way to resolve the issue of varying units of analysis may be to look at how research has been handled in a discipline with connections to public relations and communication. Hitt et al. (2007) describe three areas of management studies that have been conducted with little attempt "to integrate theory or conduct research that crossed these levels of inquiry or analysis":

> The disciplinary heritages of scholars working in these areas reinforced their differences. The micro approach was rooted in psychology and focused on understanding the thoughts, feelings, and actions of individuals. The macro approach was rooted in sociology and economics: it focused on understanding organizations and markets. The middle ground was rooted in social psychology and closely related fields such as communications.
>
> (Hitt et al., 2007, p. 1386)

These authors recommend that organizational studies that address individual-, group-, and firm-level issues should identify the level at which the researcher wants to generalize (the level of theory or focal unit), the level from which the data come (the level of measurement), and the level at which the data are analyzed (the level of analysis). Confusing these levels results in "fallacies of the wrong level" (Hitt et al., 2007, p. 1389).

Theory-building

A further suggestion to public relations and communications scholars is to extend theory-building in the area of mid-range theories. The reason for this approach is that neither the descriptive management theories nor the normative public relations and communications theories appear to account for the findings of *this study*. This discrepancy would argue for a third course, which is that of an instrumental, or predictive, approach to theory-building that might explain the data. Such an approach has been found useful in developing theory in the management field (Berman, Wicks, Kotha, & Jones, 1999), and it might prove useful in this arena, as well. One such path to theory-building could begin with evolutionary theory as the "umbrella under which all mid-range public relations and communications theories can shelter" (Greenwood, 2010, p. 469). Within that concept, the theory of the Golden Handcuffs could be developed to predict behavior within corporations as a function of the current and future rewards offered to executives.

The Golden Handcuffs

The Golden Handcuffs as theory

Two of the most important findings from *this study* were that top-ranking public relations and communications executives had significantly more favorable relationships with their employers than other respondents, and there was a significant negative difference for all relationship scales except exchange between the *Fortune 1000* study, which had twice as many top-ranking public relations and communications executives, and the *Wilshire 5000* study. This supports an earlier finding from the *Fortune 1000* study that respondents who earned more than $100,000 per year had significantly more favorable relationships with their employers than those making less than $100,000, and they also had higher scores on 68% of relationship quality outcomes than younger public relations and communications agency employees (Greenwood, 2016). The notion of the "Golden Handcuffs" as rewards that bind an employee to an organization may provide part of the explanation for those findings. In public relations and communications literature, the term Golden Handcuffs specifically referred to high salaries, extensive benefits, and the power that goes with higher-level positions, but they also may have ethical implications for public relations and communications managers (Berger, 2005).

Although *this study* did not ask about deferred compensation plans, respondents from both studies reported high average salaries; management status, which implies compensation beyond salary; and positive performance reviews. Given these findings, the notion of the Golden Handcuffs may explain the responses public relations and communications executives gave on the relationship scales in which communal relationships, satisfaction, and commitment were the highest scoring outcomes. In *this study*, the Golden Handcuffs may offer a more robust explanation for the good relationships public relations and communications executives have with their organizations than other theories. For example, resource dependence theory assumed that seriousness of wrongdoing would not protect powerful executives from retaliation, but in *this study* it appeared to do that. In addition, *this study* found that awareness of wrongdoing, whistleblowing, and retaliation had significant negative effects on relationship factors.

Further research is needed to parse out exactly how executives might feel beholden to, and invested in, their organizations, and how this affects their relationships with their employers. However, it would be reasonable to propose that these benefits, offered in exchange for work product and, presumably, loyalty or commitment, affect their relationships positively. More research is needed to understand how internal dependencies affect an organization's participation in wrongdoing and its response to whistleblowing. It also would be important to determine how the invitation to participate in company sanctioned wrongdoing affects the executive. One metatheory, evolutionary theory, along with the newly proposed theory of the Golden Handcuffs, seems best suited to explain the results of *this study* and to offer an avenue for future research.

Measuring the Golden Handcuffs

One question that could be answered at the organizational level is the extent and types of Golden Handcuffs, beyond standard employment variables of salary, job title, level in the company hierarchy, that are provided to corporate public relations and communications executives. A corollary question that could be answered at the interpersonal level is the degree to which the individual elements of the Golden Handcuffs influence public relations and communications executives' ethical decision-making. For example, a study of public relations agency employees found a high level of moral reasoning and a belief that their managers have higher ethical standards then they have (Coleman & Wilkins, 2009). The discrepancy between those findings and the finding in *this study* that corporate executives do not view reporting wrongdoing as one of their job duties raises questions about the impact on ethical decisions of the rewards given to corporate employees. Further research is needed to test whether the Golden Handcuffs compromise moral reasoning such that employees may become socialized to corrupt behaviors, resulting in the internalization of those behaviors and the normalization of corruption (Ashforth & Anand, 2003).

However, the larger issue raised by *this study* may involve the type of reasoning that occurs when those who have received professional training address issues of ethics. Coleman and Wilkins (2009) reported that increased levels of education have been found to lead to higher levels of moral reasoning. However, they also raised the possibility that increased levels of education in professional practices, such as public relations and communications, may lead to a greater ability to see all sides of an issue. As a result, those trained in professional practices may have the capacity to make finer distinctions among options. One result of that capacity may include the ability to convince oneself that one's course of action, because it is consistent with the organizational direction, is ethical.

Top-ranking public relations and communications executives were significantly more likely to be aware of wrongdoing in their organizations than others. They were no more likely to report it than others. Top-ranking public relations and communications executives were significantly more positive toward their employers than other employees. It appears that power leads to knowledge of wrongdoing but not to whistleblowing; that when power leads to whistleblowing, some power elements (education, salary, and supervision) protect the powerful from retaliation; that power influences positive relationships with the employer; but that when retaliation occurs, it has a negative effect on those relationships. Taken together, these significant results lend credence to the proposal to elevate the Golden Handcuffs from a concept to a theory: the theory of the Golden Handcuffs.

Conclusion

Despite the inherent difficulties in studying whistleblowing, the effort needs to be made because of the importance of this issue to society. What *this study* has demonstrated is that at least some of the largest U.S. companies do not have cultures that actively promote and sanction whistleblowing. Whistleblowers continue to be silenced or harmed. Public relations and communications executives do not play a role in facilitating or practicing whistleblowing. Instead, as this report on government protections for whistleblowers attests, the inclination is still to "shoot the messenger":

> In looking ahead, the prognosis for the whistleblower is not promising. While legally federal civil servants may have technical protections to rely upon, they will likely be subjected to a continuing culture that brands them as disloyal if they choose to report questionable activities. Until the idea of disclosure is seen as an ethical benefit for the entire organization, rather than a violation of trust perpetrated by the whistleblower, civil servants will remain reluctant to come forward. Ultimately, lingering perceptions of whistleblowing is all about shooting the messenger, rather than heeding the content of the message. The fact that the whistleblower is doing nothing more than handing off information as they know it to an authority illustrates the ultimate irony. The whistleblower is just the messenger wondering why they end up shot.
>
> (Saunders & Thibault, 2008, p. 22)

Thus, wrongdoing continues to occur in private industry as well as government, despite legislation such as Sarbanes-Oxley and Dodd-Frank that is designed to help prevent it, and retaliation against messengers delivering news of organizational wrongdoing persists. The question asked in 1999 about the efficacy of laws to protect whistleblowers has not yet been answered (Miceli et al., 1999). The use of the science-based study of human behavior and cross-disciplinary collaboration with the biological sciences could be used to answer that question and should become best practices for public relations and communications executives, practitioners, and scholars. "Researchers into whistleblowing should be both comforted and concerned to know that the human condition will provide ample opportunities for research into organizational wrongdoing [Machiavellian behavior], individual whistleblowing [cheater detection], and organizational and individual retaliation [reciprocity] for the foreseeable future," (Greenwood, 2011, pp. 169-170). Unfortunately, science tells us that that future is short-lived if human behavior cannot be changed significantly; time is of the essence; and there is no time to waste.

Note

1   Research Question 7 has been answered before Research Question 6 due to the length of Research Question 6 findings.

References

Aldrich, H. E., & Herker, D. (1977). Boundary spanning roles and organization structure. *Academy of Management Review, 2*(2), 217–230.

Aldrich, H. E., & Ruef, M. (2006). *Organizations evolving* (2nd. ed.). Thousand Oaks, CA: Sage.

Ashforth, B. E., & Anand, V. (2003). The normalization of corruption in organizations. In R. M. Kramer & B. M. Staw (Eds.), *Research in organizational behavior: An annual series of analytical essays and critical reviews* (vol. 25, pp. 1–52). Oxford, UK: Elsevier. https://doi.org/10.1016/S0191-3085(03)25001-2

Berger, B. K. (2005). Power over, power with, and power to relations: Critical reflections on public relations, the dominant coalition, and activism. *Journal of Public Relations Research, 17*(1), 5–28.

Berman, S. L., Wicks, A. C., Kotha, S., & Jones, T. M. (1999). Does stakeholder orientation matter? The relationship between stakeholder management models and firm financial performance. *Academy of Management Journal, 42*(5), 488–506.

Bowen, S. A. (2009). What communication professionals tell us regarding dominant coalition access and gaining membership. *Journal of Applied Communication Research, 37*(4), 418–443.

Cheney, G., & Christensen, L. T. (2001). Public relations as contested terrain: A critical response. In R. L. Heath (Ed.), *The handbook of public relations* (pp. 167–182). Thousand Oaks, CA: Sage.

Civil Service Reform Act of 1978, 5 U.S.C. § 1101 (1978).

Coleman, R., & Wilkins, L. (2009). The moral development of public relations practitioners: A comparison with other professions and influences on higher quality ethical reasoning. *Journal of Public Relations Research, 21*(3), 318–340.

Corbin, J. (1997). Lawyers and us – A synergistic relationship. *Public Relations Quarterly, 42*(4), 15–17.

Cyert, R. M., & March, J. G. (1963). *A behavioral theory of the firm* (2nd ed.). Englewood Cliffs, NJ: Prentice-Hall, Inc.

Digital Realty Trust, Inc. v. Somers, 583 U. S.___ (2018).

Dodd-Frank Act of 2010, 12 U.S.C. § 5301 (2010).

Dooley, L. M., & Lindner, J. R. (2003). The handling of nonresponse error. *Human Resource Development Quarterly, 14*(1), 99–110.

Dozier, D. A. (1992). The organizational roles of communications and public relations practitioners. In J. E. Grunig, D. A. Dozier, W. P. Ehling, L. A. Grunig, F. C. Repper, & J. White (Eds.), *Excellence in public relations and communication management* (pp. 327–355). Hillsdale, NJ: Lawrence Erlbaum Associates.

Egan, M. (2020). A government agency just paid a record $114 million to an anonymous whistleblower. *CNN* (October 23, 2020). Retrieved from https://www.cnn.com/2020/10/23/business/sec-record-whistleblower-award/index.html

Ethics & Compliance Initiative. (2018). *The state of ethics & compliance in the workplace* (978-1-5323-7114-1). Retrieved from www.ethics.org/knowledge-center/eci-recent-research/

Ethics & Compliance Initiative. (2019). *Workplace misconduct and reporting: A global look.* Retrieved from www.ethics.org/

Fitzpatrick, K. R., & Rubin, M. S. (1995). Public relations vs. legal strategies in organizational crisis decisions. *Public Relations Review, 21*(1), 21–33. http://doi.org/10.1016/0363-8111(95)90037-3

Greenwood, C. A. (2010). Evolutionary theory: The missing link for conceptualizing public relations. *Journal of Public Relations Research, 22*(4), 456–476. https://doi.org/10.1080/10627261003801438

Greenwood, C. A. (2011). *Killing the messenger: A survey of public relations practitioners and organizational response to whistleblowing after Sarbanes-Oxley.* Doctoral dissertation. Retrieved from ProQuest Dissertations & Theses (UMI No. 907550960).

Greenwood, C. A. (2015). Whistleblowing in the *Fortune 1000*: What practitioners told us about wrongdoing in corporations in a pilot study. *Public Relations Review,* (41), 490–500. https://doi.org/10.1016/j.pubrev.2015.07.005

Greenwood, C. A. (2016). Golden Handcuffs in the Fortune 1000? An employee-organization relationship survey of public relations executives and practitioners in the largest companies. *Communication Research Reports, 33*(3), 269–274. http://doi.org/10.1080/08824096.2016.1186624

Greenwood, C. A. (2020). "I was just doing my job!" Evolution, corruption, and public relations in interviews with government whistleblowers. *PARTECIPAZIONE E CONFLITTO, 13*(2), 1042–1061. https://doi.org/10.1285/i20356609v13i2p1042

Grunig, J. E. (Ed.) (1992). *Excellence in public relations and communication management.* Hillsdale, NJ: Lawrence Erlbaum Associates.

Grunig, J. E., & Huang, Y.-H. (2000). From organizational effectiveness to relationship indicators: Antecedents of relationships, public relations strategies, and relationship outcomes. In J. A. Ledingham & S. D. Bruning (Eds.), *Public relations as relationship management: A relational approach to the study and practice of public relations* (pp. 23–54). Mahwah, NJ: Lawrence Erlbaum Associates.

Grunig, L. A., Grunig, J. E., & Dozier, D. M. (2002). *Excellent public relations and effective organizations: A study of communication management in three countries.* Mahwah, NJ: Lawrence Erlbaum Associates.

Hitt, M. A., Beamish, P. W., Jackson, S. E., & Mathieu, J. E. (2007). Building theoretical and empirical bridges across levels: Multilevel research in management. *Academy of Management Journal, 50*(6), 1385–1399.

Hon, L. C., & Grunig, J. E. (1999). *Guidelines for measuring relationships in public relations* (p. 40). Retrieved from http://painepublishing.com/wp-content/uploads/2013/10/Guidelines_Measuring_Relationships.pdf

Kang, J.-A., & Berger, B. K. (2010). The influence of organizational conditions on public relations practitioners' dissent. *Journal of Communication Management, 14*(4), 368–387. https://doi.org/10.1108/13632541011090464

Karanges, E., Johnston, K., Beatson, A., & Lings, I. (2015). The influence of internal communication on employee engagement: A pilot study. *Public Relations Review, 41*(1), 129–131. http://doi.org/10.1016/j.pubrev.2014.12.003

Keenan, J. P. (1988, August). *Communication climate, whistle-blowing, and the first-level manager: A preliminary study.* Paper presented at the Annual Meeting of the Academy of Management, Anaheim, CA.

Keenan, J. P. (2000). Blowing the whistle on less serious forms of fraud: A study of executives and managers. *Employee Responsibilities and Rights Journal, 12*(4), 199–217.

Keenan, J. P. (2002). Whistleblowing: A study of managerial differences. *Employee Responsibilities and Rights Journal, 14*(1), 17–32.

Lauzen, M. M., & Dozier, D. M. (1992). The missing link: The public relations manager role as mediator of organizational environments and power consequences for the function. *Journal of Public Relations Research, 4*(4), 205–220.

Lee, J., Jares, S. M., & Heath, R. L. (1999). Decision-making encroachment and cooperative relationships between public relations and legal counselors in the management of organizational crisis. *Journal of Public Relations Research, 11*(3), 243–270.

Lee, S. T., & Cheng, I.-H. (2011). Characteristics and dimensions of ethical leadership in public relations. *Journal of Public Relations Research, 23*(1), 46–74.

Lewis, D., Devine, T., & Harpur, P. (2014). The key to protection: Civil and employment law remedies. In A. J. Brown, D. Lewis, R. E. Moberly, & W. Vandekerckhove (Eds.), *International handbook on whistleblowing research* (pp. 350–380). Cheltenham, UK: Edward Elgar Publishing Limited.

Lim, J. S., & Greenwood, C. A. (2017). Communicating corporate social responsibility (CSR): Stakeholder responsiveness and engagement strategy to achieve CSR goals. *Public Relations Review, 43*(4), 768–776. https://doi.org/10.1016/j.pubrev.2017.06.007

Merit Systems Protection Board. (1981). *Whistleblowing and the federal employee: Blowing the whistle on fraud, waste, and mismanagement—who does it and what happens.* Washington, DC: MSPB.

Merit Systems Protection Board. (1984). *Blowing the whistle in the federal government: A comparative analysis of 1980 and 1983 survey findings.* Washington, DC: MSPB.

Merit Systems Protection Board. (2011a). *Blowing the whistle: Barriers to federal employees making disclosures.* Washington, DC: MSPB.

Mesmer-Magnus, J. R., & Viswesvaran, C. (2005). Whistleblowing in organizations: An examination of correlates of whistleblowing intentions, actions, and retaliation. *Journal of Business Ethics, 62*, 277–297.

Miceli, M. P., & Near, J. P. (1985). Characteristics of organizational climate and perceived wrongdoing associated with whistle-blowing decisions. *Personnel Psychology, 38*, 525–544

Miceli, M. P., Near, J. P., & Dworkin, T. M. (2009). A word to the wise: How managers and policy-makers can encourage employees to report wrongdoing. *Journal of Business Ethics, 86*(3), 379–396. https://doi.org/10.1007/s10551-008-9853-6

Miceli, M. P., Rehg, M. T., Near, J. P., & Ryan, K. C. (1999). Can laws protect whistle-blowers? Results of a naturally occurring field experiment. *Work and Occupations, 26*(1), 129–151. https://doi.org/10.1177/0730888499026001007

Moberly, R. E. (2006). Sarbanes-Oxley's structural model to encourage corporate whistle-blowers. *Brigham Young Law Review, 2006*(5), 1107–1180.

Near, J. P., & Miceli, M. P. (1996). Whistle-blowing: Myth and reality. *Journal of Management, 22*(3), 507.

Penman, C., Fox, T., Snelling, B., & Stricker, T. (2018). *2018 Ethics & Compliance Policy & Procedure Management Benchmark Report. Benchmark*. Retrieved from NAVEX Global: Lake Oswego, OR: https://www.navexglobal.com/en-us/file-download-canonical?file=/2018-Policy-Management-Benchmark-Report_0.pdf&file-name=2018-Policy-Management-Benchmark-Report_0.pdf

PriceWaterhouseCoopers. (2009). The global economic crime survey: Economic crime in a downturn. Retrieved from http://www.pwc.com/en_GX/gx/economic-crime-survey/pdf/global-economic-crime-survey-2009.pdf

PriceWaterhouseCoopers. (2018). *2018 Global Economic Crime and Fraud Survey: US perspectives*. Retrieved from https://www.pwc.com/us/en/services/consulting/cybersecurity-privacy-forensics/library/global-economic-fraud-survey.html

Rappeport, A., & Flitter, E. (2018). Congress approves first big Dodd-Frank rollback. *The New York Times* (May 22, 2018). Retrieved from https://www.nytimes.com/2018/05/22/business/congress-passes-dodd-frank-rollback-for-smaller-banks.html

Reber, B. H., Cropp, F., & Cameron, G. T. (2001). Mythic battles: Examining the lawyer-public relations counselor dynamic. *Journal of Public Relations Research, 13*(3), 187–218.

Rehg, M. T. (1998). *An examination of the retaliation process against whistleblowers: A study of federal government employees*. Doctoral dissertation. Indiana University, Bloomington, IN.

Rehg, M. T., Miceli, M. P., Near, J. P., & Van Scotter, J. R. (2008). Antecedents and outcomes of retaliation against whistleblowers: Gender differences and power relationships. *Organization Science, 19*(2), 221–240.

Sarbanes-Oxley Act of 2002, 15 U.S.C. § 7201 nt (2002).

Saunders, K., & Thibault, J. (2008). *Whistleblowing in Canada: One step forward or two steps back?* Paper presented at the MPSA Annual National Conference, Chicago, IL.

Securities and Exchange Commission. (2020a). *SEC adds clarity, efficiency and transparency to its successful whistleblower award program* [Press release]. Retrieved from www.sec.gov/news/press-release/2020-219

Whistleblower Protection Act of 1989, 5 U.S.C. § 1201 nt (1989).

Whistleblower Protection Act Amendments of 1994, 5 U.S.C. § 101 nt (1994).

Whistleblower Protection Enhancement Act of 2012, 5 U.S.C. § 101 nt (2012).

White, C., Vanc, A., & Stafford, G. (2010). Internal communication, information satisfaction, and sense of community: The effect of personal influence. *Journal of Public Relations Research, 22*(1), 65–84. https://doi.org/10.1080/10627260903170985

White, J., & Dozier, D. A. (1992). Public relations and management decision making. In J. E. Grunig (Ed.), *Excellence in public relations and communication management*. Hillsdale, NJ: Lawrence Erlbaum Associates.

Wimmer, R. D., & Dominick, J. R. (2006). *Mass media research: An introduction* (8th ed.). Belmont, CA: Thomson Wadsworth.

Yeoh, P. (2013). Whistle-blowing laws in the UK. *Business Law Review, 34*(6), 218–224.

Appendices

Appendix A

Recruitment consent e-mail 2–24–10

Dear Public Relations Colleague:

As an Accredited member of the Public Relations Society of America, a member of the PRSA College of Fellows, and a doctoral candidate in the School of Journalism and Mass Communication at the University of Oregon, I would like to invite you to participate in my dissertation research. My study involves a survey of public relations executives and organizational response to whistle-blowing, including response to the Sarbanes-Oxley Act of 2002. You are eligible to participate in this study because you are the highest ranking public relations executive in your Fortune 1000 corporation.

The confidentiality of your information is of prime importance to this study. If you decide to participate, the encrypted link in this email, **which is being sent from my University of Oregon email account,** will take you to a survey on SurveyMonkey that should take no more than 20 minutes to complete. www.surveymonkey.com/s/Fortune_1000_Public_Relations

Your responses will be completely anonymous, and your identifying information will not appear anywhere on the survey. Please do not include any identifying information on the survey, including in the open-ended questions. You should take the survey on your home computer if you feel uncomfortable about possible work-related issues.

Remember, this is completely voluntary. You may choose to be in the study or not. Completing the questionnaire constitutes your consent to participate. Please complete the survey within one week.

Everyone contacted for this study will receive a copy of the Executive Summary of the survey results and analysis after the study is completed.

If you are willing to be contacted about future research on this topic, please **mail** the signed Permission/Release Form to me **at my private mailbox. These forms will be stored in a secure location under lock and key.** There will be no way for anyone to link your information on the Permission/Release Form to the anonymous survey data.

If you have any questions about the study, please email me at cgreenwo@ uoregon.edu or call me at 541–968–6180. You may also contact my advisor,

Dr. Patricia Curtin, at pcurtin@uoregon.edu or 541–346–3752. If you have any questions regarding your rights as a research subject, please contact the Office for Protection of Human Subjects at the University of Oregon, (541) 346–2510. This Office oversees the review of the research to protect your rights and is not involved with this study.

As the ranking public relations executive in your corporation, your participation in this survey is of the utmost importance to research on this topic. You will be doing the profession of public relations and the teaching of public relations a great service by participating in this research.

Thank you for your help.

Sincerely,

Cary A. Greenwood, APR, Fellow PRSA
Doctoral Candidate, School of Journalism and Communication
University of Oregon
1275 University of Oregon
Eugene, OR 97403–1275
541–968–6180 (PH)
cgreenwo@uoregon.edu

Appendix A: Permission/Release Form

Thank you for allowing me to contact you about my current research project. I may have future opportunities for you to participate in additional research studies on this topic. If you would be interested in hearing about these opportunities, I would be happy to contact you by phone or email when they become available.

Should you change your mind and decide that you do not want to be contacted, let me know at any time and I will destroy this form.

If you wish to be contacted, please provide the following information:

Name: _____
Phone number: _____
Email address: _____
What is the best way to reach you?
___Phone _____Email
Is it okay to leave a voicemail about research studies?
_____Yes ____No

Are there any restrictions on contacting you (e.g., don't call before 10 a.m.; don't contact after October 2010, etc.)?

Please mail this form to my private mailbox at the following address:
Cary A. Greenwood, 597 Country Club Rd. #17, Eugene, OR 97401.

Thank you for your consideration.

Sincerely,

Cary A. Greenwood, APR, Fellow PRSA
Doctoral Candidate
School of Journalism and Communication
University of Oregon
1275 University of Oregon
Eugene, OR 97403–1275
541–968–6180 (PH)
cgreenwo@uoregon.edu

Appendix A: Follow-up reminder

Dear Public Relations Colleague:

Last week you were sent information about an Internet survey on Sarbanes-Oxley and whistleblowing in the *Fortune 1000*. If you have already completed the survey, thank you for your time! Please feel free to delete this message as it is simply a reminder that your participation in this research is appreciated. If you have not completed the survey, please let me repeat the previous information.

As an Accredited member of the Public Relations Society of America, a member of the PRSA College of Fellows, and a doctoral candidate in the School of Journalism and Mass Communication at the University of Oregon, I would like to invite you to participate in my dissertation research. My study involves a survey of public relations executives and organizational response to whistleblowing, including response to the Sarbanes-Oxley Act of 2002. You are eligible to participate in this study because you are the highest ranking public relations executive in your Fortune 1000 corporation.

The confidentiality of your information is of prime importance to this study. If you decide to participate, the encrypted link in this email, **which is being sent from my University of Oregon email account,** will take you to a survey on SurveyMonkey that should take no more than 20 minutes to complete. www.surveymonkey.com/s/Fortune_1000_Public_Relations

Your responses will be completely anonymous, and your identifying information will not appear anywhere on the survey. Please do not include any identifying information on the survey, including in the open-ended questions. You should take the survey on your home computer if you feel uncomfortable about possible work-related issues.

Remember, this is completely voluntary. You may choose to be in the study or not. Completing the questionnaire constitutes your consent to participate. Please complete the survey within one week.

Everyone contacted for this study will receive a copy of the Executive Summary of the survey results and analysis after the study is completed.

If you are willing to be contacted about future research on this topic, please **mail** the signed Permission/Release Form to me **at my private mailbox. These forms will be stored in a secure location under lock and key.** There will be no way for anyone to link your information on the Permission/ Release Form to the anonymous survey data.

If you have any questions about the study, please email me at cgreenwo@ uoregon.edu or call me at 541–968–6180. You may also contact my advisor, Dr. Patricia Curtin, at pcurtin@uoregon.edu or 541–346–3752. If you have any questions regarding your rights as a research subject, please contact the Office for Protection of Human Subjects at the University of Oregon, (541) 346–2510. This Office oversees the review of the research to protect your rights and is not involved with this study.

As the ranking public relations executive in your corporation, your participation in this survey is of the utmost importance to research on this topic. You will be doing the profession of public relations and the teaching of public relations a great service by participating in this research.

Thank you for your help.

Sincerely,

Cary A. Greenwood, APR, Fellow PRSA
Doctoral Candidate, School of Journalism and Communication
University of Oregon
1275 University of Oregon
Eugene, OR 97403–1275
541–968–6180 (PH)
cgreenwo@uoregon.edu

Appendix A: whistleblowing survey questionnaire

1. **Does your organization have an anonymous communication channel to the audit committee of the board of directors?** *(Please select ONE box.)*

1.	No
2.	Yes
3.	Don't know

2. **If your organization has such a channel, did you or someone who worked with you help develop it?** *(Please select ONE box.)*

1.	No
2.	Yes
3.	Does not apply

3. **If your organization has such a channel, did you or someone who worked with you help publicize it?** *(Please select ONE box.)*

1.	No
2.	Yes
3.	Does not apply

4. **If your organization has such a channel, which of the following have been used to publicize it?** *(Please select ALL that apply.)*

1.	Electronic communication (e-mail/Internet/Intranet)
2.	Print communication
3.	Verbal communication
4.	Other
5.	Not publicized
6.	Don't know
7.	Does not apply

5. **During your entire career, have you ever been aware of some-one other than you who was aware of an illegal, wasteful, or unethical activity involving the organization for which he or she worked?** *(Please select ONE box.)*

1.	No [If No, skip to Q. 13.]
2.	Yes

6. **What was the dollar amount of this activity?** *(Please select ONE box.)*

1.	<$1,000
2.	$1,000–$49,999
3.	$50,000–$100,000
4.	>$100,000

5.	>$500,000
6.	Don't know

7. **How frequently did this activity occur?** (*Please select ONE box.*)

1.	Rarely
2.	Occasionally
3.	Frequently
4.	Don't know

8. **Did this person report this activity to any individual or group?** *(Please select ONE box.)*

1.	No
2.	Yes
3.	Don't know

9. **If this person reported this activity, was it because reporting such activity was a routine part of his or her job?** *(Please select ONE box.)*

1.	No
2.	Yes
3.	Don't know

10. **If this person reported this activity how did he or she report it?** *(Please select ALL that apply.)*

1.	Internally through chain of command
2.	Internally through anonymous channel
3.	Externally
4.	Don't know

11. **If this person reported this activity, was this person identified as the source of the report?** *(Please select ONE box.)*

1.	No
2.	Yes
3.	Don't know

12. If this person was identified as the source of the report, what happened to this person? *(Please select ALL that apply.)*

1.	Person was rewarded.
2.	Nothing happened to person.
3.	Person's co-workers were unhappy with him/her.
4.	Person's supervisor was unhappy with him/her.
5.	Someone above person's supervisor was unhappy with him/her.
6.	Person experienced retaliation.
7.	Don't know

13. What else would you like to share about this topic? *(Please do not include any identifying information.)*

_____

14. During your career with your current employer, did you ever personally observe or obtain direct evidence of an illegal, wasteful, or unethical activity involving your organization? *(Please select ONE box.)*

1.	No [If No, skip to Q. 22.]
2.	Yes

15. What was the dollar amount of this activity? *(Please select ONE box.)*

1.	<$1,000
2.	$1,000–$49,999
3.	$50,000–$100,000
4.	>$100,000
5.	>$500,000
6.	Don't know

16. How frequently did this activity occur? *(Please select ONE box.)*

1.	Rarely
2.	Occasionally
3.	Frequently
4.	Don't know

17. **Did you report this activity to any individual or group?** *(Please select ONE box.)*

1.	No
2.	Yes

18. **If you reported this activity, was it because reporting such activity is a routine part of your job?** *(Please select ONE box.)*

1.	No
2.	Yes

19. **If you reported this activity, how did you report it?** *(Please select ALL that apply.)*

1.	Internally through chain of command
2.	Internally through anonymous channel
3.	Externally

20. **If you reported this activity, were you identified as the source of the report?**

1.	No
2.	Yes

21. **If you were identified as the source of the report, what happened to you?** *(Please select ALL that apply.)*

1.	I was rewarded.
2.	Nothing happened to me.
3.	My co-workers were unhappy with me.
4.	My supervisor was unhappy with me.
5.	Someone above my supervisor was unhappy with me.
6.	I experienced retaliation.

22. **What else would you like to share about this topic?** *(Please do not include any identifying information.)*

_____

Please answer the following questions as they pertain to your relationship with your current employer.

Strongly Disagree	Somewhat Disagree	Neither Agree nor Disagree	Somewhat Agree	Strongly Agree
1	2	3	4	5

___ 23. I feel that this organization is trying to maintain a long-term commitment to me.

___ 24. This organization treats me fairly and justly.

___ 25. This organization does not especially enjoy giving others aid.

___ 26. There is a long-lasting bond between this organization and me.

___ 27. This organization believes my opinions are legitimate.

___ 28. Whenever this organization makes an important decision, I know it will be concerned about me.

___ 29. Whenever this organization gives or offers something to me, it generally expects something in return.

___ 30. Both the organization and I benefit from the relationship.

___ 31. This organization is very concerned about my welfare.

___ 32. Even though I have had a relationship with this organization for a long time, it still expects something in return whenever it offers me a favor.

___ 33. I can see that this organization wants to maintain a relationship with me.

___ 34. In dealing with me, this organization has a tendency to throw its weight around.

___ 35. This organization can be relied on to keep its promises.

___ 36. Most people like me are happy in their interactions with this organization.

___ 37. I feel that this organization takes advantage of people who are vulnerable.

___ 38. I believe that this organization takes my opinions into account when making decisions.

___ 39. This organization really listens to what I have to say.

___ 40. I am happy with this organization.

___ 41. I think that this organization succeeds by stepping on other people.

___ 42. Generally speaking, I am pleased with the relationship this organization has established.

___ 43. This organization will compromise with me when it knows that it will gain something.

___ 44. I feel very confident about this organization's skills.

___ 45. Compared to other organizations, I value my relationship with this organization more.

___ 46. This organization takes care of people who are likely to reward the organization.

___ 47. This organization has the ability to accomplish what it says it will do.

___ 48. This organization and I are attentive to what each other say.

49. What else would you like to share about this topic? *(Please do not include any identifying information.)*

_____

50. How many years have you worked for this employer?

___

51. How many years have you been in your current position?

___

52. Are you: *(Please select ONE box.)*

___ Male
___ Female

53. What is your age?

___

54. What is your highest education level? *(Please select ONE box.)*

___ No college
___ Some college

___ A 4-year college degree
___ Some graduate or professional school
___ Graduate or professional degree

55. What is your current salary range? *(Please select ONE box.)*

___ Under $100,000
___ $100,000 to $199,999
___ $200,000 to $500,000
___ More than $500,000

56. Are you: *(Please select ALL that apply.)*

___ American Indian/Alaskan Native
___ Asian/ Asian American
___ Black or African American
___ White, not Hispanic
___ Hispanic/Latino
___ Other

57. Are you the highest-ranking official in your department? *(Please select ONE box.)*

___ Yes
___ No

58. What is the location of your position in relation to the Chief Executive Officer? (Please select ONE box.)

___ I am the Chief Executive Officer.
___ I report to the Chief Executive Officer.
___ I report to someone who reports to the Chief Executive Officer.
___ I report to someone who reports to someone who reports to the Chief Executive Officer.
___ Other

59. In what department do you work? (Please select ONE box.)
___ Public Relations

___ Corporate Communications
___ Public Affairs
___ Investor Relations
___ Corporate Social Responsibility
___ Marketing
___ Advertising
___ Sales
___ Finance & Administration
___ Other (Please specify)

60. **Do you now write performance appraisals for other employees?**

___ Yes
___ No

(Note: The answer to the following question has been found to be significant in some studies of whistleblowing.)

61. **Which of the following most closely describes the performance rating you received at your last appraisal?**

___ Unacceptable
___ Minimally successful
___ Fully successful
___ Exceeds fully successful
___ Outstanding

62. **What is your company's industry sector?**

- ___ Advertising, Marketing
- ___ Aerospace and Defense
- ___ Airlines
- ___ Apparel
- ___ Automotive Retailing, Services
- ___ Beverages
- ___ Chemicals
- ___ Commercial Banks
- ___ Computer Peripherals
- ___ Computer Software
- ___ Computers, Office Equipment
- ___ Construction and Farm Machinery
- ___ Diversified Financials
- ___ Diversified Outsourcing Services
- ___ Education
- ___ Electronics, Electrical Equipment
- ___ Energy
- ___ Engineering, Construction
- ___ Entertainment
- ___ Financial Data Services
- ___ Food and Drug Stores
- ___ Food Consumer Products
- ___ Food Production
- ___ Food Services
- ___ Forest and Paper Products
- ___ General Merchandisers
- ___ Health Care: Insurance and Managed Care
- ___ Health Care: Medical Facilities
- ___ Health Care: Pharmacy and Other Services

- ___ Home Equipment, Furnishings
- ___ Homebuilders
- ___ Hotels, Casinos, Resorts
- ___ Household and Personal Products
- ___ Industrial Machinery
- ___ Information Technology Services
- ___ Insurance: Life, Health (mutual)
- ___ Insurance: Life, Health (stock)
- ___ Insurance: Property and Casualty (mutual)
- ___ Insurance: Property and Casualty (stock)
- ___ Internet Services and Retailing
- ___ Mail, Package, and Freight Delivery
- ___ Medical Products and Equipment
- ___ Metals
- ___ Mining, Crude-Oil Production
- ___ Network and Other Communications Equipment
- ___ Oil and Gas Equipment, Services
- ___ Packaging, Containers
- ___ Petroleum Refining
- ___ Pharmaceuticals
- ___ Pipelines
- ___ Publishing, Printing
- ___ Railroads
- ___ Scientific, Photographic and Control Equipment
- ___ Securities
- ___ Semiconductors and Other Electronic Components
- ___ Specialty Retailers: Apparel
- ___ Specialty Retailers: Other
- ___ Telecommunications
- ___ Tobacco
- ___ Transportation and Logistics
- ___ Trucking, Truck Leasing
- ___ Utilities: Gas and Electric
- ___ Waste Management
- ___ Wholesalers: Diversified
- ___ Wholesalers: Electronics and Office Equipment
- ___ Wholesalers: Food and Grocery
- ___ Wholesalers: Health Care

Thank you for completing the survey!

Appendix B

Relationship quality outcomes and relationship type measures

Item	% 1	% 2	% 3	% 4	% 5	M	SD	N	α
Satisfaction									
Both the organization and I benefit from the relationship.	2.1	4.2	5.6	43.0	45.1	4.25*	.901	142	
Most people like me are happy in their interactions with this organization.	4.3	8.7	17.4	47.8	21.7	3.74 i	1.034	138	
I am happy with this organization.	2.9	10.0	13.6	41.4	32.1	3.90*	1.055	140	
Generally speaking, I am pleased with the relationship this organization has established with me.	5.7	6.4	15.7	41.4	30.7	3.85*	1.105	140	
						3.94*	**1.024**		.88
Commitment									
I feel that this organization is trying to maintain a long-term commitment to me.	4.1	9.6	13.7	37.0	35.6	3.90*	1.116	146	
There is a long-lasting bond between this organization and me.	6.3	9.8	21.7	37.8	24.5	3.64*	1.141	143	
I can see that this organization wants to maintain a relationship with me.	5.0	7.1	12.9	44.3	30.7	3.89*	1.080	140	
Compared to other organizations, I value my relationship with this organization more.	6.5	6.5	16.7	34.8	35.5	3.86*	1.116	138	
						3.82*	**1.113**		.88
Trust									
This organization treats me fairly and justly.	2.7	5.5	8.9	37.7	45.2	4.17*	0.992	146	
Whenever this organization makes an important decision, I know it will be concerned about me.	9.1	20.3	34.3	28.7	7.7	3.06 i	1.080	143	
This organization can be relied on to keep its promises.	2.9	8.6	20.1	38.1	30.2	3.84*	1.044	139	
I believe that this organization takes my opinions into account when making decisions.	4.3	12.9	22.9	42.9	17.1	3.56*	1.054	140	
I feel very confident about this organization's skills.	5.8	10.1	15.8	37.4	30.9	3.78 i	1.161	139	
This organization has the ability to accomplish what it says it will do.	2.9	5.8	8.0	42.0	41.3	4.13*	0.988	138	
						3.76*	**1.053**		.90

(Continued)

Item	%	%	%	%	%	M	SD	N	α
	1	**2**	**3**	**4**	**5**				
Control Mutuality									
This organization believes my opinions are legitimate.	2.8	5.6	9.0	51.4	31.3	4.03i	0.938	144	
In dealing with me, this organization has a tendency to throw its weight around. [R]	4.3	10.8	29.5	30.9	24.5	3.60*	1.101	139	
This organization really listens to what I have to say.	4.3	10.1	26.6	39.6	19.4	3.60i	1.048	139	.80
This organization and I are attentive to what each other says.	2.2	3.6	30.7	43.1	20.4	3.76i	0.895	137	
						3.75i	**0.664**		
Communal									
This organization does not especially enjoy giving others aid. [R]	.7	9.1	11.2	26.6	52.4	4.21i	1.013	143	
This organization is very concerned about my welfare.	3.5	14.9	19.9	40.4	21.3	3.61i	1.087	141	
I feel that this organization takes advantage of people who are vulnerable. [R]	4.3	5.7	15.7	23.6	50.7	4.11i	1.130	140	
I think that this organization succeeds by stepping on other people. [R]	2.2	5.8	11.7	19.7	60.6	4.31i	1.033	137	.82
						4.06i	**1.066**		
Exchange									
Whenever this organization gives or offers something to me, it generally expects something in return.	7.0	16.9	32.4	31.7	12.0	3.25i	1.093	142	
Even though I have had a relationship with this organization for a long time, it still expects something in return whenever it offers me a favor.	10.8	15.8	38.8	26.6	7.9	3.05	1.086	139	
This organization will compromise with me when it knows that it will gain something.	20.4	10.9	39.4	24.1	5.1	2.82	1.163	137	
This organization takes care of people who are likely to reward the organization.	3.6	8.0	17.4	36.2	34.8	3.91i	1.080	138	.60
						3.26i	**1.106**		

Note: Adapted from "Golden Handcuffs in the Fortune 1000? An employee-organization relationship survey of public relations executives and practitioners in the largest companies," by C. A. Greenwood (2016), *Communication Research Reports, 33*(3), pp. 271–273. Copyright 2016 by Routledge. Adapted with permission. Scale: 1 = Strongly disagree; 2 = Somewhat disagree; 3 = Neither agree nor disagree; 4 = Somewhat agree; 5 Strongly agree. *M* = means. *SD* = Standard Deviation. *N* = sample size after pairwise deletion for missing variables. *α* = Cronbach's coefficient alpha, which measures scale reliability. *R* = reverse coded. [i] = Means less than *Fortune 1000* study; [*] = Means greater than millennial study; communal and exchange scales not included, Gallicano, Curtin, and Matthews (2012).

Appendix C

C.1. Open-ended question: third party

Fortune 1000 **Study**

1. I've worked primarily in the finance organization for 32 years of my career and only in the past year have I had responsibility for PR.
2. By and large, ethical behavior rules. I have not witnessed any unethical actions.
3. I saw fraud while at a public relations agency – saw two senior executives charge time and expenses that were not legitimate.
4. I answered "no" because the individuals were not aware of the activity at the time it was going on, but rather later.
5. We have signs posted in our buildings to make sure that team members understand how importanat [sic] of an issue ethics is.
6. n/a
7. Person cited in previous questions subsequently retired.
8. Your buttons didn't work on how the info was communicationed [sic]- we used print, electronic and face-to-face.
9. Episode I am thinking of is not SOX [Sarbanes-Oxley] related but manager-level ethical issues involving money. Whistle-blowing was done during exit interviews and ASAIK no action was taken. I left that company at mty [sic] earliest opportunity.
10. Ethics and ethical behavior if a core value of our all company. All employees are educated to report ethical violations immediately, either to their supervisors or to the compliance officer for their business unit.
11. Involvement of PR people was BECAUSE of their role, not as the person observing or reporting. Therefore virtually all questions in this section do not apply.
12. I've worked in PR for 41 years for two Fortune 500 companies. Both had very ethical management.
13. We have annual Code of Conduct training – all employees must participate.
14. The previous question to select all that applies only allowed me to choose one.

Wilshire 5000 **Study**

15. In my experience, there have been two situations regarding how this has been handled: / 1) Person with the knowledge expresses concern to manager. In most situations, this has negative impact on the person raising the issue. / 2) Person with the knowledge does not express concern because they are afraid of negative impact based on what they've seen happen to others.// I haven't seen anyone fired over this issue, but I have seen people's careers stall or move backward because of it.
16. I have never seen any retaliation taken against a person for reporting a possible integrity or compliance concern.

17. We have a channel to report ethics or treatment violations. I have received some complaints myself and forwarded them to this channel. My commpany [sic] investigates every complaint.
18. One of our VP's was attempting to make a side deal with an [sic] customer for international sourcing. They offered to handle it for them bypassing the company, which was working on this at the time.
19. All organizations I ahve [sic] ever worked with have encouraged whistle blowing strongly.
20. I got fired on 9/7/2012 for repoting [sic] the situation after they discovered it was me.
21. We have an anonymous reporting hotline and a third party method to report ethical violations. We receive annual ethics training and managers all complete an annual email certifying that they are not aware of, nor have they participated in a unethical, antitrust, anticompetitive, behaviors. We also verify taht [sic] we have not been involved with bribery or illegal political contributions.
22. i [sic] think more severe punishments are needed for those in public trust positions who violate tha ttrust [sic] . . . this includes 'Wall Street' type investment organzations [sic] who willing [sic] promote fradulent [sic] securities or who willingly manipulative [sic] information to alter stocks or stock prices.
23. There are frequent and numerous low value infractions – meals and alcohol inaccurately reported on expense reports, personal use of company purchased technology, devices and supplies, inaccurate travel and mileage expenses etc.
24. I'm not aware of how effective our process is as it is all confidential and there has never been any indication of a situation being reported as you suggest. To the best of my knowledge, it's all been confidential.
25. I'm aware of more vague reference to things in my previous jobs – nothing specific. Also aware of things that seemed unethical, but still legal. I think the FDA shut that down eventually though.
26. We had suspicions . . . began investigating as well as putting tighter controls in place. eventually identified the offense and placed cease and disist [sic] corrective actions in place
27. n/a
28. I am not sure I understand how to answer the question. At another job about 20 years ago came across some unethical behavior and reported it to a supervisor.
29. Nothing to share.
30. Person had been explicitly propositioned to pay a "finder's fee" to a foreign government representative as the basis for award of a large contract. Subsequently, because this was a large market already (and no bribes had heretofore been given or requested), this was turned over to appropriate authorities at the federal level with jurisdiction over foreign corrupt practices.
31. Annual Ethics training which includes reporting ANY unethical activities is a requirement for employment. (period)
32. Experienced [sic] described are for multiple scenarios. Half showed blatant retaliation (from the smaller offenders). For significant offenders with substantial monetary value attached to their deeds, nothing happened to the reporting person.
33. the issue was briefly reviewed but wasn't really taken seriously
34. I believe my company adheres completely to all Sarbanes Oxley guidelines.

C.2. Open-ended question: self

Fortune 1000 Study

1. It was nothing illegal, it was a consulting relationship that I felt was not useful, and thus a waste of corporate dollars.
2. One person who committed the fraud was fired. The other was not, and she retaliated against me. I eventually left the firm.
3. n/a
4. Need to clarify: We have an anonymous Ethics hotline. When there was an alleged breach of ethics against an employee it was reported to the client, a public-sector entity in an open-records state. Upon learning of the breach, our attorneys alerted PR and told the client, knowing that this would result in our termination. When the media asked for details we worked with the client to provide accurate factual information. I have no knowledge of any wrongdoing by the company itself on a SOX [Sarbanes-Oxley] related matter or anything else.
5. We are surveyed annually to ensure we have not forgotten to report and [sic] issue and also have annual training.
6. again [sic], in my position, I am involved in responding to and addressing most significant incidents in this regard. So most of these questions really do not apply at ALL. And I am becoming concerned in responding to this questionnaire, as I fear answers may not be understood. remember [sic], in this position, we are involved in addressing and/or managing almost every incident of this nature.
7. No other comments
8. Nothing
9. None of the "Select ALL" questions work. I'm only allowed to choose one. Additionally, what I encountered was not monetary.

Wilshire 5000 Study

10. Nothing happened as result of this at all. I did not report as a co worker [sic] reported this. Was never questioned, not aware that any investigation ever occurred internally at all.
11. I was fired on the spot after they found out it was me.
12. I found out about the incident after the individual was fired. There was no retaliation for the individual that reported.
13. Nothing
14. A culture exists of a 'blind eye' to minor infractions – i.e. we prohibit the reimbursement for purchase of alcohol at company events so those costs are 'obscured' within reported costs.
15. Was borderline: ordering expensive food while traveling then having a direct expense it.
16. I've been impressed at how consciencious [sic] my current employer is about supporting ethical behavior and sharing ways to report any issues./But when you see stuff that shouldn't be done, if it isn't directly harming anyone (minor expense reporting overcollection), it's tough to be the person to raise it up when the issue is from a manager above you, especially if your peers are involved as well. Lots of downside, little to no upside.
17. n/a
18. We have a good system for being able to report wrong doing, including issues related to this area. But it is not directly tied to auditing. It is anonymous.
19. Nothing to share.
20. I believe that the company for which I work is both ethical and legal in its business practices, both at home and abroad. We receive mandatory annual training on the topic and are subject to both internal and external audits to ensure compliance to known and well understood fraud and abuse statutes.

(Continued)

(Continued)

21. Not reporting unethical actions is as severe as committing the acts.
22. Whistle-blowing is frowned upon unless someone is stealing money from the organization or clients. 'Stealing' by way of questionable expenses is only used as a tool to build a case against someone they would like to see gone. It is not grounds for termination if the offender is considered 'profitable'.
23. this [sic]was an incident that the impacted individual made the complaint. I knew of the event from her statements. I would say that while she has not been directly impacted, that there is a stigma around her.
24. IF information is being reported by a lower level staff person it is rarely given much weight or taken seriously.
25. If I had reported it, my CEO et all would have gone billastic [sic].
26. My experience is that truly unethical or illegal behavior is rare. Petty theft iand [sic] inappropriate relationships are more common than major corruption. I find it a little odd that the only reporting structure you show in the survey is to the audit committee of the Board. That would assume the illegal behavior is so senior in the company that other managment [sic] would be incapable of taking care of the issue. Waste, Fraud, Abuse and HR issue hotlines certainly can and do exist for reporting, but do not necessarily go to the Board audit committee. I think the results will be skewed by people who are unfamiliar with the reporting structure you presented versus more common types that are available.
27. My current employer has a very strong code of ethics.

C.3. Open-ended question: roundup

Fortune 1000 Study

1. Remember, in the minds of many senior professionals, the CEO = the organization.
2. I am often perplexed by individuals who feel that their organization 'owes' them anything. This line of questioning seems to reinforce that mindset.
3. No other comments.

Wilshire 5000 Study

4. Not sure about these questions.
5. They fired me.
6. Really difficult survey to complete as the strongly agree column was hidden. I encourage you to ignore the results of your survey since you won't ever know if the responses are valid. Some respondents only see 4 choices and others five.
7. This moving of the bar to read and then answer is a trick page. One should be able to see the whole page.
8. This organization will make significant effort provided such effort neither causes it expend [sic] more than budgeted or place it in a situation of commitment or obligation. It is willing to give perks and benefits provided it retains the right to withold [sic] or remove those benefits at its discretion.
9. This is the best company I've ever worked for, particularly good at rewarding desired behaviors, setting clear expectations, and cultivating a learning culture.
10. Overall a good organization to work for. Most people are happy with the interactions, however there are time [sic] when senior management don't treat all employees the same.
11. As my organization is a publishing company, and publishing is going through tremendous change and evolving business models, all employees are going through the change curve and feel less empowered than in prior years.

12. Any organization which treats people poorly, steps on them or fails to listen to them will go out of business. (Unless the organization is a Government entity.) Organizations do NOT do favors. People do favors for other people. Organiztaions [*sic*] have a task to perform and objectives to meet . . .
13. Publicly-traded organization. Fortune 500 company. I've been employeed [*sic*] here for 10 years. As I've moved up the ladder, I've seen hard evidence of unscrupulous activities and have lost all respect for the firm.
14. I work for a firm with high values, moral obligations and, ethical firm with high regard for it's [*sic*] employees and their contribution. They have policies in place to guard from any illegal activity and from backlash of reporting any such activity.

Appendix D

U.S. Merit Systems Protection Board

The U.S. Merit Systems Protection Board ("MSPB" or "The Board") is an independent, quasi-judicial agency in the Executive branch that serves as the guardian of Federal merit systems. The Board was established by the Civil Service Reform Act of 1978 (CSRA), Public Law No. 95–454.

The Board's mission is to protect Federal merit systems and the rights of individuals within those systems. MSPB carries out its statutory responsibilities and authorities primarily by adjudicating individual employee appeals and by conducting merit systems studies.

The topic of this report, whistleblowing, occurs at the intersection of MSPB's two missions. As a part of its adjudicatory mission, MSPB considers, among other types of cases, appeals brought by individuals who allege that they have been subjected to retaliatory personnel actions because they have disclosed a violation of any law, rule, or regulation, or gross mismanagement, a gross waste of funds, an abuse of authority, or a substantial and specific danger to public health or safety.

As a part of the studies mission, MSPB has the statutory responsibility to study the health of the merit systems and the extent to which the public's interest in a civil service free from prohibited personnel practices is being protected. An efficient and effective civil service – a merit principle – requires a workplace in which employees feel that they can safely blow the whistle on wrongdoing. This report is issued solely under the studies function of the MSPB, and any findings or recommendations are not an official "opinion" of the Board in its adjudicatory role (Merit Systems Protection Board, 2011a, Preface).

Bibliography

Abramson, J. (2017). In defense of leaks. In E. Bell & T. Owen (Eds.), *Journalism after Snowden* (pp. 29–33). New York: Columbia University Press.

Acharya, V. V., Cooley, T. F., Richardson, M., Sylla, R., & Walter, I. (2011). Prologue: A Bird's-Eye View: The Dodd-Frank Wall Street Reform and Consumer Protection Act. In V. V. Acharya, T. F. Cooley, M. Richardson, & I. Walter (Eds.), *Regulating Wall Street: The Dodd-Frank Act and the New Architecture of Global Finance* (pp. 1–32). Hoboken, NJ: John Wiley & Sons, Inc.

Acharya, V. V., Cooley, T. F., Richardson, M., & Walter, I. (2011). Preface. In V. V. Acharya, T. F. Cooley, M. Richardson, & I. Walter (Eds.), *Regulating Wall Street: The Dodd-Frank Act and the New Architecture of Global Finance* (pp. xvii–xviii). Hoboken, NJ: John Wiley & Sons, Inc.

Acharya, V. V., Cooley, T. F., Richardson, M., & Walter, I. (Eds.). (2011). Regulating Wall Street: The Dodd-Frank Act and the new architecture of global finance. Hoboken, NJ: John Wiley & Sons, Inc.

Agence France-Presse in Washington. (2021). US government appeals UK ruling against Julian Assange's extradition. *The Guardian* (Feb 12, 2021). Retrieved from https://www.theguardian.com/media/2021/feb/12/us-government-appeals-uk-ruling-against-julian-assanges-extradition-joe-biden-wikileaks

Aldrich, H. E. (1999). *Organizations evolving*. London: Sage.

Aldrich, H. E., & Herker, D. (1977). Boundary Spanning Roles and Organization Structure. *Academy of Management Review, 2.2* 217–230. Retrieved from https://doi.org/10.2307/257905

Aldrich, H. E., & Ruef, M. (2006). *Organizations evolving* (2nd. ed.). Thousand Oaks, CA: Sage.

Alleyne, P., Hudaib, M., & Haniffa, R. (2018). The moderating role of perceived organisational support in breaking the silence of public accountants. *Journal of Business Ethics, 147*(3), 509–527. Retrieved from https://doi.org/10.1007/s10551-015-2946-0

Anonymous. (2018). I Am Part of the Resistance Inside the Trump Administration. *The New York Times* (September 5, 2018). Retrieved from https://www.nytimes.com/2018/09/05/opinion/trump-white-house-anonymous-resistance.html

Arbogast, S. V. (2013). *Resisting Corporate Corruption: Cases in Practical Ethics From Enron Through The Financial Crisis* (2nd. ed.). Hoboken, NJ: Wiley-Scrivener.

Archibald, S. J. (1979). The Freedom of Information Act Revisited. *Public Administration Review, 39*(4), 311–318. Retrieved from https://doi.org/10.2307/976206

Ashforth, B. E., & Anand, V. (2003). The normalization of corruption in organizations. In R. M. Kramer & B. M. Staw (Eds.), Research in organizational behavior: An annual series of analytical essays and critical reviews. In R. M. Kramer & B. M. Staw (Series Eds.),

Research in organizational behavior (vol. 25, pp. 1–52). Oxford, UK: Elsevier. Retrieved from https://doi.org/10.1016/S0191-3085(03)25001-2.

Ashton, J. (2015). 15 Years of whistleblowing protection under the Public Interest Disclosure Act 1998: Are we still shooting the messenger? *Industrial Law Journal, 44*(1), 29.

Axelrod, R. M. (1984). *The evolution of cooperation.* New York: Basic Books.

Banking Act of 1935, 12 U.S.C. § 228 (1935).

Barkow, J. H., Cosmides, L., & Tooby, J. (Eds.). *The adapted mind: Evolutionary psychology and the generation of culture* (pp. 3–18). New York: Oxford University Press.

Baum, J. A. C., & Singh, J. V. (Eds.). (1994). *Evolutionary dynamics of organizations.* New York: Oxford University Press.

Beck, J. R. (2000). The False Claims Act and the English eradication of qui tam legislation. *North Carolina Law Review*, 78, 539.

Bell, E., & Owen, T. (Eds.). (2017). *Journalism After Snowden: The Future of the Free Press in the Surveillance State.* New York: Columbia University Press.

Berger, B. K. (2005). Power over, power with, and power to relations: Critical reflections on public relations, the dominant coalition, and activism. *Journal of Public Relations Research, 17*(1), 5–28.

Berger, B. K., & Reber, B. H. (2006). *Gaining influence in public relations: The role of resistance in practice.* Mahwah, NJ: Lawrence Erlbaum Associates.

Berman, S. L., Wicks, A. C., Kotha, S., & Jones, T. M. (1999). Does stakeholder orientation matter? The relationship between stakeholder management models and firm financial performance. *Academy of Management Journal, 42*(5), 488–506.

Bernstein, C., & Woodward, B. (1974). *All the President's men.* New York: Simon and Schuster.

Bernstein Liebhard LLP. (2018a). *False Claims Act and whistleblower employee protections antiretaliation protections.* Retrieved from www.bernlieb.com/whistleblowers/FCA-Whistleblower-Employee-Protections/index.html

Bernstein Liebhard LLP. (2018b). *History of the False Claims Act – The Whistleblower Act.* Retrieved from www.bernlieb.com/whistleblowers/History-Of-The-False-Claims-Act/index.html

Bertalanffy, L. v. (1951). General system theory: A new approach to unity of science. *Human Biology, 23*, 302–361.

Bertalanffy, L. v. (1968). *General system theory: Foundations, development, applications.* New York: Braziller.

Boo, E. f., Terence Bu-Peow, N., & Shankar, P. G. (2016). Effects of incentive scheme and working relationship on whistle-blowing in an audit setting. *Auditing: A Journal of Practice & Theory, 35*(4), 23–38. https://doi.org10.2308/ajpt-51485

Bosua, R., Milton, S., Dreyfus, S., & Lederman, R. (2014). Going public: Researching external whistleblowing in a new media age. In A. J. Brown, D. Lewis, R. E. Moberly, & W. Vandekerckhove (Eds.), *International Handbook of Whistleblowing Research* (pp. 250–272). Cheltenham, UK: Edward Elgar Publishing Limited.

Botan, C. H. (1989). Theory development in PR. In C. H. Botan & V. Hazleton, Jr. (Eds.), *Public relations theory* (pp. 99–110). Hillsdale, NJ: Lawrence Erlbaum Associates.

Botan, C. H. (1993). Introduction to the paradigm struggle in public relations. *Public Relations Review, 19*(2), 107–110.

Botan, C. H., & Hazleton, V., Jr. (Eds.). (1989). *Public relations theory.* Hillsdale, NJ: Lawrence

Botan, C. H., & Hazleton, V. (2006). Public relations in a new age. In C. H. Botan & V. Hazleton (Eds.), *Public relations theory II* (pp. 1–20). Mahwah, NJ: Lawrence Erlbaum Associates. Erlbaum Associates.

Botan, C. H., & Hazleton, V. (Eds.). (2006). *Public relations theory II.* Mahwah, NJ: Lawrence Erlbaum Associates.

Boulding, K. E. (1956). General systems theory: The skeleton of science. *Management Science, 2*(3), 197–208.

Bowen, S. A. (2008). A state of neglect: Public relations as "corporate conscience" or ethics counsel. *Journal of Public Relations Research, 20*(3), 271–296. https://doi.org/10.1080/10627260801962749

Bowen, S. A. (2009). What communication professionals tell us regarding dominant coalition access and gaining membership. *Journal of Applied Communication Research, 37*(4), 418–443.

Bowen, S. A., Heath, R. L., & Lee, J. (2006). *An international study of ethical roles and counsel in the public relations function.* Paper presented at the International Communication Association Annual Conference, Dresden, Germany.

Bowman, M. (2008). Former White House press secretary defends tell-all book. *Voice of America News* (May 28, 2008). Retrieved from https://www.voanews.com/a/a-13-2008-05-29-voa15/401785.html

Bradbury, S. G. (2017). National Security and the "New Yellow Press". In E. Bell & T. Owen (Eds.), *Journalism after Snowden* (pp. 172–185). New York: Columbia University Press.

Bredemier, K. (1979). Tapes show Nixon role in firing of Ernest Fitzgerald. *The Washington Post* (March 7, 1979). Retrieved from https://www.washingtonpost.com/archive/politics/1979/03/07/tapes-show-nixon-role-in-firing-of-ernest-fitzgerald/048cd88e-60e5-498d-a8e2-e3b39461356b/?utm_term=.dac5c4cd35e0

Brickey, K. F. (2003). F. Hodge O'Neal Corporate and Securities Law Symposium: After the Sarbanes-Oxley Act: The future disclosure system: From Enron To Worldcom and beyond: Life and crime after Sarbanes-Oxley. *Washington University Law Quarterly, 81,* 357–402.

Broom, G. M., Casey, S., & Ritchey, J. (1997). Toward a concept and theory of organization-public relationships. *Journal of Public Relations Research, 9*(2), 83–98.

Brown, A. J. (2011). Weeding out WikiLeaks (and why it won't work): legislative recognition of public whistleblowing in Australia. *Global Media Journal: Australian Edition, 5*(1), 1–11.

Brown, A. J., Lewis, D., Moberly, R. E., & Vandekerckhove, W. (Eds.). (2014). *International Handbook on Whistleblowing Research.* Cheltenham, UK: Edward Elgar Publishing Limited.

Brown, A. J., Meyer, D. P., Wheeler, C., & Zuckerman, J. (2014). Whistleblower support in practice: Towards an integrated research model. In A. J. Brown, D. Lewis, R. E. Moberly, & W. Vandekerckhove (Eds.), *International Handbook on Whistleblowing Research* (pp. 457–494). Cheltenham, UK: Edward Elgar Publishing Limited.

Buss, D. M. (1991). Evolutionary personality psychology. *Annual Review of Psychology, 42,* 459–491.

Butan, M., Scott, R., Landesman, P., & MadRiver. (2017). *Mark Felt: The man who brought down the White House* [Video/DVD]. Culver City, CA: Sony Pictures Classics.

Byrne, R. W., & Whiten, A. (1988). *Machiavellian intelligence: Social expertise and the evolution of intellect in monkeys, apes, and humans.* Oxford, UK: Clarendon Press.

Byrne, R. W., & Whiten, A. (1997). Machiavellian intelligence. In A. Whiten & R. W. Byrne (Eds.), *Machiavellian intelligence II: Extensions and evaluations* (pp. 1–23). Cambridge, UK: Cambridge University Press.

Capelli, P. (2000). A market-driven approach to retaining talent. *Harvard Business Review, 78*(1), 103–111.

Chayes, S. (2015). *Thieves of State: Why Corruption Threatens Global Security.* New York: W. W. Norton.

Cheney, G., & Christensen, L. T. (2001). Public relations as contested terrain: A critical response. In R. L. Heath (Ed.), *The handbook of public relations* (pp. 167–182). Thousand Oaks, CA: Sage.

Cheng, X., Karim, K. E., & Lin, K. J. (2015). A cross-cultural comparison of whistleblowing perceptions. *Management and Decision Making, 14*(1), 15–31.

Chu, A. (2016). In tradition of speaking fearlessly: Locating a rhetoric of whistleblowing in the Parrhēsiastic dialectic. *Advances in the History of Rhetoric, 19*(3), 231–250. https://doi.org/10.1080/15362426.2016.1232206

Ciasullo, M. V., Cosimato, S., & Palumbo, R. (2017). Improving health care quality: the implementation of whistleblowing. *The TQM Journal, 29*(1), 167–183. https://doi.org/10.1108/tqm-06-2016-0051

Civil Service Reform Act of 1978, 5 U.S.C. § 1101 (1978).

Clark, M. S., & Mills, J. (1979). Interpersonal attraction in exchange and communal relationships. *Journal of Personality and Social Psychology, 37*(1), 12–24. https://doi.org/10.1037/0022-3514.37.1.12

Clarke, R. A. (2004). *Against all enemies: Inside America's war on terror.* New York: Free Press.

Clinton, H. R. (2017). *What happened* (First ed.): New York: Simon & Schuster.

Cobb, C. (2008). *Driving public relations: Chrysler moves PR under the HR umbrella, spurs debate about where PR reports. Strategist, 14*(3), 6–11.

Coblenz, W. (Producer) & A. J. Pakula (Director). (1976). *All the President's Men* [Motion Picture]. Los Angeles: Warner Bros.

Code of Ethics for Government Service, 72 Stat. B12 (1958).

Coleman, R., & Wilkins, L. (2009). The moral development of public relations practitioners: A comparison with other professions and influences on higher quality ethical reasoning. *Journal of Public Relations Research, 21*(3), 318–340.

Comey, J. (2018). *A Higher Loyalty: Truth, Lies, and Leadership.* New York: Flat Iron Books.

Coombs, W. T. (2001). Interpersonal communications and public relations. In R. L. Heath (Ed.), *The handbook of public relations* (pp. 105–114). Thousand Oaks, CA: Sage.

Corbin, J. (1997). Lawyers and us—A synergistic relationship. *Public Relations Quarterly, 42*(4), 15–17.

Cords, M. (1997). Friendships, alliances, reciprocity and repair. In A. Whiten & R. W. Byrne (Eds.), Machiavellian intelligence II: Extensions and evaluations (pp. 24–49). Cambridge, UK: Cambridge University Press.

Cortina, L. M., & Magley, V. J. (2003). Raising voice, risking retaliation: Events following interpersonal mistreatment in the workplace. *Journal of Occupational Health Psychology, 8*(4), 247–265.

Cosmides, L., & Tooby, J. (1992). Cognitive adaptation for social change. In J. H. Barkow, L. Cosmides, & J. Tooby (Eds.), *The adapted mind: Evolutionary psychology and the generation of culture* (pp. 163–228). New York: Oxford University Press.

Cosmides, L., & Tooby, J. (1992). The psychological foundations of culture. In J. H. Barkow, L. Cosmides, & J. Tooby (Eds.), *The adapted mind: Evolutionary psychology and the generation of culture* (pp. 19–136). New York: Oxford University Press.

Cosmides, L., Tooby, J., & Barkow, J. H. (1992). Introduction: Evolutionary psychology and conceptual integration. In J. H. Barkow, L. Cosmides, & J. Tooby (Eds.), *The adapted mind: Evolutionary psychology and the generation of culture* (pp. 3–18). New York: Oxford University Press.

Court rules small groups can bring whistleblowing claims. (2017). *People Management* (August 2017), 14. Retrieved from https://issuu.com/peoplemgt/docs/pm_aug17_web

Cronbach, L. J. (1951). Coefficient alpha and the internal structure of tests. *Psychometrika, 16*(3), 297–334. https://doi.org/10.1007/BF02310555

Cropp, F., & Pincus, J. D. (2001). The mystery of public relations: Unraveling its past, unmasking its future. In R. L. Heath (Ed.), *The handbook of public relations* (pp. 189–203). Thousand Oaks, CA: Sage.

Culiberg, B., & Mihelič, K. K. (2017). The Evolution of whistleblowing studies: A critical review and research agenda. *Journal of Business Ethics, 146*(4), 787–803. https://doi.org/10.1007/s10551-016-3237-0

Curry, B., & Wenske, P. (1979). Silkwood Family Awarded $10.5 Million in Damages. *The Washington Post* (May 19, 1979). Retrieved from www.washingtonpost.com

Curtin, P. A., & Gaither, T. K. (2005). Privileging identity, difference, and power: The circuit of culture as a basis for public relations theory. *Journal of Public Relations Research, 17*(2), 91–115.

Cutlip, S. M., & Center, A. H. (1952). *Effective public relations; Pathways to public favor.* New York: Prentice-Hall, Inc.

Cutlip, S. M., Center, A. H., & Broom, G. M. (1985). *Effective public relations* (6th ed.). Englewood Cliffs, NJ: Prentice-Hall.

Cutlip, S. M., Center, A. H., & Broom, G. M. (1994). *Effective public relations.* Englewood Cliffs, NJ: Prentice-Hall

Cyert, R. M., & March, J. G. (1963). *A behavioral theory of the firm* (2nd ed.). New Jersey: Prentice-Hall, Inc.

D'Amato, A. (2006). Porn up, rape down. *Original Law Review, 2*(3), 91–100

Darwin, C. (1871). *The descent of man, and selection in relation to sex.* London: J. Murray.

Darwin, C. (1979/1859). *On the origin of species.* New York: Gramercy Books.

Dawkins, R. (1976). *The selfish gene:* New York: Oxford University Press.

Delikat, M., & Phillips, R. B. (2011). *Corporate whistleblowing in the Sarbanes-Oxley/Dodd-Frank era* (2nd ed.). New York: Practising Law Institute.

Dennett, D. C. (1995). *Darwin's dangerous idea: Evolution and the meanings of life.* New York: Simon & Schuster.

Department of Homeland Security and Office of the Director of National Intelligence. (2016). Joint Statement from the Department of Homeland Security and Office of the Director of National Intelligence on Election Security [Press release]. Retrieved from https://www.dhs.gov/news/2016/10/07/joint-statement-department-homeland-security-and-office-director-national#content

Department of Justice Guide to the Freedom of Information Act. (2013). Retrieved from https://www.justice.gov/sites/default/files/oip/legacy/2014/07/23/intro-july-19-2013.pdf

Depoorter, B., & De Mot, J. (2006). Whistle Blowing: An Economic Analysis of the False Claims Act. *Supreme Court Economic Review, 14*(1), 135–162.

de Santis, M. D. (2021). Misconceptions About Historical Sciences in Evolutionary Biology. *Evolutionary Biology, 48*(1), 94–99. https://doi.org/10.1007/s11692-020-09526-6

Devine, T. (1997). The whistleblower's survival guide: Courage without martyrdom. Washington, DC: Fund for Constitutional Government.

Digital Realty Trust, Inc. v. Somers, 583 U. S.___ (2018).

Dille, B. (2016, Summer). [Review of the book *Thieves of State: Why Corruption Threatens Global Security.* By Sarah Chayes. New York: W.W. Norton & Company, 2015]. *Journal of Strategic Security, 9*(2), 129–132.

Dobzhansky, T. (1973). Nothing in biology makes sense except in the light of evolution. *The American Biology Teacher, 35*(March), 125–129.

Dodd-Frank Act of 2010, 12 U.S.C. § 5301 (2010).

Doherty, B., & Remeikis, A. (2019). Julian Assange's extradition fight could turn on reports he was spied on for CIA. *The Guardian(London)* (December 16, 2019). Retrieved from https://www.theguardian.com/media/2019/dec/17/julian-assanges-extradition-fight-could-turn-on-reports-he-was-spied-on-for-cia

Dooley, L. M., & Lindner, J. R. (2003). The handling of nonresponse error. *Human Resource Development Quarterly, 14*(1), 99–110.

Dozier, D. A. (1992). The organizational roles of communications and public relations practitioners. In J. E. Grunig, D. A. Dozier, W. P. Ehling, L. A. Grunig, F. C. Repper, & J. White (Eds.), *Excellence in public relations and communication management* (pp. 327–355). Hillsdale, NJ: Lawrence Erlbaum Associates.

Dozier, D. A., & Grunig, L. A. (1992). The organization of the public relations function. In J. E. Grunig (Ed.), *Excellence in public relations and communication management* (pp. 395–417). Hillsdale, NJ: Lawrence Erlbaum Associates.

Dreyfus, S., Lederman, R., Bosua, R., & Milton, S. (2011). Can we handle the truth? Whistleblowing to the media in the digital era. *Global Media Journal: Australian Edition, 5*, 1–6.

Edelman. (2018). 2018 Edelman Trust Barometer Retrieved from https://www.edelman.com/trust-barometer/

Edward Snowden Fast Facts. (2013). *CNN* (September 11, 2013). Retrieved from https://www.cnn.com/2013/09/11/us/edward-snowden-fast-facts/index.html

Egan, M. (2020). A government agency just paid a record $114 million to an anonymous whistleblower. *CNN* (October 23, 2020). Retrieved from https://www.cnn.com/2020/10/23/business/sec-record-whistleblower-award/index.html

Eggen, D., Fainaru, S., & Washington Post Staff Writers. (2002). FBI whistle-blower to testify in senate. *The Washington Post* (June 1). Retrieved from www.washingtonpost.com

Eisenberg, E. M. W., Marsha G. (1987). Reconsidering Openness in Organizational Communication. *The Academy of Management Review, 12*(3), 418–426.

Ellsberg, D. (2018a). Daniel Ellsberg. Retrieved from HYPERLINK "http://www.ellsberg" www.ellsberg.net/

Ellsberg, D. (2018b). Extended biography. Retrieved from HYPERLINK "http://www.ellsberg" www.ellsberg.net/bio/extended-biography/

Erickson, S. L., Weber, M., & Segovia, J. (2011). Using communication theory to analyze corporate reporting strategies. *Journal of Business Communication, 48*(2), 207–223. Retrieved from https://doi.org/10.1177/0021943611399728

Ethics & Compliance Initiative. (2018). *The State of Ethics & Compliance in the Workplace* (978-1-5323-7114-1). Retrieved from https://www.ethics.org/knowledge-center/2018-gbes-2/

Ethics & Compliance Initiative. (2019). *Workplace misconduct and reporting: A global look.* Retrieved from https://www.ethics.org/

Ethics Resource Center. (2007). *The 2007 national business ethics survey: An inside view of private sector ethics.* Retrieved from Arlington, VA: http://www.ethics.org/resource/2007-national-business-ethics-survey

F.B.I. agent who wrote critical memo retires at 50. (2005). *New York Times* (January 2, 2005), 16. Retrieved from https://search-proquest-com.ezproxy.lib.ou.edu/docview/92870014?accountid=12964

The False Claims Act Legal Center. (2008). *What does "qui tam" mean?* (May 30, 2008). Retrieved from http://www.taf.org/faq.htm#q2

False Claims Act of 1863, 12 U.S.C. § 696 (1863).

False Claims Amendments Act of 1986, 31 U.S.C. § 3701 nt (1986).

Fasterling, B., & Lewis, D. (2014). Leaks, legislation and freedom of speech: How can the law effectively promote public-interest whistleblowing? *International Labour Review, 153*(1), 71–92. https://doi.org/10.1111/j.1564-913X.2014.00197.x

Faunce, T., Crow, K., Nikolic, T., & Morgan, J., Frederick M. (2014). Because they have evidence: Globalizing financial incentives for corporate fraud whistleblowers. In A. J. Brown, D. Lewis, R. E. Moberly, & W. Vandekerckhove (Eds.), *International Handbook of Whistleblowing* (pp. 381–404). Cheltenham, UK: Edward Elgar Publishing Limited.

Federal Bureau of Investigation. (1974). *Watergate (Summary) Part 01 of 02.* (139–4089). Retrieved from https://vault.fbi.gov/watergate/watergate-summary-part-01-of-02/view.

Fessler, D. M. T., & Haley, K. J. (2003). The strategy of affect: Emotions in human cooperation. In P. Hammerstein (Ed.), *Genetic and cultural evolution of cooperation* (pp. 7–36). Cambridge, MA: MIT Press.

Field, A. J. (2004). *Altruistically inclined? The behavioral sciences, evolutionary theory, and the origins of reciprocity.* Ann Arbor, MI: University of Michigan Press.

Fitzpatrick, K. R., & Rubin, M. S. (1995). Public relations vs. legal strategies in organizational crisis decisions. *Public Relations Review, 21*(1), 21–33. http://doi.org/10.1016/0363-8111 (95)90037-3

Foose, A. (2017). UK financial services whistleblowing regulation survey. *Benchmark.* NAVEX Global: Lake Oswego, OR. Retrieved from https://www.navexglobal.com/en-us/file-download-canonical?file=/uk-financial-services-whistleblowing-regulation-report-emea.pdf&file-name=uk-financial-services-whistleblowing-regulation-report-emea.pdf

Foreign Corrupt Practices Act of 1977, 15 U.S.C. § 78a nt (1977).

Fraud Enforcement and Recovery Act of 2009, 18 U.S.C. § 1 nt (2009).

Freedom of Information Act of 1966, 5 U.S.C. § 552 (1966).

Frith, C. D. (2007). The social brain? *Philosophical Transactions: Biological Sciences Social Intelligence: From Brain to Culture, 362*(1480), 671–678.

Gallicano, T. D., Curtin, P., & Matthews, K. (2012). I love what i do, but . . . A relationship management survey of millennial generation public relations agency employees. *Journal of Public Relations Research, 24*(3), 222–242. https://doi.org/10.1080/1062726X.2012.671986

Gee, H., Howlett, R., & Campbell, P. (2009, January). 15 Evolutionary gems. *Nature.* Retrieved from www.nature.com/evolutiongems

Gellman, B. (2013). Edward Snowden, after months of NSA revelations, says his mission's accomplished. *The Washington Post* (December 23, 2013). Retrieved from https://www.washingtonpost.com/

Gerald R. Ford Library and Museum. (2020). *The Watergate files.* Retrieved from https://www.fordlibrarymuseum.gov/museum/exhibits/watergate_files/content.php?section=2&page=b&person=2

Gibb, J. R. (1961). Defensive communication. *Journal of Communication, XI*(3), 141–148.

Gibson, M. A., & Lawson, D. W. (2015). Applying evolutionary anthropology. *Evolutionary Anthropology, 24*(1), 3–14. https://doi.org/10.1002/evan.21432

Gigerenzer, G. (1997). The modulatory of social intelligence. In A. Whiten & R. W. Byrne (Eds.), *Machiavellian intelligence II: Extensions and evaluations* (pp. 264–288). Cambridge, UK: Cambridge University Press.

Glauser, M. J. (1984). Upward information flow in organizations: Review and conceptual analysis. *Human Relations, 37*(8), 613–643. https://doi.org/10.1177/001872678403700804

Glazer, M. P., & Glazer, P. M. (1989). *The whistleblowers: Exposing corruption in government and industry.* New York: Basic Books, Inc.

Goldfarb, A. (2009). "Golden handcuffs" can hold key to locking up top executives. Fenton Report (March 22, 2009). Retrieved from www.fentonreport.com/2009/03/22/entrepreneurs/%E2%80%9Cgolden-handcuffs%E2%80%9D-can-hold-key-to-locking-up-top-executives/684

Government Accountability Project. (2008a). S. 494 – H.R. 1317: *Whistleblower Protection Act Amendments.* Retrieved from www.whistleblower.org/template/page.cfm?page_id=146

Government Accountability Project. (2008b). *Whistleblower Protection Act & Amendments.* Retrieved from http://web.archive.org/web/20080604135422/www.whistleblower.org/template/page.cfm?page_id=121

Gower, K. K. (2006). Public relations research at the cross-roads. *Journal of Public Relations Research,* 18, 177–190.

Graham, J. W. (1986). Principled organizational dissent: A theoretical essay. *Research in Orga-nizational Behavior, 8,* 1–52. https://psycnet.apa.org/record/1988-12437-001

Gravley, D., Richardson, B. K., & Allison Jr., J. M. (2015). Navigating the "Abyss": A narrative analysis of whistle-blowing, retaliation, and identity within Texas Public School Systems. *Management Communication Quarterly, 29*(2), 171–197. https://doi.org/10.1177/08933189 14567666

Greenwood, C. A. (2007, March). *Evolutionary theory: The missing link for public relations.* Unpublished manuscript.

Greenwood, C. A. (2008, May). *Evolutionary theory: The missing link for public relations.* Paper presented at the Annual Meeting of the International Communication Association, Mon-treal, Canada.

Greenwood, C. A. (2009, August). *Whistleblowing in public relations: Call for a research agenda.* Poster presented at the Association for Education in Journalism and Mass Communica-tion Annual Conference, Boston, MA.

Greenwood, C. A. (2010). Evolutionary theory: The missing link for conceptualizing public relations. *Journal of Public Relations Research, 22*(4), 456–476. https://doi.org/10.1080/106 27261003801438

Greenwood, C. A. (2011). *Killing the messenger: A survey of public relations practitioners and orga-nizational response to whistleblowing after Sarbanes-Oxley.* Doctoral dissertation. University of Oregon, Eugene, Oregon. Retrieved from ProQuest Dissertations & Theses (UMI No. 907550960).

Greenwood, C. A. (2012, August). *Whistleblowing in the Fortune 1000: Ethical dilemma or role responsibility?* Paper presented at the Association for Education in Journalism and Mass Communication Annual Conference, Chicago, IL.

Greenwood, C. A. (2013, March). *Whistleblowing in government: What whistleblowers and reporters say about it.* Paper presented at the Association for Education in Journalism and Mass Communication Midwinter Conference, Norman, OK.

Greenwood, C. A. (2013, May). *What public relations practitioners do and what whistleblowers want.* Presentation at the PRSA/GA Annual Conference, Atlanta, GA.

Greenwood, C. A. (2013, June). *Whistleblowing in the Fortune 1000: What did public relations practitioners tell us?* Poster presented at the International Communication Association Confer-ence, London. Retrieved from http://citation.allacademic.com/meta/p640129_index.html

Greenwood, C. A. (2014, April). *Whistleblowing as an act of communication: What ethical choices do communicators face?* Panel presentation at the Eastern Communication Association Annual Meeting, Providence, RI.

Greenwood, C. A. (2014, May). *Whistleblowing in government: What whistleblowers say about it.* Paper presented at the International Communication Association Annual Conference, Seattle, WA.

Greenwood, C. A. (2014, August). *I was just doing my job! In-depth interviews with government whistleblowers.* Panel presentation at the Association for Education in Journalism and Mass Communication Annual Conference. Montreal, Canada.

Greenwood, C. A. (2015). Whistleblowing in the *Fortune 1000*: What practitioners told us about wrongdoing in corporations in a pilot study. *Public Relations Review,* (41), 490–500. https://doi.org/10.1016/j.pubrev.2015.07.005

Greenwood, C. A. (2015, April). *Whistleblowing in a national laboratory: Do whistleblower protections apply to federal contractors, and how is national security compromised when they don't?* Panel presenta-tion at the Eastern Communication Association Annual Conference. Philadelphia, PA.

Greenwood, C. A. (2016). Golden Handcuffs in the Fortune 1000? An employee-organi-zation relationship survey of public relations executives and practitioners in the largest companies. *Communication Research Reports, 33*(3), 269–274. http://doi.org/10.1080/08824 096.2016.1186624

Greenwood, C. A. (2017, April). *Whistleblowing: Can E&C programs induce reporting and reduce retaliation?* Presentation at the Ethics and Compliance Initiative Annual Conference. Washington, DC.

Greenwood, C. A. (2020). "I was just doing my job!" Evolution, corruption, and public relations in interviews with government whistleblowers. *PARTECIPAZIONE E CONFLITTO, 13*(2), 1042–1061. https://doi.org/10.1285/i20356609v13i2p1042

Greenwood, C. A. (forthcoming). Secrets, sources, whistleblowers, and leakers: Journalism in the Digital Age. [Review of the book *Journalism after Snowden: The Future of the Free Press in the Surveillance State*, E. Bell & T. Owen (Eds.)]. *Communication Booknotes Quarterly, 52*(1).

Greenwood, C. A., & Kahle, L. R. (2007, June). *Toward an evolutionary theory of marketing: Evolution and branding.* Proceedings of the Advertising & Consumer Psychology Conference. Santa Monica, CA. Retrieved from https://www.myscp.org/pdf/ACP%202007%20Proceedings.pdf

Groves, R. M., Fowler, F. J., Couper, M. P., Lepkowski, J. M., Singer, E., & Tourangeau, R. (2004). Survey methodology. Hoboken, NJ: Wiley.

Grunig, J. E. (1975). A multi-systems theory of organizational communication. *Communication Research, 2*(2), 99–136.

Grunig, J. E. (1989). Symmetrical presuppositions as a framework for public relations theory. In C. H. Botan & V. Hazleton, Jr. (Eds.), *Public relations theory* (pp. 17–44). Hillsdale, NJ: Lawrence Erlbaum Associates.

Grunig, J. E. (Ed.) (1992). *Excellence in public relations and communication management.* Hillsdale, NJ: Lawrence Erlbaum Associates.

Grunig, J. E. (1993). Image and substance: From symbolic to behavioral relationships. *Public Relations Review, 19*(2), 121–139.

Grunig, J. E. (2000). Collectivism, collaboration, and societal corporatism as core professional values in public relations. *Journal of Public Relations Research, 12*(1), 23–48.

Grunig, J. E. (2001). Two-way symmetrical public relations: Past, present, and future. In R. L. Heath & G. Vasquez (Eds.), *The handbook of public relations* (pp. 11–30). Thousand Oaks, CA: Sage.

Grunig, J. E., & Grunig, L. A. (1992). Models of public relations and communication. In J. E. Grunig (Ed.), *Excellence in public relations and communication management* (pp. 285–325). Hillsdale, NJ: Lawrence Erlbaum Associates.

Grunig, J. E., & Grunig, L. A. (2000). Public relations in strategic management and strategic management of public relations: Theory and evidence from the IABC Excellence project. *Journalism Studies, 1*(2), 303–321.

Grunig, J. E., & Grunig, L. A. (2008). Excellence theory in public relations: Past, present, and future. In A. Zerfass, B. van Ruler, & K. Sriramesh (Eds.), *Public relations research: European and international perspectives* (pp. 327–347). Weisbaden, Germany: VS Verlag für Sozialwissenschaften.

Grunig, J. E., Grunig, L. A., & Dozier, D. M. (2006). The excellence theory. In C. H. Botan & V. Hazleton (Eds.), *Public relations theory II* (pp. 21–62). Mahwah, NJ: Lawrence Erlbaum Associates.

Grunig, J. E., & Grunig, L. S. (1986). Application of general system theory to public relations: Review of a program of research. *Public Relations Review, 12*(3), 54.

Grunig, J. E., & Huang, Y.-H. (2000). From organizational effectiveness to relationship indicators: Antecedents of relationships, public relations strategies, and relationship outcomes. In J. A. Ledingham & S. D. Bruning (Eds.), *Public relations as relationship management: A relational approach to the study and practice of public relations* (pp. 23–54). Mahwah, NJ: Lawrence Erlbaum Associates.

Grunig, J. E., & Hunt, T. (1984). *Managing public relations*. New York: Holt, Rinehart and Winston.

Grunig, J. E., & Kim, J.-N. (2021). 15 The four models of public relations and their research legacy In C. Valentini (Ed.), *Public Relations* (pp. 277–312). Boston: De Gruyter Mouton. Retrieved from https://doi.org/10.1515/9783110554250-015.

Grunig, J. E., & White, J. (1992). The effect of worldviews on public relations theory and practice. In J. E. Grunig, D. M. Dozier, W. P. Ehling, L. A. Grunig, F. C. Repper, & J. White (Eds.), *Excellence in public relations and communication management* (pp. 31–64). Hillsdale, NJ: Lawrence Erlbaum Associates.

Grunig, L. A., Grunig, J. E., & Dozier, D. M. (2002). *Excellent public relations and effective organizations: A study of communication management in three countries*. Mahwah, NJ: Lawrence Erlbaum Associates.

Hair, J. F., Jr., Anderson, R. E., Tatham, R. L., & Black, W. C. (1998). *Multivariate data analysis* (5th ed.). Upper Saddle River, NJ: Prentice Hall.

Hamilton, W. D. (1964). The genetical evolution of social behaviour. I and II. *Journal of Theoretical Biology, 7*(1), 1–52.

Hammerstein, P. (2003). *Genetic and cultural evolution of cooperation*. Cambridge, MA: MIT Press.

Hansberry, H. L. (2012). In spite of its good intentions, the Dodd–Frank Act has created an FCPA monster. *Journal of Criminal Law & Criminology, 102*(1), 195–226.

Harcourt, A. H., & de Waal, F. B. M. (1992). *Coalitions and alliances in humans and other animals*. Oxford, UK: Oxford University Press.

The heavy toll of Watergate. (1975). *U.S. News & World Report*, (January 13, 1975), 16–20. Retrieved from https://advance-lexis-com.ezproxy.lib.ou.edu/api/document?collection=news&id=urn:contentItem:3SJ4-DTS0-000C-D54P-00000-00&context=1516831.

Hickson, M., III. (1973). The open systems model: Auditing the effectiveness of organizational communication. *Journal of Business Communication, 10*(3), 7–14.

Hirsh, M., Isikoff, M., Klaidman, D., Hosenball, M., Clift, E., Barry, J., & . . ., & Dickey, C. (2002). What Went Wrong. *Newsweek, 139*, 28–36.

Hitt, M. A., Beamish, P. W., Jackson, S. E., & Mathieu, J. E. (2007). Building theoretical and empirical bridges across levels: Multilevel research in management. *Academy of Management Journal, 50*(6), 1385–1399.

Holtzhausen, D. R. (2000). Postmodern values in public relations. *Journal of Public Relations Research, 12*(1), 93–114.

Holtzhausen, D. R. (2015). The unethical consequences of professional communication codes of ethics: A postmodern analysis of ethical decision-making in communication practice. *Public Relations Review, 41*(5), 769–776. https://doi.org/10.1016/j.pubrev.2015.06.008

Holtzhausen, D. R., & Roberts, G. F. (2008). *An investigation into the role of image repair theory in strategic conflict management*. Paper presented at the meeting of the International Communication Association, Montreal, Canada.

Holtzhausen, D. R., & Voto, R. (2002). Resistance from the margins: The postmodern public relations practitioner as organizational activist. *Journal of Public Relations Research, 14*(1), 57–84.

Hon, L. C., & Grunig, J. E. (1999). *Guidelines for measuring relationships in public relations* (p. 40). Retrieved from http://painepublishing.com/wp-content/uploads/2013/10/Guidelines_Measuring_Relationships.pdf

Hosenball, M., & Isikoff, M. (2002). Newsweek: FBI counterterrorism officials 'toned down' an agent's request for a warrant to search Moussaoui's computer, whistleblowing letter says. *PRNewswire* (May 26, 2002), 1. Retrieved from https://search-proquest-com. ezproxy.lib.ou.edu/docview/446796301?accountid=12964

Huang, Y.-H. (1997). *Public relations strategies, relational outcomes, and conflict management strategies.* (Doctoral dissertation), University of Maryland, College Park, MD. Retrieved from ProQuest Dissertations Publishing 9816477

Huang, Y.-H. (2008). Trust and relational commitment in corporate crises: The effects of crisis communicative strategy and form of crisis response. *Journal of Public Relations Research, 20*, 297–327. https://doi.org/10.1080/10627260801962830

Humphrey, N. (1976). The social function of intellect. In P. P. G. Bateson & R. A. Hinge (Eds.), *Growing points in ethology* (pp. 303–317). Oxford, UK: Cambridge University Press.

Humphrey, N. (1988). The social function of intellect. In R. W. Byrne & A. Whiten (Eds.), *Machiavellian intelligence: Social expertise and the evolution of intellect in monkeys, apes and humans* (pp. 13–26). Oxford, UK: Oxford University Press.

Hutton, J. G. (2001). Defining the relationship between public relations and marketing. In R. L. Heath (Ed.), *The handbook of public relations* (pp. 205–214). Thousand Oaks, CA: Sage.

Inspector General Act of 1978, 5 U.S.C. app. (1978).

Isikoff, M. (2008). The fed who blew the whistle. *Newsweek* (December 22, 2008). Retrieved from https://login.ezproxy.lib.ou.edu/login?url=https://www-proquest-com.ezproxy.lib. ou.edu/magazines/fed-who-blew-whistle/docview/214258835/se-2?accountid=12964

Jarrett, L., & Borger, G. (2017). Obama commutes sentence of Chelsea Manning. *CNN U.S.* (January 17, 2017). Retrieved from https://www.cnn.com/2017/01/17/politics/ chelsea-manning-sentence-commuted/index.html

Jo, S., Hon, L. C., & Brunner, B. R. (2004). Organization-public relationships: Measurement validation in a university setting. *Journal of Communication Management, 9*(1), 14–27.

Jo, S., & Shim, S. W. (2005). Paradigm shift of employee communication: The effect of management communication on trusting relationships. *Public Relations Review, 31*(2), 277–280.

Johnson, C. E., Sellnow, T. L., Seeger, M. W., Barrett, M. S., & Hasbargen, K. C. (2004). Blowing the whistle on Fen-Phen. *Journal of Business Communication, 41*(4), 350–369. Retrieved from https://doi.org/10.1177/0021943604265608

Kaal, W. A. (2016). Dodd-Frank Act. In A. Farazmand (Ed.), *Global encyclopedia of public administration, public policy, and governance* (pp. 1–5). Switzerland: Springer International Publishing.

Kahle, L. R. (1984). *Attitudes and social adaptation: A person-situation interaction approach.* Oxford, UK: Pergamon Press.

Kang, J.-A., & Berger, B. K. (2010). The influence of organizational conditions on public relations practitioners' dissent. *Journal of Communication Management, 14*(4), 368–387. https://doi.org/10.1108/13632541011090464

Kang, J.-A., Berger, B. K., & Shin, H. (2012). Comparative study of American and Korean practitioners' dissent with perceived unethical management decisions. *Public Relations Review, 38*, 147–149. https://doi.org/10.1016/j.pubrev.2011.12.006

Karanges, E., Johnston, K., Beatson, A., & Lings, I. (2015). The influence of internal communication on employee engagement: A pilot study. *Public Relations Review, 41*(1), 129–131. http://doi.org/10.1016/j.pubrev.2014.12.003

Katz, D. M., & Homer, J. (2008). WorldCom whistle-blower Cynthia Cooper. *CFO Magazine* (February 1, 2008), 38–40. Retrieved from http://www.cfo.com/article.cfm/10590507?f= search

Keenan, J. P. (1988, August). *Communication climate, whistle-blowing, and the first-level manager: A preliminary study*. Paper presented at the Annual Meeting of the Academy of Management, Anaheim, CA.

Keenan, J. P. (2000). Blowing the whistle on less serious forms of fraud: A study of executives and managers. *Employee Responsibilities and Rights Journal, 12*(4), 199–217.

Keenan, J. P. (2002). Whistleblowing: A study of managerial differences. *Employee Responsibilities and Rights Journal, 14*(1), 17–32.

Keller, B. (2011). Dealing with Assange and the WikiLeaks secrets. *The New York Times,* (January 26, 2011). Retrieved from http://www.nytimes.com/2011/01/30/magazine/30Wikileaks-t.html?pagewanted=all&_r=0

Kelly, K. S. (2001). Stewardship: The fifth step in the public relations process. In R. L. Heath (Ed.), *Handbook of public relations* (pp. 279–289). Thousand Oaks, CA: Sage Publications.

Ki, E.-J. (2006). *Linkages among relationship maintenance strategies, relationship quality outcomes, attitude, and behavioral intentions*. (Doctoral dissertation), University of Florida, Gainesville, FL.

Ki, E.-J., & Hon, L. C. (2007). Reliability and Validity of Organization-Public Relationship Measurement and Linkages Among Relationship Indicators in a Membership Organization. *Journalism & Mass Communication Quarterly, 84*(3), 419–438.

Kim, H.-S. (2007). A multilevel study of antecedents and a mediator of employee-organization relationships. *Journal of Public Relations Research, 19*(2), 167–197.

Kim, S.-Y., & Ki, E.-J. (2014). An exploratory study of ethics codes of professional public relations associations: Proposing modified universal codes of ethics in public relations. *Journal of Mass Media Ethics, 29*(4), 238–257. https://doi.org/10.1080/08900523.2014.946602

King, G. (1997). The effects of interpersonal closeness and issue seriousness on blowing the whistle. *The Journal of Business Communication, 34*(4), 419–436.

Kohn, H. (1977). Karen Silkwood was right in plutonium scandal. *RollingStone* (October 20, 1977). Retrieved from https://www.rollingstone.com/culture/culture-news/karen-silkwood-was-right-in-plutonium-scandal-47908/

Kraterou, A. (2020). Julian Assange will learn on January 4 whether he will be sent to US to face hacking charges that could see him jailed for 175 years. *Daily Mail* (October 29, 2020). Retrieved from https://www.dailymail.co.uk/news/article-8894665/Julian-Assange-learn-January-4-sent-face-hacking-charges.html

Krogh, E. (2007). The break-in that history forgot. *The New York Times* (June 30, 2007). Retrieved from https://www.nytimes.com/2007/06/30/opinion/30krogh.html

Kruckeberg, D. (1989). The need for an international code of ethics. *Public Relations Review, 15*(2), 6–18. https://doi.org/10.1016/S0363-8111(89)80050-5

Kruckeberg, D. (1993). Universal ethics code: Both possible and feasible. *Public Relations Review, 19*(1), 21–31. https://doi.org/10.1016/0363-8111(93)90027-A

Krumpal, I. (2013). Determinants of social desirability bias in sensitive surveys: a literature review. *Quality & Quantity, 47*(4), 2025–2047. https://doi.org/10.1007/s11135-011-9640-9

Kuhn, T. S. (1970). *The structure of scientific revolutions*. Chicago, IL: University of Chicago Press.

Lacayo, R., & Ripley, A. (2002). Persons of the year: The whistleblowers. *Time, 160*(27). Retrieved from http://content.time.com/time/subscriber/article/0,33009,1003998,00.html

Laerd Statistics. (2017). *Binomial logistic regression using SPSS Statistics. Statistical tutorials and software guide*. Retrieved from https://statistics.laerd.com/

Laerd Statistics. (2020). *Binomial logistic regression using SPSS Statistics*. Retrieved from https://statistics.laerd.com/premium/spss/blr/binomial-logistic-regression-in-spss.php

Laskin, A. V. (2018). The narrative strategies of winners and losers: Analyzing annual reports of publicly traded corporations. *International Journal of Business Communication, 55*(3), 338–356. https://doi.org/10.1177/2329488418780221

Lauzen, M. M., & Dozier, D. M. (1992). The missing link: The public relations manager role as mediator of organizational environments and power consequences for the function. *Journal of Public Relations Research, 4*(4), 205–220.

Lee, J., Jares, S. M., & Heath, R. L. (1999). Decision-making encroachment and cooperative relationships between public relations and legal counselors in the management of organizational crisis. *Journal of Public Relations Research, 11*(3), 243–270.

Lee, S. T., & Cheng, I.-H. (2011). Characteristics and Dimensions of Ethical Leadership in Public Relations. *Journal of Public Relations Research, 23*(1), 46–74.

Lee, S. T., & Kee, A. (2017). Testing an environmental framework for understanding public relations practitioners' orientation toward relationship management. *Journal of Public Relations Research, 29*(6), 259–276. https://doi.org/10.1080/1062726X.2017.1408465

Ledingham, J. A., & Bruning, S. D. (2000). *Public relations as relationship management: A relational approach to the study and practice of public relations*. Mahwah, N.J.: Lawrence Erlbaum Associates.

Leeper, R. (2001). In search of a metatheory for public relations: An argument for communitarianism. In R. L. Heath (Ed.), *The handbook of public relations* (pp. 93–104). Thousand Oaks, CA: Sage.

Leslie, G. (2003). Justice and the whistleblower. *News Media & the Law, 27*(3), 4–6.

Lewis, D. (Ed.) (2001). *Whistleblowing at work*. London: The Athlone Press.

Lewis, D. (2018). Book Reviews: Lewis, Bowers, Fodder and Mitchell, Whistleblowing: Law and Practice. [Review of the book *Whistleblowing: Law and Practice* by J. Lewis, J. Bowers QC,, M. Fodder and J. Mitchell]. *Industrial Law Journal, 47*(1), 165.

Lewis, D., Brown, A. J., & Moberly, R. E. (2014). Whistleblowing, its importance and the state of the research. In A. J. Brown, D. Lewis, R. E. Moberly, & W. Vandekerckhove (Eds.), *International Handbook on Whistleblowing Research* (pp. 1–34). Cheltenham, UK: Edward Elgar Publishing Limited.

Lewis, D., Devine, T., & Harpur, P. (2014). The key to protection: Civil and employment law remedies. In A. J. Brown, D. Lewis, R. E. Moberly, & W. Vandekerckhove (Eds.), *International Handbook on Whistleblowing Research* (pp. 350–380). Cheltenham, UK: Edward Elgar Publishing Limited.

Lewis, J., Bowers QC, J., Fodder, M., & Mitchell, J. (2017). *Whistleblowing: Law and Practice* (Third ed.). Oxford, UK: Oxford University Press.

Lewis, D., & Vandekerckhove, W. (2018). Trade unions and the whistleblowing process in the UK: An opportunity for strategic expansion? *Journal of Business Ethics, 148*(4), 835–845. https://doi.org/10.1007/s10551-016-3015-z

Lim, J. S., & Greenwood, C. A. (2017). Communicating corporate social responsibility (CSR): Stakeholder responsiveness and engagement strategy to achieve CSR goals. *Public Relations Review, 43*(4), 768–776. https://doi.org/10.1016/j.pubrev.2017.06.007

Liyanarachchi, G. A., & Adler, R. (2011). Accountants' whistle-blowing intentions: The impact of retaliation, age, and gender. *Australian Accounting Review, 21*(2), 167–182. Retrieved from https://doi.org/10.1111/j.1835-2561.2011.00134.x

Lopez, Y. P., Lavan, H., & Katz, M. (2013). Whistleblowing in organizations: A logit analysis of litigated cases. *Journal of Workplace Rights, 17*(3/4), 283–302. https://doi.org/10.2190/WR.17.3-4.c

Los Alamos National Laboratory. (1995). The Karen Silkwood Story. *Los Alamos Science*, 23, 252–255. Retrieved from PBS Frontline website: www.pbs.org/wgbh/pages/frontline/ shows/reaction/interact/silkwood.html

Lumm, D. C. (2010). The 2009 "Clarifications" to the False Claims Act of 1863: The all-purpose antifraud statute with the fun qui tam twist. *Wake Forest Law Review*, 45.

MacAskill, E., Snowden, E., & Ellsberg, D. (2018). 'Is whistleblowing worth prison or a life in exile?': Edward Snowden talks to Daniel Ellsberg. The Guardian, (January 16, 2018). Retrieved from https://www.theguardian.com/world/2018/jan/16/is-whistleblowing-worth-prison-or-a-life-in-exile-edward-snowden-talks-to-daniel-ellsberg?CMP=share_btn_link

Malek, F. (2008). The truth about the "Malek Manual". *Fred Malek Blog* (March 6, 2008). Retrieved from http://www.fredmalekblog.com/2008/03/06/the-truth-about-the-%E2% 80%9Cmalek-manual%E2%80%9D/

Marsh, C. (2012). Converging on harmony: Idealism, evolution, and the theory of mutual aid. *Public relations inquiry, 1*(3), 313–335. https://doi.org/10.1177/2046147X12448583

Marsh, C. (2013). Social harmony paradigms and natural selection: Darwin, Kropotkin, and the metatheory of mutual aid. *Journal of Public Relations Research, 25*(5), 426–441. http:// doi.org/10.1080/1062726X.2013.795861

Marsh, C. (2017). *Public relations, cooperation, and justice: From evolutionary biology to ethics.* London: Routledge Taylor & Francis Group.

Marsh, C. (2018). Indirect reciprocity and reputation management: Interdisciplinary findings from evolutionary biology and economics. *Public Relations Review, 44*(4), 463–470. Retrieved from https://doi.org/10.1016/j.pubrev.2018.04.002

Martin-Bariteau, F., & Newman, V. (2018). Lancer une alerte au Canada: une synthèse des connaissances (Whistleblowing in Canada: A Knowledge Synthesis). Elsevier SSRN. Retrieved from https://ssrn.com/abstract=3112688

Mayer, J. (2018). Christopher Steele, the man behind the Trump dossier. The New Yorker (March 12, 2018). Retrieved from HYPERLINK "http://www.newyorker.com/ magazine/2018/03/12/christopher-steele-the-man-behind-the-trump-dossier" www.newyorker.com/magazine/2018/03/12/christopher-steele-the-man-behind-the-trump-dossier

Mazumdar, S. (2013). Whistleblowers: More threatened than threatening? *Media Asia, 40*(3), 198–203. https://doi.org/10.1080/01296612.2013.11689966

McClellan, S. (2008). *What Happened: Inside the Bush White House and Washington's Culture of Deception.* New York: Public Affairs.

McGlynn, J., & Richardson, B. K. (2014). Private support, public alienation: Whistle-Blowers and the paradox of Social Support. *Western Journal of Communication, 78*(2), 213–237. https://doi.org/10.1080/10570314.2013.807436

McKie, D. (2001). Updating public relations: "New science," research paradigms, and uneven developments. In R. L. Heath (Ed.), *The handbook of public relations* (pp. 75–92). Thousand Oaks, CA: Sage.

Meintjes, C., & Grobler, A. F. (2014). Do public relations professionals understand corporate governance issues well enough to advise companies on stakeholder relationship management? *Public Relations Review, 40*(2), 161–170. https://doi.org/10.1016/j. pubrev.2013.10.003

Merit Systems Protection Board. (1981). *Whistleblowing and the Federal Employee: Blowing the whistle on fraud, waste, and mismanagement—who does it and what happens.* Washington, DC: MSPB.

Merit Systems Protection Board. (1984). *Blowing the whistle in the federal government: A comparative analysis of 1980 and 1983 survey findings*. Washington, DC: MSPB.

Merit Systems Protection Board. (1993). *Whistleblowing in the Federal Government: An Update*. Washington, DC: MSPB.

Merit Systems Protection Board. (2001). *Questions & answers about whistleblower appeals*. Washington, DC: MSPB.

Merit Systems Protection Board. (2010a). *Prohibited personnel practices a study retrospective*. Washington, DC: MSPB.

Merit Systems Protection Board. (2010b). *Whistleblower protections for federal employees*. Washington, DC: MSPB.

Merit Systems Protection Board. (2011a). *Blowing the Whistle: Barriers to federal employees making disclosures*. Washington, DC: MSPB.

Merit Systems Protection Board. (2011b). *Prohibited personnel practices: Employee perceptions*. Washington, DC: MSPB.

Merit Systems Protection Board. (2014). *Current Projects, Planned Projects, and Proposed Research Topics for 2015–2018*. Washington, DC: MSPB.

Merton, R. K. (1967). *On theoretical sociology: Five essays, old and new*. New York: The Free Press.

Mesmer-Magnus, J. R., & Viswesvaran, C. (2005). Whistleblowing in organizations: An examination of correlates of whistleblowing intentions, actions, and retaliation. *Journal of Business Ethics, 62*, 277–297.

Meyer, A. D. (1991). What is strategy's distinctive competence? *Journal of Management, 17*(4), 821–833.

Meyer, A. L., & Leonard, A. (2014). Are we there yet? En route to professionalism. *Public Relations Review, 40*(2), 375–386. https://doi.org/10.1016/j.pubrev.2013.11.012

Meyer, P. N. (2002). Making the narrative move: Observations based upon reading Gerry Spence's closing argument in the Estate of Karen Silkwood v. Kerr-Mcgee, Inc. Clinical Law Review, 9(1), 229–292.

Miceli, M., Dreyfus, S., & Near, J. (2014). Outsider 'whistleblowers': Conceptualizing and distinguishing 'bell-ringing' behavior. In A. J. Brown, D. Lewis, R. E. Moberly, & W. Vandekerckhove (Eds.), *International Handbook on Whistleblower Research* (pp. 71–94). Cheltenham, UK: Edward Elgar Publishing

Miceli, M. P., & Near, J. P. (1984). The relationships among beliefs, organizational position, and whistle-blowing status: A discriminant analysis. *Academy of Management Journal, 27*(4), 687–705.

Miceli, M. P., & Near, J. P. (1985). Characteristics of organizational climate and perceived wrongdoing associated with whistle-blowing decisions. *Personnel Psychology, 38*, 525–544.

Miceli, M. P., & Near, J. P. (1988). Individual and situational correlates of whistle-blowing. *Personnel Psychology, 41*, 267–281.

Miceli, M. P., & Near, J. P. (1992). *Blowing the whistle: The organizational and legal implications for companies and employees*. New York: Lexington Books.

Miceli, M. P., & Near, J. P. (1994). Relationships among value congruence, perceived victimization, and retaliation against whistle-blowers. *Journal of Management, 20*(4), 773–794.

Miceli, M. P., & Near, J. P. (1997). Whistle-blowing as antisocial behavior. In R. A. Giacalone & J. Greenberg (Eds.), *Antisocial behavior in organizations* (pp. 130–149). Thousand Oaks, CA: SAGE Publications, Inc.

Miceli, M. P., & Near, J. P. (2002). What makes whistle-blowers effective? Three field studies. *Human Relations, 55*(4), 455–479.

Miceli, M. P., & Near, J. P. (2013). An international comparison of the incidence of public sector whistle-blowing and the prediction of retaliation: Australia, Norway, and the US. *Australian Journal of Public Administration, 72*(4), 433–446. https://doi.org/10.1111/1467-8500.12040

Miceli, M. P., Near, J. P., & Dworkin, T. M. (2008). *Whistle-blowing in organizations.* New York: Routledge Taylor & Francis Group.

Miceli, M. P., Near, J. P., & Dworkin, T. M. (2009). A word to the wise: How managers and policy-makers can encourage employees to report wrongdoing. *Journal of Business Ethics, 86*(3), 379–396. https://doi.org/10.1007/s10551-008-9853-6

Miceli, M. P., Near, J. P., & Schwenk, C. R. (1991). Who blows the whistle and why? *Industrial and Labor Relations Review, 45*(1), 113–130.

Miceli, M. P., Rehg, M. T., Near, J. P., & Ryan, K. C. (1999). Can laws protect whistle-blowers?: Results of a naturally occurring field experiment. *Work and Occupations, 26*(1), 129–151. https://doi.org/10.1177/0730888499026001007

Miethe, T. D. (1999). Whistleblowing at Work: Tough Choices in Exposing Fraud, Waste, and Abuse on the Job. Boulder, CO: Westview Press.

Miller, G. R. (1989). Persuasion and public relations: Two "Ps" in a pod. In C. H. Botan & V. Hazleton Jr. (Eds.), *Public Relations Theory* (pp. 45–66). Hillsdale, NJ: Lawrence Erlbaum Associates.

Miller, K. S. (2000). U.S. public relations history: Knowledge and limitations. In M. E. Roloff & G. D. Paulson (Eds.), *Communication Yearbook* (Vol. 23, pp. 381–420). London: Sage.

Moberly, R. E. (2006). Sarbanes-Oxley's structural model to encourage corporate whistle-blowers. *Brigham Young Law Review, 2006*(5), 1107–1180.

Moberly, R. E. (2007). Unfulfilled expectations: An empirical analysis of why Sarbanes-Oxley whistleblowers rarely win. *William and Mary Law Review, 49*, 65–156.

Moberly, R. E. (2012). Sarbanes-Oxley's whistleblower provisions: Ten years later. *South Carolina Law Review, 64*(1), 1–54.

Moloney, K. (2006). *Rethinking public relations: PR, propaganda, and democracy* (2nd ed. ed.). New York: Routledge Taylor & Francis Group.

Moloney, K. (2008, November). *Trouble making and whistleblowing.* Paper presented at the Institute of Communication Ethics, London College of Communications, London. Retrieved from http://eprints.bournemouth.ac.uk/7996/1/Trouble_making_231108.pdf

Morse, C. T., Hall, W. E., & Lake, B. J. (1997). More than golden handcuffs. *Journal of Accountancy, 184*(5), 37–42.

Muellenberg, K. W., & Volzer, H. J. (1980). Inspector general act of 1978. *Temple Law Quarterly, 53*(4), 1049–1066.

Murphy, K. (2006). Judge Throws Out Kenneth Lay's Conviction The New York Times, (October 18, 2006). Retrieved from https://www.nytimes.com/2006/10/18/business/18enron.html?smid=em-share

Murphy, P. (1991). The limits of symmetry: A game theory approach to symmetric and asymmetric public relations. In L. A. Grunig & J. E. Grunig (Eds.), *Public relations research annual* (Vol. 3, pp. 115–131). Hillsdale, NJ: Lawrence Erlbaum Associates.

Murphy, P. (1996). Chaos theory as a model for managing issues and crises. *Public Relations Review, 22*(2), 95.

Murphy, P. (2000). Symmetry, contingency, complexity: Accommodating uncertainty in public relations theory. *Public Relations Review, 26*(4), 447–462.

Murphy, P. (2007). Coping with an uncertain world: The relationship between excellence and complexity theories. In E. L. Toth (Ed.), *The future of excellence in public relations and communication management* (pp. 119–134). Mahwah, NJ: Lawrence Erlbaum Associates, Inc.

Near, J. P., Dworkin, T. M., & Miceli, M. P. (1993). Explaining the whistle-blowing process: Suggestions from power theory and justice theory. *Organization Science, 4*(3), 393–411.

Near, J. P., & Miceli, M. P. (1985). Organizational dissidence: The case of whistle-blowing. *Journal of Business Ethics, 4*, 1–16.

Near, J. P., & Miceli, M. P. (1986). Retaliation against whistle blowers: Predictors and effects. *Journal of Applied Psychology, 71*(1), 137–145.

Near, J. P., & Miceli, M. P. (1987). Whistle-blower in organizations: Dissidents or reformers? In L. L. Cummings & B. W. Staw (Eds.), *Research in organizational behavior* (pp. 321–368). Greenwich, CT: JAI Press.

Near, J. P., & Miceli, M. P. (1990, August). *When whistleblowing succeeds: Predictors of effective whistleblowing.* Paper presented at the Annual Meeting of the Academy of Management, San Francisco.

Near, J. P., & Miceli, M. P. (1996). Whistle-blowing: Myth and reality. *Journal of Management, 22*(3), 507.

Near, J. P., & Miceli, M. P. (2008). Wrongdoing, whistle-blowing, and retaliation in the U.S. Government: What have researchers learned from the Merit Systems Protection Board (MSPB) survey results? *Review of Public Personnel Administration, 28*(3), 263–281. https://doi.org10.1177/0734371x08319153

Near, J. P., Ryan, K. C., & Miceli, M. P. (1995, August). *Results of a human resource management "experiment": Whistle-blowing in the federal bureaucracy, 1980–1992.* Paper presented at the Annual Meeting of the Academy of Management, Vancouver, B.C.

Nelson, R. R., & Winter, S. G. (1982). *An evolutionary theory of economic change.* Cambridge, MA: Harvard University Press.

Nettle, D., Gibson, M. A., Lawson, D. W., & Sear, R. (2013). Human behavioral ecology: current research and future prospects. *Behavioral Ecology, 24*(5), 1031–1040. https://doi.org/10.1093/beheco/ars222

New York Times Co. v. United States, 403 U.S. 713 (1971).

Ni, L. (2007). Refined understanding of perspectives on employee-organization relationships. *Journal of Communication Management, 11*(1), 53–70.

Ni, L. (2009). Strategic role of relationship building: Perceived links between employee-organization relationships and globalization strategies. *Journal of Public Relations Research, 21*(1), 100–120.

Norris, F. (2009). Could Skilling get a new trial? *The New York Times* (January 6, 2009). Retrieved from http://norris.blogs.nytimes.com/2009/01/06/could-skilling-get-a-new-trial/?pagemode=print

Nothhaft, H. (2016). A framework for strategic communication research: A call for synthesis and consilience. *International journal of strategic communication, 10*(2), 69–86. Retrieved from http://doi.org/10.1080/1553118X.2015.1124277

Nothhaft, H. (2017). Disagreement about the therapy, Not the diagnosis: A reply to the rejoinders. *International journal of strategic communication, 11*(3), 189–193. Retrieved from https://doi.org/10.1080/1553118X.2017.1318884

Notification and Federal Employee Anti-Discrimination and Retaliation Act of 2002, 5 U.S.C. § 2301 (2002).

Obama, B. (2012). *Presidential policy directive 19 (PPD-19) protecting whistleblowers with access to classified information.* Retrieved from https://fas.org/irp/offdocs/ppd/ppd-19.pdf

Office of the Inspector General of the Intelligence Community. (2019a). *Letter to Congressional Intelligence Committees re. Whistleblower Complaint.* Washington, DC: U.S House of Representatives Permanent Select Committee on Intelligence Retrieved from https://intelligence.house.gov/uploadedfiles/20190812_-_whistleblower_complaint_unclass.pdf

Office of the Inspector General of the Intelligence Community. (2019b). *IG Letter to the Director of National Intelligence (Acting)*. Washington, DC: U.S House of Representatives Permanent Select Committee on Intelligence Retrieved from https://intelligence.house.gov/uploadedfiles/20190826_-_icig_letter_to_acting_dni_unclass.pdf.

Orbell, J., Morikawa, T., Hartwig, J., Hanley, J., & Allen, N. (2004). "Machiavellian" intelligence as a basis for the evolution of cooperative dispositions. *American Political Science Review, 98*(1).

Oswald, R. S., & Zuckerman, J. (2010). Whistleblower provisions of the Dodd-Frank Act. *The Employment Law Group*. Retrieved from https://www.employmentlawgroup.com/in-the-news/articles/whistleblower-provisions-dodd-frank-act/

Pallant, J. (2005). *SPSS survival manual* (2nd ed.). Chicago: Open University Press.

Parmerlee, M. A., Near, J. P., & Jensen, T. C. (1982). Correlates of whistle-blowers' perceptions of organizational retaliation. *Administrative Science Quarterly, 27*, 17–34.

Pasadeos, Y., Renfro, R. B., & Hanily, M. L. (1999). Influential authors and works of the public relations scholarly literature: A network of recent research. *Journal of Public Relations Research, 11*(1), 29.

Pascal, A., Spielberg, S., & Krieger, K. M. (Producer) & S. Spielberg (Director). (2018). *The Post* [Motion Picture]. Los Angeles: 20th Century Fox.

Pavgi, K. (2012). Obama expands whistleblower protections to cover intelligence agencies. *Government Executive* (October 11, 2012). Retrieved from Factiva website: https://www.govexec.com/oversight/2012/10/obama-expands-whistleblower-protections-cover-intelligence-agencies/58728/

Peffer, S. L., Bocheko, A., Del Valle, R. E., Osmani, A., Peyton, S., & Roman, E. (2015). Whistle where you work? The ineffectiveness of the federal Whistleblower Protection Act of 1989 and the promise of the Whistleblower Protection Enhancement Act of 2012. *Review of Public Personnel Administration, 35*(1), 70–81. https://doi.org10.1177/0734371X13508414

Penman, C., Fox, T., Snelling, B., & Stricker, T. (2018). *2018 Ethics & Compliance Policy & Procedure Management Benchmark Report*. Benchmark. Retrieved from NAVEX Global: Lake Oswego, OR: https://www.navexglobal.com/en-us/file-download-canonical?file=/2018-Policy-Management-Benchmark-Report_0.pdf&file-name=2018-Policy-Management-Benchmark-Report_0.pdf

Perez-Pena, R., & Magra, I. (2018). Julian Assange's arrest warrant is again upheld by U.K. Judge. *The New York Times*, (February 13, 2018). Retrieved from https://www.nytimes.com/2018/02/13/world/europe/julian-assange-uk-warrant.html

Pfeffer, J., & Salancik, G. (1978). *The external control of organizations: A resource dependence perspective*. New York: Harper Row, Publishers.

Pfeffer, J., & Salancik, G. (2003). *The external control of organizations: A resource dependence perspective* Stanford, CA: Stanford University Press.

Perry, J. L. (1992). The consequences of speaking out: processes of hostility and issue resolution involving federal whistleblowers. In *Best papers proceedings – Academy of management* (vol. 8, pp. 311–315). Las Vegas, NV. https://doi.org/10.5465/AMBPP.1992.17516059

Pillay, S., Ramphul, N., Dorasamy, N., & Meyer, D. (2018). Predictors of whistle-blowing intentions: An analysis of multi-level variables. *Administration & Society, 50*(2), 186–216. https://doi.org/10.1177/0095399715581621

Pittroff, E. (2015). Whistle-blowing regulation in different corporate governance systems: An analysis of the regulation approaches from the view of path dependence theory. *Journal of Management and Governance, 20*, 703–727. https://doi.org/10.1007/s10997-015-9311-7

Pohle, J., & Van Audenhove, L. (2017). Post-Snowden Internet policy: Between public outrage, resistance and policy change. *Media and Communication, 5*(1), 1–6. https://doi.org/10.17645/mac.v5i1.932

Pompper, D. (2014). The Sarbanes-Oxley Act: Impact, processes, and roles for strategic communication. *International journal of strategic communication, 8*(3), 130–145. https://doi.org/10.1080/1553118X.2014.905476

Pope, K. R., & Lee, C.-C. (2013). Could the Dodd-Frank Wall Street Reform and Consumer Protection Act of 2010 be helpful in reforming corporate America? An investigation on financial bounties and whistle-blowing behaviors in the private sector. *Journal of Business Ethics, 112*(4), 597–607.

PriceWaterhouseCoopers. (2009). *The global economic crime survey: Economic crime in a downturn.* Retrieved from http://www.pwc.com/en_GX/gx/economic-crime-survey/pdf/global-economic-crime-survey-2009.pdf

PriceWaterhouseCoopers. (2018). *2018 Global economic crime and fraud survey: US perspectives.* Retrieved from https://www.pwc.com/us/en/services/consulting/cybersecurity-privacy-forensics/library/global-economic-fraud-survey.html

Prior-Miller, M. (1989). Four major social scientific theories and their value to the public relations researcher. In C. H. Botan & J. Hazleton, V. (Eds.), *Public relations theory* (pp. 67–81). Hillsdale, NJ: Lawrence Erlbaum Associates.

Public Relations Society of America. (2008). Public Relations Society of America Member Code of Ethics 2000. Retrieved from http://www.prsa.org/aboutUs/ethics/preamble_en.html

Quinn, B. (2021). Julian Assange cannot be extradited to US, British judge rules. *The Guardian* (January 4, 2021). Retrieved from https://www.theguardian.com/media/2021/jan/04/julian-assange-cannot-be-extradited-to-us-british-judge-rules

Rappeport, A., & Flitter, E. (2018). Congress approves first big Dodd-Frank rollback. *The New York Times* (May 22, 2018). Retrieved from https://www.nytimes.com/2018/05/22/business/congress-passes-dodd-frank-rollback-for-smaller-banks.html

Ratnesar, R., & Weisskopf, M. (2002). How the FBI blew the case. *Time, 159*(22).

Reber, B. H., Cropp, F., & Cameron, G. T. (2001). Mythic Battles: Examining the Lawyer-Public Relations Counselor Dynamic. *Journal of Public Relations Research, 13*(3), 187–218.

Reed, S. (2015, October). *Calling a foul.* Paper presented at the Annual International Conference on Journalism & Mass Communications, Singapore. Retrieved from http://libraries.ou.edu/access.aspx?url=http://search.ebscohost.com/login.aspx?direct=true&db=cms&AN=112931819&site=ehost-live

Rehg, M. T. (1998). *An examination of the retaliation process against whistleblowers: A study of federal government employees.* doctoral dissertation. Indiana University, Bloomington, IN.

Rehg, M. T., Miceli, M. P., Near, J. P., & Van Scotter, J. R. (2004). *Predicting retaliation against whistle-blowers: Outcomes of power relationships within organizations.* Paper presented at the Academy of Management, New Orleans, LA.

Rehg, M. T., Miceli, M. P., Near, J. P., & Van Scotter, J. R. (2008). Antecedents and outcomes of retaliation against whistleblowers: Gender differences and power relationships. *Organization Science, 19*(2), 221–240.

Reilly, K. (2017). The true story about the new movie about Watergate and Deep Throat. *Time* (October 12, 2017). Retrieved from http://time.com/4969472/mark-felt-deep-throat-movie-fact-check/

Reuters. (2017). U.S. Intelligence report identifies Russians who gave DNC emails to Wikileaks. *Time* (January 5, 2017). Retrieved from http://time.com/4625301/cia-russia-wikileaks-dnc-hacking/

Reuters Staff. (2017). Britain remains hostile to whistleblowers, statistics show. *Reuters* (November 21, 2017). Retrieved from https://www.reuters.com/article/britain-whistleblowing/britain-remains-hostile-to-whistleblowers-statistics-show-idUSL8N1NR4R9

Richardson, B. K. (2005, May). *Expanding whistle-blowing scholarship: How stakeholder theory, organizational structure, and social influence processes can inform whistle-blowing research.* Paper presented at the International Communication Association Annual Conference, New York.

Richardson, B. K., & McGlynn, J. (2007, May). *Gendered retaliation, irrationality, and structured isolation: Whistle-blowing in the collegiate sports industry as gendered process.* Paper presented at the International Communication Association Annual Conference, San Francisco.

Richardson, B. K., Wang, Z., & Hall, C. A. (2012). Blowing the whistle against Greek hazing: The theory of reasoned action as a framework for reporting intentions. *Communication Studies, 63*(2), 172–193. Retrieved from https://doi.org10.1080/10510974.2011.624396

Ripley, A., & Sieger, M. (2002). The special agent [Persons of the year]. *Time, 160*(271), 28–34. Retrieved from http://content.time.com/time/subscriber/article/0,33009,1003988,00.html

Rosenberg, M., Confessore, N., & Cadwalladr, C. (2018). How Trump consultants exploited the Facebook data of millions. *The New York Times* (March 17, 2018). Retrieved from https://www.nytimes.com/2018/03/17/us/politics/cambridge-analytica-trump-campaign.html

Rosenberg, M., & Frenkel, S. (2018). Facebook's role in data misuse sets off storms on two continents. *The New York Times* (March 18, 2018). Retrieved from https://www.nytimes.com/2018/03/18/us/cambridge-analytica-facebook-privacy-data.html

Rosenwald, M. S. (2008). Brokering power in business and politics. *Washington Post* (April 21, 2008). Retrieved from http://www.washingtonpost.com/wp-dyn/content/article/2008/04/20/AR2008042001564.html

Roth, N. L., Hunt, T., Stavropoulos, M., & Babik, K. (1996). Can't we all just get along: Cultural variables in codes of ethics. *Public Relations Review, 22*(2), 151–161. https://doi.org/10.1016/S0363-8111(96)90004-1

Saad, G. (2004). Applying evolutionary psychology in understanding the representation of women in advertisements. *Psychology & Marketing, 21*(8), 593–612.

Saad, G. (2006). Applying evolutionary psychology in understanding the Darwinian roots of consumption phenomena. *Managerial and Decision Economics, 27,* 189–201.

Saad, G. (2006). Applying Darwinian principles in designing effective intervention strategies: The case of sun tanning. *Psychology & Marketing, 23*(7), 617–638.

Saad, G. (2007). *The evolutionary bases of consumption.* Mahwah, NJ: Lawrence Erlbaum Associates.

Saad, G., & Gill, T. (2000). Applications of evolutionary psychology in marketing. *Psychology & Marketing, 17*(12).

Safina, C. (2009). Darwinism must die so that evolution may live. *The New York Times* (February 10, 2009). Retrieved from http://www.nytimes.com/2009/02/10/science/10essa.html?th&emc=th

Safire, W. (2002). The Rowley memo. *The New York Times (1923-Current File)* (May 27, 2002), A17. Retrieved from https://search-proquest-com.ezproxy.lib.ou.edu/docview/92229373?accountid=12964

Sallot, L. M., Lyon, L. J., Acosta-Alzuru, C., & Jones, K. O. (2008). From aardvark to zebra redux: An analysis of theory development in public relations academic journals into the 21st century. In T. L. Hansen-Horn & B. Neff, Dostal (Eds.), *Public relations: From theory to practice* (pp. 343–387). Boston, MA: Pearson Allyn & Bacon.

Sarbanes-Oxley Act of 2002, 15 U.S.C. § 7201 nt (2002).

Saunders, K., & Thibault, J. (2008). *Whistleblowing in Canada: One step forward or two steps back?* Paper presented at the MPSA Annual National Conference, Chicago, IL.

Schaal, D. (2008). Days in the life of a whistleblower. *The CRO Blog.* Retrieved from www.thecro.com/node/648

Scholes, M. S. (2011). Foreword. In V. V. Acharya, T. F. Cooley, M. Richardson, & I. Walter (Eds.), *Regulating Wall Street: The Dodd-Frank Act and the new architecture of global finance* (pp. xi–xvi). Hoboken, NJ: John Wiley & Sons, Inc.

Schulz, A. (2011). Sober & Wilson's evolutionary arguments for psychological altruism: a reassessment. *Biology & Philosophy, 26*(2), 251–260. https://doi.org/10.1007/s10539-009-9179-5

Scott-Phillips, T. C., Dickins, T. E., & West, S. A. (2011). Evolutionary theory and the ultimate proximate distinction in the human behavioral sciences. *Perspectives on Psychological Science, 6*(1), 38–47. https://doi.org/10.1177/1745691610393528

SEC Final rule: Management's report on internal control over financial reporting and certification of disclosure in Exchange Act periodic reports, 17 CFR PARTS 210, 228, 229, 240, 249, 270 and 274 (2003).

Securities and Exchange Commission. (2016a). *SEC announces enforcement results for FY 2016* [Press release]. Retrieved from https://www.sec.gov/news/pressrelease/2016-212.html

Securities and Exchange Commission. (2016b). *SEC: Casino-gaming company retaliated against whistleblower* [Press release]. Retrieved from https://www.sec.gov/news/pressrelease/2016-204.html

Securities and Exchange Commission. (2018). *SEC proposes whistleblower rule amendments* [Press release]. Retrieved from https://www.sec.gov/news/press-release/2018-120

Securities and Exchange Commission. (2020a). *SEC adds clarity, efficiency and transparency to its successful whistleblower award program* [Press release]. Retrieved from https://www.sec.gov/news/press-release/2020-219

Securities and Exchange Commission. (2020b). *SEC issues record $114 million whistleblower award* [Press release]. Retrieved from https://www.sec.gov/news/press-release/2020-266

Securities and Exchange Commission. (2020c). *SEC Awards Over $10 Million to Whistleblower* [Press release]. Retrieved from https://www.sec.gov/news/press-release/2020-270

Securities Exchange Act of 1934, 15 U.S.C. § 78a (1934).

Seiffert-Brockmann, J. (2018). Evolutionary psychology: A framework for strategic communication research. *International journal of strategic communication, 12*(4), 417–432. https://doi.org/10.1080/1553118X.2018.1490291

Seiffert-Brockmann, J., Nothhaft, H., Kim, J.-N., & Greenwood, C. A. (2019, July 17). *Call for Papers: Conference on Evolutionary Perspectives on Public Relations, Strategic Communication, and Organizational Communication to be presented at University of Vienna, July 10–12, 2020.* Web log post. Retrieved from https://www.linkedin.com/pulse/call-papers-evolutionary-theory-public-relations-dr-cary-a-/?trackingId=LuYPWI4CvhiZQvyWI96W9g%3D%3D

Sengupta, S., Whitfield, K., & McNabb, B. (2007). Employee share ownership and performance: Golden path or golden handcuffs? *International Journal of Human Resource Management, 18*(8), 1507–1538. https://doi.org/10.1080/09585190701502620

Shen, H. (2017). Refining Organization–Public relationship quality measurement in student and employee sample. *Journalism and Mass Communication Quarterly, 94*(4), 994–1010. https://doi.org/10.1177/1077699016674186

Shen, H., & Jiang, H. (2019). Engaged at work? An employee engagement model in public relations. *Journal of Public Relations Research, 31*(1–2), 32–49. https://doi.org/10.1080/1062726X.2019.1585855

Singh, J. V. (Ed.) (1990). *Organizational evolution*. Newbury Park, CA: Sage.

Sixel, L. M. (2018). Former Enron CEO Jeff Skilling out of prison, sent to halfway house. *Houston Chronicle* (August 31, 2018). Retrieved from https://www.chron.com/business/energy/article/Skilling-out-of-prison-sent-to-halfway-house-in-13194674.php

Skinner, R. W., & Shanklin, W. L. (1978). The changing role of public relations in business firms. *Public Relations Review, 4*(2), 40–45. http://doi.org/10.1016/S0363-8111(78)80005-8

Skivenes, M., & Trygstad, S. C. (2014). Wrongdoing: Definitions, identification and categorizations. In A. J. Brown, D. Lewis, R. E. Moberly, & W. Vandekerckhove (Eds.), *International Handbook on Whistleblowing Research* (pp. 95–114). Cheltenham, UK: Edward Elgar Publishing Limited.

Smirnov, O., Arrow, H., Kennett, D., & Orbell, J. (2007). Ancestral war and the evolutionary origins of "heroism". *Journal of Politics, 69*(4), 927–940.

Soon, J. M., & Manning, L. (2017). Whistleblowing as a countermeasure strategy against food crime. *British Food Journal, 119*(12), 2630–2652. https://doi.org/10.1108/BFJ-01-2017-0001

Specia, M. (2020). At Assange's extradition hearing, troubled tech takes center stage. *The New York Times* (September 16, 2020). Retrieved from https://www.nytimes.com/2020/09/16/world/europe/assange-extradition-hearing.html?searchResultPosition=1

Spitzer, E. (2019). New York Times Co. v. US: Supreme Court Case, Arguments, Impact. *New York Times* (November 8, 2019). Retrieved from thoughtco.com/new-york-times-co-v-u-s-4771900

Stack, L., Cumming-Bruce, N., & Kruhly, M. (2018). Julian Assange: A legal history. *The New York Times* (February 13, 2018). Retrieved from https://www.nytimes.com/interactive/2019/world/julian-assange-wikileaks.html?mtrref=undefined&gwh=1F41BB0052C5B3D7F98C87160622CEE2&gwt=regi&assetType=REGIWALL

Stateman, A. (2003). Secrets and lies: How good communication prevents leaks. *The Strategist, 9*, 36–39.

Steffy, L. (2013). An end to the Enron saga. *Forbes* (June 21, 2013). Retrieved from https://www.forbes.com/sites/lorensteffy/2013/06/21/an-end-to-the-enron-saga/#1368dbfd163d

Stephanopoulos, G. (1999). *All too human: A political education*. Boston, MA: Little, Brown.

Stroh, U. (2007). An alternative postmodern approach to corporate communication strategy. In E. L. Toth (Ed.), *The future of excellence in public relations and communication management* (pp. 199–220). Mahwah, NJ: Lawrence Erlbaum Associates.

Susskind, R. (2004). *The price of loyalty: George W. Bush, the White House, and the education of Paul O'Neill*. New York: Simon & Schuster Paperbacks.

Tabachnick, B. G., & Fidell, L. S. (2007). *Using Multivariate Statistics* (5th ed.). Boston, MA: Pearson.

Tholander, M. (2011). Mundane whistleblowing: Social drama in assessment talk. *Discourse Studies, 13*(1), 69–92.

Tapper, J., & Herb, J. (2020). Author of 2018 'Anonymous' op-ed critical of Trump revealed. *CNN* (October 28, 2020). Retrieved from https://www.cnn.com/2020/10/28/politics/anonymous-new-york-times-oped-writer/index.html

Tarzie. (2017). Edward Snowden, frenemy of the state. *American Journal of Economics and Sociology, 76*(2), 348–380. https://doi.org10.1111/ajes.12179

Trivers, R. (1971). The evolution of reciprocal altruism. *Quarterly Review of Biology, 46*(March), 35–57.

Trivers, R. (1985). *Social evolution. Menlo Park*, CA: Benjamin/Cummings.

Tucker, R. K. (1971). *General systems theory application to the design of speech communication courses* Speech Teacher, 20(3), 159–166.

U.S. Department of Justice. (2016). *Justice Department recovers over $4.7 billion from False Claims Act cases in fiscal year 2016* [Press release]. Retrieved from HYPERLINK "http://www.justice.gov/opa/pr/justice-department-recovers-over-47-billion-false-claims-act-cases-fiscal-year-2016" www.justice.gov/opa/pr/justice-department-recovers-over-47-billion-false-claims-act-cases-fiscal-year-2016

U.S. House of Representatives Committee on Commerce and Energy. (2018). *Facebook: Transparency and use of consumer data* (Committee Print No. 30-956). Washington, DC: G.P.O. Retrieved from https://www.govinfo.gov/content/pkg/CHRG-115hhrg30956/pdf/CHRG-115hhrg30956.pdf

U.S. House of Representatives Permanent Select Committee on Intelligence. (2016). *(U) Review of the unauthorized disclosures of former national security agency contractor Edward Snowden.* (114 H. Rpt. 891). Washington, DC: G.P.O. Retrieved from https://www.govinfo.gov/app/details/CRPT-114hrpt891/CRPT-114hrpt891

U.S. House of Representative Permanent Select Committee on Intelligence. (2019). *House Intelligence Committee Releases Whistleblower Complaint,* [Press release]. Retrieved from https://intelligence.house.gov/news/documentsingle.aspx?DocumentID=708

U.S. House of Representatives Subcommittee on Manpower and Civil Service of the Committee on Post Office and Civil Services. (1976). *Final report on violations and abuses of merit principles in federal employment, together with minority views, 94th Cong., 2nd* (Committee Print No. 94-28). Washington, DC: G.P.O.

U.S. Senate Committee on Commerce, Science, & Transportation and the Senate Committee on the Judiciary. (2018). *Facebook, social media privacy, and the use and abuse of data.* (Serial No. J-115–40). Retrieved from https://www.govinfo.gov/content/pkg/CHRG-115shrg37801/pdf/CHRG-115shrg37801.pdf

U.S. Senate Committee on Governmental Affairs. (1978). *The whistleblowers: A report on federal employees who disclose acts of governmental waste, abuse, and corruption.* (CMP-1978-SGA-0004). Washington, DC: G.P.O.

U.S. Senate Committee on the Judiciary. (1986). *Confirmation hearings on appointments to the Federal Judiciary and the Department of Defense (testimony of Robert M. Tobias).* (S. Hrg. 99–141/Pt. 2). Washington, DC: G.P.O.

U.S. Senate Committee on the Judiciary. (2018). *Hearing on Cambridge analytica and future of data privacy (Testimony of Christopher Wylie).* Washington, DC: U.S. Senate Retrieved from https://www.judiciary.senate.gov/meetings/cambridge-analytica-and-the-future-of-data-privacy

U.S. Senate Select Committee on Intelligence. (2017). *Nomination of Christopher Sharpley to be the Inspector General of the Central Intelligence Agency.* (S. HRG. 115–303). Washington, DC: G.P.O. Retrieved from https://www.govinfo.gov/content/pkg/CHRG-115shrg27396/pdf/CHRG-115shrg27396.pdf

Vallejo, J. (2020). Whistleblower Edward Snowden granted permanent residency in Russia, reports say. *The Independent* (October 22, 2020). Retrieved from https://www.independent.co.uk/news/world/americas/edward-snowden-cia-nsa-surveillance-whistleblower-russia-asylum-residency-b1234646.html

Vandekerckhove, W., Uys, T., Rehg, M. T., & Brown, A. J. (2014). Understandings of whistleblowing: Dilemmas of societal culture. In A. J. Brown, D. Lewis, R. E. Moberly, & W. Vandekerckhove (Eds.), *International handbook on whistleblowing research* (pp. 37–70). Cheltenham, UK: Edward Elgar Publishing Limited.

Vaughn, R. G. (2005). America's first comprehensive statute protecting corporate whistleblowers. *Administrative Law Review, 57*(1), 1–105.

Verčič, D., & Grunig, J. E. (2000). The origins of public relations theory in economics and strategic management. In D. Moss, D. Vercic, & G. Warnaby (Eds.), *Perspectives on public relations research* (pp. 9–58). London: Routledge Taylor & Francis Group.

Volk, S. C. (2016). A systematic review of 40 years of public relations evaluation and measurement research: Looking into the past, the present, and future. *Public Relations Review, 42*(5), 962–977. https://doi.org/10.1016/j.pubrev.2016.07.003

Von Drehle, D. (2005). FBI's no. 2 was 'Deep Throat': Mark Felt ends 30-year mystery of the Post's Watergate source. *The Washington Post* (June 1, 2005). Retrieved from http://www.washingtonpost.com

Wade, N. (2009). Darwin, ahead of his time, is still influential. *The New York Times* (February 10, 2009). Retrieved from http://nytimes.com/2009/02/10/science/10evoluton.html?_r=1&th=&em=th&pagew

Wahl-Jorgensen, K., & Hunt, J. (2012). Journalism, accountability and the possibilities for structural critique: A case study of coverage of whistleblowing. *Journalism, 13*(4), 399–416. https://doi.org/10.1177/1464884912439135

A warning / Anonymous, a senior Trump administration official. (2019). (1st ed.). New York: Twelve, an imprint of Grand Central Publishing.

Wasserman, E. (2017). Safeguarding the news in the era of disruptive sources. *Journal of Media Ethics, 32*(2), 27–85. https://doi.org/10.1080/23736992.2017.1294020

The Watergate Story Part 2: The government investigates. (2008). *The Washington Post.* Retrieved from http://www.washingtonpost.com/wp-srv/politics/special/watergate/part2.html

The Watergate Story Part 4: Deep Throat Revealed. (2005). *The Washington Post* (June 1, 2005). Retrieved from https://www.washingtonpost.com/wp-srv/politics/special/watergate/part4.html

The Watergate Story: John Dean. (2008). *The Washington Post.* Retrieved from http://www.washingtonpost.com/wp-srv/politics/special/watergate/dean.html

Watson, T. (2014). IPRA Code of Athens—The first international code of public relations ethics: Its development and implementation since 1965. *Public Relations Review, 40*(4), 707–714. https://doi.org/10.1016/j.pubrev.2013.11.018

Weaver, A. J., & Wilson, B. J. (2009). The role of graphic and sanitized violence in the enjoyment of television dramas. *Human Communication Research, 35*(3), 442–463.

Westin, A. F. (Ed.). (1981). Whistle blowing! Loyalty and dissent in the corporation. New York: McGraw-Hill.

Wexler, M. N. (1981). The Biology of Human Altruism. *Social Science, 56*(4), 195–203.

Whewell, W. (1840). *Aphorisms concerning ideas, science & the language of science.* London: Harrison & co., printers.

Whistleblower Protection Act Amendments of 1994, 5 U.S.C. § 101 nt (1994).

Whistleblower Protection Act of 1989, 5 U.S.C. § 1201 nt (1989).

Whistleblower Protection Enhancement Act of 2012, 5 U.S.C. § 101 nt (2012).

White, C., Vanc, A., & Stafford, G. (2010). Internal communication, information satisfaction, and sense of community: The effect of personal influence. *Journal of Public Relations Research, 22*(1), 65–84. https://doi.org/10.1080/10627260903170985

White, J., & Dozier, D. A. (1992). Public relations and management decision making. In J. E. Grunig (Ed.), *Excellence in public relations and communication management* (pp. 91–108). Hillsdale, NJ: Lawrence Erlbaum Associates.

Whiten, A., & Byrne, R. W. (1988). The Machiavellian intelligence hypotheses: editorial. In R. W. Byrne & A. Whiten (Eds.), *Machiavellian intelligence: Social expertise and the evolution of intellect in monkeys, apes, and humans.* Oxford, UK: Clarendon Press.

Whiten, A., & Byrne, R. W. (1997). *Machiavellian intelligence II: Extensions and evaluations.* Cambridge, UK: Cambridge University Press.

Wilbanks, C. (2013). Ex-Enron CEO Jeff Skilling to leave prison early. *CBS News* (June 21, 2013). Retrieved from CBS News website: https://www.cbsnews.com/news/ex-enron-ceo-jeff-skilling-to-leave-prison-early/

Wild, D. (2003). Profile: Sherron Watkins, Enron whistleblower. *Accountancy Age* (December 18, 2003). Retrieved from https://www.accountancyage.com/2003/12/18/profile-sherron-watkins-enron-whistleblower/

Williams, J., & Toropin, K. (2017). Russia extends Edward Snowden's asylum to 2020. *CNN U.S.* (January 1, 2017). Retrieved from https://www.cnn.com/2017/01/18/europe/russia-snowden-asylum-extension/index.html

Wilmarth, J., & Arthur, E. (2011). The Dodd-Frank Act: A flawed and inadequate response to the Too-Big-to-Fail problem. *Oregon Law Review, 89*(951), 97

Wilson, D. S. (2009a). Truth and reconciliation for group selection II: The original problem. *The Huffington Post* (January 1, 2009). Retrieved from www.huffingtonpost.com/david-sloan-wilson/truth-and-reconciliation_b_154660.html

Wilson, D. S. (2009b). Truth and reconciliation for group selection XIII: Hamilton speaks. *The Huffington Post* (May 21, 2009). Retrieved from www.huffingtonpost.com/david-sloan-wilson/truth-and-reconciliation_b_206248.html

Wilson, D. S., & Sober, E. (1994). Reintroducing group selection to the human behavioral sciences. *Behavioral and Brain Sciences, 17*(4), 585–608. https://doi.org/10.1017/S0140525X00036104

Wilson, E. O. (1975). Sociobiology: *The new synthesis.* Cambridge, MA: Harvard University Press.

Wilson, E. O. (1998). *Consilience: The unity of knowledge.* New York: Knopf.

Wimmer, R. D., & Dominick, J. R. (2006). *Mass media research: An introduction (8th ed.).* Belmont, CA: Thomson Wadsworth.

Wolff, M. (2018). *Fire and fury: inside the Trump White House* (First ed.): New York: Henry Holt and Company.

Woodward, B. (2005). *The secret man: The story of Watergate's "Deep Throat".* New York: Simon & Schuster.

Yamey, G. (2000). Protecting whistleblowers: Employers should respond to the message, not shoot the messenger. *British Medical Journal, 320*(7227), 70–71.

Yang, S.-U. (2007). An integrated model for organization-public relational outcomes, organizational reputation, and their antecedents. *Journal of Public Relations Research, 19*(2), 91–121.

Yang, A., Taylor, M., & Saffer, A. J. (2016). Ethical convergence, divergence or communitas? An examination of public relations and journalism codes of ethics. *Public Relations Review, 42*(1), 146–160. Retrieved from https://doi.org/10.1016/j.pubrev.2015.08.001

Yeoh, P. (2013). Whistle-blowing laws in the UK. *Business Law Review, 34*(6), 218–224.

Yeoh, P. (2014). Whistleblowing: motivations, corporate self-regulation, and the law. *International Journal of Law and Management, 56*(6), 459–474. https://doi.org/10.1108/IJLMA-06-2013-0027

Zuckerberg, M. (2021). *Mark Zuckerberg.* Retrieved from https://m.facebook.com/zuck

Zuckerman, J. (2012). Congress strengthens whistleblower protections for federal employees. *ABA LEL Flash* (November-December 2012). Retrieved from https://www.zuckermanlaw.com/wp-content/uploads/2019/01/Whistleblower-Protection-Enhancement-Act.pdf

Index

Note: Page numbers in **bold** indicate a table on the corresponding page.

executives' whistleblowing 151; acceptance or retaliation 145; choice of channels 170–171, 173–174, 176–180; comparison with federal studies 130, 146, 148, 151; comprehensiveness of retaliation 147; corporate-level variables 141–147; corporate-level variables compared with federal surveys 146–147; individual-level variables compared with federal surveys 146, **148**, 169; internal or external 145; relationship demographics 149; relationships, impact of rank on 154–156; retaliation 148; relationships, impact of awareness of wrongdoing on 152–154; relationships, impact of whistleblowing on 153–154; relationships, impact of retaliation on 153, 154–155

exit culture 93–94

external whistleblowers 73

Facebook 57

Fair Work Act 2009 89

False Claims Act (FCA) 54, 111n2; *False Claims Act of 1863*; *False Claims Amendments Act of 1986* 44, 111n2

False Claims Amendments Act of 1986 111n2

Fastow, Andrew 49

federal laws 38

federal laws after 9/11 46–48; *Notification and Federal Employee Antidiscrimination and Retaliation Act of 2002* 46; Presidential Policy Directive (PPD-19) 48; *Whistleblower Protection Enhancement Act of 2012* (WPEA) 48; whistleblower protections, failure of 46; whistleblower protections for federal employees 47

federal laws after Watergate 44–45; *Civil Service Reform Act of 1978* 44; *False Claims Amendments Act of 1986* 44; *Inspector General Act of 1978* 44; *Whistleblower Protection Act of 1989* (WPA) 45; *Whistleblower Protection Act of 1994* (WPA) 45

federal whistleblowing research 67–69

Felt, W. Mark 1, 42

Fire and Fury: Inside the Trump White House 109

Fitzgerald, A. Ernest 41

follow-up reminder 192–193

food industry sector 94

Foreign Corrupt Practices Act (FCPA) 53

formal type retaliation 80

France 90

Fraud Enforcement and Recovery Act of 2009 (FERA) 52

Freedom of Information Act of 1966 39

Fulbright, J. William 41

further research needs: qualitative research 179; responsibility for whistleblowing channels 177–180; whistleblowing knowledge and understanding 178; whistleblowing laws 178–179

gender 72; demographic variables as 128–129, 137–139, 156, 159nn7–8, 160n15, 160n19, 161n26, 170–171; power variables as 120, 130nn1–2, **150**, 172; predictors of retaliation as (female) 78, 95, 122, 151–152, **151**, 157, 171–172

Germany 90, 93

Gibb, J. R. 100

global whistleblowing research 90–92; Australia 91–92; Italy 91; Public Interest Disclosure Act (PIDA) of 1998 90; public sector 90–92; Scotland 91; United Kingdom 90–91

Golden Handcuffs 3–5, 25–26, 122–124, 130nn1–2, 158, 182–184; measuring 183–184; as theory 4, 182–185

Government Accountability Project (GAP) 46

Great Britain 94; finance sector 94; food industry sector 94

Greenwood, C. A. 26–27, 107, 176–177

Group of Twenty (G20) 90

group selection 25, 124

Grunig, J. E. 13, 19–20, 27n2, 110, 121–123, 125, 149, 162n45, 181

Grunig, L. A. 13, 27n2

Hamilton, W. D. 25

health care 82

Higher Loyalty: Truth, Lies, and Leadership, A 109

Hitt, M. A. 181

Hon, L. C. 110, 121–123, 125, 149, 162n45, 181

Hoover, J. Edgar 42

human behavior 22, 185

Iceland 81

inactive observers, whistleblowers versus 73

incidence of retaliation 71, 128, 131n20, 145, **146**, 147, 169

incidence of whistleblowing 71, 128, 131n16, **146**, 147, 167

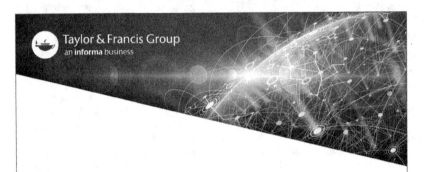

Printed in the United States
by Baker & Taylor Publisher Services